Tarik Sabry is Senior Lecturer in Media and Communication Theory at the University of Westminster. He is the author of *Cultural Encounters in the Arab World: On Media, the Modern and the Everyday* (I.B.Tauris, 2010) and is co-editor of the *Middle East Journal of Culture and Communication*.

ARAB
CULTURAL
STUDIES
Mapping the Field

EDITED BY
TARIK SABRY

I.B. TAURIS
LONDON · NEW YORK

Published in 2012 by I.B.Tauris & Co Ltd
6 Salem Road, London W2 4BU
175 Fifth Avenue, New York NY 10010
www.ibtauris.com

Distributed in the United States and Canada
Exclusively by Palgrave Macmillan
175 Fifth Avenue, New York NY 10010

ISBN: 978 1 84885 558 8 (HB)
      978 1 84885 559 5 (PB)

A full CIP record for this book is available from the British Library
A full CIP record is available from the Library of Congress

Library of Congress Catalog Card Number: available

Printed and bound in Great Britain by TJ International Ltd, Padstow, Cornwall
from Camera-ready copyedited and supplied by the author

This book is dedicated to Mohamed El-Bou'zizi
and others who sacrificed their lives for
a free and democratic Arab world.

Contents

Acknowledgements

This volume is the outcome of a conference organized by the Communication and Media Research Institute's Arab Media Centre in 2008 as well as continuous and lengthy discussions with colleagues from London, Oxford, New York and different parts of the Arab world, to whom I am humbly grateful for accepting my invitation to be part of this project. Special thanks go to each one of them. I also thank Philippa Brewster and Helen Sabry for their continual support and Jodie Robson and Maria Way for going over the manuscript.

Notes on Contributors

Atef Alshaer completed his first degree in English Language and Literature at Birzeit University in Palestine. He completed his Masters in Linguistics at the School of Oriental and African Studies, University of London, where he also recently completed his PhD in Sociolinguistics. His interests include linguistics, literature and politics of the Arab world and Europe. He has published several academic and magazine articles concerned with the literary, sociolinguistic, cultural and political life of the Arab world. He is based at SOAS.

Walter Armbrust is Hourani Fellow and University Lecturer in Modern Middle Eastern Studies. He is a cultural anthropologist whose research interests focus on popular culture and mass media in the Middle East. He is the author of *Mass Culture and Modernism in Egypt,* and the editor of *Mass Mediations: New Approaches to Popular Culture in the Middle East and Beyond*. He is currently working on a cultural history of the Egyptian cinema.

Muhammad Ayish is a Jordanian media scholar based in the United Arab Emirates. He holds Masters and Doctoral degrees in communication from the University of Minnesota – Twin Cities (1983 and 1986 respectively). He has worked at universities in Jordan and the United Arab Emirates, most recently as Dean of the College of Communication, University of Sharjah, UAE. His most recent book is: *The New Arab Public Sphere* (2008). He also contributes regular columns on media and culture to the Abu Dhabi-based newspaper, *The National*.

Riadh Ferjani is Lecturer at the Institut de Presse et des Sciences de l'Information, Tunis-Manouba University, and Associate Researcher at CARISM (Centre d'analyse et de recherche interdisciplinaire sur les medias), Université Panthéon-Assas – Paris 2. He is the author of several articles and book chapters, on international television and information and communication technologies (ICT). His recent publications include

'Religion and television in the Arab world: Towards a Communication studies approach' in *Middle East Journal of Culture and Communication*.

Layal Ftouni is currently a doctoral candidate at the University of Westminster where she was awarded a CREAM scholarship. She is also a visiting lecturer at the same university. Her thesis, entitled 'Dismantling or Reproducing the Orientalist Canon' examines Neo-Orientalism in contemporary visual arts. Layal's research is interdisciplinary, crossing fields such as Cultural and Gender Studies, Photographic and Film Studies, and Art History and Philosophy.

Abdullah Al-Ghathami is a Saudi scholar, teaching at King Sa'ud University in Riadh. He is one of the earliest, if not the first, advocates of Arab cultural studies. His books, all published in Arabic include, *Cultural Criticism* (2000), *Feminizing the Poem and the Different Reader* (1999), *Women and Language* (1996), *The Poem and the Oppositional Text* (1994), *Writing Against Writing* (1991), *The Culture of Illusion* (1998), *The Story of Modernity in Saudi Arabia* (2005) and *Deconstructing the Text* (1987). His most recent book is entitled *Television Culture* (2006; also published in Arabic).

Iman Hamam teaches Rhetoric and Composition at the American University in Cairo. She received her BA in English and Comparative Literature from the AUC before moving to the UK to complete her MA in Modern Literature (University of Kent, Canterbury, 1998) and PhD in Culture and Communication Studies (University of Sussex, 2002). Her research focuses on Egyptian film and popular culture and she is currently noting the transformations occurring in Egypt's contribution to satellite television and the city of Cairo. She writes mostly across the disciplines, looking at visual culture in medicine, film and urban studies.

Rosser Johnson is Senior Lecturer and Head of Postgraduate Studies in the School of Communication Studies at AUT University, New Zealand.

Marwan M. Kraidy is Professor of Global Communication at the Annenberg School for Communication at the University of Pennsylvania and the Edward Said Chair of American Studies at the American University of Beirut. He is a Fellow of the John Simon Guggenheim Memorial Foundation and of the Woodrow Wilson International Centre for Scholars. His publications include *Reality Television and Arab Politics: Contention* *in Public Life* (Cambridge, 2010), which won the 2010 Best Book Award in Global Communication and Social Change, from the International Communication Association, and the 2011 Diamond Anniversary Best Book Award from the National Communication Association; *Arab Television Industries* (BFI/Palgrave, 2009, with J. Khalil), *Hybridity, or, The Cultural Logic of Globalization* (Temple, 2005), and the co-edited volumes *Global Media Studies: Ethnographic Perspectives* (Routledge, 2003), and *The Politics of Reality Television: Global Perspectives* (Routledge, 2010).

Dina Matar is Lecturer in Media and International Political Communication at the Centre for Film and Media Studies at the School of Oriental and African Studies. She is the author of *What it Means to be Palestinian: Stories of Palestinian Peoplehood* (2010) and co-founder and co-editor of *The Middle East Journal of Culture and Communication*. She has published several journal and book chapters on the Palestinian Diaspora in Britain, cultural politics, Arab women and media, and is currently working on a research project on Hezbollah.

Susan O'Rourke is Programme Coordinator (Communication Studies) for the Oman project. She is also Senior Lecturer and Head of Undergraduate Programmes in the School of Communication Studies at AUT University, New Zealand.

Tarik Sabry is Senior Lecturer in Media and Communication Theory at the University of Westminster, where he is member of the Communication and Media Research Institute. He is the author of *Cultural Encounters in the Arab World: On Media, the Modern and the Everyday* (2010) and the co-founder/co-editor of the *Middle East Journal of Culture and Communication*. His research interests focus on media and migration, contemporary Arab philosophical thought, Arab popular culture and Arab cultural studies.

Naomi Sakr is Professor of Media Policy at the Communication and Media Research Institute (CAMRI), University of Westminster, and Director of the CAMRI Arab Media Centre. She is the author of *Arab Television Today* (2007) and *Satellite Realms: Transnational Television, Globalization and the Middle East* (2001), and has edited two collections, *Women and Media in the Middle East: Power through Self-Expression* (2004, reprinted 2007) and *Arab Media and Political Renewal: Community, Legitimacy and Public*

Life (2007). Her research interests centre on the political economy of Arab media, including relationships between corporate cultural production, media law and human rights.

Helga Tawil-Souri is Assistant Professor in the Department of Media, Culture and Communication at New York University. Her research is on Palestinian internet practices, broadcasting and cinema, and contemporary spaces of social, political and technological control/resistance. She is also a photographer and documentary filmmaker.

Mohamed Zayani is Associate Professor of Critical Theory at the Georgetown University School of Foreign Service in Qatar. His research interests lie in the intersection between critical theory, media studies and cultural studies. He is the author of several scholarly articles and books. His works include *Reading the Symptom* (1999), *Arab Satellite Television and Politics in the Middle East* (2004), *The Al Jazeera Phenomenon: Critical Perspectives on New Arab Media* (2005) and *The Culture of Al Jazeera: Inside an Arab Media Giant* (2007).

1

Introduction

Arab Cultural Studies: Between 'Reterritorialisation' and 'Deterritorialisation'

Tarik Sabry

[...] beginning with beginning will consist of an operation which [...] will have already begun. Even though this means that a procedure has already been identified, more will still be at stake here in this particular beginning than what would amount to nothing other than an assessment of the viability of a procedure which was itself advanced in terms of a beginning that did no more than concern itself with beginnings. In this instance there will be a different point of departure involving a substitution of that which is taken to be central. What this will mean at this stage is that the strategy that comes to be articulated within the terms set by the posited centrality of beginnings will itself be taken as central. (Andrew Benjamin, 1993: 3)

Beginning with *beginning*

Over the last decade, while many scholars researching 'Arab media', both in Western and Arab academe, worked ceaselessly thinking and writing about different aspects of this relatively new area of research, I found myself pre-occupied with epistemic questions, a persistent one being: how can the deficit in the contemporary Arab cultural repertoire benefit from a critical

Arab cultural studies[1] project? This intellectual interest was driven by even more nagging questions around the cultural *spatialities* and *temporalities* within which the field was being framed, its hermeneutics and the historical moment(s) to which it was responding. Grappling with such concerns, as a way of beginning with *beginning*, at a time when most scholars have been preoccupied with unpacking the structures of Arab transnational/digital media and their 'effects' on Arab societies, seemed in comparison to be far less urgent and, perhaps, discouragingly, unimportant. However, now that what I like to call the 'hyperbolic-fetishism' (that usually comes with technologically deterministic ways of seeing the world), has given way to a more sobering *analysis*, I hasten, like any opportunist, to exploit this *écart* (a swerve/gap), to use the Derridian terminology, as an opening or even *interlude*, in which to reflect and engage in a meta-narrative discussion on the nascent field of Arab cultural studies and its development. Taking on beginning with *beginning*, as a central object of enquiry, is by no means a strategy through which to re-do or undo what has already been said and written, nor is it, in any shape or form, an attempt to discredit any kind of *a priori* beginnings. Arab cultural studies is already 'there' in different treatises, PhD theses, journal articles and books, but the problem with such a compendium, I contend, is that it is not, epistemologically that is, 'conscious' of itself or its parts-of-the-whole. Nor is it, dare I add, conscious of the historical and conjunctional moments to which it is responding. Such consciousness and self-assuredness, I argue, can only take place once we, as scholars, begin to engage with our subject, Arab cultural studies, from a position of *différance*, and as a thinking-about-*thinking* sort of exercise – and this, I believe, has yet to be done in any meaningful or systematic way. Dealing with this *écart*, as a moment of reflection, is, by way of a *beginning*, the main *telos* of this book. The chapters that follow, that come from both established and emerging scholars in the field, engage, in an interdisciplinary and reflexive fashion, with what I think are key issues facing this area of study and its development. They allow for a reflexive articulation/rearticulation of the field's many facets, including, in no particular order, language and discourse, language and culture, media and modernity, gender studies, media historiography, culture and history, the state and cultural production, political economy of the media, popular culture, epistemology and institutionalisation. This book is, I believe, the first conscious effort to enunciate the parameters of, and visions for, a critical and creative Arab cultural studies. Its main objective is thus one of reflexivity par excellence.

Reterritorialisation and deterritorialisation as ways of doing *beginning*

How does one acquire/institute an epistemologically 'connected creativity' without losing sight of the 'infinite-sieve': the plane on which human thought plunges, deterritorialises, moves and creates, without 'stealing' or alienating the thought of the other? In this introductory chapter, and as a way of *beginning* or, as Benjamin puts it, making the *beginning* central, I argue that to articulate the new kinds of hermeneutics and the new language upon which Arab cultural studies can rely to interpret social and cultural phenomena, all the while maintaining what Lalande calls '*la raison critique nécessaire*', it is essential to work through and follow a double-critique mechanism; ensuring that both *endogenous* and *exogenous* cultural phenomena, forms of knowledge, their interpretation and the types of conjectural immanence/metaphysics they produce, are always subjected to a distanciated double-refutation. However, this dual critical process is, by itself, I argue, not methodologically sufficient to help us meet our *telos*: the creation of a 'conscious' critical cultural project that is aware not only of its own temporality (*time-consciousness/a sense of historical time that looks towards the future*) and spatiality (*epistemic/theoretical situatedness*), but also of its relational positionality to the 'Other', to other temporalities, its 'being otherwise' and of being in and out of its time. This necessitates the invention and incorporation of a whole new ethics of 'otherness', not just in its ontological sense, but also as a necessary prerequisite for an ethical form of rationality. For it to function, this kind of ethical rationality must be articulated through a two-way epistemic trajectory: reterritorialisation and deterritorialisation. Here, the idea is to oscillate upon a *plane* of thoughts, ideas/concepts and paradigms, back and forth from 'immanence' to 'transcendence', and vice-versa; a ceaseless move from/between a culture of immanence to a culture of transcendence – and here I mean the transcendence of any form of immanence. The objective here is the initiation of an ethics and ontology of otherness, a 'transcendental kind of empiricism', where thought and being are determined not merely through the ontologising of *experience* and the championing of *creativity*, as I will later propose, but also through an unconditional form of engagement with 'otherness' – the other's thought/the other's technique, thus avoiding the traps, into which it is easy to fall, that come with 'reverse orientalisms' and battles associated with disciplinary boundaries. An ethical and critical and/or creative Arab cultural studies must transcend this kind of violence, and engage in processes of negotiation; an inter-marriage with the others' thought and perhaps even, why not, it may learn to stammer in his/her language(s). Navigating from reterritorialisation or 'connectivity' to deterritorialisation/dislocation, while concurrently building and destroying, is one way to protect *thinking* from the arborescence of the tree as a structure of power, cultural immanence, and types of 'ontological imperialisms', as well as the kinds of cultural 'salafisms' and rigid binaries that come with this. It is through the double take that arises from reterritorialising and deterritorialising that thought, as a tool, can again create, creating not only from within and for its repertoire, but also for-the-other.

Reterritorialising as necessary epistemic 'connectivity'

I have argued elsewhere (2007, 2010) that a 'conscious' articulation of Arab cultural studies/media studies cannot take place without connection to key debates and problematics that are inherent to contemporary Arab thought, for what epistemic purpose would Arab cultural studies have if it were unable to inform or deal with problems intrinsic to contemporary Arab thought and social theory? To not reterritorialise; to ignore this kind of epistemic dislocation – and I cannot make this point strongly enough – means to work upon a *plane* that is simply unconscious of its own history, its own time and even of the moments to which it may be responding. The result is likely to be a highly superficial repertoire – mere epiphenomenal froth: a baseless project and a failed *beginning*. Since 'the structures and processes of social communication are deeply embedded within the wider structures and processes of a given social formation'[2] and because the moral/rational subject is always socially formed, it is imperative when articulating the notion of an Arab cultural studies, not only to engage with social theory, but it is also equally necessary, in order to understand 'the wider processes and structures' that determine Arab media, culture and society, 'to make a diversion by way of philosophy in order to understand how and why the debates have been set up the way they have and what they are in fact about'.[3] To reterritorialise Arab cultural studies on a *plateau* that is conscious of the structures of its social formations, and since the discipline of cultural studies has developed elsewhere as a reaction to modernity's ambivalence, a serious engagement with key debates on modernity in contemporary Arab philosophical thought becomes a necessary intellectual exercise. It is only through this epistemic positioning, as a *beginning*, I would argue, that we can distil from the multiplicity of positions that which we think is sound enough to become the interlocutor of a critical/ethical Arab cultural studies project. It is important to add that this kind of exercise must not only be framed within the context of de-Westernisation, for it is fundamental to both Western and non-Western contexts that there is a diversion by way of philosophy. To engage with the task of reterritorialisation, by way of beginning from the beginning, I revisit, and quote in full, a typology that I devised elsewhere (2010: 30–35) to describe four key Arab philosophical standpoints, some more dominant than others, in relation to modernity and tradition, a relationship, which I think is still at the heart of contemporary Arab philosophical discourse.

The historicist/Marxist position

The key figure in this position is Abdullah Laroui, a Marxist historian who dedicated his cultural/historical project to the question of modernity.[4] As he put it, in *Mafhum al-'aql* (The Meaning of Reason): 'All I have written so far can be considered as parts in one volume, on the meaning of modernity.'[5] Laroui's call for a radical/decisive epistemological break with the past, what he calls *hassm*, has been a key contribution to the Arab philosophical discourse on modernity. Progress and development in the Arab world, asserts Laroui, can only be achieved if and when a decisive break with the past and its heritage takes place, and also when Arabs are conscious of their own history and their role in it. Western historical materialism (Marxist historicism, to be precise) and its revolutionary politics is, for Laroui, the only viable strategy to escape from cultural *salafism*, the superficialities of liberalism, technocracy, and the only route to modernity.[6] However, Laroui's radical break with the past (Laroui 1973, 1996, 2001) must not be confused with an outright rejection of *ussul*, or cultural heritage. For Laroui, this still remains a very important object of enquiry. What he rejects, however, are the Arab-Islamic heritage's value systems. As he put it: 'If, as the theologian/philosopher thinks value is the absolute, then the modern man is the man of non-value, he who expects nothing to be definitive.'[7] For Laroui, the main reason for Arab intellectual digression is the Arab's inability to realise the historical split that took place between secular realities in the Arab world and its cultural heritage.

The rationalist/structuralist position

Mohammed Abed al-Jabri (whose is the key voice in this position) has a different take on *turath* (heritage). Rather than breaking with the past aesthetically, ethically and epistemologically, al-Jabri repudiates Laroui's 'universalism' (Western historical materialism), arguing for the historicisation of *turath* by modernising it from within, so that it is reconciled with the present and with the new realities of Arab cultures. Al-Jabri calls for *al-infissal min ajl al-ittissal* (to disconnect in order to reconnect) as a strategy through which to solve the problem of the 'unconscious' in Arab cultural temporality. For al-Jabri, the main problems with Arab thought and the Arab intellectual crisis are inherent to a structural/epistemological problem in modes of Arab reasoning. The *turath* and modernity problematic, observes al-Jabri, is not moved by class struggle, but 'by cultural and conceptual issues dealing with thought and its structure'.[8] Al-Jabri, like any intellectual, is the product of historical moments. He, like a number of the predominant pan-Arab intellectuals, Laroui included, have had their intellectual formations shaped by key historical events: the occupation of Palestine in 1948, the nationalisation of the Suez Canal by Nasser in July, 1956, and the Arab-Israeli wars of 1967 and 1973. These events have shaped a whole political consciousness, and have dictated the kind of hermeneutics relied upon to interpret 'Arabness' and 'Arab culture' by a whole generation of Arab intellectuals. The pan-Arab interpretation of culture's function is an interesting one. The term 'Arab world' is divided into two unifying terminologies: *Al-watan al-Arabi* and *al-ummah al-Arabiya*. The first denotes geographic unity; the second alludes to some sort of spiritual ('Din' religion) common experience.[9] According to al-Jabri, the main historical characteristic of 'culture' is inherent to its function as a unifier. Here, the awakening of Arab consciousness is predicated on culture's ability to unify. Culture's historical function and purpose, according to al-Jabri, a pan-Arabist *par excellence*, is to help transform the Arab world from a mere geographic space (*al-watan al-Arabi*) to *al-ummah al-Arabiya*, a space bound by common experience and consciousness.[10]

The cultural *salafist/turatheya* position

The Arab-Islamic heritage is a key component of Arab culture and makes for the best, if not the only, possible and coherent civilisational model. This position is intricate[11] and contested and can easily be unpicked through a dozen different positions (some of which are even contradictory). The term '*turatheya*' comes from '*turath*', meaning heritage. Taha Abdurrahman (2006) differentiates between *turatheya* and *turathaweyah*. The former refers to schools of thought that privilege *turath* (cultural heritage) as a civilisational model and reference point. The latter (*turathaweyah*), how-ever, is a more orthodox position within turatheya that considers Islamic heritage to be the *only* acceptable narrative for happiness, and it vehemently and defensively rejects all others. There is no room for otherness, toler-ance or double-identity in this position. Abdurrahman also distinguishes between *hadatheyah* and *hadathaweyah*. A *hadathi* refers to an intellectual who embraces modernity as a necessary phase of human development and who is prepared to negotiate a local narrative of the modern (al-Jabri is a good example of this). A *hadathawi*, however, is the kind of radical intel-lectual, perhaps like Laroui, who is not afraid to argue for a decisive break with the past. The culturally salafist position varies from the *turathi* to the *turathawi*. What gives the culturally salafist position some sort of coher-ence, as a discursive formation, is its adherents' hanging on to the 'utopian idea of a recoverable past',[12] the thinking/methodology, perhaps illusory, that answers to the Arab/Islamic world's present problems can be found in a past or timeless temporality (the golden Islamic era of *al-salaf al-salih*).[13] From this position, the struggle is driven by the privileging of the past over the present and an illusory *authenticity* over *difference*.

The anti-essentialist position: deterritorialisation as double-critique

Running parallel to these three dominant positions lies a fourth discourse that has remained almost unnoticed at the margins of contemporary Arab thought. Its advocates call their philosophy that of *tajawuz* (a philoso-phy promising to surpass the duality problematic between modernity and tradition). This group may hold the key to the Arab intellectual impasse, but they face both endogenous and exogenous obstacles, and the two are inter-related. Historically, when under outside threat (and here I refer to imperialism), Arab scholars have tended to veer from being enlightened rationalists to becoming traditionalists (Laroui, 1976). Here, the first casualty is thought itself, as it shifts from the rational to the dogmatic. This also explains why the work of contemporary Arab thinkers, such as Abdelkabir Khatibi (1980),[14] 'Abdel-Salam Binabdal'ali (1983, 2000, 2002), Abdul-Aziz Boumesshouli (2001, 2003, 2005, 2006, 2007), Fatima Mernissi and the late Edward Said (there are, of course, other examples) has never found the same resonance or reception on the Arab intellectual scene, as work that is embedded in the essentialist ideologies of cultural unity: nationalism, pan-Islamism and pan-Arabism. The threat of imperialism prompted defensive reactionary positions; ones that justified intoxicated discourses of unity and salafism. Imperialism, it is important to add, is a system that subverts not only consciousness and institutional structures, but also thought and its development. This fourth position can be encapsulated in the philosophy of *tajawuz*.[15] Its key intellectuals reject ideological discourses of identity, and situate heritage, and even modernity, within a position of *différance*, where both tradition and philosophy become objects of critique and subversion, thus Khatibi's famous call for a double-semiotics and *double-critique* as *double death* (here, 'death' implies the birth of difference as the source of new questions, new écarts and ways of knowing). The advocates of this position, headed by Khatibi, constitute a very small minority in contemporary Arab thought. They champion otherness, alterity, pluralism, fragmentation, non-linearity and the constant questioning of essentialised Arab discourses around *becoming. Turath*, for them, to use Khatibi's phrase, is nothing other than 'the return of the forgotten dead'.[16] Khatibi finds the 'savage difference' *vis-à-vis* the West and what he calls 'blind identity', naïve, patriotic, nationalist, ideological and leading to nothing but a theoretical trap. Instead, he calls for critical work that disturbs the metaphysical soils monopolising Arab thought, mainly: the metaphysics of God or *lahut*, the metaphysics of sects or *mazahib*, and the metaphysics of technique.[17] Khatibi's take on history and *turath* is different from Laroui's, as he refuses to articulate *turath* through any philosophy of History.[18] He critiques Laroui's ideological take on history for its generalisations (*shumuleyat*) and considers it a type of metaphysics that champions organisation, continuity and *will*, but does not consider difference, otherness, chaos or non-linearity (1980). Binabdal'ali, on the other hand, stresses that Arab thought cannot move forward unless its problematics are framed within key changes or 'revolutions' in world contemporary thought: a) a semiological revolution that led to a re-examination of *interpretation* and the creation of meaning; b) an epistemological revolution that disturbs the philosophy of the *cogito*, and c) the philosophical revolution that reversed Platonism, championing the truth of the body.[19] Thought in the Arab cultural repertoire has become stagnant, affirms Binabdal'ali, because it has become disconnected from *event*[20] and thus calls for a reconnection between Arab philosophy and event. Both Khatibi and Binabdal'ali champion universalism and the deterritorialisation of thought. Binabdal'ali uses Heidegger's take on *metaphysics* and Derrida's deconstructionist approach to articulate his position in relation to *turath* and to other key aspects of thought in the Arab philosophical repertoire. He calls for a rereading of *turath* with *différance* as a way of surpassing it. His take on *différance*, as a way of dealing with essentialised forms of identity and *turath*, can also be traced back to Hegel's *dialectics*, but Binabdal'ali argues for a different kind of *dialectics*, one that liberates difference from fixed and absolute forms of oppositionality. He calls for a distancing of the two opposites, so they are brought nearer – and that is exactly what Heidegger means by '*ontological difference*'.[21] Binabdal'ali and his followers from the same intellectual position, seek to surpass not only naive *metaphysics*, as we live it in the Arab Islamic world, but also philosophical metaphysics.[22]

To reiterate, it is this epistemic position within contemporary Arab thought; its ethics of 'otherness' and its nuanced take on knowledge and self-identity, which needs to be strengthened and developed. The task here is to reposition this school of thought, shifting it from the margins of Arab thought to the centre of our thinking about Arab culture and society and, indeed, Arab cultural studies. Of course, this typology by no means encompasses, or even represents contemporary Arab thought. It is merely a metonym for a vast compendium, and to pretend otherwise would be misleading. There remain many acts of 'divergence' yet to be attempted and, as such, the intellectual task of reterritorialisation has to be seen as a process, an ongoing project. Especially important to the development of a reterritorialised Arab cultural studies are debates centred on Arab modes of political reasoning, to which both Abdullah Laroui's work on the 'state' and Mohammed Abed al-Jabri's critique of 'Arab political reason' remain extremely important. Equally important is the work of Abdullah Al-Ghathami on Arab 'cultural criticism'.

On the necessity to ontologise and temporalise as creative processes

In his seminal work *A Critique of Arab Reason*, Mohammed Abed al-Jabri pointed to a major deficit in contemporary Arab thought: that of the confusion in Arab cultural temporality, or what he calls the unconscious in Arab thought. As he puts it:

> The temporal in recent Arab cultural history is stagnant ... for it does not provide us with a development of Arab thought and its movement from one state to another, instead, it presents us with an exhibition or a market of past cultural products, which co-exist in the same temporality as the new, where the old and the new become contemporaries. The outcome is an overlapping between different cultural temporalities in our conception of our own cultural history ... This way, our present becomes an exhibition of our past, and we live our past in our present, without change and without history (al-Jabri, 1991: 47).

However, al-Jabri, who was convinced that the problem of 'unconscious time' was the result of a deficit in modes of reasoning (for which he provided the following epistemic solution: we solve the problem of 'unconscious time' by re-organising our cultural repertoire from within, in such a way that it is made answerable to the present, using answers and solutions from the present) has, nonetheless, failed to tackle a rather urgent question: how do we go about studying the present tense of Arab cultures, in all its sacredness and imperfections? Here, I do not suggest that there is no benefit to be gained from the study of Arab cultural history or the past, or let us say, the history of Arab media.[23] Nor am I suggesting that Arab cultural studies should only focus on the present (see Walter Armbrust's contribution in this book). The past, as we learn from Hobsbawm, 'remains the most useful analytical tool for coping with constant change'.[24] Rather, I argue that the deficit in Arab cultural temporality – its unconsciousness – cannot be resolved through the re-organisation of Arab cultural history alone. An anthropological approach is needed to claim the present tense of Arab everydayness in all its cultural manifestations, to bring it to the fore so that it is assured of its time, its being and this, I suggest, is a task for which Arab cultural studies is best suited. What the Arab discourse on the 'modern' is not about, as yet, however, is Man and lived experience. We

simply cannot make sense of modernity in the Arab world today without
making sense of what it means to be modern, and if living in a mass mediated world is part of modern experience, then a philosophical discourse
that ignores this is surely lacking in contemporaneity; a key component
of modernity. Equally, the cultural time-consciousness of Arab modernity
cannot be reassured of its time solely through *Cartesian* doubt or through
its historicist/rationalist schools, and certainly not through its salafist
schools. Furthermore, the Arab discourse on modernity is so influenced
by Western thought and methodology, (especially the 'rationalist' and 'historicist' positions) that it has unwittingly inherited a much debated problematic in modern Western epistemology, which can be traced to Descartes
whose starting point in thinking the world was not 'the facticity (the actual
matter-of-factness) of the actually existing living world', but the 'contents
of his own mind'.[25] This is, to quote Scannell, 'where an awful lot of modern philosophers and others start'.[26] The Arab philosophical discourse on
modernity has yet to ontologise or humanise its take on modernity, that
is, to become able to deal with its sociological and anthropological significance. Those who threaten to do just this (the anti-essentialist position) are
sidelined as ahistorical and marginal, therefore, if we are to make use of the
Arab discourse on modernity as a bridge by which we can understand contemporary Arab media, culture and society, we must then begin by removing it from its discourse or, should I say, metaphysics, making it an object
of critique before it can become a tool of critique.

Deterritorialising articulations of Arab culture

The role of deterritorialisation is as important as that of reterritorialisation.
Both serve a particular epistemic task, in which thought, as a creative tool,
is able to be creative, always making space for swerves and gaps, and initiating new ways of seeing and interpreting the world. There are dozens of
books, theses and journal articles on 'Arab culture', its modes, problems and
future. The majority are written in Arabic, though there are also numerous
publications on the subject in French, English and other European languages. The Centre for the Study of Arab Unity[27] alone has produced dozens of books (both single-authored and edited collections) that attempt
to deal, through different capacities and specificities, with the future and
challenges that face 'Arab culture'.[28] While the number of publications that
deal with the challenges facing 'Arab culture' (and here I use the category

'Arab culture' in the most generic and unreflexive fashion), demonstrates the importance that this category occupies in the contemporary Arab cultural repertoire, it would be facile and simplistic to use 'abundance' or quantity as measures for, or assessments of, the quality of this repertoire. The undeniable richness and diversity of such work is undermined by key problems that have prevented the study of Arab culture's metamorphosis from a fragmented whole into a conscious and conjunctional intellectual project. When I say 'conscious', I do not exactly mean 'political consciousness', for much of the work on 'Arab culture' is driven by a clear historicist telos. What is somewhat ironic is that while the historicisation of the category 'Arab culture' has encouraged its development into a politically conscious and coherent intellectual project, it has simultaneously alienated other types of hermeneutics about 'culture', especially those competing for broader and non-essentialist definitions, thus limiting what can be said, thought and studied about this category beyond the prism of the ideological and the kinds of *metaphysics* this brings with it. This epistemic deficit has already had a clear effect on the level of media research in the Arab world, where academics tend to consider information/news-led research as being more important, let us say, than media research centred on entertainment or other aspects of popular culture (see Walter Armbrust's chapter in this book). The framing of 'Arab culture' within pan-Arabist, nationalist, Islamicist and Salafist discourses has indeed contributed to the historicisation of the category 'Arab culture', but this process, I contend, has, in the meantime, led to an *epistemological* impasse, underlined by the dominance of very few interpretations of 'Arab culture'. Here, the political historicisation of 'culture' becomes a mere philosophical metaphysics, as it limits what can be said about Arab culture or identity to a narrow and fixed frame of analysis. So, by the 'unconscious' in the discourse on 'Arab culture' in the first instance, I am referring to an epistemic and paradigmatic deficit, and not necessarily to a political one (although the two are, of course, not entirely unrelated). Just as there are multiple discourses on the 'modern' and 'modernity' in the Arab cultural repertoire (some more dominant than others), there are also different discourses on 'culture'. These two contested thought positions are relational, since those discourses that dominate debate on modernity and tradition also dictate how the category 'culture' is articulated, thought of and appropriated. All three dominant positions in Arab thought (the historicist, the rationalist/structuralist, the cultural salafist) articulate the category culture within frames that justify the *telos* of that ideological position. This leaves the fourth and less dominant position (the anti-essentialist position), discussed, yet again, on the margins of Arab cultural/identity discourse. The dominant discourses on 'Arab culture' are still frozen at a metaphysical, *Cartesian* and, one might add, an aesthetic/élitist stage, almost oblivious to the anthropological factors and the socio-economic and cultural transformations that determine contemporary Arab cultures and societies. What is required here is not so much a task of bridging or reterritorialisation, as argued above, but one of *dislocation* and deterritorialisation. Here, the intellectual task is to expose the artificial, discursive conjunction between Arab thought (the philosophical repertoire/its historicised discourses of becoming) and its articulations of culture – that is to say, to break and unveil this artificial conjunction by removing it from its discourse. The point of dislocating/disturbing the conjunction between articulations of culture and the discourses of Arab *becoming* should not be confused with an attack on any possible form of Arab historicity. This would be to miss the point. Nor should this be confused with an attempt to depoliticise Arab cultures or, indeed, discourses on Arab cultures. If we are to consider 'Arab cultures' as objects of scientific enquiry, we must be prepared for the archaeological task that comes with this. We must be prepared to implement Khatibi's *double-critique* (1980) by questioning, interrogating and disturbing the continuities, totalisations and teleologies inherent to Arab discourses on culture and identity. The task of *dislocation* is useful here, as it will open up space that allows broader and less totalising articulations of Arab culture/identity to emerge. Dislocation is also a way to accommodate and free new political expressions and new spaces of resistance. So, rather than *dislocation/deterritorialisation* being a tool of de-historicisation or de-politicisation, *dislocation/deterritorialisation* may lead to the creation of new and alternative discourses of *becoming* and may broaden the spectrum of research on Arab culture.

Framing 'Arab culture' within essentialist discourses of *authenticity* and unity masks difference (social and cultural stratification) and undermines anthropological interpretations of the everyday. Arab intellectuals' attempts to mobilise the masses through a historicised articulation of culture have ironically failed: a) to recognise the role of 'popular culture' as a site for the production of political meaning, and, b) by downplaying the centrality of 'the everyday' to the Arab masses and their cultures. A second problematic is an outcome of the first, and is manifest in the analytical vacuum that exists between 'official', homogenising mediations of Arab cultures, and the extraordinary range of contemporary and resistant heterogeneous forms of artistic and carnivalesque expressions, which remain notoriously under-studied. What is more, and to highlight a third methodological problem-atic, I am not convinced that Arab popular cultures have been thought of through a concrete structural framework that acknowledges the problem-atic conjunctions and the fluid, yet interdependent, moments that deter-mine their nature. Arab popular cultures have yet to be rationalised within a relational/conjunctional structure, or through a concretised foreground-ing that explores the conjunctions between the social, political, economic, existential and the anthropological, as well as the dynamics that result from the interface between the 'local' and the 'global' (see Sakr's analysis of Saudi Cinema in this book). Both rationalist and salafist positions attack popu-lar culture. While the latter sees popular culture, especially mass mediated culture, as an extension of Western capitalist discourse and its consumerist culture,[29] the former sees everyday popular culture as 'unconscious' and ahistorical.[30] In these conditions, the culture that prevails (although it has always been resisted in different ways) is 'the culture of the ear',[31] i.e., that of deference to the state, its intellectuals (both rationalists and salafists), their 'multiplex ideologies'[32] and different discourses of *becoming*. The result is rather predictable: Arab popular cultures and lived experiences, profane culture, remain, not only on the periphery of Arab intellectual discourse and academic research, but also on the periphery of political discourses that, ironically, champion the Arab working classes and their concerns (see Sabry 2010).

The everyday

The everyday, asserts Lefebvre, is 'not only a concept but one that may be used as a guide-line for an understanding of society'.[33] However, 'doing everyday life', as we learn from Lefebvre and, much earlier, Adorno, who urged us to distinguish between popular or folk culture and the cultural industries (1991), can also be a site of control and ideology. Modernity and its institutions, Lefebvre maintains, are responsible for the reification of the everyday by detaching leisure from its festive nature and replacing the latter with a mere 'generalised display': television, cinema and tourism.[34] It is not difficult to find examples from within Arab 'popular cultures' where the 'popular' is reified to serve the state's ideological telos. However, are the articulations of 'the everyday' within discourses of reification, or 'false consciousness', in themselves types of ideological positioning that need to be questioned? Lefebvre's account of the everyday draws much from French structuralism, to be precise, from he whom Scannell satirically calls the 'Pope of structuralist Marxism', Althusser. For this position, or positioning, of the everyday, 'lived experience cannot be taken as the ground for anything because it is unconscious in a double sense: it is unreflective (unselfconscious if you like) and therefore gives no account for itself. And it is also unconscious in psychoanalytical terms, and therefore cannot *account* for itself'.[35] Positioning everyday and lived experience along this line of thinking clearly limits what can be said about everyday, popular culture, and certainly has serious implications for the ways in which the media and their audiences are articulated (see Ferjani's contribution in this book). Perhaps, a more nuanced critique of the everyday that would be more useful is one that combines a critique of ideology with a more culturalist positioning, for instance, that advocated by Raymond Williams, who took lived experience as the ground for a conscious and reflective analysis of culture. Such a paradigmatic reconciliation was the objective of Hall's (1980) *Media, Culture and Society* article: 'Cultural Studies: Two Paradigms', but where, according to Scannell, Hall fails in this attempt, is in his privileging of Althusser over Williams. What I find more exciting about Lefebvre's critique of the 'quotidian' is his insistence on objectifying it by rediscovering it as a crucial arena for study, and also his prompting to find a new language or discourse with which to do so. 'The answer', observed Lefebvre 'is everyday life, to rediscover everyday life – no longer to neglect and disown it, elude and evade it – but actively to re-discover it while contributing to its transfiguration; this undertaking', he notes, 'involves the invention of a language ... the transfiguration of everyday life is the creation of something new, something that requires new words'.[36] Reducing manifestations of the everyday, or everyday popular culture, to mass media is to also limit the everyday and its dynamics to the realm of the institutional. The 'everyday' or 'quotidian' is certainly a much wider and more varied phenomenon, as it encompasses a whole set of human activities and non-institutional social settings, from shopping to cooking, having sex, following fashion, queuing, worshipping and dancing. What kind of language, semiotics or even hermeneutics, do we rely on to study everyday Arab popular cultures? Inventing a new language to deal with them can only succeed if preceded by another intellectual task, that of democratising and freeing the category 'Arab culture' from: a) the grip of the aesthetic as *discourse* (see Al-Ghathami's chapter in this book) and, b) the discourses of *becoming* that downplay all other forms of artistic and carnivalesque expressions, including entertainment (see Sabry 2010).

Otherness as ethics and ethics as *otherness*

An ethics of otherness does not have to conform to any immanent discourse of religiosity for it to be ethical. The focus here is on 'otherness' as a heuristic and necessary ethical modality, a kind of precursor to a more universally inclusive and non-immanent way of thinking the others or/and their cultures, ideas, languages and histories. Knowledge, in this case, would be described as 'the relation of man to exteriority, the relation of the same to the Other, in which the other finally finds itself stripped of its alterity, in which it becomes interior to my, in which transcendence makes itself immanence'.[37] An ethical Arab cultural studies project, as a form of knowledge, should not take as its role the need to preach 'otherness' and the kind of ethical disinterestedness that comes with it beyond what it already is: a fore-given ethical category – that of 'care'. I am, and everyone else is, always and everywhere, the 'other' since I am; and, we are always, the other's other. Otherness is, therefore, not just an ethical transcendental category, one that precedes the ontological, as Levinas would have us believe; it is also that which determines our being and is in this sense also an ontological category *par excellence*. By otherness, I am here referring to respect and engagement with for all forms of *othering*: religious, opinion, racial, gender, class, linguistic and intellectual. That is, by always making sure that our relation to exteriority is one of radical disinterestedness and respect, no matter how different the other is. Embracing 'otherness', as ethics and as an epistemic strategy, is a precursor not only to an ethical society, but also to an ethical rationality and even, to use Taha Abderrahman's words, an 'ethical modernity'. One of the key shortcomings of orthodox thought and thinking in contemporary Arab thought, be it that of the cultural salafist, the Marxist-historical materialist, the Pan-Islamist-Arabist, and there are other forms of essentialisms and salafisms, is their automatic alienation and exclusion of the other. They lay out a plane of immanence, an essentialised, teleological way of *becoming*, not realising that all planes of immanence are, in the end, always replaced or transcended. It is, as Polyani puts it, 'almost axiomatic that the distinction between a free and totalitarian society lies exactly at this point: a free society is regarded as one that does *not* engage, on principle, in attempting to control what people find meaningful, and a totalitarian society is regarded as one that does, on principle, attempt such control'.[38] A radical ethics of otherness/difference/exteriority is the only way to avoid this intellectual/theoretical trap. An ethical-critical Arab cultural studies has to act as a plateau where the line of flight/escape, what Deleuze calls 'deterritorialisation', is always open, always prepared for flight; *escape*. Deterritorialisation, however, must not be understood as 'inaction', or as mere intellectual arbitrariness (bourgeois indifference), but as an intentional, creative mechanism. The flight here is not from responsibility or engagement/historicity, but from decaying and redundant ideas, from metaphysics and the myths that come with essentialised narratives of *becoming*. Nothing is, in fact, 'more active than a flight'.[39] Let us put the other/othering/*al-ghayriah* at the heart of Arab cultural studies; an ethics where the purpose of objectification is not one of mere reciprocity, but one of 'radical exteriority', of 'disinterestedness', otherness-as-care, an otherness 'for-the-other', and a way of 'being otherwise'.

On creativity, concepts and *planes*

It is within the manoeuvring processes of reterritorialisation and deterritorialisation and the operationalising of 'otherness' as a form of ethics, that creativity within Arab cultural studies, and Arab thought, in general, can take root. The usefulness of the double-critique method – as advanced by Khatibi – lies in its promise to engage with both local and universal concepts in a relation of différance, submitting both to a continuous active process of destruction and rebuilding. With this method, we are guaranteed flight or escape from all sorts of ontological imperialisms as well as from the many intoxicated discourses of *becoming* that are described above. It is, I contend, within this critical analytic frame and type of mechanisation that creativity can materialise. To be creative, or to create, is to be able to destroy and build anew, without being paralysed or rendered impotent by texts, thought or concepts, universal or local, which have, over time, acquired a status of immanence or sacredness. One way to de-sacralise (and desacralisation as an intellectual ritual has to be performed if we are to be creative) such forms of knowledge and to ensure their usefulness and relevance, is to put them to the empirical test. When and if concepts prove irrelevant, redundant or out of sync with social and cultural realities, we then need to rethink them or to create new ones.

Here, it is important to differentiate between the creative process (the creation of concepts/paradigms) and the space (the *plane*) within which the creative process takes place. I have argued elsewhere (2007, 2009, 2010) that a serious articulation of Arab cultural studies, as a field of enquiry into Arab media, culture and society, cannot take place outside a conscious epistemic space, which then becomes the home or plane where concepts and paradigms co-exist and are created. This kind of epistemic historicity – if we can call it so – is fundamentally important for the coherence of the field and for the creation of concepts. A concept, as Deleuze and Guattari put it in their *Introduction to Philosophy*, is 'a matter of articulation'; a 'multiplicity of possible worlds', 'existing face' and 'real language or speech'. The creation of concepts can also take place through a rearticulation of borrowed/stolen concepts, which, because of the arbitrariness of historical moments, may not cohere in interpreting local cultural phenomena. This is because every concept has a history, and every concept is there, in the first place, to deal with specific problems. Since concepts require not only problems, but also a junction of problems that combine other existing concepts, it is fundamental that the articulation of borrowed or 'stolen' concepts, as a creative process, is performed with *a priori* awareness of their conjectural problematics. To give an example, before we borrow concepts, such as the 'public sphere', 'habitus', 'postmodernity' and the kind of 'mad-hyper-textualities' that come with them, we need to first trace the problems to which they were or are responding, and that is the *beginning* of rearticulation as a creative process. To further highlight the distinction between the creative process and the *plane* upon which it takes place, Deleuze and Guatarri observe that concepts are:

> concrete assemblages, like the configurations of a machine, but the plane is the abstract machine of which these assemblages are the working parts. Concepts are events, but the plane is the horizon of events, the reservoir or reserve of purely conceptual events: not the relative horizon that functions as a limit, which changes with an observer and encloses observable states of affairs, but the absolute horizon, independent of any observer, which makes the event as concept independent of a visible state of affairs in which it is brought about.[40]

This differentiation between 'concepts', or their creation, and the 'plane', is key to understanding what I think is a fundamental epistemic deficit in the nascent field of Arab cultural studies; and by this I mean the confusion between a fragmented compendium of writings on Arab media, culture and society, as *events* for the *plane* itself which, in this instance is Arab cultural studies. The key reason for such a confusion or deficit is that the writing and thinking on Arab media, culture and society that has developed in the last decade did so outside a serious articulation of the epistemic problematics that come with the development of new fields of enquiry, and it is quite unfortunate to note that where attempts have been made to situate the field epistemologically, the prevailing objective has remained, largely, one of essentialisation and authentication. Once the *plane* upon which we are going to work becomes conscious of itself; once a definition of what it is, what it can do and how it can do it, is in place, we can then begin the process of connective creating; a kind of creativity that is conscious and assured of its own time and place. To be unable to identify the *plane* upon which one writes and creates (here, in our case, the enquiry into Arab media, culture and society) is to unconsciously, naïvely and glibly offer one's services as a native orientalist.

To summarise, what I have set out to do in this opening chapter, and by way of a beginning, is to demarcate a double-critique, an analytic framework through which a critical and creative episteme, Arab cultural studies, can be thought and studied, in ways that make it, through ongoing processes of reterritorialisation (creative connectivity), grounded in and answerable to Arab contemporary thought and realities; and through deterritorialisation (dislocation), as a mechanism of différance and constant flight that guarantees self-reflexion and creativity. This double-critique, I maintained, must be motivated by a broadening of the notion of Arab culture and by the enunciation of an ethics of 'otherness', so that the creative process forms part of an ethical rationality that transcends binarisms, essentialisms and the teleological entrapments that come with authenticity and its intoxicated discourses of becoming.

The book

Capturing the moment of Arab cultural studies as a new field of enquiry into Arab media, culture and society is, in the first place, an epistemic task, a way of making the field conscious of its existence in time and space. It is exactly this epistemic *telos* that motivates the contributions in this book.

This edited book is an attempt to establish Arab cultural studies as a conscious epistemic space or *plane* where the study of Arab culture and society
follow some kind of systematic scientific and intellectual rigour; a process
where not only are new fields established, but where new concepts and paradigms of thought can take shape, solidify and then vanish to make way for
other new ones, in a constant oscillation between building and destroying,
continuity and discontinuity, where new immanent teleologies are ceaselessly countered and transcended. This book is thus a reflexive account of
how the field ought to be thought, and how it may develop in the future.
I have divided the book in such a way as to create a movement or, dare I
say, an illusion of movement, from the general to the specific, which I hope
will give the book a more logical and coherent order. Whereas the first
five chapters introduce the reader to the state of Arab cultural studies in a
holistic way, the remaining chapters engage with specific themes (such as
gender, modernity, language, the state, popular culture, institutionalisation
and cultural criticism) and, in certain instances, specific geographic contexts are deployed to tackle wider processes and structures (such as Sakr's
study of Saudi Cinema; Hamam's work on Egyptian comedy and O'Rourke
and Johnson's chapter on the Omani Media Studies programme).

In Chapter 2, Walter Armbrust outlines the justification and rationale for his most recent intellectual endeavour: a cultural history of new
media in Egypt between 1919 and 1975. Focusing on six potential themes,
Armbrust enunciates a timely and emphatic critique of recent Arab media
studies scholarship, exposing it for its 'presentism' and 'technological determinism'. The problem with the literature on Middle Eastern media, argues
Armbrust is that it 'has assumed the primacy of one media category – information, when the overall mediascape in the era of "big media" might reveal
that, in terms of the categories, information occupies a place inverse to
our own academic preoccupation with news'. Armbrust enunciates a more
perceptive cultural history of Arab media which approaches modernity by
'foregrounding the increasingly ubiquitous fact of mass mediation – a fact
that touches on both "thought" and on European hegemony, but cannot
be reduced to the terms of either. Such a history ideally', he adds, 'would
grapple with concrete social facts and processes, elucidating institutions,
political and legal frameworks, key individuals, important themes in the
content of the various media, discourses on how media should disseminate
modernity'.

In his contribution, Mohamed Zayani examines recent 'noteworthy' scholarship in the field, and argues for future interdisciplinary, 'theoretically informed and culturally attuned' research on Arab media that does away with the 'more narrowly conceived pursuits, based on media-centric models'. As he puts it, 'in the absence of a developed theoretical framework that takes into account the specificity of the area of study, much of the work that is produced is based, in large part, on a set of unrevised assumptions, which are insufficient to explore a region-specific set of dynamics that have been accentuated and altered by the forces of globalization'. Zayani advocates a focus on 'the quotidian' as a frame within which to understand 'the significance of media-mediated experiences in their full complexity, giving attention to the political, economic and social dimensions underlying the multiple discourses of everyday life'. This, he argues, needs to rest on theoretical frameworks that 'situate the configurations of the evolving Arab media sphere within larger cultural dynamics, taking into account the interconnectedness of the micro and the macro, the specific and the general, the local and the global'.

Muhammad Ayish's chapter outlines key deficits in media and communication programmes in Arab universities, noting that their failure to establish 'intellectual links with relevant humanities and social sciences, imbued with critical cultural orientations' is due to both endogenous and exogenous elements. On the one hand, and with the exception of the countries of the Maghreb, the intellectual foundations of media and communication programmes in the Arab world, observes Ayish, 'remain captive' to uncritical, 'functionalist American mainstream social science traditions'. On the other, Arab universities, Ayish writes, have 'developed their communication curricula to serve national development and not to be critical of it'. Media and communication courses are, therefore, either descriptive or technical, thus 'mirroring the technical-intellectual communicator dichotomy'. He also explains how the boundaries dividing proponents of cultural studies, as studies of culture and as cultural criticism in the Arab world are 'not formalistic, but intrinsically ideological'. He introduces the reader to 'cultural criticism', as a nascent and emerging discipline in the Arab cultural repertoire, with the potential to serve as a route to establishing an indigenous form of Arab cultural studies and he demonstrates, using an extensive range of literature, how Arab universities and the Arab public sphere at large, have turned into 'battlegrounds for a conflict between two orientations with respect to cultural criticism': 'the traditional orientation aligned with the establishment, and the critical orientation associated with private (often non-conformist) individuals and groups'. The first orientation, he adds, is 'intrinsically "culturalist" and seeks to perpetuate the study of culture as a descriptive intellectual practice, drawing on its conception as a sacred entity, while the second (grounded in mainly secular cultural and literary traditions) takes on a more critical approach to cultural values and practices as the driving engines of political and social change'. Although the author believes that Arab societies, 'have not yet commanded the liberal culture needed to accommodate such critical orientations' as have those that have been celebrated by the tradition of critical cultural studies, he still sees the latter and its emancipatory potential, as a rich subject area for which it is worth fighting and institutionalising in Arab academia.

Riadh Ferjani enunciates a sociological reading of the development of media and cultural studies in the Arab academe, which moves beyond 'the examination of published texts to focus on the conditions of their production'. Ferjani exposes media studies programmes in the Arab world as a site of social control, and provides a nuanced and critical historiography of media studies in Arab universities, shedding light on the material and sobering realities (institutional, political, conceptual and methodological) of academia in the Arab world. Ferjani also dissects key paradigms in Arab media studies whilst critiquing their 'developmentalist' and 'technological determinist' discourses. Under the section, entitled, 'Lost in Translation', Ferjani traces the problematic ways in which cultural studies has been introduced to the Arabophone reader. A project of critical Arab cultural studies, argues Ferjani, 'does not have to be frightened to note its divergences from institutional research, which tends by conviction, obligation or ignorance to legitimate the social order and its violence'.

Dina Matar engages in a theoretical debate on the relationship between the state and culture in the Arab world and warns of the intellectual enclosures that come from the abstraction of communication practices and the new spaces for cultural expression from the wider systems within which they operate. Focusing on the role of the Arab state, she further advances that a grounded and critical Arab cultural studies cannot 'ignore the dynamic and changing links between the state, as a system of power, rooted in discursive practices, and culture, understood as a crucial terrain for struggle over power'. Matar proposes that incorporating a 'thick' understanding of the Arab state and its discursive practices into a cultural studies analysis 'would provide a more instructive articulation of the sites, and instances, of power and how it is negotiated'. Such an analysis, informed by history and empirical evidence, can help us examine, she argues, the Arab state's shifting strategies and discourses.

Helga Tawil-Souri complains that Palestinian 'contemporary cultural artefacts share a common "lack" of creativity' and asks 'whether there is something intrinsic to the Palestinian (political) condition that makes only a specific kind of cultural expression and hermeneutics possible'. Focusing on the relationship between the 'cultural' and the 'political', Tawil-Souri demonstrates how the resistance at the heart of the two 'analytics', culture and cultural studies, is imperative, and shows how, in the case of the Palestinians, the very act of 'creating culture' is a form of political resistance. She explores under-examined Palestinian forms of artistic expression, including film, music and broadcasting, as tools of political expression, or as she puts it: 'bulwarks against historical erasure', an intellectual 'means of resistance that is not just in the realm of the abstract but has very real consequences'. She also shows how these sites can, at times, as in the case of Palestinian rap, have strenuous relationships with the 'political'. Tawil-Souri also points to an inherent tension within Palestinian cultural studies, which she terms 'the predicament of the political'. On the one hand, Palestinian cultural studies 'continues to be hostage to the political conditions of the culture it is studying; on the other, the political is an order it is trying to negate'.

Sifting through key literature on gender/women's studies in the Arab and Middle East by North African, Middle Eastern and Western scholars, Layal Ftouni provides an emphatic critique of both 'reactionary' and 'deconstructivist' feminist discourses and calls for an Arab feminist epistemology. Ftouni finds the recent debates in social science and anthropology on the positionality of the female researcher and her 'epistemic privilege' to be 'far more promising than the invisible voice of God that modern epistemology permeates'. However, acknowledging the researcher's position *vis-à-vis* her research and the women she is speaking for, Ftouni argues, is not enough. For her, the main intellectual challenge lies in finding ways to reinscribe an Arab feminist epistemology through social scientific and historical research, without falling into the traps of sexism, ethnocentrism or reverse Orientalism.

Iman Hamam's chapter, 'Disarticulating Arab Popular Culture: The Case of Egyptian Comedies', provides a rare and highly nuanced analysis of Egyptian comedies as a site where discourses of the popular, class, gender, the modern, the temporal and self-identity are both constructed and negotiated. Giving wonderful and, at times, hilarious examples from different comical moments, Hamam makes a connection between certain oral narrative media structures and shifts in 'the experience of time'. The randomness and illogicality of the sequencing in the studied comedies is, for Hamam, neither an intentional discursive technique (there to mock), nor evidence of the *ahistoricity* or unconsciousness of the popular text, but of a kind of intellectual dilemma, which Hamam leaves open for the readers to think about, digest and ponder over. Comedy, observes Hamam, 'mocks us because we don't know who "we" are, or because we, it, suspects that we do. We act as if we know who we are and comedy calls us in on this joke of presumptions'.

Focusing on the case of Saudi Cinema, Naomi Sakr demonstrates what can be achieved by a political economy approach to the understanding of culture. Sakr begins her chapter by exploring 'distinctions and overlaps between a political economy of culture and cultural studies'. She then goes on to apply a political economy perspective to five years of struggle (2005–09) over the future of cinema in Saudi Arabia. The insights provided by Sakr from the initial review and the case study 'allow conclusions to be drawn about cinema's place in Saudi power relations and about political economy's distinctive research agenda'. She shows how cinema in Saudi Arabia, 'as a medium of expression and entertainment, is also a means by which investors seek to make financial gains, and figures endowed with political or religious authority try to shape the future of the country'. All these aspects, reasons Sakr, 'are fused, so that, far from determining outcomes, economics and the flow of capital are subject to obstacles created by rule-making structures that were put in place half a century ago'. On the more general question of what can be achieved by a political economy approach to understanding culture in the Arab world, Sakr advocates 'an exploration of geographic and historic contingency' that untangles 'the complex web of bargains made by those who exercise authority and uncover the unequal distribution of communicative resources'. The bargains and resource allocations discussed in her contribution show that 'the moments of production, distribution and consumption of film are analytically inseparable'.

Marwan Kraidy tells the story of modernity in Saudi Arabia through a compelling analysis of Abdullah Al-Ghathami's autobiographical work *The Tale of Modernity in the Kingdom of Saudi Arabia*. Kraidy's analysis unravels a fascinating 'picture of the litigious and abiding debate over the elaboration of an Arab-Muslim modernity'. He elucidates this picture through a systematic analysis, citing copiously from Al-Ghathami's book to reflect as much as possible his 'definition and theorizing of modernity'. Kraidy then moves on to analyse the role of the media in the struggle over modernity, as seen and witnessed by Al-Ghathami. Kraidy also uses some of Al-Ghathami's ideas as a 'prism through which contentious debates about media, culture and identity in the Arab world can be comprehended'. He further explores the heuristic potential of Al-Ghathami's notion of the 'symbolic event' for Arab thought about media and culture, and in thinking through some of the implications of the Saudi modernity wars in their regional context, managing all the while to delineate theoretical elements that could be significant for the development of Arab cultural studies, as a theoretical project.

In this first translation from the Arabic of his seminal work 'Theory and Method' (*Cultural Criticism*, 2000) Abdullah Al-Ghathami's chapter argues for a shift in the Arab cultural repertoire away from 'literary criticism' towards 'cultural criticism'. His aim is to make a jump from a critique of texts to a critique of the systems embedded in the texts, thus reversing the role of the critic. The divide between Arab 'high' culture, mainly the literary tradition known as *adab*, and Arab 'popular' culture, contends Al-Ghathami, is the product of a process and an embedded system that he calls *nassaq*, ceaselessly engineered by an official élitist discourse that privileges certain aesthetics and forms of artistic expression over others. Using examples from Arab poetry, both old and 'modern', Al-Ghathami shows how the system (*nassaq*) inherent to Arab literary aesthetics, is laden with a largely anti-modern and chauvinistic culture that is so old that it predates Islam. Arab literary aesthetics, he advances, need to be freed from both the institutional rhetorical discourse that reproduces them, and from 'aesthetics' as an official discourse. Literary criticism has failed as a tool of language and analysis because it focused on the text's beauty and ignored the hidden meaning system that is camouflaged by the text's aesthetic quality. Al-Ghathami proposes that we remove the aesthetic in Arab culture from its discourse and expose it to constant critique and subversion.

Atef Alshaer's chapter highlights the theme of language in respect to its cultural relevance, particularly in the context of the Arab world. He provides an overview of key schools of thought and debates, focusing on the relationship between language and culture and argues for the 'cultural consideration of language 'as a system of communication that expresses social and political orientations and attitudes'. He then delves into Arab cultural history and the location of Arabic within it. For Alshaer, the 'centrality of language to culture is captured in the phrasal term, 'culture of communication'. This term, he advances, has 'the potential to institute cultural embodiment through language use'. A sensible understanding of language, explains Alshaer, will take into consideration its natural, its cultural and political components, which are shown in various ways within a broader culture of communication.

Susan O'Rourke and Rosser Johnson's chapter provides a very rare insight into the kind of theoretical and practical problems that arise when trying to institutionalise one body of knowledge, in this case a Media Studies programme taught in New Zealand, into a traditional Arab country, here, Oman. The chapter focuses on the intricate cultural differences between the two countries and how these have informed the 'reversioning' of New Zealand's oldest media studies degree, a Bachelor of Communication Studies, into Oman's first Bachelor of Communications.

Notes

1. For many scholars, media studies is a separate field, but in my view cultural studies include studies of media, since media in all their forms reflect and spring from the cultures and societies in which they are found.
2. Garnham, Nicolas (2000) *Emancipation, the Media and Modernity: Arguments about the media and social theory*, Oxford University Press, p. 4.
3. Ibid: 7.
4. The concepts that this Arab Historian/philosopher articulated in his books: *Mafhum al-ideolujeya* (The Meaning of Ideology) (1980), *Mafhum al-hurreya* (The Meaning of Freedom) (1981), *Mafhum Addawlah* (The Meaning of the State) (1981), *Mafhum attarikh* (The Meaning of History) (1992), and *Mafhum al-Aql* (The Meaning of Reason) (1996, 2001), all dealt with modernity.
5. Laroui, Abdullah (2001) *Mafhoum al-'aql*, The Arab Cultural Centre, p. 14.
6. Laroui, Abdullah (1973) *al-'Arab wa al-Fikr Attarikhi*, Dar al Haqiqua.
7. Author's translation from French, Laroui, 2001, p. 72.
8. al-Jabri, Abed Mohammed (1989) *Ishkaleyat al-Fikr al-Arabi al-Mua'ssir*, Banshra, p. 24.

9. al-Jabri, Abed Mohammed (1994) *al-Mass'alat attakafeyah*, The Centre for the Studies of Arab Unity, p. 25.
10. Ibid: 25–27.
11. Although known for being a 'moderniser' and against *taqlid* (opting for imitation rather than independent reasoning), Mohammed Abduh, the highly influential nineteenth-century 'reformist' from Egypt, equated 'reform', with learning from the lessons of the past (from *al-salaf al-salih*, to be precise), which seems to contradict the whole logic of reform, which should be understood in terms of change, progression and a move away from past methods, structures and ideas (al-Jabri, 2005). Muhammad Abduh divided the *raison d'être* of his 'reform' to two main purposes: a 'restatement of what Islam really was' and a 'consideration of its implications for modern society' (Hourani, 1983: 140–41). Describing the first purpose, Abduh observed: 'First to liberate thought from the shackles of *taqlid*, and understand religion as it was understood by the elders of the community before dissention appeared; to return, in the acquisition of religious knowledge, to its first sources...' (ibid.). I have used the case of Abduh here to highlight the intricacy and fluidity within the key four intellectual positions described in this chapter. The case of Abduh is certainly an ambivalent one, but since he understands and seeks reform through a return to the past (regardless of the 'timelessness' of its ideas) places him, intellectually, as a 'cultural salafist'. What this also highlights is the difference between the ways in which the concept 'reform' has been used/articulated by scholars from the four different intellectual positions.
12. al-Azmeh, Aziz (1993) *Islams and Modernities*, Verso, p. 51.
13. *Ahl al-salaf al-saleh* refers to the companions of the prophet Mohammed (pbuh).
14. Abdelkabir Khatibi (1938–2009) is a Moroccan sociologist, literary critic, novelist and poet. His work, both fictional and non-fictional, is, in many ways, an exploration of complex postcolonial traits, such as 'double-identity' and 'hybridity'. 'Double-critique', a method he uses to reconcile and deal with his own double-identity, is conspicuous in his literary work. This includes: *La blessure du nom propre* (1974); *La mémoire tatouée* (1979) [an autobiographical piece, also his most acclaimed literary work]; *Amour bilingue* (1983); *Maghreb pluriel* (1983) [articulating the diversity and plurality of cultures in the Maghreb]; *Un été à Stockholm* (1990); *Le livre de sang* (1979); *Ombres japonaises* (1988); *Le prophète voilé* (1979); *White vomit* (1974) [criticising Zionism]; *Le même livre* (1985) [exploring the similarities between Arabs and Jews]; *Le roman maghrébin* (1958); *L'art calligraphique arabe* with Mohammed Sijilmassi (1976); and *Le livre de l'aimance* (1995).
15. I was introduced to the idea and concept of *tajawuz* 'transcendence' (meaning the transcendence of the duality problematic between turath and modernity) by two of its advocates, during an interview in Marrakech 2008: Abdul-Aziz Boumesshouli and Abdessamad Ghabass.

16. Khatibi, Abdelkabir (1980) *Annaqd al-Mujdawij*, Dār al-'Awdah, p. 17–18.
17. Ibid.
18. Binabdal'ali, Abdal-Salam (2002) *Baina al-ittissal wa al-Infi ssal: dirassat fi al-Fikr al-Falssafi bi al-Maghrib*, Dār Tubqal, p. 60.
19. Ibid: 18–19.
20. Binabdal'ali, Abdal-Salam (1983) *al-Fikr al-Falssafi fi al-Maghrib*, Dār attali'a.
21. Sheikh, Mohammed (2007) *Al-maghareba wa al-Hadatha*, Ramsis, p. 44.
22. Boumesshouli, Abdul-Aziz (2006) *al-Falssafa al-Maghribiyah*, The Moroccan Centre for Philosophical Research, p. 45.
23. See Walter Armbrust's chapter in this book.
24. Hobsbawm, Eric (1997, 2007) *On History*, London: Abacus, p. 23.
25. See Scannell, Paddy in Sabry, Tarik (2007a) 'An Interview With Paddy Scannell' in *Westminster Papers in Communication and Culture*, Volume: 4, Number: 3, pp. 3–23.
26. Ibid.
27. See the Centre's list of publications, published in 2005, for examples of academic publications dealing with the subject of 'Arab culture'.
28. See also analytical work by Ben Shekroun, 1980; Tarabishi 1993; Binabdal'ali 1994; al-Jabri 1994; Belqziz 2000; Abu Zaid 2002; Bundoq 2003; Ussfur 2003; Wakidi 2007; Oumlil, 2005.
29. Johnson, Nels (1987) 'Mass Culture and Islamic Populism' in Stauth, Georg and Zubaida, Sami (eds) (1987) *Mass Culture, Popular Culture, and Social Life in the Middle East*, Colorado: Westview Press, p. 165.
30. Al-Jabri, 2001.
31. Binabdal'ali, 1994, pp. 7–8.
32. Johnson, 1987, p. 171.
33. Lefebvre, Henri ([1984], 1999) *Everyday Life in the Modern World*, New Jersey: Transaction Publishers, p. 28.
34. Ibid: 54.
35. Scannell, P. in Sabry, T. 2007a, p. 12.
36. Lefebvre, 1999, p. 202.
37. Levinas, Emmanuel ([1991] 1998) *On the thinking-of-the-other: entre nous*, New Columbia University Press, p.180
38. Polanyi, Michael and Prosch, Harry (1975) *Meaning*, Chicago: University of Chicago Press, p.182.
39. Deleuze, Gilles (2002) *Dialogues II*, London: Continuum, p. 27.
40. Deleuze, Gilles and Guattari, Felix (1994) *What is Philosophy?* New York: Columbia University Press, p. 36.

Bibliography

Adorno, W. Theodor (1991) *The Culture Industry: Selected Essays on Mass Culture*, London: Routledge.

al-Azmeh, Aziz (1993) *Islams and Modernities*, Verso: London.

—— (1992) *al-Assala aw siyassat al-hurub mina al-waki'*, London: Dar al-Saqi.

Al-Ghathami, Abdullah (2005) *Attaqafa Atilivisyoniyat*, Casablanca: The Arab Cultural Centre.

—— (2000) *qiraa' fiannaqd athkafi*, Casablanca: The Arab Cultural Centre.

—— (1999) *ta'neet al-qassida wa al-qaari'al-mukhtalif*, Casablanca: The Arab Cultural Centre.

al-Jabri, Abed Mohammed (2005) *Finaqd al-hajat Ila al-islah*, Beirut: The Centre for the Study of Arab Unity.

—— (2001) *al-'aql al-akhlaqi al-'Arabi 4: A Critical Analytical Study of Ethical Models in Arab Culture*, Casablanca: Dār al-Nashr al-Maghribiyah.

—— (2000) *Naqd al-aql al-'Arabi 3: Arab Political Reason*, Beirut: The Centre for the Study of Arab Unity.

—— (1996) *Naqd al-aql al-'Arabi 2: The Structure of Arab Reason*, Casablanca: Arab Cultural Centre.

—— (1994) *al-Mass'alat attakafeyah*, Beirut: The Centre for the Studies of Arab Unity.

—— (1991) *Naqd al-'aql al-'Arabi 1: The Construction of Arab Reason*, Beirut: The Arab Cultural Centre.

—— (1989) *Ishkaleyat al-Fikr al-Arabi al-Mua'ssir*, Casablanca: Banshra.

Benjamin, Andrew (1993) *The Plural Event*, London: Routledge.

Binabdal'ali, Abdal-Salam (2002) *Baina al-ittissal wa al-Infissal: dirassat fial-Fikr al-Falssafibi al-Maghrib*, Casablanca: Dār Tubqal.

—— (2000) *al-Fikr fi'assr al-Techneya*, Casablanca: Ifrequiya al-Sharq.

—— (1994) *thakkafat al-udun wa thakafat al-'ain*, Rabat: Dār Tubqal.

—— (1983) *al-Fikr al-Falssafi fial-Maghrib*, Beirut: Dār attali'a.

Boumesshouli, Abdul-Aziz (2006a) *al-Falssafa al-Maghribeya, Sua'l al-Kawneyawa al-Mustaqbal*, Marrakech: The Moroccan Centre for Philosophical Research.

—— (2006) *al-Falssafa al-Maghribiyah*, Marrakech: The Moroccan Centre for Philosophical Research.

—— (2005) *Akhlā qu al-ghair: Nahwa falssafa Ghairiyah*, Marrakech: The Moroccan Centre for Philosophical Research: Walili Printers.

—— (2001) *al-ussus al-falsafeyat li nadareyat nihayat al-akhlaq*, Marrakech: The Moroccan Centre for Philosophical Research: Matba'at Walili.

Boumesshouli, Abdul-Aziz and Ghabass, Abdessamad (2003) *Azzamān wa al-fikr*, Casablanca: The Centre for Philosophical Research: Dār attakafa.

Deleuze, Gilles (2002) *Dialogues II*, London: Continuum.

—— (2001) *Pure Immanence*, New York: Zone Books.

Deleuze, Gilles and Guattari, Felix (1994) *What is Philosophy?*, New York: Columbia University Press.

Garnham, Nicolas (2000) *Emancipation, the Media and Modernity: Arguments about the Media and Social Theory*, Oxford: Oxford University Press.

Heidegger, Martin ([1962] 2007) *Being and Time*, Oxford: Blackwell Publishing.

Hobsbawm, Eric (1997, 2007) *On History*, London: Abacus.

Johnson, Nels (1987) 'Mass Culture and Islamic Populism' in Stauth, George and Zubaida, Sami (eds) (1987) *Mass Culture, Popular Culture, and Social Life in the Middle East*, Boulder: Westview Press, pp. 165–87.

Khatibi, Abdelkabir (1980) *Annaqd al-Mujdawij*, Beirut: Dār al-'Awdah.

Lalande, André (1948) *La Raison et Les Normes*, Paris: Librairie Hachette.

Laroui, Abdullah (2006) '*Awaeq al-tahdith*, Morocco: Manshurat Itihad Kutab al-Maghrib.

—— (2001) *Mafh oum al-'aql*, Casablanca: The Arab Cultural Centre.

—— (2001) *Modernité et L'Islam*, Casablanca: The Arab Cultural Centre.

—— (1992) *Mafh oum attarikh*, Casablanca: The Arab Cultural Centre.

—— (1981) *Mafh oum addawlah*, Casablanca: The Arab Cultural Centre.

—— (1980) *Mafh oum al-hurreya*, Casablanca: The Arab Cultural Centre.

—— (1977) *Les Origines Sociales et Culturelles du Nationalisme Marocain*, Paris: Maspero.

—— (1976) *The Crisis of the Arab Intellectual: Traditionalism or Historicism?*, Berkeley: California University Press.

—— (1973) *al-'Arab wa al-Fikr Attarikhi*, Beirut: Dar al Haqiqua.

—— (1970) *L'histoire du Maghreb*, Paris: Maspero.

Lefebvre, Henri (1995) *Introduction to Modernity*, London: Verso.

—— ([1984], 1999) *Everyday Life in the Modern World*, New Jersey: Transaction Publishers.

Levinas, Emmanuel (1998) *On the Thinking-of-the-Other: Entre nous*, New York: Columbia University Press.

—— (1994) *L'intrigue de L'infini*, Paris: Flammarion.

—— (1993) *Dieu, la Mort et le Temps*, Paris: Bernard Grasset.

—— (1987) *Collected Philosophical Papers*, Dordrecht: Martinus Nijhoff Publishers.

—— (1978) *Existence and Existents*, London: Kluwer Academic Publishers.

Mernissi, Fatima (1991) *Women and Islam*, Oxford: Blackwell.

—— (1975) *Beyond the Veil, Male-Female Dynamics in Modern Muslim Society*, London: John Wiley and Sons.

Polanyi, Michael and Prosch, Harry (1975) *Meaning*, Chicago: University of Chicago Press.

Sabry, Tarik (2010) *Cultural Encounters in the Arab World: On Media, the Modern and the Everyday*, London: I.B.Tauris.

—— (2009) 'Media and Cultural Studies in the Arab world: Making Bridges to Local Discourses of Modernity' in Daya Thussu (ed.), *Internationalising Media Studies*, London: Routledge, pp. 196–214.

—— (2008) 'Arab Media and Cultural Studies: Rehearsing New Questions' in Kai Hafez (ed.), *Arab Media: Power and Weakness*, New York: Continuum, pp. 237–51.

—— (2007a) 'An Interview With Paddy Scannell' in *Westminster Papers in Communication and Culture* 4.3: 3–23.

—— (2007) 'In search of the Present Arab Cultural Tense' in N. Sakr (ed.), *Arab Media and Political Renewal: Community, Legitimacy and Public Life*, London: I.B.Tauris, pp. 154–68.

Scannell, Paddy (2007) *Media and Communication*, London: Sage.

—— (2006) *Broadcasting and Time*, Ph.D. Dissertation, University of Westminster.

—— (2000) 'For-anyone-as-someone structures' *Media, Culture and Society* 22.1: 5–24.

—— (1999) 'Cultural Studies and the Meaning of Life', unpublished manuscript.

Sheikh, Mohammed (2007) *Al-maghareba wa al-Hadatha*, Rabat: Ramsis.

Zylinska, Joanna (2005) *The Ethics of Cultural Studies*, London: Continuum.

2

History in Arab Media Studies: A Speculative Cultural History

Walter Armbrust

Although my purpose in this essay is to outline some thoughts about the value of history to the study of Arab media, one might equally consider the value of history to cultural studies. In either case, as an anthropologist I am a somewhat odd proponent of history. I am, to be sure, not a historian, though I have contributed to history publications.[1] Nor do I conjure with the academic formation of 'cultural studies' in my research or teaching, which is perhaps unsurprising, on the grounds that anthropology and cultural studies are famously uneasy with each other. Anthropology devours critical theory voraciously while simultaneously mounting a zealous defence of its disciplinary boundaries, usually on grounds of method, specifically, participant observation.[2] The quasi-discipline of cultural studies self-consciously appropriates 'the culture concept', which anthropology had regarded as its own, but not as anthropology's method. As of the millennium a 'cultural studies reader' assembled by Simon During (a scholar of English literature) included only two anthropologists among thirty-eight contributors.[3] However, as an anthropologist hired by the Faculty of Oriental Studies at Oxford, I am in some ways an outlier from my own discipline, and hence, not greatly concerned with disputes over the boundaries between anthropology and cultural studies, but history is, by some measures, as wary of cultural studies as anthropology, or perhaps the wariness comes from the opposite direction. During's cultural studies reader counts only one historian among its thirty-eight contributors, so in his formulation of the field anthropologists outnumber historians two to one; collectively they are dwarfed by such fields as English literature, film and communications studies.[4]

I mention all of this at the outset to establish first, that I have no disciplinary axe to grind or boundaries to defend in this essay and, secondly, that a historical perspective may be as lacking in cultural studies as it is in Arab media studies. I am therefore a double outlier (to both history and anthropology) speaking to twin deficiencies (in both cultural studies and Arab media studies). Given the general dissociation of history from Arab media studies (my main concern here), it may be that an outlier position is the only position from which to think about the two fields together. I will not devote a great deal of energy to exploring the reasons for ahistoricism in cultural studies, and I recognise that there are many important exceptions to the ahistoricism implied in During's attempt to synthesize his field. There are likewise many exceptions to the ahistorical rule in Arab media studies, and I *will* discuss those. My main agenda is a positive one: to suggest some historical problems that should be addressed, but I will expend some effort to outline the consequences of ahistoricism to Arab media studies, because an argument for historical engagement can hardly ignore them.

A case study

My historical project, which I will outline in purely speculative terms here, focuses on Egypt as a case study. This is partly a matter of convenience; Egypt is my primary research site, but my case study for historical engagement in Arab media studies is itself also a product of history. For much of the nineteenth and twentieth centuries Egypt was one of the main producers of printed media content in the Arabic-speaking world (the other being Lebanon, and no other Arab countries had effective pan-Arab ambitions). In the context of audio and audiovisual media, Egypt was unquestionably *the* dominant producer until quite late in the twentieth century. Consequently, the academic literature on Egyptian media is considerably richer than is comparable writing on other Arab countries. Egyptian scholars are well aware of the importance of their country's media heritage, and foreign researchers have experienced few disruptions in access compared, for example, to places like Iraq, Lebanon and Algeria (where long periods of war and civil strife prohibited research by foreign scholars and greatly narrowed research agendas at home), or Syria (where political restrictions have often had a crippling effect on all research). Furthermore, attempting to cover the entire Arab world in a single essay in any case requires paying too high a price in generalisation,[5] thus, if I focus a discussion of 'Arab media' through a case study, then I would first argue that a case study stands a far better chance of usefully articulating my topic, and secondly, that this particular case study should be seen as the most broadly productive point of entry to a conceptual problem.

The project

My positive agenda is a cultural history of new media in Egypt between 1919, when a print culture can be said to have been consolidated, and 1975, when the audiocassette was introduced. Radio, cinema, television and a flourishing illustrated press emerged in this period, and were central to the experience of modernity in Egypt. We lack basic institutional histories of all the media from this period, but for present purposes (a book on cultural studies and Arab media), I will outline some of the issues raised by the cultural effects of these new media, focusing on the following areas: 1) sensory culture; 2) the impact of colonialism; 3) the politics of language; 4) the place of religion in media; 5) the functional distribution of media; and 6) tensions between continuity and transformation, but first let me elaborate on some of the contextual features of my project.

Preliminary considerations

The period should not be viewed as sharply bounded, but there are good reasons for defining it as such. Printing was an important social phenomenon in Egypt by the late nineteenth century. One can cover the early history of printing in Egypt through secondary literature,[6] hence, the logic of defining the nominal starting point as 1919; this is roughly when print culture reached a critical mass. Both institutions for publishing and the emergence of a public trained to read printed materials had crystallised. The 1970s make sense as an endpoint, because this was when the audiocassette entered the global mediascape. For the Middle East, the audiocassette was a 'game changer'. Audiocassettes are a 'small medium',[7] characterised by decentralised production potentially targeted to specific audiences. Small media include inexpensive and flexible technologies for print reproduction (photocopiers) and telephony (fax machines), but in Egypt and the wider Middle East the audiocassette was (and in many places, remains) by far the most important small medium; its capacity to bypass cultural, religious and political gatekeepers dramatically altered the structure of media production and consumption, enabling the formation of 'counterpublics'.[8] Audiocassette technology is really more akin to what we conventionally call 'new media' (i.e., digital media, most prominently satellite broadcasting and information technology) than to the relatively more centralised media regimes salient before the 1970s. There is no precise date on which the audiocassette was introduced to Egypt. Local businessmen had to acquire it and learn to market it, the public had to become familiar with its capacities, and local content producers had to learn how to use the new medium. None of these processes took place overnight, but certainly by the mid-1970s the audiocassette was a palpable presence in Egypt, and its flexibility, cheapness, ease of duplication, and hence, counter-hegemonic potential, marked the beginning of a new era in Egyptian mass media history.

The accession to power of the Free Officers in 1952 is a conventional watershed in Egyptian history. Many social, political and economic processes relevant to mass media ran across the 1952 divide. These include the expansion of mass education and rising literacy; state ownership of radio broadcasting (starting in 1934); the proliferation of illustrated magazines and periodicals; the growth of mass mediated musical production, including the dominance of institutional gatekeepers; and the business model of the cinema, which eschewed Hollywood-like vertical monopolies, despite a public embrace of a 'Hollywood on the Nile' label. In other ways, 1952 is highly significant to Egyptian media history. The scope and ambition of radio broadcasting were famously expanded by Nasser; nationalisation of the cinema took place in the 1960s, partly as a solution to economic contradictions that reached back to the 1930s, but also in response to ideological imperatives that took shape starting with independence. Egyptian state television broadcasting was initiated entirely in the Nasser era. Research on the history of Egyptian media should account for both continuities and changes across the 1952 divide but, on the whole, the institutional and cultural logic of 'big media' transcends the divide.

If one were to approach the history of Egyptian media in this period culturally, there would be of course many potential avenues of inquiry. Here I suggest six potential themes that highlight the ways new media shaped Egyptian society and culture during most of the twentieth century.

The senses

Arab-Islamic societies generally can be characterised by tension between audiocentric (hearing-centred) modes of authority now associated with tradition, and ocularcentric (vision-centred) techniques of European provenance, either imposed or consciously adopted by colonised societies (Mitchell 1988; Messick 1993). Audiocentrism emphasises the linking of texts to the people who create and transmit them; it is predicated on the status of the Qu'ran as a 'recitation text',[9] meant to be spoken and memorised before it was read, and functioning as the cornerstone of literacy. Ocularcentrism, by contrast, places texts in a world of representable objects distinguished from the mind of a thinking subject, thereby dispersing authority to the texts themselves. This is not to say that pre-colonial Arab societies somehow 'lacked' visual culture. Superficial readings of certain Qu'ranic and Hadith texts undoubtedly made Arab-Islamic aniconism seem more clear-cut than it actually was,[10] but in reality 'the relation between the visual world and ocular experience and its representation' is always complex and fluid,[11] a point also made eloquently for European culture by Jay (1993). Ethnographic studies suggest that Arab-Islamic writing practice gives a central place to audition even in contemporary societies.[12]

It cannot be doubted that in Egypt from 1919 to 1975 vision was ascendant. Even radio broadcasts and audio recordings were yoked to the visual sphere by an increasingly insistent marketing logic requiring audio production to be known through visual representations (in print, cinema or television) of their 'authors'. However, while the expansion in technologies of vision was a prominent feature of the period, it does not necessarily follow that we must interpret the history of media in Egypt as a straightforward replacement of audiocentric authority with European-style ocularcentrism. A history of the senses as they pertain to Egyptian mass media should therefore be attentive not just to the emerging authority of vision, but also to its limits. Does a significant tension between ear-centred and eye-centred practices remain, even when audiocentrism was apparently in recession during much of the twentieth century? At a certain point, one might argue that the balance of power between audiocentrism and ocularcentrism began to shift. In this vein, the 'resurgence' of Islam as a political force in the 1970s can be interpreted through the lens of sensory culture. Islamic resurgence was (and remains) marked not just by audiocentrism, but by tangible anti-ocularism expressed most famously through debates over women's dress, but also in the promotion of putative prohibitions against representation that had been either ignored in practice, or at least debated (rather than simply accepted) for centuries.[13] The rise of audio-centric discourses and practices in the 1970s may have come in reaction to vision-centred modes of authority, or it may be that the history of pre-1970s Egyptian media will show a less decisive hegemony of the eye. It is therefore important to explore tensions between vision and hearing as they occur across a wide range of media during a time in which vision was nominally ascendant.

Colonialism

It is, to some degree, necessary to decentre European colonialism as the primary agent of Egyptian modernity in the interest of foregrounding Egypt's own engagements with that modernity. The point in doing so is, as Timothy Mitchell puts it, to 'look at particular examples of the local articulation of modernity, the way the modern is staged and performed'.[14] By this logic it does not follow that colonialism was irrelevant. How did colonialism affect the adoption of (or resistance to) mass media in Egypt? The experience of modernity under colonial domination was intrinsically ambivalent. Like all colonial societies, Egypt was compelled to both distinguish itself from Europe and, at the same time, to replicate European form.[15] Mass mediation was a prominent stage on which this dialectic of replication and difference was performed. Implicitly, scholars took the replication of European form in Egyptian mass media for granted. Until quite recently it was assumed that important debates on how Egypt should make itself modern took place in art (almost exclusively writing – novels, short stories, or poetry – in our scholarship) or in 'thought' (non-fictional, secular or Islamic texts that engaged with various aspects of Egyptian modernity). Little attention was paid to how the experience of even our conventional categories of literature and thought were, for Egyptians, *mediated*, and not just in the form of printed books, but in cinema, recorded music, the popular press, radio and television. The cultural capital of 'thinkers' and artists – and certainly not just writers – became the basis of an ongoing construction of cultural icons. A central issue in the relationship of media and colonialism is the question of how Egyptians elaborated differences from a putatively universal European standard of modernity in their own repetitive mass mediated 'sketchpads', on which such differences were staged.

Language

How did increasingly diversified mass media articulate with the politics of language? Conventionally, Arabic-speaking communities are considered 'diglossic', characterised by a functional differentiation between a 'high' prestige variant used in writing, and a 'low' variant used for specific spoken purposes.[16] Academic linguists now tend to focus more on performative code switching,[17] or the sociology and politics of language standardisation,[18] than on diglossia, which now seems overly descriptive. However, aside from the issues of how the language actually works in Arab societies, 'diglossia' is a useful summary of folk ideologies about Arabic, and it powerfully inflects the significance of mass mediation. In Arabic-speaking societies, the perceived difference between spoken and written language is distinctive, and far more ideologically charged than in most other places.[19] Nominally, all writing is in the 'high' variant of Arabic, though there have always been important exceptions.[20] Audiovisual mass media, in which the vast majority of expression is colloquial, essentially reverses the proportions of 'high' and 'low' language. A history of Egyptian mass media must therefore examine the status of audiovisual recorded discourse as 'text'. Much of the material screened or broadcast in cinema, recorded music, radio and television was, in fact, written prior to being recorded. This was also the case with most theatrical drama, which though not mediated in the same way as films or television shows, was closely linked to both through writers and performers, and was in any case presented in a commercial setting comparable to mediated performance (available to 'paying customers', more or less on demand, rather than linked to holidays, rites of passage, or élite patronage, as was the case with pre-modern performing arts). The vernacular character of audiovisual mass media presented thorny problems in a number of areas. One was art. By definition, any verbal art should be in the 'high' language. This is why Arabic literature departments in both Europe and the Arab world focus almost exclusively on literature in the 'high' language, and largely ignore vernacular production. Nonetheless, it was never feasible for Egyptian intellectuals to, for example, dismiss the cinema in its entirety as non-artistic; or to deny the artistic credentials of many intensely admired singers who performed vernacular texts. An implicit imperative to create national canons in the arts made it impossible to simply 'write off' entire art forms, even if their 'colloquial-ness' could never receive formal recognition. Overall, the situation with regard to language was that an official rhetoric of instilling the 'high' language through education, national institutions, and national bureaucracy paralleled a vast audiovisual production of colloquial expression which had ambiguous credentials as 'text', but which impinged on many areas of importance to Egyptian nationalism.

Religion

What was the relationship between media and religious discourse? The role of print media in facilitating the interpretation of religious texts by non-specialists has been articulated in contemporary contexts,[21] and the point would not be lost on anyone writing about the history of the Muslim Brotherhood (e.g., Goldberg 1991). However, other forms of mediated religious discourse in Egypt prior to the 1970s are a *tabula rasa* in academic writing. Radio programmes in the 1930s show that religion was part of state broadcasting agendas, but there is no academic writing on the topic. There is no academic writing on any aspect of early Egyptian television. Given the Egyptian state's longstanding practice of maintaining a stake in religious discourse, even if only in the interest of trying to limit its role in modern society,[22] one cannot assume the absence of religion in the television programme. Scholarship has not engaged with discourses on religion in putatively secularising media, such as cinema or the mainstream press. Did audiovisual media amplify the capacity of printing to push religious interpretation outside the authoritative institutions, particularly al-Azhar? Or, on the contrary, did 'big media', which were easily controlled by the state, buttress the conventional religious authority of 'big institutions'?

Functional distribution

Information, education, and entertainment are conventional categories of media analysis.[23] How were these categories distributed in Egyptian media, and can they be applied cross culturally? Academic literature on Middle Eastern media concentrates very heavily on information (news) in the satellite era. To the extent that we have paid attention to news in the 'big media' era, we focus entirely on the press. Even in this case, we use news as a source for the writing of history, but never examine it as an artefact of mediation. Academic literature on the other standard categories of media analysis – education and entertainment – is impoverished. In examining the entire mediascape of this period, we should start to ask questions about the distribution of mediated expression that falls into these categories. The categories themselves are useful as a starting point for analysis, and one may assume that the actual function of a given instance of mass mediated expression may not line up neatly with any of the three. The problem is that the literature on Middle Eastern media *has* assumed the primacy of one media category – information (more about this below). However, a view of the overall mediascape in the era of 'big media' might reveal that, in terms of the categories, information occupies a place inverse to our own academic preoccupation with news – in other words, a rather small place – but functionally entertainment informs in ways that we might not have expected. The widest circulating periodicals of the interwar era carried only small amounts of 'news'. They instead featured a wide variety of commentary on current events blended into an entertainment package that featured short stories, opinion, often in the form of satire, poetry, caricature and photojournalism (see the discussion below on the magazine *al-Ithnayn*). Similarly, the early radio programme, in the 1930s, was almost devoid of news – news only came into the picture during World War II, when the British began to broadcast it. Cinema was obviously entertaining, but the preoccupation of films with love (in a nominally Westernising form) can also be seen as a long slow-moving discussion of patriarchal authority, and hence, an educational medium. In the end, the categories may well have had a kind of common-sense quality to Egyptians of the interwar era, just as they do to us now, and yet we should not confuse common-sense labels with potentially much more complex social functions.

Continuity vs. 'apocalyptic transformation'

The advent of new media is often seen in apocalyptic terms, as erasing stable social practices that had been predicated on older media but, as Thorburn and Jenkins put it, 'the actual relations between emerging technologies and their ancestor systems proved to be more complex, often more congenial, and always less suddenly disruptive than was dreamt of in the apocalyptic philosophies that heralded their appearance'.[24] This sense of apocalypse is underwritten by implicit assumptions about the fundamental importance of writing and printing. For example, Ong argued that secondary orality (based on audiovisual recording technology rather than on direct speech) is 'essentially a more deliberate and self-conscious orality, based permanently on the use of writing and print'.[25] In this vein, it pays to ask whether there was significance in the historical compression of printing and successive waves of audiovisual innovation in Egypt, as opposed to Europe, where print culture had been established for several centuries before the advent of audiovisual technology? Longue durée histories of media encompass everything from parchment to digital hypermedia;[26] or they can focus more closely on eras,[27] or even points of transition.[28] However, all such histories are Eurocentric, as are more speculative 'global' histories implied in such theoretically inspired work as that of Ong (1982) and McLuhan (1994). Crucially, print culture in Egypt took shape under the pressure of colonial rule. Previously, the culture of writing and reading was geared to manuscripts, and it remained so to the end of the nineteenth century. Consequently, the introduction of new media technologies in Egypt, *including printing*, was compressed into a short time frame relative to the European case. Audiovisual technologies, invented and commercialised starting in the nineteenth century, became global phenomena, but the mediascapes into which they spread were more diverse than 'global' histories of media acknowledge. The emergence of grass-roots modernity in Egypt from the late nineteenth century was accompanied by assumptions about the best ways to communicate to presumably illiterate sectors of the population, *without* having to teach them to read in either the traditional (religious) schools or in the modern schools that were still inaccessible to most Egyptians. Hence, the dominance of print culture looks very different in Egypt than it is assumed to have been in Europe. The practical implication of this is that a history of mass media in Egypt benefits from keeping the relation between writing and audiovisual media as an open question, rather than assuming the primacy of writing and print as a kind of bedrock upon which audiovisual media build. To put it differently, the history of Egyptian print culture can be seen as closely intertwined with that of audiovisual culture, in contrast to Europe, where the idea of the 'permanent use of writing and print' seems like common sense. As things stand, the default position on the history of Egyptian print culture is that printing is connected to the rise of mass literacy, and is therefore strictly a matter of the history of education and the history of texts; the history of other media is a separate issue. A more perceptive cultural history might well offer an alternative to this default position by maintaining a focus on connections *between* mass media, rather than implicitly assuming that printing was fundamental to subsequent media practices.

The bigger picture

A cultural history of media would illuminate key aspects of the history of modernity in Egypt and the wider Middle East, and to the decentring of modernity from a Western model without, however, losing sight of the tangible presence of Euro-American hegemony. It might well also crystallise a picture of Egyptian modernity that transcends both intellectual history (modernity as the inevitable unfolding of coherent 'modern thought'), and the centrality of Western hegemony that animates postcolonial scholarship. To put it differently, a cultural history of Egyptian media would approach modernity by foregrounding the increasingly ubiquitous fact of mass mediation – a fact that touches on both 'thought' and on European hegemony, but cannot be reduced to the terms of either. Such a history ideally would grapple with concrete social facts and processes, elucidating institutions, political and legal frameworks, key individuals, important themes in the content of the various media, discourses on how media should disseminate modernity, linguistic issues, and articulations with nationalism. However, beyond the goal of creating a fine-grained history of a number of important Egyptian media, a cultural studies approach to such a history would focus on new media or, more precisely, of the social effects associated with technological innovation.

Elements of such a history can already be extrapolated from existing scholarship, including the history of sound recording,[29] and mass mediated popular music generally,[30] and the history of cinema as art and socio-political expression.[31] The basic history of the press in the Middle East has been outlined.[32] Academic literature on Egyptian television begins in the 1990s,[33] and says little about the early history of Egyptian television broadcasting, but we suffer from serious deficiencies in a number of key areas, including the histories of illustrated magazines, radio, cinema (as a medium), and television – the 'biggest' of the media introduced to Egypt between 1919 and 1975.

It is at this point that the confluence of cultural studies and the study of Arab media should feel a keen need for historical engagement. Literature on new media in the Middle East focuses narrowly on post-1990s digital media – satellite television broadcasting and the Internet.[34] However, the Middle East has, like the rest of the world, experienced successive waves of new media over the past two centuries. A substantial historical literature addresses the social effects of these innovations in Europe and the United States.[35] There is no comparable attention to such phenomena in histories of the Middle East. Regional literature engages with the early effects of the printing press,[36] and links printing and nationalism.[37] At the other end of this historical period a lively literature examines the impact of the audiocassette.[38] Middle East-oriented literature on new media in the conventional (digital) sense is completely ahistorical.

The consequences of this ahistoricism can be illustrated productively through a further consideration of the issue of functional distribution, which was raised above. How were information, education, and entertainment distributed through Egyptian media?

The categories themselves are conventional entry points to analysing media – both their production and their use by people. In one book, a *Social History of Media from Gutenberg to the Internet* by Asa Briggs and Peter Burke (2005), they are described as the 'holy trinity' of media studies. No doubt this is only true of a certain kind of academic literature, but what is most significant in the present context is that the categories are implicit in the structure of much of the literature on Middle Eastern media. As we all know, most academic literature on Middle Eastern media concentrates very heavily on information, which we call 'news', and they often sloppily equate news with 'media' itself. Arab media studies are by no means the only offenders. As Lisa Gitelman puts it, 'naturalizing, essentializing, or ceding agency to media is something that happens at a lexical level every time anyone says "the media" in English, as if media were a unified natural entity, like the wind'.[39] Nonetheless, while Arab media studies are by no means exceptional in this regard, it cannot be overemphasised that 'Arab media', as artefacts of the digital age, remains a spectacularly unexamined assumption that is strongly mirrored at the institutional level. Furthermore, to the extent that we have paid attention to news in previous historical eras, we focus entirely on the printed press. Even in this case, we use news occasionally as a source for the writing of history, but never examine it as an artefact of mediation. It is worth emphasising that academic literature on the other standard categories of media analysis – education and entertainment – is small, though it must be acknowledged that the situation is changing rapidly. Many scholars are in fact beginning to think more perceptively about the overall social environment in which Arab media occur, though historical engagement is still rare.[40]

As for 'information, education, and entertainment', the first observation that one ought to make about these three categories – which the media historians Briggs and Burke do make, and most of us writing about the Middle

East have not made – is that in and of themselves, they are manifestly crude. My point in raising them, of course, is that they should *not* be taken for granted, as they have been taken for granted in Arab media studies. The purpose of distinguishing between mediated information, education and entertainment is not just to slot instances of media production into one or the other category. The categories are not ends in themselves. Far more importantly, there are all sorts of overlaps, exchanges and ambiguities between the categories, and *these* are their most analytically productive aspect. It is precisely the functional hybridity around the edges of the categories to which we should pay attention.

A historical perspective helps us to see this more clearly than the relentlessly presentist view of Arab media has been able to do. Hence, if we view the overall mediascape of the period, that is implicitly assumed to be an unproblematic predecessor to the digital revolution – in other words, 1919 to 1975, as my project frames it, or everything before 1995 (before the practical applications of the digital revolution began to become tangible) as Arab media studies implicitly defines its object of study – then we might well discover that in terms of the broad categories of information, education and entertainment, *information* occupies a place *inverse* to our own academic preoccupation with news – in other words, a rather more limited place than our academic and political preoccupations might suggest.

Consider, in this vein, that the widest circulation weekly in the Egyptian interwar era was not a news publication, but was, as mentioned above, a publication called *al-Ithnayn* (Figure 1). *Al-Ithnayn* – literally 'the two', named as such because it combined two previous publications, *al-Fukaha* and *al-Kawakib*, which covered humour and show business – was an illustrated variety magazine that carried only small amounts of 'news'. Instead it mixed commentary on current events into an entertainment package. To put it bluntly, it simply did not fit the conventional categories of information, education, and entertainment; it was instead inherently a creature of thematic overlaps, exchanges, ambiguities, and functional hybridity.

Figure 1 shows a sample of covers from the interwar era. In Figure 2, we see a brief reference to the contents. *Al-Ithnayn's* very popular and much-emulated package was, of course, adapted from a foreign model. The parallel with the present is obvious; the variety magazine format is just like 24-hour news programmes and reality television, both nominally forms 'copied' from Western models, but very quickly customised

Figure 1   The highest-circulating weekly of the Egyptian interwar era: *Al-Ithnayn* (1934–1960)

to local needs and realities. The specific convention of *al-Ithnayn* was that its contents varied from year to year, but over the long haul, it featured short stories, opinion, often in the form of satire (such as the 'disciplinary court' series invoked in Figure 2),[41] but also opinion expressed in poetry (such as a poem displayed on the bottom of Figure 2, which comments on radio, and was written by a staff poet who wrote under the pen name Abu-Buthayna). It also had caricature and photojournalism, and often the 'news' it carried was about show business, but show business itself should not be taken for granted. It is worth mentioning that aside from print media, academics have barely even thought about other media of the pre-digital age. If we did, we would find that it makes more sense, as suggested a moment ago, in the context of thematic overlaps, exchanges, ambiguities and functional hybridity. More sense, that is, than if one just assigns a given instance of media content to a category – information,

Satire in *al-Ithnayn*: in the "Maglis al-Ta'dib" (disciplinary court) a jury of show business luminaries and mostly lower-tier intellectuals tries case against British High Commissioner Miles Lampson

Poetic commentary in *al-Ithnayn*: staff poet "Abu-Buthayna" extolling the achivement of a national radio broadcasting program in 1934

Figure 2   Cover of issue no. 2 (June 25, 1934) of *al-ithnayn*

entertainment or education – and then elevate one category above the others, as we have done in Arab media studies. Egyptian radio began in the 1920s through haphazard individual efforts, and was nationalised in 1934, as memorialised by Abu-Buthayna's poem (Figure 3). The poem extols radio as a serious and important national achievement,[42] but early radio programmes, in the 1930s, were almost devoid of news, which only came into the picture during World War II when the British began to broadcast it.[43] Most of the programming consisted of music, and there was, even then, a bit of religious content broadcast alongside the entertainment. The Abu-Buthayna poem comments on both. The poet extols the new accessibility of 'national singers', such as Umm Kulthoum, to ordinary people,[44] and when discussing religion, exhorts the new national radio service to give the public the clear and simple religious instruction they craved and deserved in the eyes of the poet.[45] Early radio was therefore at least nominally about entertainment and education, though not at all in a straightforward way. The entertainment served national goals, and the religion

Figure 3 'He's sleeping heavily ... we'll wake him up'

subtly undermined confidence in the ability of conventional institutions to give the people what they should have. It is easy to imagine the nascent Muslim brotherhood in the wings, stoking up pressure on the state to react to their message. So one can either ignore early radio, on the assumption that its entertainment profile was insufficiently 'serious' – a comment often made about entertainment media in Arab media conferences during the first decade of the new millennium – or better, one might want to ask more questions about what radio meant to people in the 1930s and 1940s. It is not as if they failed to regard it as an important and serious development, even if the content was mostly music. The problem is that we are not equipped to see the phenomenon of early radio; it was not 'news', therefore, by the standards of Arab media studies, it must have been 'mere entertainment', which is surely one of the most regrettable phrases ever uttered at a media conference, and yet it has been lamentably common in Arab media conferences over the previous decade.

Conclusion: the presentism of Arab media studies

One might well ask, why bring up history in a book on Arab media? As we all 'know' (or more precisely, assume without really thinking very much about it), 'Arab media', as an emerging academic concentration, is essentially a digital phenomenon. Arab media studies are relentlessly 'presentist' – our historical horizon is roughly from the mid-1990s to now, and it encompasses primarily digital and transnational media. Quite possibly, if I say we need greater historical perspective, most readers from within the field of Arab media studies would be inclined to agree, but as I write this essay, I would bet a large sum that most would do so tepidly. 'History? Sure, why not'. Nobody who responds in this way would follow up through publications, teaching, recruitment priorities or research. Why is that so? Why are Arab media studies so presentist?

I have already alluded to some of the consequences of ahistoricism in Arab media studies. Let me now speculate on some of the reasons for it. In my opinion, the field of Arab media studies is dominated by a form of technological determinism that is a strand of media studies everywhere, but is particularly marked in Arab media studies. In the context of the issue that I have outlined as my case study within a case study – the implicit organisation of what we research by content categories; 'information, education, entertainment' – technological determinism has had the effect of casting the categories as a hierarchy: information (essentially news) above everything else, particularly over entertainment. The technological determinist assumes that once a new technology is introduced it causes the teleological unfolding of a set of inexorable changes. For example, the essence of the so-called 'Al Jazeera effect', however one interprets it, was that the new medium, harnessed to the function of providing information, would cause dramatic change. As mentioned above, Kraidy put his finger on why this is so problematic in his recent book on reality television. As he put it, Arab media studies are 'deliberative-rationalistic', assuming a straightforward cause and effect relationship between the provision of 'objective' information and the emergence of the sort of liberal politics characteristic of a Habermasian public sphere. He instead recommends a 'deliberative-performative' approach, which is a way to say that we should be attentive to how media does what it does, rather than select in advance to enable a particular outcome, blinding ourselves to alternative possibilities. What Kraidy suggests has actually been taken up by many scholars;

Arab media studies now enjoys a lively engagement with religion, popular culture, social networking, activism, blogging, political economy, and many other topics that can't be easily shoehorned into the conventional categories of content. The days in which anyone could say with a straight face at a conference that Arab media is all about news, and everything else is 'mere entertainment', are thankfully over. However, there is still a fact that ought to be faced, and this is that we do not seem to regard the presentism of Arab media studies as a problem. Or, to put it differently, lurking just below the surface of a field that is fantastically diverse by the standards of its recent history, we are still taking as a given that 'new media', by which we mean digital media introduced since the 1990s, must be seen as the harbinger of *dramatic change*. Consequently, we still suffer from an unexamined technological determinism. I do not mean to argue that the solution to this problem is to become social determinists instead. An extreme social determinist would completely deny the transformative effect of technology; 'culture' would always nullify it, leaving the social landscape essentially unchanged. Many of my colleagues in the Faculty of Oriental Studies fall into this trap, assuming that 'Islamic history' must always carry forward an Islamic essence that remains unchanging. We are all familiar enough with criticisms of that kind of intellectual mistake, but I do not think we quite appreciate the degree to which we've set ourselves up as 'technological orientalists', assuming that the march of technology always somehow decisively shapes history. Presumably nobody would want to adopt the extreme positions of either technological or social determinism, but to avoid falling into the trap of one or the other we have to first recognise the problem. Mass media do not necessarily 'cause' dramatic change, for the simple reason that change is more often a gradual process of slow sedimentation; in other words, the gradual changing of habits and practices over long periods. Consequently, history is important, because without it we fundamentally misunderstand what we look at today. Every new medium becomes a 'great white hope'; a new champion that will slay whatever beast we fear, whether it takes the form of authoritarianism, terrorism, Western dominance or patriarchy. A more vigorous engagement with history will put to rest such false hopes that we have implicitly laid on technological innovation, but it will certainly do so without making us lose sight of much more fundamental social changes, such as the pre-eminence of vision over hearing, or vice versa; or the recasting of beliefs about what constitute proper and improper modes of linguistic expression, or what it really means to mass mediate religious experience. History will cause us to lose a bit of the breathless quality of Arab media studies that comes from the belief that every new medium is bound to change everything, but we would be more than adequately compensated by what we would gain through understanding how the world actually works.

Notes

1. Armbrust, Nettler and Ryzova 2007; Armbrust 2006; 2002; 2008a; 2008b; 2008c, 2010.
2. Nugent and Shore 1997.
3. The anthropologists tapped by During (2000) as key contributors to cultural studies were James Clifford and Arjun Appadurai.
4. The historian in During's volume is Carolyn Steedman. Many of the other contributors have written histories, but like myself, they all have degrees in other disciplines and teach in other departments.
5. Boyd's survey of radio and television broadcasting in the Arab world demonstrates the high cost of making geographic coverage a higher priority than local depth. His volume works as a very basic reference tool, but one could never assign it, or even parts of it, to a class at any level. It is 'consult-able' without being at all readable.
6. Ayalon 1995; Fahmy 2007.
7. Sreberny-Mohammadi and Mohammadi 1994.
8. Hirschkind 2006.
9. Nelson 2001.
10. Baghdadi 2006.
11. Ibid: 10.
12. Eickelman 1987; Messick 1993.
13. Baghdadi 2006.
14. Mitchell 2000, xxvi.
15. Ibid.
16. Ferguson 1959.
17. Bassiouney 2006.
18. Haeri 2003.
19. Ibid.
20. Fahmy 2007; Booth 1992.
21. Eickelman and Anderson 2003.
22. Starrett 1997.
23. Briggs and Burke 2005.
24. Thorburn and Jenkins 2003: 2.
25. Ong 982: 136.
26. E.g., Diebert 1997.

27. Briggs and Burke 2005.
28. Eisenstein 1997; Gitelman 2006; Marvin 1988; Thorburn and Jenkins 2003.
29. Racy 1977.
30. Danielson 1996; El-Shawan 1977.
31. Shafik 2007; Gordon 2002; Armbrust 2004.
32. Ayalon 1995.
33. E.g., Abu-Lughod 2005; Armbrust 1996.
34. Sakr 2007; Kraidy 2010.
35. Briggs and Burke 2005; Deibert 1997; Eisenstein 1979; Thorburn and Jenkins 2003.
36. E.g., Ayalon 1995; Robinson 1993; Roper 1995.
37. Armbrust 1996; Fahmy 2007; Gershoni 1995; Shryock 1997.
38. Hirschkind 2006; Miller 2007; Sreberny-Mohammadi and Mohammadi 1994.
39. Gitelman 2006: 2.
40. Note Georgetown conference; new publishing venues that define the field more flexibly.
41. On the 'disciplinary court' see Dougherty 2000.
42. 'At first the Radio was like getting a bad shave [the sound presumably]; now it has become an exalted institution from which we take lessons / A voice which the people of Europe and the Syria hear; not like before, when it felt like we were going to sleep / Now we listen to something fine, rising up without bashing [our ears]; whoever resists it is in error or stupid'.
43. Reference to Annabelle Sreberny's paper 'BBC Television for the Middle East: Diplomatic Competition for Publics?', Georgetown University Conference: 'Information Evolution in the Arab World' 22, 23 March 2010.
44. 'At first the radio was recorded on disks, like the phonograph; now we hear every singer, of every type / Fathiya [Ahmad], and Suma [Umm Kulthoum], and Salih Abd al-Hayy and lots more; if you heard them in the theatre you'd go broke and your salary would fly away / Listen to them at home with your kids and your friends; listening to them will cost you no more than a millime'.
45. 'If the director invited me to be on the show; I'd say 'there's something that bugs me, and I'll say it because I'm a listener' / Why don't you broadcast the Quran in the morning; if Shaykh Rif'at is sleeping heavily let's wake him up / Also, we don't want long boring sermons; we want just to learn grammar and inflection, and with a long explanation'.

Bibliography

Abu-Lughod, Laila (2005) *Dramas of Nationhood: The Politics of Television in Egypt*, Chicago: University of Chicago Press.
Armbrust, Walter (2010) 'Cinema and Television in the Arabic-speaking World' in Robert Hefner (ed.), *New Cambridge History of Islam* (Muslims and Modernity: Culture and Society Since 1800). Vol. 6. Cambridge: Cambridge University Press.

—— (2008c) 'Long Live Love: Patriarchy in the Time of Muhammad Abd al-Wahhab', *History Compass* 6 (http://www.blackwell-compass.com/subject/history/).

—— (2008b) 'The Formation of National Culture in Egypt in the Interwar Period: Cultural Trajectories', *History Compass* 6 (http://www.blackwellcompass.com/subject/history/).

—— (2008a) 'The Formation of National Culture in Egypt: Social, Cultural and Ideological Trajectories', A special issue of *History Compass* 6 (http://www.blackwell-compass.com/subject/history/).

—— (2006) 'Audiovisual Media and History of the Middle East' in Amy Singer and Israel Gershoni (eds), *History and Historiographies of the Modern Middle East*, Seattle: University of Washington Press, pp. 288–312.

—— (2004) 'Egyptian Cinema On Stage and Off' in Andrew Shryock (ed.), *Off Stage/On Display: Intimacy and Ethnography in the Age of Public Culture*, Palo Alto: Stanford University Press, pp. 69–100.

—— (2002) 'Manly Men on the National Stage (and the Women Who Make Them Stars)' in Ursula Wokoeck, Hakan Erdem, and Israel Gershoni (eds), *Histories of the Modern Middle East: New Directions*, Boulder: Lynne Rienner Publishers, pp. 247–78.

—— (1996) *Mass Culture and Modernism in Egypt*, Cambridge: Cambridge University Press.

Armbrust, Walter, Nettler, Ronald and Ryzova, Lucie (2007) 'The Formation of National Culture in Egypt: Social, Cultural and Ideological Trajectories' A special issue of *Maghreb Review* 33.1.

Ayalon, Ami (1995) *The Press in the Arab Middle East*, Oxford: Oxford University Press.

Bagdadi, Nadia (2006) 'Introduction to "Mapping the Gaze – Vision and Visuality in Classical Arab Civilisation"', A special issue of *The Medieval History Journal* 9.1, 1–16.

Bassiouney, Reem (2006) *Functions of Code-Switching in Egypt*, London: Brill.

Booth, Marilyn (1992) 'Colloquial Arabic Poetry, Politics, and the Press in Modern Egypt', *International Journal of Middle East Studies*, 24.3 (August 1992).

Briggs, Asa and Burke, Peter (2005) *A Social History of the Media from Gutenberg to the Internet*, London: Polity Press.

Danielson, Virginia (1996) *The Voice of Egypt: Umm Kulthum, Arabic Song, and Egyptian Society in the Twentieth Century*, Chicago: University of Chicago Press.

Deibert, Ronald (1997) *Parchment, Printing and Hypermedia: Communication in World Order Transformation*, New York: Columbia University Press.

Dougherty, Roberta L. (2000) 'Badi' a Masabni, Artiste and Modernist: The Egyptian Print Media's Carnival of National Identity' in Walter Armbrust (ed.), *Mass Mediations: New Approaches to Popular Culture in the Middle East and Beyond*, Berkeley: University of California Press, pp. 243–68.

During, Simon (2000) *The Cultural Studies Reader*, 2nd edn, London: Routledge.

Eickelman, Dale (1978) 'The Art of Memory: Islamic Education and Its Social Reproduction', *Comparative Studies in Society and History* 20.4: 485–516.

Eickelman, Dale and Anderson, Jon (2003) *New Media in the Muslim World*, Bloomington: Indiana University Press.

Eisenstein, Elizabeth (1979) *The Printing Press as an Agent of Change: Communications and Cultural Transformations in Early-modern Europe*, Cambridge: Cambridge University Press.

El-Shawan, Salwa (1977) *Al-Musika Al-Arabiyya: A Category of Urban Music in Cairo*, Egypt, 1927–1977, Ph.D. Dissertation, Columbia University.

Fahmy, Ziad. (2007) *Popularizing Egyptian Nationalism: Colloquial Culture and Media Capitalism, 1870–1914*, Ph.D. Dissertation, University of Arizona.

Ferguson, Charles (1959) 'Diglossia', *Word* 15: 324–340.

Gershoni, Israel and Jankowski, James (1995) *Redefining the Egyptian Nation, 1930–1945*, Cambridge: Cambridge University Press.

Gitelman, Lisa (2006) *Always Already New: Media, History and the Data of Culture*, Boston: MIT Press.

Goldberg, Ellis (1991) 'Smashing Idols and the State: The Protestant Ethic and Egyptian Sunni Radicalism', *Comparative Studies in Society and History* 33.1: 3–35.

Gordon, Joel (2002) *Revolutionary Melodramas: Popular Film and Civic Identity in Nasser's Egypt* (Middle East Documentation Centre).

Haeri, Niloofar (2003) *Sacred Language, Ordinary People: Dilemmas of Culture and Politics in Egypt*, New York: Palgrave Macmillan.

Hirschkind, Charles (2006) *The Ethical Soundscape: Cassette Sermons and Islamic Counterpublics*, New York: Columbia University Press.

Jay, Martin (1993) *Downcast Eyes: The Denigration of Vision in Twentieth-Century French Thought*, Berkeley: University of California Press.

Kraidy, Marwan (2010) *Reality Television and Arab Politics: Contention in Public Life*, Cambridge: Cambridge University Press.

Marvin, Carolyn (1988) *When Old Technologies Were New: Thinking about Communication in the Late Nineteenth Century*, New York: Oxford University Press.

McLuhan, Marshall (1994 [1964]) *Understanding Media: The Extensions of Man*, Cambridge: MIT Press.

Messick, Brinkley (1993) *The Calligraphic State: Textual Domination and History in a Muslim Society*, Berkeley: University of California Press.

Miller, Flagg (2007) *The Moral Resonance of Arab Media: Audiocassette Poetry and Culture in Yemen*, Cambridge: Harvard Centre for Middle Eastern Studies.

Mitchell, Timothy (2000) *Questions of Modernity*, Minneapolis: University of Minnesota Press.

—— (1988) *Colonising Egypt*, Cambridge: Cambridge University Press.

Nelson, Kristina (2001 [1985]) *The Art of Reciting the Quran*, Cairo: American University in Cairo Press.

Nugent, Stephane and Shore, Cris (eds). (1997) *Anthropology and Cultural Studies*, London: Pluto Press.

Ong, Walter (1982) *Orality and Literacy: The Technologizing of the Word*, London: Methuen.

Racy, Ali (1977) *Musical Change and Commercial Recording in Egypt, 1904–1932*, Ph.D. Dissertation, University of Illinois at Urbana-Champaign.

Robinson, Francis (1993) 'Technology and Religious Change: Islam and the Impact of Print', *Modern Asian Studies* 27.1: 229–51.

Roper, Geoffrey (1995) 'Fares al-Shidyaq (d.1887) and the Transition from Scribal to Print Culture in the Middle East' in Attiyeh, G. (ed.), *The Book in the Islamic World*, Albany: SUNY Press.

Sakr, Naomi (2007) *Arab Television Today*, London: I.B.Tauris.

Shafik, Viola (2007) *Popular Egyptian Cinema: Gender, Class, and Nation*, Cairo: American University in Cairo Press.

Shryock, Andrew (1997) *Nationalism and the Genealogical Imagination: Oral History and Textual Authority in Tribal Jordan*, Berkeley: University of California Press.

Sreberny-Mohammadi, Annabelle and Mohammadi, Ali (1994) *Small Media, Big Revolution: Communication, Culture, and the Iranian Revolution*, Minneapolis: University of Minnesota Press.

Starrett, Gregory (1997) *Putting Islam to Work: Education, Politics and Religious Transformation in Egypt*, Berkeley: University of California Press.

Stein, Sally (1992) 'The Graphic Ordering of Desire: Modernization of a Middle-Class Women's Magazine, 1914–1939' in Richard Bolton (ed.), *The Contest of Meaning: Critical Histories of Photography*, Cambridge: MIT Press, pp. 145–162.

Thorburn, David and Jenkins, Henry (eds). (2003) *Rethinking Media Change: The Aesthetics of Transition*, Cambridge: MIT Press.

3

Arab Media Studies Between the Legacy of a Thin Discipline and the Promise of New Cultural Pathways

Mohamed Zayani

The rapid and substantial development of Arab media in the past few years has attracted increased research interest, turning what was a small and in many ways marginalised area of study into a burgeoning field. This relatively new field, however, remains unevenly developed, partly because of the fragmentation of the subject of analysis and partly because of the lack of adequate theoretical frameworks to examine the emerging dynamics and thought processes around the intricacies and implications of the changes engendered. Particularly challenging is the weight of disciplinarity, which often delineates the field of study in narrow communication terms. A media-centric approach is likely to undermine the fact that media speaks of wider processes at work.[1] In a richly complex region like the Middle East, the tight connection between media, political communication, political economy and, in fact, culture at large has not been sufficiently emphasised. A cultural studies perspective can go a long way towards rejuvenating the study of Arab media and unravelling the unfolding of a region-specific set of dynamics, of which the media are arguably only a pointed manifestation. An examination of recent noteworthy scholarship, which weaves together the cultural, the anthropological and the socio-political can help situate rich possibilities for future interdisciplinary, theoretically-informed and culturally-attuned research on Arab media, which eschews the more narrowly-conceived pursuits based on media-centric models that are characteristic of much of what is produced in the field.

The state of Arab media research

Over the past decade or so, there has been a rapid and dramatic change in the media scene in the Arab world in general, and the Middle East in particular, the implications of which are only starting to manifest themselves. Although the unprecedented development of Arab media and of expanding audience access have spurred increased research interest, particularly after 9/11, and have also yielded a number of studies and scholarly works (turning what was, only a decade ago, a small and marginalised area of study into a burgeoning field[2] and morphing Arab media and culture from an area of negligible interest to a hot topic[3]), the attention the field attracts remains intermittent, the research output uneven, and the theoretical impetus undeveloped. Overall, the study of Arab media is constrained by the relative newness of the field and is hindered by the notable dispersion, fragmentation and incommensurability of the subject of analysis.[4] In spite of the growing interest in the field, keenness to understand the changing Arab media scene remains hampered by the nature and quality of the research available. Much of the published work in this area is predominantly essayistic or exploratory, leaving it devoid of a significant analytical framework. In fact, the research landscape is teeming with survey studies and is informed by descriptive and historical accounts of media institutions and events.[5] Likewise, a great number of the existing studies suffer from empirical weakness or deficit, while others tend to be unrepresentative in nature, often reducing Arab media to Al Jazeera and internet dynamics in the region to the Egyptian blogosphere.[6] The theoretical thinness, which characterises the corpus of work on Arab media,[7] is particularly flagrant. Broadly speaking, much of the available research tends to be insufficiently informed by communication theories and methodologies.[8] Many studies suffer from a weak theoretical underpinning; and where theory is used, it is limited in scope.

Several factors have contributed to the absence of solid media and communication research in the Arab world. Not only is there an absence of a strong research tradition in that part of the world to start with, but also research in the field has not kept pace with an evolving Arab media scene driven by fast-unfolding, technologically-induced changes in an era marked by intense communication and global interconnectedness. Not only are the institutional conditions for research in the Arab world inhibiting, but also the intellectual and institutional investment in research is blatantly weak.[9] If the thrust of research in the Arab world is more redundant than cumulative, so to speak, it is partly because research cooperation and collaboration are still not fully ingrained in Arab academic institutions. This necessarily results in undeveloped networking mechanisms among Arab scholars and researchers, who then find themselves working in isolation.[10] Similarly, the lack of serious communication journals in the Middle East and the absence of a reward structure in most government institutions does not favour research productivity. For Hussein Amin, as for Muhammad Ayish, 'the politically repressive atmosphere that has for so many years prevailed in Arab national universities has pushed research into narrow channels', thus hampering the development of an indigenous Arab communication scholarship.[11] The restrictive political and social conditions under which the Arab world subsists, along with governments' sensitivity to media research, have further contributed to this superficiality as researchers work in an environment, characterised by political authoritarianism and dominated by social and cultural taboos, which mitigates against the production of new research, innovative scholarship and indigenous knowledge.[12] As Arab governments grow increasingly wary of the likely security implications and potentially destabilising power of a new and rapidly evolving, and dramatically changing, Arab and information media environment, research in the field becomes a sensitive endeavour.[13]

A case in point is Arab audience research. The dearth of studies on audience and reception can be related to the relatively short history of audience research. Previous work in this area has been largely exploratory and descriptive in nature.[14] The few existing studies suffer from various problems and their quality is affected by a number of challenges in the field. The first set of challenges is empirical in nature, and has to do with registering, monitoring, measuring and assessing media uses and effects. In fact, there is hardly any current, reliable, independent data with which to analyse viewing habits, patterns and preferences. Research on Arab media reception is thus constrained by a lack of institutionalised rating systems, such as the Nielsen ratings, which provide audience measurements and, being quantitative, such assessments give little indication as to how programmes engage viewers.[15] Furthermore, reliable data is either hard to come by or impossible to obtain because of political consciousness, hesitation to disclose financial information, or fear of regional competitors. Government restrictions and procedures make the process of conducting opinion polls and survey research both cumbersome and problematic.[16] Although, increasingly, media firms and advertising companies in the Middle East region commission audience research, this tends to be limited in value and use, as it is either narrow in scope (targeting a particular segment of the market) or limited in value (being proprietary research for in-house use and consumption). These practices are not without consequences. In Hussein Amin's view:

> [...] the lack of sufficient data on audience demographics, opinions, viewing habits, uses and gratifications, and preferences has hindered the ability of communications researchers to conduct in-depth research. With little reliable data on demographics, viewing habits and preferences, advertisers are forced to rely on guesses and instinct.[17]

Opinion polls on media consumption patterns and political behaviour in the Arab world are equally problematic. In some ways, audience research remains a sensitive topic. Overall, although empirical political research in the Arab world has improved significantly in the past few years, it is still hampered by considerable limitations and challenges due to political restrictions and various other impediments, some of which are social and cultural in nature,[18] which necessarily translate into problems of reliability, representativeness, scientific merit, validity and significance.[19]

A way out of the discipline's cul-de-sac

One notable weakness in Arab media studies is the lack of a strong theoretical grounding; and where the research is informed by theoretical models, it is notably low in 'indigenous theoretical features',[20] as it tends to uncritically use a body of scholarship which has evolved in the West and which has developed around specific institutions, technologies and political systems and so is either normative, or not adequately suited to account for the specificity of Arab world media and communication.[21] For some media scholars and critics, research in the Arab world continues to be driven by 'deep convictions concerning the media's power and guided by Western-oriented conceptual models'.[22] Traditionally, Western academic discourse on the Middle East was dominated by theories which were produced outside the region and which were not always suited to the study and understanding of the intricacies of regional phenomena in their full complexity.[23] This is why the tendency to apply Western theory indiscriminately and uncritically to the study of Arab media is particularly problematic. In the absence of a developed theoretical framework that takes into account the specificity of the area of study, much of the work that is produced is based, in large part, on a set of unrevised assumptions, which are insufficient to explore a region-specific set of dynamics that have been accentuated and altered by the forces of globalisation. For Muhammad Ayish, dealing with this lacuna requires generating new indigenous conceptions of communication that are anchored in Arab traditions:

> [...] more research should be directed to documenting modern transitions in Arab social, cultural, economic, political and media trends to generate solid scientific perspectives on the Arab media scene, perhaps utilizing totally different concepts and methods relevant to Arab culture.[24]

The search for more adequate theorisations of the Arab media scene motivates Ayish's own endeavours to offer a revisionist reading of the rather newly conceived Arab public sphere, as epitomised in the sophisticated formulations of Marc Lynch.[25]

For Lynch, the emergence of a vibrant media scene in the Arab world has ushered in a new Arab public sphere. Yet, what makes the public sphere what it is, is not the media in and of themselves, but the public arguments the latter entertain in an increasingly open, participatory and interactive media context. As such, the new independent political transnational media that are emerging in the Arab world constitute largely 'a rational and two-way communication stream'[26] which values debate and rational arguments:

> I define the public sphere in terms of active arguments before an audience about issues of shared concern. These dialogues require media that can bring arguments before a relevant audience, but media alone do not a public sphere make. Indeed, the mobilizational media characteristics of authoritarian Arab states can be seen as the antithesis of a public sphere with a single voice driving out all dissent, questioning, and critical

reason. Nor does argument alone make a public sphere. Private arguments, carried out behind closed doors, lack the critical dimension of publicity. What makes a public sphere is the existence of routine, ongoing, unscripted arguments before an audience about issues relevant to many.[27]

As an arena of public argument that falls outside the official channels of the state, the public sphere offers a zone of free and critical reason that tends to influence collective action, but is not reduced to it.[28] This new Arab public sphere stands in marked contrast to the dynamics of an era marked by 'the production and manipulation of an Arab consensus'.[29] In lieu of conformity and public consensus, a public disagreement is starting to emerge, ushering in a culture of pluralistic and contentious politics and giving birth to a new populist and identity-driven Arab public that is increasingly aware of its ability to challenge the *status quo*.[30] Defining this new Arab public sphere, Lynch notes, is 'the rapidly expanding universe of Arabs able and willing to engage in public arguments about political issues within an ever-increasing range of possible media outlets'.[31]

Insightful as it may be, Lynch's celebration of the emergence of a media-mediated Arab public sphere conveniently falls back on models and presumptions that are associated with a different tradition. In the words of Lena Jayyusi, the critical commentary on the new Arab public sphere 'tends to presume that the only genuinely valid form of the public sphere is a liberal one, not in the sense of having various voices in mutual debate, but in the sense that it should espouse Western liberal understandings of the world and a Western liberal set of goals'.[32] Similarly, Ayish notes that the appropriation of the notion of the public sphere in the context of political communication in the Arab world calls for an interdisciplinary analysis which pays special attention to the moral, cultural and political, which give the evolving Arab public sphere its unique identity.[33] To eschew a conceptualisation of the Arab public sphere, which is embedded in a West-specific tradition, Ayish proposes an Islamic public sphere, which is premised on a more original and complex Arab and Islamic tradition. Accordingly, he uses the concept of Islamocracy, or Islamic democracy, as a basic conceptual foundation for the theorising of the public sphere in the Arab world.[34] At the same time, Ayish takes pains to note that in a world of diminishing physical boundaries, theorising about the Arab public sphere is hardly conceivable outside the discourse on globalisation.[35]

Other judicious and rigorous theoretical attempts were made by Dale Eickelman, Armando Salvatore, Jon Anderson, Mehdi Abedi and Michael Fischer, to articulate the unfolding of a more all encompassing Muslim public sphere.[36] However, such attempts, which question the very terms of analysis and provide refreshing analytical frameworks, are not all that common and where they exist, they have not been able to decisively redefine the terms of Arab media analysis. This is partly because the inter-disciplinarity and the social science thrust of such formulations mitigate their widespread adoption in a more empirically attuned communications field. For the most part, the tendency is to use Western media theories and methodologies and to fall back on foreign analytical frameworks to examine internal dynamics, an endeavour which does not sufficiently heed the interpretative challenges posed by various media developments in the Arab world. As Jon Alterman points out, there is a need:

> [...] to free our studies of new media and technology in the Middle East from the straitjacket of the Western experience [...] to be more sensitive of how identical technologies can have vastly different impacts in different regions.[37]

The fast development of Arab media means that the need for theoretical orientations that go beyond normative frameworks is more insistent than ever before.

The theoretical imperative between Western formulations and indigenous knowledge

Overall, the emergence of media as an important force in the Arab world has not yet sufficiently induced rigorous theoretical and empirical approaches amenable to Arab media dynamics in their full complexity. For Tarik Sabry, there tends to be an over-reliance on Western critical theory as a knowledge frame for the articulation of a whole field of enquiry into media culture and society in the modern Arab world.[38] The study of Arab media which, for the most part, has been left to Western theorisations, should be renewed with the injection of new, mostly indigenous theories and methodologies, and the generation of region-specific knowledge.[39] However, these initiatives should not be taken as an argument in favour of media-exceptionalism in the Middle East, which risks also entrapping the analysis in a framework narrowly focused on Arab and Islamic issues, nor should they be considered as a call to eschew the wealth of research in Western media and communication studies; rather, they should be taken as part of a concerted effort to graft onto Arab media research reflections on the specificity of the field of study, the complexity of the region, and the idiosyncrasy of the local context, culture and systems. West-centric approaches, standard analytical tools and normative preoccupations cannot be transposed willy nilly from Western contexts; they can help to inform our understanding of the nascent field of Arab media if infused with new concepts built from the ground up.[40] To say that existing theories are not adequate, then, is not to say that they are inappropriate but that they are insufficient, for it is hardly possible to imagine a quintessentially Arab critical theory, given the history of intellectual encounters between East and West, and especially when considering the ways in which communication flows and contra-flows under globalisation are marked by an increasingly intense, interlaced, multi-dimensional and multi-centric impetus, such that an understanding of the Arab mediascape calls not only for the adoption of a three-pronged approach in which the quantitative, qualitative and comparative complement each other, but also through the development of a reflexive theoretical instinct which favours the referent (whether Arab media or its Western counterpart).[41] In this sense, the reinvigoration of Arab media studies does not require a completely different set of theories as much as it calls for a nuanced understanding, a critical approach and an interdisciplinary investigation of the field. It requires more than simply the de-Westernisation (or internationalisation) of media and communication theory; it calls for a critique of de-Westernisation, as a discourse, and argues for a dialogic approach between Arab and Western views, which enacts a double critique that enables de-Westernisation itself, as a tool of critique, to be criticised.[42]

These considerations are not without significance, as they point to a related issue: the need for a cultural underpinning of Arab media research. As Annabelle Sreberny perceptively argues, 'broader conceptual frameworks and more nuanced, grounded and subtle forms of media and contemporary cultural analysis can contribute to a better understanding of both the region and of media studies'.[43] It is important to consider how to approach a relatively new and dynamic field in a richly diverse region outside existing exogenous theories and away from assumptions about culture and media dynamics, which are often imposed on the subject, for, as Thomas Patterson reminds us, media are shaped by society's cultural values.[44] Take, for instance, the conceptualisation of the political effects of media. There is a fundamental difference between the media's role in Western democracies and Arab autocracies.[45] The analysis of the political significance or political effects of media in ways which indigenise the very study of Arab media, while at the same time drawing on and learning from a rich tradition of Western theories in and outside the field of media studies *strictu sensu*, is particularly challenging. There is a need to develop theories that can adequately conceive of the changing relationship between programming, attitudes, and political outcomes in non-democratic settings. Such queries necessarily hinge on broader questions pertaining to the role of media and the relationship between media and politics in Arab societies. These inquiries have to go through a conceptualisation of the cultural underpinning of media and a theorisation of the relationship between media and culture, a task that has only just started to attract serious critical attention.

Cultural studies and the reinvigoration of the field

The theoretical thinness that marks Arab media studies can be ascribed to a variety of reasons. Among the challenges facing the researcher are the constraints imposed by the weight of disciplinarity, whereby the field of study is often delineated in narrow communication terms. Conceiving of Arab media studies as a stand-alone discipline can be severely constraining. At the same time, the interdisciplinary potential of Arab media studies has neither been adequately tapped into nor capitalised on. While Arab media research lies, theoretically, at the crossroads of larger disciplines, like Middle Eastern studies and media and communication sciences, in practice, neither field has done justice to it. As Kai Hafez explains:

> [...] because Middle Eastern studies are traditionally inspired by political science, economics, cultural studies, philology, and anthropology, they often lack theoretical and methodological ingredients needed for the study of Arab media; meanwhile, media and communication studies, which could provide such qualifications, have for years, almost totally neglected the non-Western world.[46]

Where the study of media has benefited from this interdisciplinarity, it has made an impact.

As it can go a long way toward mediating the relationship between various fields of study, cultural studies has the potential to reinvigorate study of Arab media. Not only are media difficult to study independently of other aspects of Arab society,[47] and outside the historical, social and political contexts in which they operate,[48] but the various disciplines capable of informing the study of media are increasingly converging on the terrain of cultural studies. There has been some momentum in this direction in emerging theory. Timely and interesting work has been done in this area by scholars working on Arab and Middle Eastern media, providing a theoretical impetus for the conception of the field.[49] For instance, arguing against 'media-centrism'[50] when studying a richly complex region like the Middle East, Annabelle Sreberny emphasises the interconnection between media, on the one hand, and political communication, political economy and cultural studies, on the other. An insistently 'media-centric' model operative within international communication studies tends to obscure context-specific forces of a social, political and cultural nature.[51] The field, she argues, 'must connect with other and older disciplines to avoid a naïve sense of discovering new topics that in fact have long and distinctive pedigrees of scholarship'.[52] Media processes in the region speak of much wider processes at work.[53] While drawing on existing conceptual tools, Sreberny insists that the field needs to build new concepts from the ground up. Insightful as they may be, international (mostly Western) communication theories and analyses function independently from, and are developed outside, existing local systems so that congeries of historical, social, political and cultural forces (which emanate from the inside, so to speak) are often obscured.[54] Accordingly, Sreberny calls for an added sensitivity to the specificity of the forces that operate 'within':

> We need to explore the manner in which both broader conceptual frameworks and more nuanced, grounded and subtle forms of media and contemporary cultural analyses can contribute to a better understanding of both the region and of media studies. We need better analysis of the political economies of the region, the nature of their politics and more grounded cultural studies and far, far better conversations across the registers. A sensitivity to varied and competing special orders and levels of

analysis can thicken the conceptual soup and produce innovative thinking. The Middle East is a highly complex region, and any attempt to describe its processes of political change and democratisation has to be mindful of the real historical and contingent differences and particular political economies that exist. No essentialist or culturalist models will suffice. Further, the region's insertion into the global political economy, indeed the differential roles of particular states within the global order and the varying impacts of markets, migration and media, have to be considered. The pressures toward and dynamics of political change need to be examined both from outside and from inside the region.[55]

For Sreberny, then, a holistic and analytic approach to media issues in the Arab world does not necessarily privilege one perspective over the other. What it does, instead, is to seek to 'examine the conjunction and effects of global processes within specific, localised settings, exploring the dynamics of external forces combined with internal processes'.[56]

Similarly, pointing out how media, being at the end of a historical and social process, are more than a simple technological development, Tarik Sabry emphasises the need for 'thinking through the methodological considerations and epistemological implications to be used for the study of the region' and the need for the development of an interdisciplinary academic field which takes culture and the media as objects of enquiry,[57] which would provide a theoretical exploration of 'the region's reaction to modernity and its disorders',[58] particularly as it relates to the interdependence of the local and the global. So far, though, the development of a sociology which lies at the intersection between Arab media and cultural studies has been hampered by a notable weakness in the research in this field which, in turn, can be related in some ways to 'authoritarian states' sabotaging any form of critical reason'.[59] Being at odds with parochial regime interests, the study of media remains a low state priority, if not a liability.

Arab media, popular culture and the sociology of everyday life

Even if these shortcomings are overlooked, the field of Arab media studies remains constrained by the very conception of what constitutes a legitimate subject of study. The field of enquiry subsides under the tyranny of the aesthetic discourse[60] and is constrained by scientific frames which often obfuscate the relevance of common mediated experiences, practices and realities which cover a wide cultural spectrum and cut across a number of popular social settings embedded in what Henri Lefebvre refers to as the realm of everyday life.

For Lefebvre, everyday life (and its corollaries, the everyday and every-dayness) is the arena where capitalism, as a system of the production of relations, renews, rejuvenates and prolongs itself in pervasive ways.[61] The imposition of capitalism and its generalisation necessarily imply the expansion of relations of exchange in the different spheres of vital activities. What distinguishes the system is its ability to reproduce itself incessantly and indiscriminately in the different enclaves of the social totality and to extend its logic in territories that are not purely or exclusively economic. For Lefebvre, the realm of the *quotidian* is particularly noteworthy as the locus of dynamics which disaggregate the system, multiply its manifestations and enlarge its production so that the most trivial and the least suspect aspects of everyday life become concrete sites conducive to the (re-)production of the social existence of human beings. Theoretically, seizing the full significance of everyday life requires eschewing the reductionist traditional understanding of super-structural phenomena as a mere reflection of the economic base. If the architectural metaphor of levels is to be retained, it has to be conceived of as part of a totality that proceeds at all levels of sociality. Everyday life thus encompasses space, fashion, tourism and mass media, among other spaces. Ironically, and to the extent that nothing escapes everyday life, the realm of the *quotidian* remains highly elusive, escaping even the most concerted attempts to capture it. Further complicating this issue is the fact that everyday life is increasingly mediated in the technological and social sense, so much so that the media and everyday life, as Roger Silverstone reminds us, are inseparable.[62]

For the purpose of this enquiry, the concept of everyday life is particularly useful, as it is amenable to understanding social structures and dynamics, which are embedded in media genres, forms and programmes. From a cultural studies perspective, the attention to everyday life puts into question the often-held distinction between highbrow and lowbrow or, more pointedly, between elite and popular culture. Advocating 'a cultural science of communication' which pays particular attention to the 'mass' component of the field of 'mass media', James W. Carey, who took his cue from Raymond Williams, draws attention to the analytical value of what may seem on a surface level to be mundane cultural products and practices of contemporary life, ranging from mediated leisure rituals to television drama and talk shows, through music and graffiti.[63] Communication research acquires an added value when related to the cultural experience of particular groups or individuals, and is conceived within a critical study of media that heeds the three interconnected aspects: production, circulation and consumption.[64]

The attention to the cultural dimension, as it manifests itself in the realm of the *quotidian,* has considerable potential for the reinvigoration of the study of Arab media. The media-induced changes the Arab world has been witnessing over the past few decades manifest themselves in everyday cultural practices, habits or products which are not traditionally deemed worthy of examination. Typically, topics such as TV drama series, entertainment shows, music channels, Ramadan programmes and sermons, are not usually perceived as subjects worthy of rigorous study and serious enquiry. Recently, though, such indifference has given way to a number of theoretically informed investigations anchored in an Arab mediatised cultural space that is marked by its increased intensity and pervasiveness. Interesting works have been produced that articulate key and subtle links between Arab media and culture, opening up new paths of research and enquiry in a field that is largely undeveloped. Using cultural, sociological and anthropological frameworks, authors and critics like Lila Abu-Lughod, Charles Hirschkind, Walter Armbrust, Dale Eickelman, Christa Salamandra and Marwan Kraidy have produced a sophisticated body of work which explores current developments in Arab media and society, paying attention to everyday practices along with the social, political and cultural beliefs which underlie them. More than putting into perspective cultural practices, which are not typically privileged as subjects of enquiry and analysis, these authors provide theoretical reflections on what are ordinarily 'taken-for-granted features of everyday life'.[65] As such, they provide insights into what Walter Armbrust calls a mass mediated popular culture, which defines, as much as it is defined by, the character of social, political and religious interaction.[66]

In their work on television drama Lila Abu-Lughod and Christa Salamandra thus map out spaces of engagement and resistance in what is otherwise a unidirectional flow of information characteristic of a predominantly state controlled media environment. For Abu-Lughod, while the political messages that are embedded in television drama reinforce the hegemony of the nation state, highlight citizenship and construct a wide sense of social belonging, the genre conventions promote a new conception of selfhood which is shaped by the producers and scriptwriters who, as mediators articulating and translating an ambitious project of modernisation, contribute to the construction of a national cultural identity, the thrust of which is not 'a process of creating identities to counter the national but rather the rearguard action of an identity politics meant to shore up the nation-state'.[67] Primarily framed in the context of the tension between two competing stands, Islamism and secularism, television both reinforces and redefines values. Not unlike Abu-Lughod, Salamandra examines the ways in which television functions as an instrument of modernity in the context of a competing tradition in Arab media and cultural production: the Syrian drama. Reconciling the progressive politics of TV makers with the demands of the market, the affinities of the conservative Gulf sponsors and the sensibilities of audiences, is a source of a comforting ambiguity. Here, the religious dimension of television drama is relegated to a colourful, but safely remote, past, such that Islam figures as a cultural referent more 'folklorised' than politicised.[68]

The traditional Egyptian and Syrian interest in TV drama is matched only by recent Saudi and Lebanese investment in entertainment programmes, in general, and reality TV – in particular – a genre that is deceptively a-political. Arguing for an understanding of the dynamics of Arab media which does not reduce them to broadcast political journalism, Marwan Kraidy draws attention to the political elements inherent to what is often dismissed as mere entertainment for the masses.[69] Interestingly, such an account also complicates our understanding of what we consider to be publics and audiences.[70] The movement from passive to active to interactive audiences, which Kraidy identifies as one of the consequences of the immersion of Arab consumers in a hyper-media environment, blurs the distinction between consumption and citizenship in ways that have potential political significance. Reality TV can thus facilitate linkages between specific socio-political contexts and new media.[71] Activities which draw on democratic rituals, such as participating in contests, or voting for participants in a televised artistic context, foster a certain ease with and awareness of the potential of information and communication technology.[72] Similarly, the use of mobiles to send messages in support of a contestant in entertainment programmes, like *Star Academy,* creates consumer habits that are readily transferable to politically charged settings. In an ethnically diverse country like Lebanon, which has been witnessing added political turmoil since the assassination of the Prime Minister, Rafik Hariri, the consumer habits fostered by entertainment shows are amenable to political activism and popular mobilisation.

In much the same way Kraidy examines the significance of a TV genre which has attracted what may be loosely described as a young and liberal segment of the Arab world, Charles Hirschkind explores the implications arising from the cassette-recorded sermons of popular Muslim preachers and orators on the lower end of an Egyptian society that is marked by a renewed concern with Islam.[73] Taking issue with the reductive common perception of Islamic cassette sermons as epitomising the world of militant and radical Islam, Hirschkind draws attention to a more subtle 'politics of sound'.[74] The everyday, common media practices in question foster deliberative practices oriented not so much towards a political engagement with the state, but at shaping their collective existence within an Islamic society. Conceived as such, these popular media practices, which are an integral part of everyday life for a large part of the Egyptian populace, not only make the distinction between the moral and the political irrelevant, but also call into question the normative understanding of what should be considered to be the political arena and the public sphere.

The foregoing examples, associated with a mediated Arab popular culture, articulate unsuspected complexities and dynamics embedded in the realm of everyday life and associated with common media practices, the full implications of which have for a long time eluded analysis. What the aforementioned authors and critics have in common is an interest in Arab media that emanates less from the field of communication *per se* than from area studies. Here, the media are of interest as an epitome of more encompassing cultural, social and political practices, beliefs and transformations in the Arab world. The on-going media changes are not without implications. To the extent that different mass mediated forms, whether they are television dramas, reality television shows or audiocassettes, create different scales of communication, Armbrust notes, they usher in new transnational dimensions of modernity and sociality.[75] Looking at cultural, social and political processes, the works under consideration open up new pathways for theoretically sophisticated research on Arab media that is anchored in a broad cultural framework which taps into the unsuspected richness of the *quotidian,* and is informed by the insights and methodologies of cultural studies, anthropology and sociology. Together, these works evince the relevance and usefulness of an analysis of everyday life as a defining characteristic of a critical approach to an increasingly more entangled and more complex media-mediated culture in the Arab world.

More broadly, attention to the integration of media in everyday life can prove useful in understanding the manifestation and implications of the changing media ecology in the Middle East. The experience of media in its dailiness, as Roger Silverstone puts it,[76] makes a media-centric approach largely inadequate. Understanding the significance of media-mediated experiences in their full complexity necessitates attention to the political, economic and social dimensions underlying the multiple discourses of everyday life. Engaging such dimensions in an interdisciplinary way can only enrich the study of mediated cultural practices. Yet, for an analysis of everyday life to be compelling, it has to be supported theoretically. It needs to rest on conceptual frameworks that situate the configurations of the evolving Arab media sphere within larger cultural dynamics. This requires attention to the interconnectedness of the micro and the macro, the specific and the general, the local and the global. Processes of mediation, which affect the social totality, are ensconced within the various enclaves of that lived totality and they manifest themselves in uneven ways which spawn counter-dynamics, shifts and disjunctions. Heeding the interrelatedness of the intrinsic and the extrinsic, the micro and the macro, the static and the dynamic, as they manifest themselves in the mediated experience of everyday life, can go a long way towards reinvigorating the study of Arab media.

Notes

1. Nicholas Garnham, 'Class Analysis and the Information Society as Mode of Production'. *Javnost: The Public* 11.3: 93–104.
2. Helga Tawil-Souri, 'Arab Television in Academic Scholarship', *Sociology Compass* 2.5: 1400.
3. Tarik Sabry, 'Media and Cultural Studies in the Arab World: Making Bridges to Local Discourses of Modernity', in Daya K. Thussu (ed.), *Internationalizing Media Studies* (London: Routledge, 2009), p. 196.
4. Marc Lynch, 'Political Opportunity Structures: Effects of Arab Media', in Kai Hafez (ed.), *Arab Media: Power and Weakness*, New York: Continuum, pp. 28–23.

5. Muhammad Ayish, 'Arab World Media Content Studies: A Meta-Analysis of a Changing Research Agenda', in Kai Hafez (ed.), *Arab Media: Power and Weakness*, New York: Continuum, p. 106.

6. On this point see Marwan Kraidy, 'From Activity to Interactivity: The Arab Audience', in Kai Hafez (ed.), *Arab Media: Power and Weakness*, New York: Continuum, pp. 91–102.

7. Annabelle Sreberny, 'Television, Gender and Democratization in the Middle East', in James Curran and Myung-Jin Park (eds), *De-Westernizing Media Studies*, London: Routledge, p. 66.

8. Hafez, *Arab Media: Power and Weakness*, p. 7.

9. See 'Universities and scientific Research in the Arab World', <http://www.al-jazeera.net/NR/exeres/FD18838E-F41B-4958-B521–2B66AE8D1048.htm>.

10. Ayish, 'Arab World Media Content Studies', p. 105.

11. See Muhammad I. Ayish, 'Communication Research in the Arab World: A New Perspective', *Javnost: The Public* 5.1 (1998): 35; Hussein Amin, 'Arab Media Audience Research: Developments and Constraints', in Kai Hafez (ed.), *Arab Media: Power and Weakness*, New York: Continuum, pp. 70–75.

12. Ayish, 'Arab World Media Content Studies', p. 117.

13. Marc Lynch, 'Globalization and Arab Security', in Jonathan Kirshner (ed.), *Globalization and National Security*, New York: Routledge, pp. 171–200; Jabbar Audah Al Obaidi, *Media Censorship in the Middle East*, Lewiston: The Edwin Mellen Press.

14. Safran Al-Makaty, Douglas A. Boyd, and Norman G. Van Tubergen, 'A Q-Study of Reactions to Direct Broadcast Satellite Television Programming in Saudi Arabia', *Journal of South Asian and Middle Eastern Studies* 20.4 (1997): 50–64.

15. Kraidy, 'From Activity to Interactivity', p. 99.

16. Amin, 'Arab Media Audience Research', p. 69.

17. Ibid.

18. Ellen Feghali, 'Arab Cultural Communication Patters', *International Journal of Intercultural Relations* 21.3 (1997): 345–78.

19. See David Pollock, *Slippery Polls: Uses and Abuses of Opinion Surveys from Arab States*, Washington, D.C.: The Washington Institute for Near East Policy, pp. 26–27; Mark Tessler and Amaney Jamal, 'Political Attitude Research in the Arab World: Emerging Opportunities', *Political Science and Politics* 39.3 (2006), pp. 1–5, <http://journals.cambridge.org/download.php?file=%2FPSC%2FPSC39_03%2FS1049096506060781a.pdf&code=8d682fbda43aa184d990e75cf703ee45 >; Marc Lynch, *Voices of the New Arab Public: Iraq, Al Jazeera, and Middle East Politics Today*, New York: Columbia University Press, pp. 66–68; Robert M. Entman, *Projections of Power: Framing News, Public Opinion, and Foreign U.S. Policy,* Chicago: University of Chicago Press; John Zogby, 'Testimony before the Subcommittee on National Security, Veterans Affairs and International Relations of the House of Representatives Committee on Government Reform', *Are we Listening to the Arab Street?*,

(8 October 2002), p. 104, <http://frwebgate.access.gpo.gov/cgi-bin/getdoc. cgi?dbname=107_house_hearings&docid=f:88885.pdf>; Carmon Yigal, 'What Makes the Arab Street Rage: Testimony before the Subcommittee on National Security, Veterans Affairs and International Relations of the House of Representatives Committee on Government Reform', *Are we Listening to the Arab Street?* (8 October 2002), p. 125, <http://frwebgate.access.gpo.gov/ cgi-bin/getdoc.cgi?dbname=107_house_hearings&docid=f:88885.pdf>; Robert Satloff, 'Survey Says: Polls and the Muslim World', *New Republic Online* (30 September 2005), <http:www.washingtoninstitute.org/tem-plateC06.php?CID=873>; Pollock, *The Arab Street*, pp. 21–27; Kifner, 'The New Power of Arab Public Opinion'; Adam Powell, 'No Independent Arab Media Exist, Say Arab Journalists', *Washington Journal* (4 March 2004), <http://uscpublicdiplomacy.com/index.php/newsroom/journal_detail/ 770/>; Mohamed Zayani, 'Courting and Containing the Arab Street', *Arab Studies Quarterly* 30.2 (2008): 45–64.

20. Muhammad I. Ayish, 'Communication Research in the Arab World', p. 52.

21. See Amin, 'Arab Media Audience Research', p. 74; see also Ayish, 'Communication Research in the Arab World'.

22. Ayish, 'Arab World Media Content Studies', p. 106.

23. Yasir Suleiman and Paul Anderson, 'Conducting Fieldwork in the Middle East: Report of a Workforce held at the University of Edinburgh on 12 February 20007', *British Journal of Middle Eastern Studies* 35.2 (2008): 152.

24. Ayish, 'Communication Research in the Arab World', p. 53.

25. Muhammad I. Ayish, *The New Arab Public Sphere* (Berlin: Frank and Timme, 2008); Lynch, *Voices of the New Arab Public*.

26. Lynch, *Voices of the New Arab Public*, pp. 36–37.

27. Ibid: 32.

28. Lynch, 'Globalization and Arab Security', p. 33.

29. Marc Lynch, *State Interests and Public Spheres: The International Politics of Jordan's Identity*, New York: Columbia University Press, p. 5.

30. Lynch, *Voices of the New Arab Public*, pp. 2–3.

31. Lynch, 'Globalization and Arab Security', p. 21.

32. Lena Jayyusi, 'Internationalizing Media Studies: A View from the Arab World', *Global Media and Communication* 3 (2007): 254–55.

33. Ayish, *The New Arab Public Sphere*, p. 11.

34. Ibid: 14.

35. Ibid: 16.

36. See Dale F. Eickelman, 'The Religious Public Sphere in Early Muslim Societies', in Hoexter, Mariam, Shmuel N. Eisenstadt and Nehemia Levtzion (eds), *The Public Sphere in Muslim Societies*, Albany: State University of New York Press, pp. 1–8; Dale F. Eickelman and Armando Salvatore, 'The Public Sphere and Muslim Identities', *European Journal of Sociology* 43 (2002): 92–115; Jon W. Anderson, 'New Media New Publics: Reconfiguring the Public Sphere of Islam',

Social Research, 70.3 (2003): 887–906; and Mehdi Abedi and Michael M.J. Fischer, 'Thinking a Public Sphere in Arabic and Persian', *Public Culture*, 6.1 (1993): 219–30.

37. Jon Alterman, 'Arab Media Studies: Some Methodological Considerations', in Mohamed Zayani (ed.), *The Al Jazeera Phenomenon: Critical Perspectives on New Arab Media* (London: Pluto Press, 2005), p. 204. See also James Curran and Myung-Jin Park, 'Beyond Globalization Theory', in James Curran and Myung-Jin Park (eds), *De-Westernizing Media Studies*, London: Routledge, pp. 3–18.

38. Sabry, 'Media and Cultural Studies in the Arab World', p. 201.

39. Hafez, *Arab Media: Power and Weakness*, p. 7.

40. Annabelle Sreberny, 'The Analytic Challenges of Studying the Middle East and its Evolving Media Environment', *Middle East Journal of Culture and Communication* 1.1 (2008): 14–18.

41. Ann-Sophie Lehmann, 'Reflexivity as Theoretical Concept in Media Studies', <http://www.mediaengager.com/tutorial1.pdf>.

42. Sabry, 'Media and Cultural Studies in the Arab World', pp. 197, 202–03. See also Daya K. Thussu, 'Internationalize Media Studies', *Television and New Media* 10.1 (2009): 162–64.

43. Sreberny, 'The Analytic Challenges of Studying the Middle East', p. 20.

44. Thomas E. Patterson, 'Political Roles of the Journalist', in Doris A Graber, Denis McQauil, and Pippa Norris (eds), *The Politics of News*, 2nd edn, Washington, DC: CQ Press, p. 28.

45. Mahmoud El Sherif, 'The Arab Attitude to Mass Media', *Intermedia* 8.2 (1989): 28.

46. Hafez, *Arab Media: Power and* Weakness, p. 9.

47. Sreberny, 'Television, Gender and Democratization in the Middle East', p. 66.

48. Mamoun Fandy, (Un)Civil War of Words: Media and Politics in the Arab World, Westport, CT: Praeger, p. 40.

49. Sreberny, 'The Analytic Challenges of Studying the Middle East and its Evolving Media Environment', pp. 8–23; Tarik Sabry, 'Arab Media and Cultural Studies: Rehearsing New Questions', in Kai Hafez (ed.), *Arab Media: Power and Weakness*, New York: Continuum, pp. 237–51.

50. Sreberny, 'The Analytic Challenges of Studying the Middle East', p. 16.

51. Sreberny, 'Television, Gender and Democratization in the Middle East', p. 64.

52. Sreberny, 'The Analytic Challenges of Studying the Middle East', p. 17.

53. Sreberny, 'Television, Gender and Democratization in the Middle East', p. 66.

54. Sreberny, 'Television, Gender and Democratization in the Middle East', p. 64.

55. Sreberny, 'The Analytic Challenges of Studying the Middle East', p. 20.

56. Sreberny, 'Television, Gender and Democratization in the Middle East', p. 64.

57. Sabry, 'Arab Media and Cultural Studies', pp. 239–40.

58. Ibid: 243.

59. Ibid: 247.

60. See Tarik Sabry, 'Arab Popular Cultures and Everyday Life', in *Cultural Encounters in the Arab World: On Media, The Modern and the Everyday*, London: I.B.Tauris, 2010.

61. See Henri Lefebvre, 'The Everyday and Everydayness', *Yale French Studies* 73 (1987): 7–11; *Everyday Life in the Modern World*, London: Allen Lane; and *Fondements d'une sociologie de la quotidienneté*, Paris: L'Arche.

62. Roger Silverstone, 'Complicity and Collusion in the Mediation of Everyday Life', *New Literary History* 33 (2002): 761–80. See also Paddy Scannell, *Radio, Television and Modern Life: A Phenomenological Approach*, Oxford: Blackwell.

63. James W. Carey, *Communication as Culture: Essays on Media and Society*, New York: Routledge, pp. 67–68.

64. Christian Fuchs, 'A Contribution to Theoretical Foundations of Critical Media and Communication Studies', *The Public* 16.2 (2009): 5–24.

65. Wes Sharrock and Wil Coleman, 'Seeking and Finding Society in the Text', in Paul L. Jalbert (ed.), *Media Studies: Ethnomethodological Approaches*, Lanham: University Press of America, p. 2.

66. Walter Armbrust, *Mass Mediations: New Approaches to Popular Culture in the Middle East and Beyond*, Berkeley: University of California Press, p. 1.

67. Lila Abu-Lughod, *Dramas of Nationhood: the Politics of Television in Egypt*, Chicago: University of Chicago Press.

68. Christa Salamandra, 'Through the Back Door: Syrian Television Makers between Secularism and Islamization', in Kai Hafez (ed.), *Arab Media: Power and Weakness* (New York: Continuum, 2008), pp. 252–62; Christa Salamandra, 'Television and the Ethnographic Endeavour: The Case of Syrian Drama', *Transnational Broadcasting studies* 14 (2005), pp. 1–22, <http://www.arab-mediasociety.com/articles/downloads/20070312081604_TBS14_Christa_Salamandra.pdf >.

69. Marwan Kraidy, *Reality Television and Arab Politics: Contention in Public Life*, Cambridge: Cambridge University Press.

70. Sonia Livingstone, 'On the Relation between Audiences and Publics', in Sonia Livingstone (ed.), *Audience and Publics: When Cultural Engagement Matter for the Public Sphere*, Bristol: Intellect Books, pp. 17–42.

71. Kraidy, 'Saudi Arabia, Lebanon and the Changing Arab Information Order', p. 141.

72. Ibid: 147.

73. Charles Hirschkind, *The Ethical Soundscape: Cassette Sermons and Islamic Counterpublics*, New York: Columbia University Press.

74. Hirschkind, *The Ethical Soundscape*, p. 6.

75. Armbrust, *Mass Mediations*, ix.
76. Roger Silverstone, *Television and Everyday Life*, London: Routledge, p. 2.

Bibliography

Abedi, Mehdi and Michael M.J. Fischer (1993) 'Thinking a Public Sphere in Arabic and Persian', *Public Culture* 6.1: 219–30.

Abu-Lughod, Lila (2005) *Dramas of Nationhood: the Politics of Television in Egypt*, Chicago: University of Chicago Press.

Al Obaidi, Jabbar Audah (2007) *Media Censorship in the Middle East*, Lewiston: The Edwin Mellen Press.

Al-Makaty, Safran, Douglas A. Boyd, and Norman G. Van Tubergen (1997) 'A Q-Study of Reactions to Direct Broadcast Satellite Television Programming in Saudi Arabia', *Journal of South Asian and Middle Eastern Studies* 20.4: 50–64.

Alterman, Jon (2005) 'Arab Media Studies: Some Methodological Considerations' in Mohamed Zayani (ed.), *The Al Jazeera Phenomenon: Critical Perspectives on New Arab Media*, London: Pluto Press, pp. 203–08.

Amin, Hussein (2008) 'Arab Media Audience Research: Developments and Constraints' in Kai Hafez (ed.), *Arab Media: Power and Weakness*, New York: Continuum, pp. 70–75.

Anderson, Jon W. (2003) 'New Media New Publics: Reconfiguring the Public Sphere of Islam', *Social Research* 70.3: 887–906.

Armbrust, Walter (2000) *Mass Mediations: New Approaches to Popular Culture in the Middle East and Beyond*, Berkeley: University of California Press.

Ayish, Muhammad (2008) *The New Arab Public Sphere*, Berlin: Frank and Timme.

—— (2008) 'Arab World Media Content Studies: A Meta-Analysis of a Changing Research Agenda' in Kai Hafez (ed.), *Arab Media: Power and Weakness*, New York: Continuum.

—— (1998) 'Communication Research in the Arab World: A New Perspective', *Javnost: The Public* 5.1: 33–57.

Carey, James W. (1992) *Communication as Culture: Essays on Media and Society*, New York: Routledge.

Charles Hirschkind (2009) *The Ethical Soundscape: Cassette Sermons and Islamic Counterpublics*, New York: Columbia University Press.

Curran, James and Myung-Jin Park (2000) 'Beyond Globalization Theory' in James Curran and Myung-Jin Park (eds), *De-Westernizing Media Studies*, London: Routledge, pp. 3–18.

Eickelman, Dale F. (2002) 'The Religious Public Sphere in Early Muslim Societies' in Mariam Hoexter, Shmuel N. Eisenstadt, and Nehemia Levtzion (eds), *The Public Sphere in Muslim Societies*, Albany: State University of New York Press, pp. 1–8.

Eickelman, Dale F. and Armando Salvatore (2002) 'The Public Sphere and Muslim Identities', *European Journal of Sociology* 43: 92–115.

El Sherif, Mahmoud (1989) 'The Arab Attitude to Mass Media', *Intermedia* 8.2: 28–29.

Entman, Robert M. (2004) *Projections of Power: Framing News, Public Opinion, and Foreign U.S. Policy*, Chicago: University of Chicago Press.

Fandy, Mamoun (2007) *(Un)Civil War of Words: Media and Politics in the Arab World*, Westport, CT: Praeger.

Feghali, Ellen (1997) 'Arab Cultural Communication Patters', *International Journal of Intercultural Relations* 21.3: 45–78.

Fuchs, Christian (2009) 'A Contribution to Theoretical Foundations of Critical Media and Communication Studies', *The Public* 16.2: 5–24.

Garnham, Nicholas (2004) 'Class Analysis and the Information Society as Mode of Production' *Javnost: The Public* 11.3: 93–104.

Hafez, Kai (ed.) (2008) *Arab Media: Power and Weakness*, New York: Continuum.

Helga Tawil-Souri (2008) 'Arab Television in Academic Scholarship', *Sociology Compass* 2.5: 1400–15.

Jayyusi, Lena (2007) 'Internationalizing Media Studies: A View from the Arab World', *Global Media and Communication* 3: 254–55.

Kraidy, Marwan (2009) *Reality Television and Arab Politics: Contention in Public Life*, Cambridge: Cambridge University Press.

—— (2008) 'From Activity to Interactivity: The Arab Audience' in Kai Hafez (ed.), *Arab Media: Power and Weakness*, New York: Continuum, pp. 91–102.

Lefebvre, Henri (1987) 'The Everyday and Everydayness', *Yale French Studies* 73: 7–11.

—— (1971) *Everyday Life in the Modern World*, London: Allen Lane.

—— (1961) *Fondements d'une sociologie de la quotidienneté*, Paris: L'Arche.

Lehmann, Ann-Sophie. 'Reflexivity as Theoretical Concept in Media Studies', (http://www.mediaengager.com/tutorial1.pdf).

Livingstone, Sonia (2005) 'On the Relation between Audiences and Publics' in Sonia Livingstone (ed.), *Audience and Publics: When Cultural Engagement Matter for the Public Sphere*, Bristol: Intellect Books, pp. 17–42.

Lynch, Marc (2008) 'Political Opportunity Structures: Effects of Arab Media' in Kai Hafez (ed.), *Arab Media: Power and Weakness*, New York: Continuum, pp. 17–31.

—— (2006) 'Globalization and Arab Security' in Jonathan Kirshner (ed.), *Globalization and National Security*, New York: Routledge, pp. 171–200.

—— (2006) *Voices of the New Arab Public: Iraq, Al Jazeera, and Middle East Politics Today*, New York: Columbia University Press.

—— (1999) *State Interests and Public Spheres: The International Politics of Jordan's Identity*, New York: Columbia University Press.

Patterson, Thomas E. (2008) 'Political Roles of the Journalist' in Doris A. Graber, Denis McQuail, and Pippa Norris (eds), *The Politics of News*, 2nd edn, Washington, DC: CQ Press.

Pollock, David (2008) *Slippery Polls: Uses and Abuses of Opinion Surveys from Arab States*, Washington: Washington Institute for Near East Policy.

Powell, Adam (2004) 'No Independent Arab Media Exist, Say Arab Journalists', *Washington Journal* (4 March 2004) (http://uscpublicdiplomacy.com/ index. php/newsroom/journal_detail/770/).

Sabry, Tarik (2010) *Cultural Encounters in the Arab World: On Media, the Modern and the Everyday*, London: I.B.Tauris.

—— (2009) 'Media and Cultural Studies in the Arab World: Making Bridges to Local Discourses of Modernity' in Daya K. Thussu (ed.), *Internationalizing Media Studies*, London: Routledge, pp. 196–214.

—— (2008) 'Arab Media and Cultural Studies: Rehearsing New Questions' in Kai Hafez (ed.) *Arab Media: Power and Weakness*, New York: Continuum, pp. 237–51.

Salamandra, Christa (2008) 'Through the Back Door: Syrian Television Makers between Secularism and Islamization' in Kai Hafez (ed.), *Arab Media: Power and Weakness*, New York: Continuum, pp. 252–62.

—— (2005) 'Television and the Ethnographic Endeavour: The Case of Syrian Drama', *Transnational Broadcasting Studies* 14: 1–22.

Satloff, Robert 'Survey Says: Polls and the Muslim World', *New Republic Online* (30 September 2005) (http:www.washingtoninstitute.org/templateC06. php? CID=873).

Scannell, Paddy (1996) *Radio, Television and Modern Life: A Phenomenological Approach*, Oxford: Blackwell.

Sharrock, Wes and Wil Coleman (1999) 'Seeking and Finding Society in the Text' in Paul L. Jalbert (ed.), *Media Studies: Ethnomethodological Approaches*, Lanham: University Press of America.

Silverstone, Roger (2002) 'Complicity and Collusion in the Mediation of Everyday Life' in *New Literary History* 33: 761–80.

—— (1994) *Television and Everyday Life*, London: Routledge.

Sreberny, Annabelle (2008) 'The Analytic Challenges of Studying the Middle East and its Evolving Media Environment', *Middle East Journal of Culture and Communication* 1.1: 14–18.

—— (2000) 'Television, Gender and Democratization in the Middle East' in James Curran and Myung-Jin Park (eds), *De-Westernizing Media Studies*, London: Routledge, pp. 63–78.

Suleiman, Yasir and Paul Anderson (2008) 'Conducting Fieldwork in the Middle East: Report of a Workforce held at the University of Edinburgh on 12 February 2007', *British Journal of Middle Eastern Studies* 35.2: 151–71.

Tessler, Mark and Amaney Jamal (2006) 'Political Attitude Research in the Arab World: Emerging Opportunities', *Political Science and Politics* 39(3): 1–5, (http://journals.cambridge.org/download.php?file=%2FPSC%2FPSC 39_03% 2FS1049096506060781a.pdf&code=8d682fb da43aa184d990e75cf 703ee45).

Thussu, Daya (2009) 'Internationalize Media Studies', *Television and New Media* 10.1: 162–64.

'Universities and scientific Research in the Arab World'(http://www.aljazeera. net/ NR/exeres/FD18838E-F41B-4958-B521-2B66AE8D1048.htm).

Yigal, Carmon (2002) 'What Makes the Arab Street Rage: Testimony before the Subcommittee on National Security, Veterans Affairs and International Relations of the House of Representatives Committee on Government Reform', *Are we Listening to the Arab Street?*(http://frwebgate.access.gpo. gov/cgibin/ getdoc.cgi?dbname=107_house_ hearings&docid=f:88885.pdf).

Zayani, Mohamed (2008) 'Courting and Containing the Arab Street', *Arab Studies Quarterly* 30(2): 45–64.

Zogby, John (2002) 'Testimony before the Subcommittee on National Security, Veterans Affairs and International Relations of the House of Representatives Committee on Government Reform', *Are We Listening to the Arab Street?* (8 October 2002), (http://frwebgate.access.gpo.gov/cgibin/getdoc.cgi? dbname= 107_house_hearings&docid=f:88885.pdf).

4

Cultural Studies in Arab World Academic Communication Programmes: The Battle for Survival

Muhammad Ayish

In many ways, 'cultural studies', as a subject area of critical analysis, is clearly a rare commodity in the Arab world. A host of political and cultural factors seem to have militated not only against the institutionalisation of 'cultural studies' in many of the region's academic programmes, but also against the very legitimacy of this orientation as a sound intellectual pursuit. If we take account of Stuart Hall's remarks about cultural studies' endeavours to make a connection between matters of power and cultural politics,[1] then we would find little evidence of such a regulated view of culture in Arab world-based higher education. In the region, culture is perceived as too sacred for exploration because it is this very culture that provides us with the safe haven we need to protect ourselves against foreign invasions.[2] National culture in the Arab world's postcolonial state has long been perceived as the final frontier in the defence line for survival in struggles against Western domination, especially in former French-colonised countries in North Africa and the Middle East. In a way, this pride in culture has led to its conception as a sacred system of thought that is immune to criticism; an exclusively patriarchal state concern, often seen as a national asset off limits for private players, including mass media.[3] In contemporary Arab intellectual and academic traditions, while the phrase 'cultural studies' seems almost non-existent, its closest conceptual equivalent is referred to as 'cultural criticism', a nascent discipline, which suggests that culture can be used to understand the dynamics of social change.[4]

In recent years, Arab universities and the public sphere at large have turned into battlegrounds for a conflict between two orientations with respect to cultural criticism: the traditional orientation aligned with the establishment, and the critical orientation associated with private (often non-conformist) individuals and groups.[5] The first orientation is intrinsically 'culturalist' and seeks to perpetuate the study of culture as a descriptive intellectual practice drawing on its conception as a sacred entity, while the second (grounded in mainly secular cultural and literary traditions) takes on a more critical approach to cultural values and practices as the driving engines of political and social change.[6] Critical intellectual forms of expression like literature, music, theatre, art, film, television and feminist works, of course, abound in the Arab world, yet they have developed more in the bookshop and on the fringes of the public sphere than in the institutional frameworks of academia.

I argue in this chapter that, since 'cultural studies' as a distinctive discipline is almost non-existent at Arab institutions of higher education, it is virtually inconceivable and perhaps immature to speak about integrating this area into communication and media studies, especially in Arab *Mashreq* (Middle Eastern) countries as compared to Arab *Maghreb* (North African) countries. In the former, American social science theoretical traditions and functional media models enjoy sweeping dominance. Hence, I call first for laying down the foundations for 'cultural studies' as an academic area of intellectual investigation before we can harness it to enrich media and communication programmes. It is clear that cultural criticism in the Arab world remains more an affair of the bookshop and the street than of institutions of higher education. Relating cultural forms of expression to matters of political and social power in Arabian societies will continue to be cautiously addressed by academic programmes in humanities and social sciences primarily because Arab societies have not yet commanded the liberal culture needed to accommodate such critical orientations. This deficit is induced by complex patriarchal social and political traditions and narrow-minded interpretations of religious scriptures that preclude competing points of views and exclude 'the other' as a legitimate counterpart.[7] In a consensus-based culture, pluralism as a defining political and cultural concept is hardly accorded any legitimacy. In this context, I argue that though media study programmes have witnessed impressive expansions over the past two decades in tandem with a growing communications sector, the intellectual foundations of those programmes remain captive to American mainstream social science traditions. As a result, they have shown strong resistance in accommodating competing global research traditions, including cultural studies.

Is there 'cultural studies' in the Arab world?

Though the term 'cultural studies' was first coined in 1964 by Richard Hoggart, founder of the Birmingham Centre for Contemporary Cultural Studies (CCCS), it is Stuart Hall who is credited with the elaboration and development of this study area. As an academic discipline, 'cultural studies' in its basic configuration combines political economy, communication, sociology, social theory, literary theory, media theory, film/video studies, cultural anthropology, philosophy, museum studies and art history/criticism to understand social change. 'Cultural studies' researchers often seek to demonstrate how a particular phenomenon relates to matters of ideology, nationality, ethnicity, social class, and/or gender. During the past four decades, Hall's pioneering work, along with his colleagues Paul Willis, Dick Hebdige, Tony Jefferson and Angela McRobbie, created an international intellectual movement to promote the study of cultural phenomena. Many 'cultural studies' scholars employed Marxist methods of analysis to explore relationships between cultural forms and the political economy; however, major shifts in Britain's political spectrum in the mid-1980s exposed the deficiencies in Marxist perspectives, provoking scholars to draw on Gramsci's arguments that capitalists not use only brute force to maintain control, but also penetrate the everyday culture of working people.[8]

'Cultural studies' has come to generate varying perspectives around the world as regards the nature and role of culture in social change. British 'cultural studies', for example, includes overtly political, left-wing views, and criticisms of popular culture as 'capitalist' mass culture, while 'cultural studies' scholarship in America was initially concerned more with understanding the subjective and appropriative side of audience reactions to, and uses of mass culture.[9] Furthermore, 'cultural studies' is not a unified theory, but a diverse field of study encompassing many different approaches, methods and academic perspectives. This diverse nature has induced debates pertaining to its legitimacy as a sound intellectual pursuit. Some academics from other fields have dismissed 'cultural studies' as an academic fad and a vehicle of careerism used by academics to promote eccentric ends.[10] Sokal refers to the 'fashionable nonsense' of postmodernists working in cultural studies, noting that 'this silliness is emanating from the self-proclaimed Left.[11] In response to critical remarks about the claimed impotence of the field to address real contemporary woes, 'cultural studies' scholars argue that what 'cultural studies' can do is to demonstrate the way in which finding solutions for our problems is embedded in a political context in which representations, metaphors and other semiotic processes come to have enormous power.[12]

When the above debates are positioned in contemporary Arab World academic contexts, one finds little relevance, especially as new voices continue to question the legitimacy of an Arabised version gaining currency as 'cultural criticism'. Of course, critical orientations to culture, in the broad sense of the word, have been around in the Arab World for the past century, often represented by diverse works of literature, fine art, film, feminist discourse, journalism, television and popular culture. Their development took place most commonly in the bookshop, often represented by voices of dissent and opposition to the establishment. Towering figures in this critical cultural landscape have ranged through nineteenth-century religious reformists, such as Mohamed Abdu, Jamal Din Al Afaghani, Abdul Rahman Al Kawakbi and Ali Abdul Raziq, to twentieth-century men of letters such as Taha Hussein, Abbas Mahmoud al Aqqad, Abdeul Rahman Munif, and Adonis, to feminists like Nawal Sadawi and Fatima Mernissi, literary critics like Kamal Abu Dheib and Abdul Aziz Hamoudi, sociologists like Hisham Sharabi and George Tarabishi, philosophers such as Hassan Hanafi, Mohammed Abed al-Jabri and Mohamed Jaber Al Ansari, to popular culture icons like Abdul Rahman Al Abnoodi and Sheikh Imam. It is clear that the majority of these figures evolved their critical cultural perspectives outside state-patronised institutions, often in the bookshop and in independent intellectual centres, like the Beirut-based Arab Unity Studies Centre and the Arab Cultural Centre. The employment of 'cultural studies' perspectives to understand those cultural productions and to relate them to matters of social and political power in the Arab World has not been a popular practice in institutions of higher education developed under state control.

Even when claims about Arab universities offering programmes on these subjects are validated, it can be seen that their contributions are classified more as studies of culture than as cultural studies in the Western sense of the words. If we take account of Hall's remarks about cultural studies' endeavours to make a connection between matters of power and cultural politics, i.e., an exploration of representations of and for marginalised social groups and the need for cultural change, we would find little evidence of such a regulated view of culture in the region's higher education. Culture has been viewed as an independent entity that may be investigated on its own terms with no connections to existing power relations. As Giroux et al. (2004) note, the rationale of traditional humanistic education is that it offers students assured access to a storehouse of cultural materials constituted as a canon. Such a canon is, of course, relatively flexible in its definition insofar as it can incorporate and take cognisance of both marginal and recondite materials; as a thesaurus of sorts it cannot pass up anything of value. Hence, we notice the production of intellectual efforts on the part of Arab literary critics, anthropologists, sociologists, feminists and culturalists that draw on the intellectual traditions of Marxism, structuralism, poststructuralism, modernism and postmodernism. They have used a variety of methodological tools, including field surveys, ethnography and textual approaches, such as semiotics, narrative theory and deconstructionism, yet, their endeavours have been viewed as lacking a coherent interdisciplinary character that enables the use of culture as an anchor point of analysis.

In the Arab World, cultural criticism may be viewed as an emerging field that seems to experience a great deal of ferment in its conceptual foundations and methodological tools. In the recent decades, cultural criticism in Arab societies has been largely a function of interactions with Western, especially European experiences, which view the production of theoretical knowledge as a political practice. In this sense, the past two decades have been formative years for the formulation of critical cultural orientations in a region long known for its full allegiance to cultural heritage, both as a source of identity and as a shield against the onslaught of what has been termed as the Western cultural invasion. Some institutions of higher education – generally, those with a clear Western academic thrust – have begun to give more attention to this subject area in a manner different from traditional cultural studies programmes which address descriptive and aesthetic features of the written text: this is highly characteristic of university study programmes in arts, humanities and social sciences in North African countries shaped by strong French academic traditions.[13] All in all, despite some development, 'cultural studies' in the Western sense of the words remains far off limits for Arab universities that have arisen within state-delineated patriarchal and political boundaries.

The genesis of this deficiency in the role of 'cultural studies' in enhancing our understanding of social change is not grounded in current social and political conditions, but runs deeper in the region's history. In the colonial and postcolonial eras, the Arab World's intellectual landscape was bustling with many cultural productions, but most were developing under state patronage and few of them were reflecting voices of dissent outside institutional frameworks. Some reasons may be cited for this patriarchal and institutional straightjacketing of cultural activities in the Arab World. First, national culture in the postcolonial state has long been perceived as the final frontier in the struggle against other colonial nations. To criticise or question culture amounted to an act of treason or flouting of national pride. Culture must be accorded loyalty and allegiance because it provides a safe haven against foreign invasions. Within the national–colonial dichotomy, the critical use of culture as a weapon in the struggle for liberation and independence was sanctioned, as is evident in Arab nationalist cultural productions of novels, poetry, radio broadcasts, films, folkloric cultural expressions and arts.

In the 1960s and 1970s, literary, art and film studies dealing with anticolonial themes sought to highlight the patriotic spirit embedded in literature, music, films, arts and media content at a time when the defence of national culture was synonymous with the struggle for independence and liberation from the shackles of colonialism and later imperialism. When the media imperialism and cultural dependency argument began to gain popularity at the height of the global debates on a new world information and communication order, many Arab culture and media researchers – for instance, Mustapha Masmoudi, Awatef Abdul Rahman (1996, 1998), Nawal Saadawi, and Samir Amin, literary critics such as Edward Said and philosophers such as Mohammed Abed al-Jabri and Hassan Hanafi – were gaining recognition in their communities as well as abroad. The advent of satellite television and the World Wide Web to the Arab region has accentuated traditional debates on Arab culture as coming increasingly under attack in an era of globalisation.[14]

Second, in addition to its view as a safe haven for Arabs in the struggle with the West, culture has also been viewed as a sacred system of thought that is immune to criticism. When anti-colonial sentiments were escalating in the 1980s and 1990s, the failure of national development projects across the Arab World produced wave after wave of frustration culminating in the questioning of many aspects of conventional wisdom and inducing a search for new visions drawing on both cultural heritage and contemporary realities.[15] It has been widely realised that culture stands at the centre of social transformation, both as a tool for reinforcing the status quo and for bringing about desired changes. A more defiant breed of intellectual traditions began to surface, mainly centring on the notion of not taking things for granted and of questioning the practicality of traditional cultural elements in a contemporary world.[16] As noted earlier, such orientations have been viewed with suspicion and fear on the part of well-entrenched institutionalised cultural and political traditions.

Third, culture in the Arab World has been largely a patriarchal, state concern, viewed as a national asset and not for private players.[17] From an operational point of view, the state has been the dominant force in defining cultural production, with many countries establishing ministries for culture and national guidance. A serious implication of this trend has been the pre-empting of an independent and sustainable cultural industry. In the West, private cultural industries are the main players in the public sphere, consequently taking the brunt of criticism in academic and policy research. As culture in the Arab World is deeply engrained in religious and tribal belief systems, the nascent private cultural players have had to grapple with a wide range of taboos that render their works ineffective. Voices originating outside institutional academic arrangements are alienated from mainstream cultural entities, often billed as antisocial heretics or lunatics. If we were to examine the harvest of the state censorship machine for the past 20 years, we would be horrified at the huge number of creative films, TV shows, websites, books, novels, poems and musical compositions that have found their way into the trash while their authors face imprisonment.

With significant social and political transformations sweeping the Arab World in the 1990s and beyond, it is clear that Arab universities and the wider public sphere have become battlegrounds for a fierce conflict over cultural criticism between two orientations: the traditionalist faction aligned with the establishment, and the critical faction aligned with non-institutional individuals and groups. This intellectual battle is taking place in the shadows of a fiercer conflict between established cultural, media and educational institutions on the one hand and rival fringe institutions enjoying significant grassroots concerns over the nature and direction of social change envisioned for their communities. The traditionalist faction seeks to perpetuate the study of culture as a descriptive intellectual practice drawing on the notion of Arab culture as a sacred entity that gives substance and shape to present existence and future development. This tradition embraces literary criticism as well as empirical social sciences with functionalist and structuralist outlooks. For this tradition, culture is the epitome of identity and national pride as well as an inspiration for futurist orientations. The study of all cultural forms should be delineated by immediate contexts of time and space with no room for inferential reasoning. Cultural criticism is limited to stylistic and aesthetic features of the text in literature and to descriptive features of community practices in different social settings.[18]

The critical tradition, on the other hand, as manifested in the diverse sub-subject areas of literature, anthropology, philosophy, feminism, media and sociology, has developed mainly in the bookshop, beyond institutional frames. The underlying theme uniting those affiliated with this tradition is their defiance of conventional wisdom and their search for a more intellectually balanced and rational view of culture in its miscellaneous manifestations in Arabian communities. The rise of this fringe stream of popular culture suggests deep-running disenchantment with the political and cultural establishment. Examples include Egyptian popular poet Ahmad Fuad Najm whose critical poems are widely circulated on Web-based social networks. In the 1980s, Iraqi poet Muzaffar al Nawwab was represented an anti-establishment voice that gained popularity in the context of successive Arab political and military failures. Such voices have gained more ground in recent years with the introduction of the World Wide Web and satellite television as new outlets of expression. The Al Jazeera Satellite Channels have always been viewed as a platform for dissident voices in politics, religion and culture at large; promoting itself as 'The Platform of Those Who Have No Platform', Al Jazeera has incurred the wrath of a range of states and non-state actors in the region, including Arab governments, fundamentalist groups, and even the Bush administration, for playing host to controversial personalities.

It is now also clear that the boundaries dividing proponents of cultural studies as studies of culture and as cultural criticism in the Arab World are not formalistic, but intrinsically ideological. The common denominator of critical cultural figures was their encounter with Western cultural criticism experiences. Such exposure was both a blessing and a curse. As much as they have harnessed modern conceptual tools to help understand the dynamics of Arab culture, they have been viewed with both suspicion and animosity in their societies for embracing modernity as a defining frame for their analysis. News of the rise and fall of a Bahraini cultural criticism association in 2006 was received with enthusiasm among culturalists, as it was portrayed as an alien body lacking vision and clarity; its members acted in constant fear and uncertainty.[19] This runs in parallel to the mushrooming of scores of literary criticism societies which receive bountiful support from the state because their mission is to develop literary craftsmanship and enhance modes of indigenous expression.

Literary criticism and feminist studies

Although the battle arenas for cultural criticism in the Arab public sphere, including the academic sphere, are diverse, two significant areas have received a good deal of attention in the ongoing debates: *literary criticism* and *feminist studies*. Literary critics have been the staunchest opponents to the diffusion of cultural criticism in higher education because they have seen in this tradition a threat to their domination of the field. Some writers have portrayed cultural criticism as a hoax culture that thrives on stretching meanings beyond their potential, causing confusion and disorientation. It is also viewed as a replica of a Western thought system that has intruded on Arab life, corrupting communications, literature and religion. Opponents of cultural criticism do not wish to dispense with a long tradition of literary criticism that has sought to enhance literary text effectiveness, yet without connecting it to social and political variables. Literary aesthetics, according to this perspective, should be the central tenet of literary criticism, focusing on the writer's endeavour to bring about change in society by means of effective communication of moral and cultural values through poetry and prose.[20]

Although opponents of cultural criticism in the Arab World often base their arguments on aesthetic (depoliticised) grounds, it is clear that the main theme uniting them is intrinsically ideological, centring on the scope and depth of how culture should be investigated as a subject area.[21] For literary critics, it is the text or the written word that needs to be highlighted in critical works. Critics need to study the aesthetics of text production in an attempt to enhance methods of expression, especially in classical poetry, which has been a central platform for promoting tribal and nationalist interests. Cultural criticism goes beyond textual analysis to explore connections between texts that embrace the whole cultural spectrum, on the one hand, and power relations in society, on the other. For cultural critics, as noted earlier, text is a broad topic that embraces camera shots and angles, colours, folkloric dances, music, costumes, written text, architectural designs, and spoken language. The conversion of literary criticism into a study of text as a political signifier goes against the institutional nature of literary scholarship in Arab universities. This same ideological feature also applies to empirical anthropological and sociological traditions that draw on the investigation of social culture as an independent quantifiable entity with no affinity to social and political contexts. All forms of cultural expression are viewed as discrete units that could be empirically studied on their own as features of social development. Once social change is seen from a critical cultural perspective as reflecting discursive processes in a community's political life, then its investigations are bound to take new and risky directions that institutional higher education cannot afford. We could also say the same when it comes to jurisprudence and scripture interpretations that draw wholly on the notion of submission to the sacredness of the text.[22]

Literary criticism has won more durability in the region for numerous reasons, the most outstanding of which has been its exclusive obsession with text as separate from the social and political context that has given rise to it. Arabic, as the spoken not written language of poetry and oration, has always cast a spell on its audiences, elite and masses alike. In a highly oral culture, Arabic has been utilised to communicate with the ear more than with the eye; as the famous Arab poet Bashhar bin Burd once noted: 'The ear sometimes falls in love before the eye'.[23] The oral features of Arabic were always under a process of critical scrutiny to produce the best the human ear could appreciate, not only for aesthetic reasons, but also for political and ideological ones. In traditionally tribal Arabian societies, poets have served as official spokesmen for tribal chiefs and nationalist leaders, receiving extra attention for their creative ability to deliver the best oral expression, one marked more by formalistic structure than substantive meaning. Although classical Arab literary traditions have embraced different categories of poetry used to praise, discredit or encourage tribal cohesion, these traditions were analysed in the context of a culture whose orientations were taken for granted as being socially stratified. In the postcolonial era, new poetic traditions with nationalist orientations received a great deal of attention because their subject was the Arab states' struggle for liberation and independence, and many of them were integrated into school and university curricula as integral components of national heritage.

The second area from which cultural criticism has drawn is feminist studies that have sought, among other things, to explore different forms of women's expression on social, political and cultural subjects and how these expressions relate to gender issues. Surfacing feminist studies have been located in very few institutional frameworks, such as universities and women's studies centres or in bookshops. Studying culture as signifying power relations, and the use of culture as text, has been well utilised in feminist studies across the Arab World. The revival of classical and modern women's works, as evident in Buthaina Shaaban's *100 Years of the Arab Woman's Novel*, falls into this category. Shabaan is the author of several works that explore themes regarding Arab women in the twentieth century. Her work, *Women Talking About Themselves* was published in both Great Britain and the United States.[24] Shaaban challenges male claims to exclusive writing on social and political issues, and finds women's approaches to political and social issues to be as astute, if not more so, as men's work. When women write on day-to-day concerns, such as commerce, trade, and transportation, the value of their contribution has been downplayed when compared to hardcore political issues, like the Balfour Declaration and the Partition of Palestine. Shabaan wonders whether we had 'become aware of these issues at the time we would not be in a better position today?'

Another widely-celebrated work on women's cultural contributions has been produced by Joseph Zeidan, who focuses on modern Arab women's literature in several of his recent publications, and most notably in his *Arab Women Novelists: The Formative Years and Beyond* (1995). Fatima Mernissi's *The Veil and the Male Elite: A Feminist Interpretation of Women's Rights in Islam* (1991) has been another outstanding contribution to this cultural studies tradition. Mernissi views the recent rise of women's repression in some Muslim countries as a rejection of colonial influence. She remarks that the fact that Western colonisers took over the paternalistic defence of the Muslim woman's lot meant that any changes in her condition were categorised as concessions to the coloniser.[25] Since the external aspects of women's liberation, for example, dropping use of the veil for Western dress, were often emulations of the practices of Western women, women's liberation was readily identified as succumbing to foreign influences.[26]

Leading cultural critics

As noted earlier, although modern Arab cultural traditions offer a wide range of works harnessing different forms of expression to critically address social and political conditions, only a few scholars have publicly declared their support for this orientation and Abdullah Al-Ghathami, a professor of literature at King Saud University in Saudi Arabia, is a leading figure in this field. Over the past decade, Al-Ghathami has established himself as the prime proponent of cultural criticism in an area extremely hostile to this subject. In recent years, Al-Ghathami has initiated a new drive to restore credibility to cultural criticism and his works have found a good deal of popularity in the region. Al-Ghathami has not only introduced cultural studies to the Arabian intellectual community, but he has also harnessed it in order to scrutinise different aspects of Arab culture, past and present. These features have been off limits for traditional literary criticism traditions, which Al-Ghathami has frequently noted, are put forward by critics who have confined themselves to the aesthetics of the literary text, seeking primarily to unravel the beauty of style and the metaphorical expressions which, he observed, hide a great deal of ugliness. For Al-Ghathami, one of the functions of cultural criticism is to demystify literary criticism and to delve behind the presumed aesthetic foundation of its inquiry. He notes that cultural criticism has to draw on literary criticism because the latter has a well-established tradition with a notable presence in the cultural and literary landscape. He suggests the implausibility of separating literary criticism from cultural criticism since both disciplines share a symbiotic relationship, especially when we talk about literary criticism, which has proven itself as a credible and popular field from which to approach one aspect of the cultural phenomena in the region.[27]

In his analysis of the literary discourse in general and poetic discourse in particular, Al-Ghathami noted that literary text has implicit value systems that, in Arabian societies, have produced a hegemonic cultural system that has caused a number of problems. This embedded system has remained beyond criticism, although it has been unravelling for quite some time, overshadowed by aesthetic inquiries. He notes that literary studies had become a fortress guarded by relentless critics as the only field of cultural inquiry throughout Arabian history, and one which had been turned into an institution in its own right. One implication of this development has been in the separation of cultural production from cultural consumption, with literary criticism turning into an elitist sphere with no relevance to the average person, The narrow scope of literary criticism and its tendency to be oblivious to central questions of cultural production and consumption beyond institutional frameworks has opened the way for cultural criticism, which is seen to be more comprehensive in its domain and more concerned with issues of production and consumption in political, social and economic contexts. Further, Al-Ghathami notes that, in traditional Arabian cultural forms, poetry has been the bastion of cultural expression and has been used as the Trojan horse in which to carry political, social and psychological value systems that perpetuate the status quo as the only viable option available to communities. Poetry has taken up a central position in classical and contemporary cultural expressions, permeating the social and cultural fabric of society with deep-reaching effects.

Another central contributor to the diffusion of cultural criticism in the Arab World is the Syrian critic, Nouri Jarah, who has described the Arab cultural scene as amounting to a 'black market'. In his newspaper articles, Jarah notes that the predicament of the Arab creative person begins with *al-thaqfa al-rasmiyyah*, official or state-sponsored culture, or the culture of the establishment. Jarah takes issue with some of the excuses for this predicament, including the notion that the intellectual has fallen victim to 'popular culture', as well as what he calls the game of the 'margin', 'marginalised', and 'marginalisation'. Official culture, according to Jarah, legitimises the status of the person as an established poet. The decisions of culture, Jarah believes, are based on exchanges of power and influence.[28] The manipulative decisions of Arab press editors and the critics distort the cultural scene, both in the homeland and in the Diaspora. He describes the dominant forces as 'cultural militias'. They use the carrot and stick approach, employing incentives as well as subtle threats, at times going so far as to deprive authors and critics of their livelihoods, namely their jobs. Membership in the 'militia' is not arranged through contracts, but rather through 'aesthetic and 'ideological causes', and soon the 'militia' becomes an 'aesthetic gang, excluding its dissident members' from this newspaper or that magazine's cultural pages, or withdrawing an invitation to this panel or that festival.[29]

Impact on communication programmes

The previous section has shown that, while cultural criticism remains a fringe intellectual pursuit in the Arab World, most discussions of its legitimacy have not trickled down into academic programmes at universities. Since the establishment of the first communication programme in 1939 in Egypt as part of the Higher Journalism Institute, Arab media study programmes have come a long way in their development and numbers, yet, they continue to suffer from being hostage to traditional views of communication as a technical function concerned with the transmission of messages to mass audiences, as James Carey (1989) once noted. By the early 1970s, Egypt and Iraq seemed to have the only full-fledged academic communication programmes in the Arab region. In the early 1980s, however, mass communication programmes mushroomed in many Arab universities, and as the third millennium dawned on the Arab World, almost all institutions of higher education had some form of academic programme in media studies. From a historical perspective, communication studies in the Arab World have evolved in three distinctive post-World War II contexts: the modernisation paradigm context; the dependency paradigm context, and the globalisation paradigm context. In the three contexts, communication has developed in tune with Western-oriented perspectives about politics, culture and social change. Daniel Lerner's classic statement about the 'passing of traditional Society' seems to have focused research on a presumed media role in socio-economic modernisation. To a large extent, academic programmes share some common feature: they largely cater to undergraduate students; focus more on professional preparation; and lean more towards Western theories of media and society.[30]

In early 2008, there were 70 communication programmes offered at different government and private Arab universities. Those programmes primarily sought to provide students mainly with technical professional skills in print, broadcast and electronic media as well as in public relations and promotional activities. Those programmes are styled on Western academic offerings that address the mass communication phenomena along technological lines as marked by print media, broadcasting, public relations, advertising and online communications.[31] These programmes seek to prepare students in specialised areas of communication with little emphasis on the interdisciplinary nature of the field. However, as convergence continues to come to bear on the Arab World media market, these programmes find themselves, more than ever before, under pressure to adapt to evolving realities. The changing face of Arab media suggests that new media jobs are surfacing and so new academic and professional training orientations need to be adopted. Unfortunately, most Arab World academic programmes seem very slow in responding to these changes and their offerings continue to be obsessed with classical mass communication phenomena.[32]

Although the Arab World has witnessed an impressive proliferation of academic communication programmes, the production of scholarly research has been limited. It is noted that Arabs' earliest encounter with communication scholarship took place mainly during the post-independence era, when mass media infrastructures were being established as part of national development projects. Communication theorisation was viewed as a luxury that Arab researchers could not afford when their societies were preoccupied with nation-building concerns. Research works reflected not only a visible Western influence in framing communication problems, but also in determining how they were methodologically approached. A survey of research works carried out over the past four decades reveals a range of areas and themes: propaganda, national development, cultural identity, Arab stereotypes, media hegemony, communication Islamisation, women's representation, new technology, and globalisation. To some extent, psychological warfare studies were carried out in the spirit of Cold War politics, when the media were entrusted with huge mobilisation functions. The 'development communication' research tradition was induced by a growing interest in the role of media in social change in newly independent states. Yet, although this tradition has spawned a wide range of works, the perpetuation of economic and social inequalities in Arab societies in the 1970s and 1980s gave rise to more critical research works drawing on anti-Western perspectives. Arab countries were central parties to global debates over a New World Information and Communication Order in the 1970s and 1980s. Imbalances and biases in news flows from and into the Arab World were important topics of research that sought to shed light on the nature, direction and orientation of news transmitted by major international news agencies and carried by Arab print and broadcast media.[33] Most of the studies found notable discrepancies in news flow patterns, with Western agencies dominating the news scene in the Arab World.

A tradition of research known as 'Islamic communication' gained vogue in the mid- 1980s. In its basic configuration, this tradition was no more than an exposition of how mass media could be used to propagate Islamic ideas and concepts around the world.[34] Such efforts fell short of meeting the minimum requirements of model building in theoretical and methodological terms. With the advent of globalisation in the early 1990s, communication research in the Arab world shifted more towards scrutinising the potentially negative effects of satellite television and the World Wide Web, yet the conceptual tools used to address these issues have been descriptive rather than analytical.

The genesis of media studies in the Arab World is technical rather than intellectual, going back to postcolonial societies that needed technical communicators who would run the media for the purposes of national development. Arab countries needed media practitioners who could operate cameras, broadcast stations and printing shops, while writers and intellectuals were responsible for content. The US was the best place to find professors of communication, and American-based curricula were more technically oriented in contrast to the European traditions of communication education, where media students could come from a background in sociology or political science, later adding technical training in media work. The first wave of communication scholars attended graduate programmes in the United States in the 1980s; they were embraced by the American tradition of communication, the transmission model as opposed to the ritualistic model.[35] When they returned to their home countries, they carried with them a whole social science tradition of communication as a powerful agent of social change.

Arab universities developed their communication curricula to serve national development and not to be critical of it.[36] Courses are either descriptive or technical, thus mirroring the technical/intellectual communicator dichotomy, with some exceptions in communication study programmes in North African universities where French interdisciplinary traditions are clear. At Algiers University, for example, a student may get a degree in sociology, political science or anthropology, then gain some technical media training, graduating as an effective communicator with credible intellectual skills. In the Arab East, meanwhile, students spend four years grappling with highly technical subjects while gaining fewer intellectual and liberal education skills.

A survey of communication programmes at 20 Arab universities has revealed little visibility of 'cultural studies' perspectives being integrated into the curriculum. All media study programmes, both at graduate and under-graduate levels, have communication theory, history, ethics, technology and research methods components, yet these subjects are addressed from a heavily American social science perspective. The percentage of specialised communication courses in overall study plans ranges from 35 per cent to 70 per cent, meaning that students are not exposed to important disciplines in the humanities and social sciences. The departmentalisation of communication studies through their isolation from other related disciplines has been underlain by a clear tendency to emphasise the technical rather than the intellectual aspects of communication training, something that seems congruent with dominant trends to neutralise media practitioners and to maximise their detachment from their surrounding contexts. In media study programmes in Algeria, Tunisia and Morocco, a more interdisciplinary character is conferred on curricula with an emphasis on philosophy, sociology, political science and anthropology.[37] In the absence of clear cultural perspectives in Arab universities, media study programmes are likely to be limited in their conceptual and methodological features for years to come.

Conclusions

It is clear that cultural criticism in the Arab World remains more related to the bookshop than to institutions of higher education. Relating cultural forms of expression to matters of political and social power in Arab institutions of higher education will continue to be cautiously viewed as a heresy, primarily because Arabian societies have not yet commanded the liberal culture that is needed to accommodate such critical orientations. During the past century, the Arab World has generated a wide range of critical works whose authors were often aligned with the anti-establishment camp. Whether they reflected reformist religious views, feminist discourse, anti-colonialist and anti-imperialist perspectives, humanist-universal orientations and anti-establishment ideology, critical cultural works in the Arab World have flourished in the street rather than in state institutions. Regulated views of such works as addressing matters of power remain limited, except for works dealing with colonialist and postcolonialist hegemony, where cultural production seemed to be converging with state ideologies. Exceptions to this dominant paradigm in academic programmes may be found in some North African universities, where bitter colonial experiences seem to have generated enduring anti-Western features in those programmes. I have noted that, as a result of a dominant American functionalist social science tradition, most communication programmes have failed to establish intellectual links with relevant humanities and social sciences that are imbued with critical cultural orientations.

I have also contended that, as 'cultural studies' goes international, we will see more diversity in its conceptualisation. This suggests that while the basic tenets of the discipline can provide us with appropriate intellectual and methodological tools for addressing social change from a cultural perspective, we can also develop an Arab perspective on this field. The regulated view of culture as a signifying system with substantive implications for existing power relations was bound to generate considerable uproar among traditional culturalists associated with literary criticism, establishment historians, empirical sociologists and anthropologists and religious scholars. If cultural studies is about the discursive construction of meanings in societies as they reflect specific power relations at gender, family, colonial, social and political levels, then we have a rich subject area that could enable us to understand ourselves and communities in a manner conducive to a smooth and balanced transformation. In this case, cultural studies should be concerned with providing insightful perspectives on society rather than making value judgments about the soundness of their social and political systems. I argue that this understanding is central for initiating change, yet on our own terms. Past experience has demonstrated that the importation of wholesale modes of thinking into Arab societies has disastrous consequences for future decades. The failing development model of the 1960s and 1970s has been a case in point. An important implication of this failure is that we must evolve our own 'cultural studies' perspective for the Arab World – one which seeks to enlighten and educate, rather than to make judgments. Such a perspective could be instrumental not only for enhancing our understanding of the dynamics of social change in Arabian societies, but in demonstrating how communication can be viewed as an integral component of that change.

Notes

1. Hall 1980.
2. Al-Jirari 2002.
3. Al-Jabri 2001, 2004; Hanafi 2003.

4. Al-Ghathami 2000.
5. An example of this is the controversial interview conducted in June 2005 with Saudi cultural critic Abdallah Al-Ghathami, aired on the Al Arabiya television network. For details, see http://www.alarabiya.net/programmes/2005/06/04/13630.html
6. The culturalist orientation is popular in state-sponsored institutions, including universities and schools while the critical orientation is characteristic of mostly dissident voices operating outside the institutional public sphere.
7. Sharabi 1988.
8. Hall 1986.
9. Sardar 2005.
10. Chow 2002.
11. Sokal 1996.
12. See Cultural Studies Central, 'The Nutty Professor: Reaction to the Sokal Hoax', accessed at: http://www.culturalstudies.net/sokal.html
13. French traditions emphasise textual analysis, semiotics and discourse analysis in addition to fostering an interdisciplinary nature in study programmes as evident in social sciences and humanities studies at Algiers University, the Higher Institute for Journalism and Mass Communication in Morocco, and the Tunis Institute for Journalism and News Sciences.
14. This is clear in academic programmes at universities in Egypt, Syria, Iraq, Libya and Algeria where the anti-colonialist slant defined many humanities and social sciences.
15. Hanafi 2003.
16. Al-Jabri 1986.
17. Sharabi 1988.
18. Al-Ghathami 2000.
19. See Al Waqt Newspaper online: 'Cultural criticism: An imaginary epithet falling down', 7 July 2007 at: http://www.alwaqt.com/art.php?aid=63604&hi, and 'Cultural criticism society: Development and end', Al Waqt Newspaper online, at: http://alwaqt.com/art.php?aid=63609
20. See 'Cultural criticism and literary criticism: One mirror or two different faces', al Majallah al Thaqafiyya, 16 February 2004, accessed 12 August 2008 at: http://www.al-jazirah.com/culture/16022004/aguas9.htm and 'cultural criticism is a strategy not ideology', in Elaph e-portal, 19 July 2007, accessed 10 August 2008 at: http://www.elaph.com/ElaphWeb/Culture/2007/7/249031.htm?sectionarchive=Culture
21. See 'The rise and fall of cultural criticism', Al Waqt newspaper, 7 July 2007, accessed 8 July 2008 at: http://alwaqt.com/art.php?aid=63604
22. Literary criticism programmes are offered mostly within graduate Arabic language and literature study degrees in almost all Arab World universities, with a focus on the aesthetic features of the poetry and prose text. However, with many faculty members gaining their graduate education from Western universities,

literary criticism and linguistic analysis have taken on a more critical tone as critical Western intellectual scholarship is brought to bear on Arabic text analysis. In this respect, Noam Chomsky's linguistic theories as well as semiotic and discourse analysis tools have become familiar in study programmes. However, these efforts have more or less failed to position literary criticism within any well-defined cultural perspective.

23. Quoted from: http://www.geocities.com/alwafi90/f/bashar.htm
24. See *Al Jadid magazine* 7:34 (Winter 2001) accessed at: http://www.aljadid.com/
25. Al Mernissi 1991.
26. Feminist or gender-based study programmes have been established in Jordan, Tunis, Egypt, Syria, Bahrain and Lebanon universities mostly with support from international women's organisations.
27. Al-Ghathami 2000.
28. http://leb.net/~aljadid/editors/0734chalala.html
29. Elie Chalala, editor's notebook, 'Lamenting Standards of Arab Literary Criticism, Rushing Poetry into Translation, at: http://leb.net/~aljadid/editors/0734chalala.html
30. Ayish 1998.
31. Examples include study programmes at Algeria University, Morocco's Higher Institute for Journalism and Mass Communication and Tunisia's Institute of Journalism and News Sciences. Study curricula offered by these institutions focus on related subjects like political science, psychology, sociology and anthropology as compared to the technically-oriented programmes offered by universities in *Mashreq* countries. The main goal espoused by those institutions is to foster critical and varied intellectual traditions in media studies to enable future communicators to serve as active players in their communities.
32. Ayish 2007.
33. Ayish 1989; MacBride et al. 1980/1984; Nordenstren and Varis 1974; Katz and Wedell 1978.
34. Imam 1983; Hatem 1985; Shanqiti n.d.; Hamza 1979; Khatib 1985; Yousof 1993; Najib 1991; Jareesha 1989.
35. Carey 1989.
36. Bou Khnofa 2008.
37. Programmes surveyed by the author are offered by universities in Jordan, Lebanon, Saudi Arabia, Egypt, United Arab Emirates, Qatar, Oman, Algeria, Morocco, Tunisia and Sudan.

Bibliography

Abdul Rahman, Awatef (1998) 'The Crisis of Critical Communication Research', *Communication Studies* (Cairo), 90 (January–March): 18–27 (in Arabic).
—— (1996) *The Arab Press: Confronting Dependency and Zionist Penetration*, Cairo: Dar Al Fiqr Al Arabi (in Arabic).

Al-Ghathami, Abdullah (2000) *Cultural criticism: A Theoretical Introduction into Arab Cultural Systems*, Beirut: Arab Cultural Centre (in Arabic).

Al-Jabri, Mohammed Abed (2004) *Structure of the Arab Mind*, Beirut: Arab Unity Studies Centre (in Arabic).

—— (2002) 'Status of the Sacred in Contemporary Culture', a paper presented at the 'Land of life: Cultural forum of the seekers of sense', Paris, 28 November–1 December. Also published in Islamic States Scientific, Educational and Cultural Organization (ISESCO) website (15 August 2008) (http:// www.isesco.org.ma/ english/publications/Islamtoday/20/P3.php).

—— (2001) *The Arab Ethical Mind: An Analytical Critical Study of the Value System in Islamic Culture*, Beirut: Arab Cultural Centre (in Arabic).

Ayish, Muhammad (2007) 'Communication as an Academic Field in the Arab world', *The International Encyclopaedia of Communication*, Wolfgang Donsbach (ed.), Oxford: Blackwell Publishing, pp. 620–25.

—— (1998) 'Communication Research in the Arab World: A New Perspective', *Javnost: The Public*, European Institute of Communication, Slovenia, 5.1:33–57.

—— (1989) 'Newsfilm in Jordan Television's Arabic Nightly Newscasts', *Journal of Broadcasting and Electronic Media* 33.4: 453–60.

Barakat, Halim (1985) *Contemporary Arab Society: An Exploratory Social Study*, Beirut: Arab Unity Studies Centre.

Bou Khnoufa, Abdelwahab (2008) 'The Epistemological Position of Media and Communication in the Arab world', Arab media studies portal (accessed 25 September 2008) (http://www.arabmediastudies.net/index.php?option=com_ content task=view&id=236&Itemid=101).

Carey, James (1989) *A Cultural Approach to Communication*, New York: Routledge.

Chow, Rey (2002) 'Theory, Area Studies, Cultural Studies: Issues of Pedagogy in Multiculturalism' in Miyoshi, M. and Harootunian, H. (eds), *Learning Places: the Afterlives of Area Studies*, Durham, NC: Duke University Press, pp. 103–118.

Giroux, Henry et al. (2004) 'The Need for Cultural Studies: Resisting Intellectuals and Oppositional Public Spheres' in *Eserver Cultural Studies and Theory Website* (accessed August 12, 2008) (http://theory.eserver.org/need.html).

Hall, Stuart (1986) 'Gramsci's Relevance for the Study of Race and Ethnicity', *Journal of communication Inquiry* 10.2: 5–27.

—— (1980) 'Cultural Studies: Two Paradigms', *Media, culture and society* 2: 57–72.

Hamza, Abdellatif (1979) *Communication in Early Islam*, Cairo: Arab Thought Publishers (in Arabic).

Hanafi, Hassan (2003) *Rhetoric and Action: Current Cultural Deadlock in the Arab-Muslim World*, Cairo: Al Fikr Publishing (in Arabic).

Hatem, Abdul Qader (1985) *Communication in the Holy Quran*, Cairo: Al Ahram Press (in Arabic).

Hijab, Munir (1983) *Theories of Islamic Communication*, Alexandria: Egyptian Book Publishing Foundation (in Arabic).

Imam, Ibrahim (1983) *Broadcast Communication*, Cairo: Arab Thought Publishers (in Arabic).

Jabra, Jabra Ibrahim (1988) 'Arabic Language and Culture' in M. Adams (ed.) *The Middle East*, New York: Facts on File Publications.

Jareesha, Ali (1989) *Towards an Islamic Communication System*, Cairo: Wahba Bookshop (in Arabic).

Katz, Elihu. and Wedell, George (1978) *Broadcasting in the Third World: Promise and Performance*, Cambridge: Harvard University Press.

Khateeb, Mohamed Ajaj (1985) *Lights on Communication in the Light of Islam*, Beirut: Risala Foundation (in Arabic).

MacBride, Sean et al. (1980/1984) *Manny Voices, One World*, Paris: UNESCO.

Mernissi, Fatima (1991) *The Veil and the Male Elite: A Feminist's Interpretation of Women's Rights in Islam*, Reading, MA: Addison-Wesley Publishing.

Najib, Amara (1991) *Communication in Light of Islam*, Riyadh: Maaref Bookshop (in Arabic).

Nordenstreng, Kaarle and Varis, Tapio (1974) *Television Traffic: A One-Way Street?* Paris: UNESCO.

Sardar, Ziauddin (2005) *Introducing Cultural Studies*, London: Icon Books.

Shanqiti, Sayyed (n. d.) *Islamic Communication*, Riyadh: Alam Kutub (in Arabic).

Sharabi, Hisham (1988) *Neopatriarchy: A Theory of Distorted Change in Arab Society*, New York: Oxford University Press.

Sokal, Alan (1996) 'A Physicist Experiments with Cultural Studies', *Lingua Franca* (May/June 1996): 62–64.

5

In Search of the Great Absence: Cultural Studies in Arab Universities

Riadh Ferjani
Translation from the French by Maria Way

I have accepted the request for a contribution to this book with a certain apprehension. First, because what has been asked of me could be the subject of five theses, because the Arab world is so vast and complex (I would say it is ever more complex) and, finally, because I will be both judge and jury. I began by asking myself a set of hard questions: Can one speak of Arab cultural studies, or Arab media studies? Can one, more modestly, limit the field of investigation to the Maghreb area, or to the Middle East? At the risk of surprising the non-Arabic speaking reader confronted with the abundant literature on Arab media published since 11 September 2001, the answer to this question is negative, doubly negative, not least because the most common denomination 'al Bouhouth al arabia fi al i'lam wal ittisal' (Arab media and communication studies), recognises neither the interdisciplinarity nor the creative heterogeneity that fostered the internationalisation of cultural studies.

The answer to our initial question is always negative, because its formulation hides an implied representation, which is quite widespread in the academic milieu. The division of scientific research into geographical and cultural entireties (and sub-entireties) may lead to a theoretical closure which postulates that concepts and methods that have developed elsewhere and, more particularly, in the West, are in principle inoperable in our societies, and that the understanding of our reality is not possible except from the moment when researchers conceive their theoretical frameworks and develop their methodologies within the borders of Arab-Muslim culture. This approach goes beyond the binarism of 'The West and the rest', which has been underlined by many researchers.[1] These most recent formulations can result in forms of closure that are akin to an insular melancholy.

Rather than seeking an ideal model, this contribution attempts to question the absence or/and the clandestine appropriation of cultural studies in Arab universities. For this, I propose a sociological reading, which tends to underline the convergences/continuities, but also the fracture lines that are inherent to the research on and around the questions of information and communication in the region. This sociological perspective leads us to expand our field of investigation beyond the commonly accepted approach that examines the published literature (books and articles) to focus also on their production conditions.

We start, then, from a definition of a scientific field as an articulation between institutions and objects, sustained by concepts and methods. This definition does not intend to undermine existing research, nor the conditions of its production in determined places and times. The passage through history seems to us necessary, not only in order to reach a better understanding of the social mechanisms that orient the practice of research, but also to make researchers 'masters and owners'[2] of the process – i.e., to be conscious that the autonomy of the research field is the condition of its existence.

Arab media studies institutions: gatekeepers without gateways

'Despite the multiplying of faculties of human and social sciences as well as centres of public and private research, research into the human sciences remains the poor relative of the scientific research system and does not benefit from any taking into account of reports on knowledge in the Arab world'.[3] This may seem banal, but its very banality makes it apparent that this 2009 statement could also have been made in 1999, and during the birth of postcolonial states. There also exists a form of continuum in the marginalisation of social sciences research, which is intensified or diminished, depending on the interest it has in questions that touch on people's lives and the positions taken by researchers, either through their own choice or under duress. On this last question, while M'hammed Sabour (1993) emphasises the central role played by institutional powers in determining different positions, Ali El Kenz (2004) shows how 'the academic values are [...] eroded by the professional conditions and, above all, by the conditions of life that are rapidly deteriorating'.

Optimistically, one could argue that media and communication studies do not present any specificity, in so far as they are animated by the same stakes and suffer from the same hindrances. Meanwhile, a closer examination will allow us to observe that these outlines are more influential in media studies than in other disciplines of the human and social sciences. The organisational bodies continue to play a determinant role in the structuring of this specific field, for they constitute the matrix from which knowledge is diffused/taught and, occasionally, produced.

It is very difficult to draw up an exhaustive map of media and communication studies in Arab universities. The ALECSO[4] report on Higher Education (1996) is among the rare sources that touch on the question. This report gives a number of around twenty Arab university institutions with academic education in journalism and/or information and communication sciences. Their geographical distribution[5] shows the contrasting interest and financial resources given to this type of formation by each country in the region. In this way, one can see that in 1996 there were countries that still did not give any formation on communication, for instance, Mauretania and the Sudan. There is also a majority of countries where only a single institution (department or institute of journalism, of information and, more rarely, of information and communication) exists. While there are many non-State universities in Egypt and Lebanon, they offer relatively little specialised formation (seven in Egypt and three in Lebanon). In this landscape, Saudi Arabia presents an atypical case, with four institutions, of which two are specifically religious: the Faculty of Preaching and Information of the University of Jeddah, and the Department of Islamic Information in the Faculty of Theology, Mecca.

Today, it seems impossible to give a quantitative estimation of the phenomenon, not only because of the exponential growth of courses that are more or less attached to the information and communication industries,[6] but also because of the dissemination of teaching communication in the other disciplines of human and social sciences (management, sociology, psychology, linguistics, foreign languages, comparative literature, etc.) or in subjects related to visual arts (design, cinema, graphic arts, etc.).

In contrast to other geographical and cultural areas, where the institutional bodies are found in the substrata of studies that are often considered as the founding moments of a discipline, the pre-existing institutional bodies have strongly marked, and continue to mark, the research on media in the Arab world. From the Department of Journalism at the University of Cairo, created in 1939, to the recent foundation of departments of information in the Gulf countries, and by way of journalism schools in the Maghreb from the end of the 1960s, it is the political will to train the 'state servants of the truth' that constitutes the field's foundation.

With the sole exception of the École Supérieure de Journalisme (ISJ),[7] Rabat, which had long belonged to the Ministry of Information and the Interior under the direction of Driss Basri[8] (the figure at the helm of Hassan II's regime), almost all the institutions in question depend legally on the Ministries of (Higher) Education. However, such legal guardianship neither guaranteed institutional independence, nor academic freedom. Much more than with the law or political science, the training of journalists and of communicators in Arab universities espouses, today as yesterday, the contours of the officials' changing moods and, most profoundly, that of the political culture prevailing in each country. With some exceptions, the teaching of journalism and of communication is more akin to an apparatus than to a field.[9] It is the incarnation of the voluntary or forced submissiveness of the academic world to political power. This submission can elsewhere take extreme forms, which are far from being anecdotal. In the early 1970s, Habib Bourguiba, first Tunisian President of the Republic, taught a course called 'History of the National Liberation Movement' at the Institut de Presse et des Sciences de l'Information.

Sometimes, the curriculum can itself become a testing ground for the authoritarian logics at work in society, thus, the ISJ in Rabat had almost disappeared in the mid-eighties after having been transformed by the regulators into a post-masters institute. Since the beginning of the 1990s, the IPSI in Tunis has undergone cyclical reforms, the prominent features of which are the drastic reduction of fieldwork, to the profit of language courses or of 'general culture', and the marginalisation of specialised methodological and theoretical teaching. Today, many media studies departments are facing a paradoxical situation, since they are torn between two imperatives: the subjects' 'professionalisation', sometimes overdone, that brings them closer to being vocational training centres, and the necessity to put in place doctoral degrees due to the exponential growth of student numbers.

One can readily understand that the research bodies and mechanisms have never been a priority for supervisory authorities. Many of the pioneering generation's teachers found themselves torn between the prestige of publication and the necessity to ward off what was more urgent, i.e., pedagogic and administrative tasks: daily management of departments, designing the timetables of programmes, offering graduation to their students and inscribing media and communication courses into an academic tradition. Apart from the Research Centre on Public Opinion at the University of Cairo, and some stuttering Maghrebi attempts to put in place research units, there are no real structures dedicated to media studies in the Arab world.[10] The rare learned societies that began to appear in Saudi Arabia, Lebanon or Tunisia found it difficult to exist outside infrequent colloquia. In the absence of national research centres and of dynamic learned societies, the interstate bodies, like ASBU[11] or ALECSO, had, at the end of the 1970s and the beginning of the 1980s, raised the hope of unlocking research through permitting exchange and scientific debate. However, the institutional framing at work in each country could only reproduce itself on a regional scale. The demands for expertise, caring little for epistemological enquiries, have indeed deepened these structures, centred on topics anchored in a political mobilisation heritage and responding only to the imperatives of the moment: yesterday, the role of information in national development, today 'Arab satellite channels in the service of Arab-Islamic culture'.

A closer analysis can certainly situate more precisely the moments and places that still maintain the minor position of media studies within the social sciences in Arab universities. This brief outline of the institutions nonetheless permits us to underline a major insufficiency: the absence of a scientific community with clear academic pathways (PhD, publications submitted to the different criteria of scientific rigour) and, above all, of peer recognition, the only guarantee against slippage, clientelism, abuses of power and plagiarism. Even if we recognise, following El Kenz (2004), 'that a scientific community cannot be created by political decree', and that it is 'the result of a long intellectual and institutional process [...] often tormented', we can acknowledge that the existing institutional bodies confine research to reduced spaces and times. Membership of the faculty, as a forum for transmitting knowledge and, rarely, for debate on scientific issues, is less and less synonymous with belonging to a community of researchers. Following this same logic, the various kind of meetings (colloquia, seminars, conferences, etc.) organised by media studies departments in the Arab world tend to exacerbate the standardisation of the younger generation's profiles, warding off any threat of a break with the dominant paradigms.

Media studies objects: social control sciences

Despite the risks entailed in a field that is particularly marked by institutional rigidity, disciplinary reflexivity is not totally absent. From the beginning of the 1980s, some researchers with different theoretical horizons pitched concerns that were less than complaisant about media studies in the Arab world.[12] If some had a greater tendency to regret the Western-oriented perspectives, others were more inclined to denounce the conformity of researchers and the redundancy of their objects of study. They all agreed in criticising the descriptive, empirical and case-studies approaches. A diachronic examination of these texts shows, beyond the initial preoccupations of their authors, the recurrence of the grievances against media studies, but also the recurrence of explanatory factors on this continuum. Arguments such as the lack of structure in the field, the feeble theorising attempts in other regions of the world, or, again, the pioneers' fervour and its risks, are no longer acceptable today. My hypothesis is that the reasons for this eternal reporting on the launching of media studies in the Arab world are to be sought within the permanence of two paradigms that are far from being local in origin, but which have been transposed, reformulated and/or adapted to national contexts.

The fatal attraction of the developmentalist ideology

The permanence and sometimes the survival of developmentalist themes in media research lie in a misunderstanding. A number of researchers in the Arab world have leant towards developmentalist hypotheses and, more particularly, to the founding work of Daniel Lerner, *The Passing of Traditional Society* (1958). This work has never been translated into Arabic. Fifty years after its initial publication, its title and its cover design that put oil derricks and mosques into competition, update all the aspects of essentialist reductionism and its pitfalls. The global success of the modernisation theory originates from Wilbur Schramm's *Mass Media and National Development,* published in 1964 under the aegis of UNESCO. Schramm's work, translated into Arabic in 1966, is silent on the polemical aspects of Lerner's enquiry,[13] enshrining the fundamental thesis of the 'Master' who affirms that 'As a mobility multiplier, Mass Media are both index and agent of change in a total social system'.[14] Whether individuals do or do not expose themselves to the media, they are still classed under three categories: traditional, transitional and modern.[15] This classification is not sheltered from the dangers of functionalist evolutionism, since Lerner upholds that 'Traditional man [sic] has habitually regarded public matters as none of his business. For the modern men in a participant society, on the contrary, such matters are fraught with interest and importance'.[16]

It seems interesting to raise two points in order to explain the permanency of developmentalism as a dominant paradigm in our area: first, highlighting knowledge which is superficial when it is not a complete misunderstanding of the founding works and major authors of the modernisation school. The references to Schramm are often given to offer an academic legitimacy to a discourse that erodes and, at times, destroys the borders of that discourse with opinion journalism and political mobilisation. Yet, with hindsight, one knows today that Lerner and Schramm were, with Klapper, Lasswell, Merton, Pye and de Sola Pool, militant scholars; 'a group of very prominent social scientists working together in different combinations on projects for various US government agencies'.[17] Tristan Mattelart[18] explained the nature of this relationship between the academic and the militant by affirming that 'the model of development proposed by Daniel Lerner [...] converged largely with the interests of enterprises of the United States government in a region that was, in the context of the Cold War, the object of a bitter battle of influence between the great powers. This propensity to attempt to serve as the discourse that accompanies private or public American strategies, is one of the great common traits of the collection of works that have been produced around the "theory of modernisation" or, better, the theory of development/modernisation'. On the theoretical plane, Lerner declined to discuss the paradigmatic question of the 'world communications revolution' and its influence on the 'social system' and thought it out with a joke: 'Once the modernizing process is started, chicken and egg in fact cause each other to develop'.[19] A more detailed study of the developmentalist paradigm may reveal the xenophobic character of a theory which gives great importance to media effects in dominated countries, and which relativises the same power when it comes to United States and European contexts. [20]

'New technologies', endless promises

The notion that technological change necessarily implies social change is not exclusive to media studies in the Arab world. The developmentalist reference in both the region and in its geostrategic context (the Palestinian drama; the management of petroleum resources) has anchored determinist belief to academic production. The launch of ARABSAT in the mid-1980s was accompanied by a plethora of texts that celebrated the technology that wiped out distance and participated in development. In a previous study, we asked if the failure of ARABSAT was not an illustration of the ideological character of determinist belief. The prospective discourse on 'the Arab village'[21] and 'Arab satellite channels'[22] or, again, more recently on 'the digital revolution',[23] contrast with the reality of neo-patrimonialism, of media instrumentalisation, and of the institutionalisation of attacks on press freedom.[24]

The renewal of the developmentalist theses, without any interrogation of their theoretical grounding, as well as determinist prospecting, both continue in the same way. They separate the communicational from the social, as if it sufficed to change the type of communication to achieve the objectives of development and to overcome 'social dysfunctions'. From this perspective, the use of the development paradigm in the Arab universities was a double obstacle to the sociological understanding of media. The confusion between linear transmission and communication, upheld by the use of the term *Itissal*, rather than *tawassol*, is often in relationship to belief in the unilateral and direct influence of powerful devices on credulous and atomised individuals. This theoretical substratum, which has not been debated, but which is largely shared by generations of researchers, partly explains the evacuation of social structures and power relations in media studies.

There is, meanwhile, another way to envisage the question of development, by taking note of it within a social context. This intellectual task has been performed by several sociologists since the 1960s, working on the concept of social change and also, for some, on social movements,[25] while trying to de-mythologise the vision of development as a linear advance towards Western modernity. The important work of François Chevaldonné (1982) about unequal communication in the Algerian countryside, for example, has received little attention from Arab researchers working on the rural world or, more generally, on reception.

Media culture: insignificant, trivial, dangerous – for whom?

If developmentalism generally draws an abstraction from society, rare sociological incursions have been carried out to assert that society is a coherent whole, and that the media assume a social responsibility that can be understood in a Laswellian sense.[26] This fixation on early functionalism has today led to an abyss between social transformations and media practices, on one hand, and the means used to analyse these phenomena, on the other.

While researchers consider tackling social and political taboos, they find themselves with the obligation of taking some precautions which we can connect to two positions: that of researchers who are more or less concerned with theoretical interrogation and methodological rigour, but who construct the Arab world as an homogenous entity, and see it as an abstraction without any delimitation of terrain or the identification of various actors. The second position depends on the commitment level of the authors, which may eventually overshadow the researcher's status, to the benefit of the conciliating expert who is summoned to find solutions in order to save the besieged citadel. At times, the reality put forward for study is caught between (un)constructed subjects and methodological (non-)choices. To study emerging phenomena, they choose to work on institutions – rather than on professionals or the audiences – where the questionnaire seems to impose itself *de facto*. Quantification thus becomes a tool for the pacification of the social world.

What seems to be important to underline in this context is that scientific innovation necessarily requires the renewal/adaptation not only of conceptual frameworks, but also of methodological approaches. The novelty of Arab Media studies is therefore more related to a journalistic signification of the term than to an academic sense. Said in another way, institutional research on media seems to confuse apparent thematic novelty with a paradigmatic rupture. Annabelle Sreberny[27] thinks that the 'the field must connect with other and older disciplines to avoid a naïve sense of discovering new topics that in fact have long and distinctive pedigrees of scholarship'. The subject of 'Arab culture in the era of satellite images', can perfectly illustrate this confusion/illusion, since some authors, who may appear to be diametrically opposed in their curriculum and their research assumptions, come to defend converging positions. Two recent publications seem to be symptomatic of this tendency: the work of Aberrahman Azzi (2005), and that of Nahawand Kadri-Issa (2008). Published by the Centre of Arab Unity Studies, Beirut, the two works study media productions through the cultural prism, the main difference being that it is the ambition of the first to put forward a new 'endogenous' theoretical body, while the work of the second lies in an empirical study enlightened by 'exogenous' theoretical contributions.

Azzi's book is quite original in the way it seeks to extend the field of the study of communication beyond the media. Following Erving Goffman, he considers 'Social Relations as Drama'[28], but his proposition of 'determinist value theory' comes close to the islamisation of knowledge project and puts the author towards the Right of the media studies spectrum. Although the author shows reservations[29] about this project, he systematically links the contemporary problematics of the media's imaginary, public opinion, or information and communication technologies, to the Qu'ranic text[30] and articulates cultural heritage as a set of precepts and knowledge given once and for all. This framing leads the author to construct the notion of culture 'as a phenomenon that is essentially religious, which takes on a social dimension through the proximity or the distancing of foundational religious values'.[31] This culturalist reductionism is embedded in a broader vision that assigns to communication social functions that are (over-)determined by moral values. 'The disturbance of the social system means the rupture or the dislocation of the engaged communication (*al ittisal al hadif*) which is demonstrated by the vacillation or collapse of the values underpinning self-esteem, community membership and belief in a system of values'.[32] Far from providing new keys to the intelligibility of transformations in the cultural/communicational field in the Arab world, Azzi's approach, meanwhile, evolves through a series of theoretical closures that finally locate the author's theses on the threshold of science, through the way in which his argumentation seems to be self-evident, neither exposed for discussion nor for verification, and through a vague and implied appropriation of the Frankfurt School's melancholy about 'the images and the eclipse of the meaning'.[33] This second tendency emerges in the beginning of Chapter Two, which focuses on an epistemological reading of information and communication technologies.[34] Cut out of the theoretical debate, this reading takes, on its own account, the outworn idea of the immanence of media images, i.e., the possibility to understand them outside the context of their production and reception, in this way opening up, once again, a route to the fatality of technological determinism.[35]

Kadri-Issa's work raises less conventional questions, which are sometimes in opposition to those of Azzi. The author asks: in what way can 'Arab satellite channels propose to their public [in the singular] a culture of citizenship founded on accountability, participation and a sense of responsibility? In what way can they permit a balanced relationship between the ruling powers and civil society?' [36] Despite the critical stance of the problematisation, the notion of culture that is at the heart of this author's enquiries remains hollow. The reader is made to wait until page 32 to find a cryptic definition of this notion: 'Culture is a way of life, a device of adaptation and creation, a factor of differentiation and openness to the world. Calcification strangles it and the unbridled race behind novelty kills it, whereas its rooting boosts its fruition and preserves its renewal'. In its brevity, this excerpt shapes the entire book, which proceeds through successive shifts from analysis to enchantment.

If we can recognise Kadri-Issa's courage in approaching the Arab broadcasting landscape as 'a missing link between [the model of] information for development in its authoritarian sense and [that of] "free' information" in the sense of financial power', her demonstration falls short, insofar as she locates novelty in 'the reinforcement of the entertaining function for television viewers, [...] who appear as victims of' not only 'the interests of the ruling classes, but also of those of global capitalism'.[37] This incapacity to think of communication outside the transmission model, putting face to face a receiver/target and an all powerful transmitter, is all the more surprising, especially as the author seems to be relatively informed about the evolution of the theoretical debate on reception.[38] There again, the incantatory slippage seems to be inevitable, so that the position of the intellectual dominates that of the analyst:

> it is natural that the good civic/national sense puts ordinary people in an oppositional standing when it comes to their existence and their national causes. The adherence to, or rejection of, what we see and hear in the media relates in great part to our beliefs, to our history and experiences. It is there that notions like selective exposition and the memorising of media messages become meaningful.[39]

Beyond its enunciation, this uncertain reconciliation between the negoti-ated reading of cultural studies and the limited media effects of behaviour-ism, remains disconnected from the author's hermeneutic. The notions of distortion, hybridisation or the misuse of the dominant culture that are conveyed/produced by media, seems to be inconceivable to Kadri-Issa. She thus concludes that 'the mimesis of transnational consumerist culture has ravaged the foundations of Arab culture [...] while flooding all of us, includ-ing the satellite channels themselves, in the deep waters of insignificance'.[40]

Between Azzi's moralising approach and Kadri-Issa's enchantment, we can extricate some converging positions with one or other of these two ends of the media studies spectrum.[41] Beyond these differentiations, the common denominator of the different authors is less the belonging to a disciplinary field, with its theoretical and methodological debates, than a flawless consen-sus on two essential and interdependent points: thus an oppositional/binary conception of culture – the ideal culture (original, inherited, transmitted, seen to be given once and for all) and an 'insignificant' culture, conveyed by the media.[42] This second type of culture is, at the same time, perceived to be dangerous because it is exogenous. Its hermeneutic also became *mission impossible* in the way that different authors seem to agree on the design of this subaltern culture[43] as a 'culture of the image', *Thakafat Assoura*, thus for-getting that image can be understood, like text, as a narration (among many others) of the world, where signification is embedded in the social contexts of their reception and their production. As John Fiske[44] formulated:

> A close reading of the signifiers of the text – that is physically present [...] recognises that the signifieds exist not in the text itself, but extra-textually in the myths, counter-myths and ideology of their culture. It recognises that the distribution of power in society is paralleled by semiotic struggle for mean-ings. Every text and every reading has a social and therefore political dimension, which is to be found partly in the structure of the text itself and partly in the relation of the reading subject to that text.

Lost in translation

The theoretical and methodological aporiae characterising the analysis of changes in the media field and, more particularly, the dismissive attitude towards secular culture, are related to the ways in which cultural studies has been presented to the Arabophone reader, i.e., institutionalised by the theoretical handbooks. At first, we dealt with books written by Arab scholars working in Arab universities. In the absence of translations of cultural studies' founding texts, I focused on two Arabic translations of Armand and Michèle Mattelart's book *Histoires des théories de la communication*[45] which offers epistemological insights into the Birmingham School. The choice to consider handbooks, sometimes published at their authors' expense, or as pirate translations, as study materials, can disconcert the polyglot reader who has the (material as well as cultural) possibility of taking up authors' thoughts in their original languages. In reality, this eclectic material offers the possibility of a cross-reading: that of the analyst aiming to grasp the prisms through which a theory is institutionalised, but also that of the student who, for sociological reasons,[46] has no other choice than to use this composite material to construct his/her object of study.

A first reading of a dozen handbooks published in Arabic since 2000 shows the redundant structure of the manuals, as well as the secondary sources used by all of the authors.[47] Two among them seem to be representative of the filters through which cultural studies continue to be introduced to Arabophone readers: the work of Fodhaïl Dalio (2003),[48] and that of Muhammed Abdelhamid (2004).[49] The first,[50] like the second,[51] refers to only one collection edited by Stuart Hall (1980),[52] which certainly heralds the ethnographic turn of the 1980s, but which is far from being capable of covering the whole trajectory of cultural studies. The lack of knowledge about major works leads the two authors to approximations that obscure, and often distort, both the epistemological positioning and the political stance of the cultural theorists. Foudhaïl Dalio dedicates one single page to all of the critical school's themes and, before reducing the Encoding/Decoding model to three interchangeable possibilities of media reception, proceeds through ellipses and contradictions and comes to classify cultural imperialism and 'critical cultural theory' (without ever mentioning cultural studies) as 'holistic approaches that give great importance to the ideological factor', and affirms that this last 'considers the cultural role of the media in terms of a hegemonic (*haymana*) relationship between the haves and the have-nots [...] refuting the Marxist economists' explication which denies any balance between wealth (*Atharwa*) and political thought'. Muhammad Abdelhamid's handbook seems to avoid the traps of excessive simplification and deals with critical theory at length,[53] but his tendency to prefer secondary sources with a functionalist inspiration to the works themselves, encloses his presentation of cultural studies and the whole of the critical school (the distinction is not always obvious) in the reductive prism of insularity as 'a theory [that] appeared in Western Europe' and of condescension towards its 'contemplative'[54] methodology. The key concepts of hegemony, of preferred reading, of popular culture, are also bonded to the text's surface in such a way that their explication seems to be anchored in binary oppositions (rich/poor, infrastructure/superstructure), nearer to common sense than to scientific rigour.

Armand and Michèle Mattelart's book (1995) offers two relatively succinct but 'thick' ways of introducing cultural studies to the reader: underlining firstly the interlocked and sometimes divergent offerings of Richard Hoggart, Raymond Williams, E.P. Thompson and Stuart Hall, and retracing, secondly, the beginnings of the ethnographic turn and then the feminist one. There again, however, translation into Arabic proves to be a euphemistic undertaking of the Birmingham School's radicality. It would add nothing in this context to recall the two translations back to back, since there are strong contrasts in terms of terminological research, of contextualisation and of reflexivity.[55] Instead, here, I am more interested in stressing that, in a certain way, both reflect the paradigmatic/institutional forces' that (un)balance Arab universities.

On the methodological level, one can identify different translations of the expression 'common sense'. For Khadhour, it is simply '*Fitra salima*',[56] literally, the healthy/natural instinct, or '*Annadhra assalima*',[57] healthy/natural view. For Iyadhi and Rabah, it is sometimes '*adhawk al âm asha'bi*'[58] (general or popular public taste),[59] but also sometimes '*Al hiss al âm*' (general or public sense).[60] The real problem with this terminological hesitation is not semantic but epistemological, in the way that it hides the problematic status of common sense in the social sciences. It is the same for the key concept 'hegemony'.

Armand and Michèle Mattelart, most correctly, highlighted the Gramscian legacy to cultural studies and its economic reductionism rebuttal. The two Arabic translations, however, disclose a sort of discrepancy between the translated text and the intellectual position of the translators. Since the 1970s, the translation of hegemony as '*Haymana*' seems to have won the support of many sociologists and intellectuals from the left. This translation is not absent from the two texts studied, but the explanation for a 'dominant reading' that corresponds to that of Stuart Hall's 'hegemonic points of view', can strangely become '*anniqat al mousaytira lirra'y*',[61] dominant points of opinion [sic], for Khadhour, and '*wojhat annadhr al ghaliba*',[62] the majority's points of view, for Iyadhi and Rabah. Other less problematic notions, as they are part of the common language of the social sciences, witness to other intrusive forms in the text that come from the enunciator/ translator. In their translation, therefore, national interest becomes '*maslahat al Umma*', the interests of the community of believers;[63] a conceptual matrix becomes '*qalib mafahimi*', a conceptual mould; heterodox Marxism '*markssiya tawfiqiya*', conciliating Marxism, or Marxism of compromise; conditions of life: '*chourout al-hayat*', conditions *sine qua non* of life.[64] These different levels of analysis show that translation is more than a stylistic composition. To be rigorous, there is no choice but to submit oneself to a truly reflexive examination, to confront the complexity of methodological processes and to face conceptual aridity, otherwise translations, like the Arabophone handbooks, will continue to hamper the calm examination of cultural studies, its subversive strength, and also its domestication.[65]

Provisional conclusions

If institutional, conceptual and methodological normativity tends to impose itself as a general norm, given once and for all, there have been many attempts, since the mid-1990s, to break with institutional media studies by interrogating the social status of communication with the help of (sometimes crossed) contributions, from political economy, history, sociology and anthropology.

In this way, and against the tendency to consider international televisual flows from only the narrow angle of their threat to national (Arab-Muslim) identities, we have tried, with other researchers, to emphasise a different perspective. Notwithstanding the international strategies of cultural domination, the national fields of communication have been shaped as battlefields between different categories of actors who occupy different positions and defend totally different interests.[66] On a micro-sociological scale, other studies have leant towards the diversity of media readings and efforts made by individuals to negotiate content.[67] The work of Lila Abou Lughod (2005) on Egyptian soap operas is one of the rare pieces that has linked both the macro and micro-perspectives, structural analysis and thick description, critical political economy and cultural studies.

These research works were carried out outside Arab universities, although some cited authors are attached to them as teachers. Moreover, they are far from being able to shape a new trend in critical research. As

Sabry put it: 'there is no cultural studies in the Arab world as such, only fragmented works in the area, which remain largely unconscious parts of an incoherent whole'.[68] However, the common denominator is a plural invitation to decentralisation from the insular melancholy of institutional research and its essentialist corollary, which is living a second life since 11 September 2001. If the emergence of these works coincides with the internationalisation of cultural studies, the relationship that they entertain with this school depends on the disciplinary affiliation of their authors, on their degree of familiarity with the texts, but also with greater or lesser reservations *vis-à-vis* the progressive dilution of the notion of power. In an Arab world, where the reality of media power takes on hybrid forms that mix authoritarianism and consumerism, pre-colonial state forms and international finance, the violence of occupation and entertainment, cultural studies can, paradoxically, represent a way to (re)construct media culture as an object of study, with the only condition being that the media should be considered not as a discipline, but as a crossroad discipline, i.e., unresponsive to the romance of resistance and attentive to the many forms of inequality.

A project of Critical Arab cultural studies should not be fearful of marking its divergences from institutional research, which tend, by conviction, obligation or ignorance, to legitimate the social order and its violence. For now, the most visible dividing line is neither conceptual nor methodological – although this is obvious[69] – but linguistic. The attempts to renew critical research seem to be forced into exile, since works that are articulated around the concepts of active reception, resistance and hegemony (against unidirectional influence), public spheres (against the advent of democracy), the uses and users of by ICT (information and communication technologies), and internationalisation (against cultural invasion), find a means of publication in languages other than Arabic – mainly in English, but also in French. The reader will thus understand why this modest contribution remains partially unachieved until it finds the path to publication in its author's mother tongue: Arabic.

Notes

1. Curran and Park, 2000; Sreberny, 2008.
2. Bourdieu, 2001: 7.
3. UNDP, 2009: 183.
4. Arab League Education Culture and Science Organisation.

5. According to Sjögren (2005: 68–69), there are sixteen departments of Journalism in Egypt, seven in Lebanon, two in Syria and one each in Algeria, Jordan, Morocco and Tunisia.
6. In 2009, there were 15,000 students in eleven Information and Communication Departments in Algerian universities, but only one National Higher School of Journalism.
7. In 1996 this became l'Institut Supérieur de l'Information et de la Communication (ISIC).
8. For Moroccan public opinion, from the beginning of the 1980s until his fall in 2000, Driss Basri embodied the arbitrary incarnation of Hassan II's regime.
9. On the distinction between field and apparatus, see Bourdieu, 1980: 136.
10. In the 1970s and 1980s, the review *Bouhouth* was edited by the Arab Centre for Research on the Audience in Baghdad. This example, among many others, inscribed a cyclical logic of eternal re-beginning.
11. Arab States Broadcasting Union.
12. See Ben Cheikh et al, 1982: 11–12, Chouika, 1994: 25; Hassan, 1994: 22; Talal, 1999: 90; Ayish, 1998: 34–35; Abdul Rahman, 2002; Hammami, 2007: 47–50.
13. Such as the stigmatisation of Middle Eastern nationalist élites, compared to the Nazis on three occasions (pp. 278, 284 and 355), or condescension towards Nasser and Mossadegh.
14. Lerner, 1958: 56.
15. It may seem strange that neither Lerner nor Schramm makes reference to the work of Malinowski (1945), which was the first to propose these ideal–type divisions in a study of cultural change in the colonial context.
16. Lerner: 70.
17. Sparks, 2007: 6.
18. Matellart, 2002: 19–20.
19. Lerner, 1958: 58.
20. Ferjani, 2001: 39.
21. See Chevaldonné, 1988: 73–95.
22. ALECSO, 1998.
23. Al Askari et al., 2004.
24. Ferjani, 2001: 40.
25. See Ben Salem, 1998: 6.
26. Talal, 1999: 87. In the context of the start of the Cold War, Harold Lasswell (1948) attributed three functions to the media: the surveillance of the environment, integration and the transmission of heritage.
27. Sreberny, 2008: 17.
28. Azzi, 2005: 90.
29. See http://forums.2dab.org/archive/index.php/t-3832.html
30. Page 43, the footnotes contain ten references to the Qu'ran. Azzi's approach is far from being iconoclastic. Other researchers seem to be seduced by the same way of proceeding. However, Abdallah (2008: 88) meanwhile regrets 'the rarity of

researchers [in media studies] capable of understanding the results of Western research in order to remodel the function of the Arab environment, in which characteristic traits come from divine revelation with its two components: the Holy Qu'ran and the *sunna* of our Lord Muhammad, praise be upon Him'.

31. Ibid: 103.

32. Ibid: 99.

33. Ibid: 49.

34. Ibid: 33–50.

35. In his latest work, Abderrahman Azzi (2009) takes up his theses with more detail. While he allows himself to use notions like 'symbolic capital' to analyse 'the identity and the sociology of the satellite channels in the Arab region', the whole work is structured around the proposal that the media are responsible for 'the moral structure decay in Arab region'.

36. Kadri-Issa, 2008: 13.

37. Ibid, 2008: 63.

38. The author briefly discusses (p. 103) the encoding/decoding model through a quotation from a Québécois handbook (1991), with no reference to Stuart Hall.

39. Ibid: 103.

40. Ibid: 340.

41. See Hijazi, 1998; Al-Ghathami, 2005.

42. Élitist interpretations of culture go beyond the work of media scholars and include a wide range of intellectuals who seek various kinds of legitimacy. In her diatribe against Arab pop stars, and particularly the *Raï* singer Khaled, Ahlam Mostaghanmi (2010), the author of the bestseller *Dhakirat al jasad* (Memory in the Flesh) wrote: 'I was coming from Paris [to Beirut], with the manuscript of "The Flesh". I spent four years to sculpt, sentence by sentence, four hundred pages, trying to include a half-century history of Algerian struggle, to save our past, and to tell the Arab world about our glory and our pains. As soon as I introduced myself, there was always someone to ask: "Ah ... You are from the country of Cheb Khaled ... Right?". I find no answer about this man, who wears earrings and appears on French television accompanied by his dog, other than a stupid laugh. Immediately, the question comes to the meaning of "Dee Dee Wah"? When my questioners realise that I also do not grasp the meaning of the lyric, they lament the fate of Algerians, who, because of colonialism, do not understand the Arabic language!'

43. The term 'subaltern' is used in its first sense and bears no reference at all to the Indian strand of 'Subaltern Studies' and its postcolonial critique of modernity.

44. Fisk, 1987: 273.

45. The third edition of this book was published in 2004. Since the first edition in 1995, it has been translated into 13 languages. The English translation appeared with the title *Theories of Communication: A Short Introduction*, London: Sage, 1998. The first Arabic translation (2003) is a pirate edition taken from

the English translation. In contrast, the second (2005) obtained copyright permission. Further, Armand Mattellart is the author, with Erik Neveu, of the first critical francophone study of cultural studies, which appeared in 1996 in *Réseaux No. 80*, and was then re-edited as a book in 2003. As at 2009, this last book has still not been translated into Arabic.

46. Contrary to the idea that is largely shared about the falling level of students, we think that the mastery of conceptual and methodological means relates to the decrease in public teaching budgets, academic liberty and the creeping professionalisation of media courses, extended as a tendency to formalise knowledge in oversimplified models, rather than to improving students' abilities in the professional world.

47. Denis McQuail's *Mass Communication Theory* (1987) is the most frequently cited work, since it was translated into Arabic in 1995. With regard to the critical school and, more particularly, to cultural studies, the different handbooks consulted use, almost exclusively, the work of Stanley J. Baran and Dennis K. Davis (1995).

48. Scholar at the University of Constantine, Algeria, and author of numerous publications on methodology and communication theories.

49. Professor, Education Department, University of Helwan, Egypt.

50. Dalio, 2003: 28.

51. Abdelhamid, 2004: 211.

52. For both authors, the year of the collection's publication is 1982, and they only refer to Stuart Hall's article, 'Encoding/Decoding'.

53. Abdelhamid, 2004: 209–22.

54. Ibid: 209.

55. In contrast to Khadhour's translation (2003), that of Iyadhi and Rabah (2005) includes an appendix with an Arabic/French lexicon of 350 notions and a surprising introduction that retraces Armand Mattelart's theoretical pathway (with no reference to Michèle Mattelart) and, takes up the formula 'to translate is to betray'.

56. Khadhour, 2004: 119.

57. Ibid.

58. Iyadhi and Rabah. 2005: 124.

59. Ibid.

60. Ibid: 149.

61. Khadhour, 2004: 119.

62. Iyadhi and Rabah, 2005: 123.

63. Khadhour, 2004: 119.

64. Iyadhi and Rabah: 119–20.

65. See Mattelart and Neveu, 2003.

66. See Ferjani, 2003 and 2009; Hadj-Moussa, 1996, Madani, 2002; Sakr, 2002 and 2007.

67. See Chouikha, 1995; Khawaga, 1995; Sabry, 2004.

68. Sabry, 2007: 160.

69. Following the perspective outlined by Raymond Williams, Tarik Sabry (2007: 161) considers that 'the working out of the idea of culture in the Arab world has to be seen as a process, an ongoing intellectual project [...] However, this reworking of the idea of culture also requires a space where the study of contemporary culture can become a legitimised scientific practice, a space where "culture" as a category is re-articulated and unpicked as the product of a system of relations, and as a process not a conclusion'.

Bibliography

Abdallah, May (2008) 'Ichkaliyat 'ouloum al i'lam wal ittisal wa in'kassouha ala waqi' al Abhath al i'lamiya' in Al Razou et al., *Thawrat al Ittisal: Al Machhad al I'lami wa fadha' al waq'*, Beirut: Markaz Dirassat Al Wihda Al Arabiya.

Abdelhamid, Muhammad (2004) *Nadhariyat al I'lam wa Ittijahat Atta'thir*, Cairo: Alam Al Koutob.

Abdul Rahman, Awatef (2002) *Annadhariya annaqdiya fibouhouth al ittisal*, Cairo: Dar al Fikr al Arabi.

Abu-Lughod, Lila (2005) *Dramas of Nationhood: the Politics of Television in Egypt*, Chicago: The University of Chicago Press.

al-Askari, Suleiman Ibrahim et al. (2004) *Mostaqbal athawra arraqmiya. Al Arab wa'ttahaddi al qadim*, Kuwait: Kitab Al Arabi.

ALECSO (1998) *Al qanawat al fadha'iya al arabiya fikhidmat ath'thaqafa al arabiya al islamiya*, Tunis: ALECSO.

—— (1996) *Dalil mo'assasat attaâlim al âli fil watan al arabi*, Tunis: ALECSO.

Al-Ghathami, Abdallah (2005) *Athakafa attilfizyounia: souqout annoukhba wa bourouz ashaâbi*, Beirut-Casablanca: Markaz al Fikr al Arabi.

Ayish, Muhammad (1998) 'Communication Research in the Arab World: A New Perspective', *Javnost: The Public* 5.1: 33–57.

Azzi, Abderrahman (2009) *Al I'lam wa Tafakouk al Binyat al Qimiya fil Mintaqa al Arabiya*, Tunis-Dubaï: Addar al Moutawassitiya Linnachr-Muhammad Bin Rashid Al Maktoum Foundation.

—— (2004) *Fi Nadhariyat Al Ittisal: Nahwa fikr I'lami moutamayiz*, Beirut: Markaz Dirassat Al Wihda Al Arbiya.

Baran, Stanley J. and Davis, Dennis K. (1995) *Mass Communication Theories: Foundations, Ferment and Future*, Belmont: Wadsworth.

Ben Cheikh, Abdelkader et al. (1982) 'Al bahth al ilmi fimajal al idhaâ wat'talfaza', *Revue Tunisienne de Communication* 2: 7–15.

Ben Salem, Lilia (1998) 'Le statut de "l'acteur social" dans la sociologie tunisienne', *Correspondances* 49: 3–10, Tunis: IRMC.

Bourdieu, Pierre (2001) *Science de la science et réflexivité*, Paris: Raisons d'agir.

—— (1980) *Questions de sociologie*, Paris: Minuit.

Curran, James and Park, Myung-Jing (eds) (2000) *De-westernizing Media Studies*, London: Routledge.

Chevaldonné, François (1988) 'Médias et développement socio-culturel: pour une approche pluraliste. Lunes industrielles, les médias dans les pays arabes', *Revue de l'Occident Musulman et de la Méditerranée* 47: 11–21.

—— (1981) *La communication inégale: L'accès aux médias dans les campagnes algériennes*, Paris: CNRS.

Chouikha, Larbi (1995) 'Le patrimoine familial dans le Ramadan 'télévisuel': Le cas des familles "modernes" de Tunis', *Communication* 16.2: 106–129.

—— (1994) 'Ébauche d'une réflexion sur l'évolution des études et de la recherche relatives à l'état de l'information au Maghreb', *Revue Tunisienne de Communication* 25: 25–33.

Dalio, Foudhaïl (2003) *Al Ittisal, Mafahimouhou, Nadhariyatouhou wa Wasa'ilihou*, Cairo: Dar Al Fajr.

El Kenz, Ali (2004) 'Les sciences sociales dans les pays arabes: cadres pour une recherche', *Savoirs et Développement*, available at www.ur105.ird.fr/ spip. php?article154.

Ferjani, Riadh (2009) 'Arabic-Language Television in France: A Postcolonial Transnationality', *Global Media Journal* 5.3 (2009): 405–28.

—— (2003) 'Du Ræle de l'Etat dans le champ télévisuel en Tunisie: Les paradoxes de l'internationalisation' in Franck Mermier (ed.) *Mondialisation et nouveaux médias dans l'espace arabe*, Paris: Maisonneuve & Larose, 2003, pp. 153–65.

—— (2001) La construction sociale des technologies de l'information et de la communication. *Revue Tunisienne de Communication* 37–38: 35–48.

Fisk, John (1987) 'British Cultural Studies and Television Criticism' in Robert Allen (ed.), *Channels of Discourse: Television and Contemporary Criticism*, London: Methuen, pp. 254–90.

Hadj-Moussa, Ratiba (1996) 'Les antennes célestes, les généraux apparatchiks, les émirs et le peuple', *Anthropologie et Société* 20.2: 129–55.

Hall, Stuart et al. (1980) *Culture, Media, Language*, London: Hutchinson.

Hammami, Sadok (2007) 'Irhassat namoudhaj tawasoli jadid: Al majal al 'ilami al arabi', *Al Moustakbal al Arabi* 335: 47–66.

Hassan, Mustapha (1994) 'L'état des recherches tunisiennes sur la presse (1881–1986), une approche globale', *Revue Tunisienne de Communication* 25: 7–23.

Hijazi, Mustapha (1998) *Hisar Athaqafa Bayna al Qanawat al Fadha'iya wa Addaâwa al Oussouliya*, Beirut-Casablanca: Markaz al Fikr al Arabi.

Kadri Issa, Nahawand (2008) *Qiraâ fithakafat al fadha'iyat al'arabiya: Al Woukouf ala toukhoum attafk ik,* Beirut: Markaz dirassat al wihda al arabiya.

Khawaga, Dina (1995) 'Le feuilleton "Ochine" vu par les Egyptiens', *Naqd* 8–9: 71–84.

Lasswell, Harold (1948) 'Structure and Functions of Communication in Society' in L. Bryson (ed.), *The Communication of Ideas*, New York: Harper, pp. 37–51.

Lerner, Daniel (1958) *The Passing of Traditional Society: Modernizing the Middle East*, New York: The Free Press.

Madani, Lotfi (2002) 'L'antenne parabolique en Algérie, entre dominations et résistances' in T. Mattelart (ed.), *La mondialisation des médias contre la censure.* Paris–Brussels: INA–Deboeck, pp. 177–210.

Malinowski, Bronislaw K. (1945) *The Dynamics of Culture Change: An Inquiry into Race Relations in Africa*, New Haven/London: Yale University Press/Oxford University Press.

Mattelart, Armand and Michèle (1995) *Histoire des théories de la communication*, 1st edn, Paris: La Découverte. Arabic trans. Adib Khadhour (2003) *Nadhariyat al Ittisal* Damascus; Adib Khadhour; Iyadhi, Nassreddine and Rabah, Sadak (2005), *Tarikh Nadhariyat al Ittisal,* Beirut: Al Monadhama Al Arabiya Littarjama.

Mattelart, Armand and Neveu, Erik (2003) *Introduction aux Cultural Studies: La domestication d'une pensée sauvage?*, Paris: La Découverte.

Mattelart, Tristan (2002). 'Le Tiers Monde à l'épreuve des médias audiovisuels transnationaux: 40 ans de controverses théoriques' in Tristan Mattelart (ed.), *La mondialisation des médias contre la censure*, Paris–Brussels: INA–Deboeck, pp. 17–80.

Mosteghanemi, Ahlam (2010), 'Bilad al Motribina. Awtani', *Mokarabat* (http://www.mokarabat.com/s7622.htm).

Sabry, Tarik (2007) 'In search of Arab Present Cultural Tense' in Naomi Sakr (ed.), *Arab Media and Political Renewal: Community, legitimacy and public life.* London: I.B.Tauris, pp. 154–168.

—— (2004) 'Young Amazighs, the Land of Eromen and Pamela Anderson as the Embodiment of Modernity', *Westminster Papers in Communication and Culture* 1: 38–51.

Sabour, M'hammed (1993) 'La lutte pour le pouvoir et la respectabilité dans le champ universitaire arabe', *International Social Science Journal* 135: 107–18.

Sakr, Naomi (2007) *Arab Television Today*, London: I.B.Tauris.

—— (2001) *Satellite Realms: Transnational Television, Globalization and the Middle East*, London: I.B.Tauris.

Sjögren, Roger (2005) *A Comparative Study on the Media Situation in Algeria, Egypt, Jordan, Lebanon, Morocco, Syria and Tunisia*, Oslo: The Olof Palme International Center.

Sparks, Colin (2007) *Globalization, Development and the Mass Media*, London: Sage.

Sreberny, Annabelle (2008) 'The Analytic Challenges of studying the Middle East and its Evolving Media Environment', *Middle East Journal of Culture and Communication* 1: 8–23.

Talal, Muhammad (1999), 'waqî addirasset wal bouhouth al i'lamiya wal ittisaliya fil watan al arabi', *Revue Marocaine de Recherche en Communication* 11: 79–105.

UNDP (2009) *The Arab Knowledge Report*, Dubai: UNDP-Muhammad Bin Rashid Al Maktoum Foundation.

6

Rethinking the Arab State and Culture: Preliminary Thoughts

Dina Matar

Any visitor to the Arab world these days cannot fail to notice growing signs of capitalism and the visible expansion of new spaces in which culture, as a system of meaning, is made, contested and performed. While there is little doubt that these spaces are products of interconnected regional, global and local imperatives, driven as much by economic considerations and competition for funds and audiences as by shifting local, regional and international political contexts, the changing landscape throws up a host of analytical concerns for media and cultural studies scholars, not the least which conceptual frameworks and modes of analysis can best address these transformations without relying on readily available frames that offer assumptions about media dynamics and society, and that are, for the most part, embedded in the historical experiences of Western industrial capitalism and liberal democracy. This chapter arises out of these concerns, and is, therefore, an attempt to rehearse diverse ways and means to meaningfully articulate the role of media in contemporary Arab culture and society without falling into the trap of cultural essentialism and historical determinism. I write this in response to a call from my colleague, the editor of this collection, Tarik Sabry, to explore the merits of an 'Arab Cultural Studies' that addresses media's role in what he terms 'the present tense', or the temporal in Arab culture and society, an exploration, he proposes, that would necessarily require building epistemological bridges to problematics inherent in contemporary Arab thought.[1]

While building bridges to Arab thought, along with a thick 'description' of culture (building concepts from the ground up through solid empirical research), is necessary to broadening our understanding of the temporal, or the 'here' and the 'now' in contemporary Arab societies, such endeavours, this chapter suggests, must remain wary of abstracting communication practices and new spaces for cultural expression from the wider systems, including the state's, within which they are situated. It goes further, proposing that a grounded study of contemporary cultural formations (and media systems) in Arab societies cannot ignore the dynamic and changing links between the state, as a system of power rooted in discursive practices, and culture, understood as a crucial terrain for struggle over power. These links, I argue, have developed *over time* (my emphasis), and, thus, cannot be studied only as being of the 'here' and 'now', but as formed within and out of 'genealogies' – particular histories of nation-states, religion(s), capitalist class formations, national, regional and international politics. Genealogies, in this sense, can provide non-teleological, non-universalist, and non-totalising ways of understanding the world.[2] Keeping the normative and explanatory potential of cultural studies as a central concern, this chapter proposes that incorporating a 'thick' understanding of the Arab state and its discursive practices into a cultural studies analysis would provide a more instructive articulation of the sites, and instances, of power and how it is negotiated. Such an analysis, informed by history and contemporary evidence, can help us examine the state's shifting strategies and discourses that are constructed in, and according to, particular contexts and conjunctions, and that co-exist with and against resistive or counter-hegemonic forces and discourses that emerge in everyday practices, in dramas, comedies, plays, novels and other forms of popular culture.[3]

The 'absent' state in media and communication studies

The relationship between the state and cultural production no doubt remains one of the central concerns of social theory, as well as of international communication and globalisation debates that broadly focus on the strategies of transnational corporations to create markets and attract audiences outside, and despite of, state interventions and national policies. Financial considerations, ownership, structure and state censorship have, too, anchored the debate in the political economy paradigm, one of the three key analytic paradigms that have dominated media and communication scholarship. In much of this scholarship, as Gholam Khiabany notes, concepts such as 'public' and 'private', 'restricted' and 'free', 'state' and 'market' have formed some of the pairings of categories in modern liberal societies. However, while success, progress and freedom in this narrative have been measured according to the degree of separation between these pairings and the increased 'undermining' of the role of the state through resistance or contestations of the political, the state has mostly been seen as a problem or as irrelevant, and has remained 'one of the main blind spots' of media theory.[4] These binaries, along with the additional and crucial pairing of the 'state' versus 'civil society', have also underpinned political science debates and thinking about the state, including the non-Western state, while throwing up questions as to whether the state is one single entity, while society is another and, if that were the case, what are the boundaries between them.[5] In much of this latter scholarship, a serious interrogation of 'culture' is largely missing, or, put differently, little consideration has been paid to the 'cultural' as a terrain for doing politics, or engaging with the 'political', partly because of a narrow, instrumentalist definition of politics, and, in the Arab context, partly because of elitist interpretations of culture that dominated Arab intellectual thought for much of the twentieth century.

Likewise, the state remains a largely abstract 'hegemonic' construct and structure in cultural studies, the third major analytic paradigm used in contemporary media scholarship, where it is often seen as an entity to be resisted without paying attention to how it, too, is pre-occupied with culture. Here, as indeed in postcolonial and feminist studies and in work on the marginalised in societies, the focus has been on the emergence and existence of resistance cultures and how these negotiate power relations. Such work is mostly informed by Foucault's de-centred concept of power, favoured by many poststructuralist critics, which, along with the neo-Gramscian term 'hegemony', has underpinned micro-politics and/or the 'resistance' perspective and its empowering potential. Power and counter-power, in this perspective, do not exist in binary opposition, but as the outcome of a complex, ambivalent and perpetual 'war of struggle' between hegemonic powers and counter-hegemonic or resistance forces in and over culture. However, while this theorisation has provided valuable and rich insights into the politics of the everyday, cultural politics, individual and/or collective agency and empowerment, it both underestimates the power of the state in cultural production, and fails to acknowledge that power circulates unevenly,[6] particularly in capitalist societies and those moving towards capitalism.

The state: an unresolved entity?

The debate on what the state is; of what it consists; its features and institutions; its dissolution or continued relevance in the age of increasing globalisation and technological advances, is vast and inconclusive. Geographically and historically speaking, the state, as an idea, if you wish, and as a reality, is a Western European phenomenon that developed between the sixteenth and twentieth centuries, though the recognition of an entity called the 'state' goes back in European political thought at least as far as Machiavelli. However, the most productive and significant period of intellectual debate around the state began in the late eighteenth century, when the concept was defined and redefined by a series of thinkers, including Hegel, culminating in what remains as the most influential definition of all, Max Weber's notion of the state as 'a human community that (successfully) claims the monopoly of the legitimate use of physical force within a given territory'.[7]

Broadly speaking, the state, addressed as a concept, or defined as a set of institutions, has been discussed through the employment and analysis of sets of binary oppositions – state/society, public/private, formal/informal – leading to some confusion and to simplistic assumptions about these binaries and how they interact. Most accounts of how the state functions refer to control of territory, sovereignty, civil organisation, legitimacy and authority. Legitimacy, as most scholars agree, is a mushy concept, yet it continues to be used widely by political and social scientists to address how states persist over time without facing serious challenge, and, as such, has been adopted by Arab political and social scientists. For example, drawing on Max Weber, Hesham al-Awadi has conceptualised how legitimacy, defined as political stability without resort to coercion, is pursued in the Arab world.[8] For him, legitimacy includes charismatic legitimacy of the type that the late Egyptian President Gamal Abdel-Nasser possessed in abundance; traditional legitimacy that encompasses the struggle over the mantle of Islam; rational legal legitimacy that emphasises the value and procedures of formal institutions; eudemonic legitimacy that is largely based on promises of an improvement in peoples' living standards; nationalist legitimacy and ideological legitimacy, enforced through cultural and symbolic production.

Though Arab countries moved fairly quickly in adopting the structural features of the European state and its bureaucracy, they were slow in internationalising the concept of the state itself, or in implementing an ethics of public service and attitudes of collective action. In fact, Arab thought in much of the nineteenth and twentieth centuries 'concerned itself with various concepts of unity and integration, except that of the state'.[9] The lack of a systematic intellectual engagement with the state may be partly due to conceptual difficulties related to the meaning of the state and how it functions in the Arab world. In Arabic, the word for state is *dawla*, which, unlike the European concept of the state, suggests temporality and change,[10] but its usage has mostly been restricted to questions of usurpation and coercion and to an obsession with power and strength, resulting in classifications of the Arab state as strong/weak or moderate/liberal, binaries that deflect attention from the nature of states. Many scholars have ditched the concept of 'state' altogether, choosing to classify modern Arab states according to the nature of their regimes; 'the radical, populist republics' vs. 'the conservative, kin-ordered monarchies', 'socialist-republics' vs. 'liberal monarchs', or 'single-party-regimes' vs. 'family rule'.[11] Different types of regimes are associated with different types of political institutions, a variety of political cultures, as well as complex relationships between different regimes and societal groups, but what remains clear is that processes of state formation in the Arab world have played, and continue to play, a significant role in explaining the nature of politics.[12]

As with other concepts in social sciences, the concept of the state emerged within an historical and purely European experience that cannot be easily transported to other contexts without paying attention to complex and specific historical and cultural environments. Furthermore, as Tamim al-Barghouti has argued, the literature has often overlooked the difference, almost the contradiction, in the 'etymologies of the two concepts (that of the "Western" concept of the state and its Arabic equivalent, *dawla*) and in their usage as political terms in Arab and Western traditions respectively. ... The static state of the state is one of the principle differences between it and the concept of the *dawla*. ... and it is a feature that corresponds with its relations to the nation (*Umma*) as its end and purpose'.[13] Irrespective of these epistemological problems, the perceived failure of democratisation to take root in the Arab world has spurred arguments in favour of Arab 'exceptionalism', embedded within ahistorical and essentialised notions of Arab-Muslim culture that treat the Arab world as a coherent, self-explanatory space with Islam as the main obstacle hindering the transition to modernity. Such arguments have been taken to extremes by Orientalist scholars, like Bernard Lewis, who maintains that Arab-Muslim culture is incompatible with democracy because concepts such as 'representative government', 'freedom' and 'the separation of religion and state' are unknown within Islam and Arab political tradition.[14] Recent efforts to quantitatively test the alleged association between Islam and authoritarian governments have produced contradictory results.[15] Though not falling within the Orientalist tradition, more recent work on media culture(s) in the Arab world and the broader Middle East, also carry the burden of a historical legacy in which Islam remains the vital and, in many cases, essential ingredient,[16] detracting from other explanations and inquiries. In the field of media studies, some of the debates aimed at formulating anti-Eurocentric media theories have also taken place in the context of cultural differences and/or specificities, with the 'Islamic' nature of societies in the Global South taken as the starting point,[17] implicitly repeating assumptions of homogeneity, cultural essentialism and exceptionalism.

The Arab state and culture

In reality, Arab states reveal remarkable differentiation along many indicators, type of government, language, economy, religion and ethnic makeup, to name a few. Some countries, like the United Arab Emirates, have particular compositions of population with significant proportions of non-nationals, and others, like Egypt, experience considerable internal population mobility for economic purposes. Foreign intervention and interest, long-term conflicts and regional struggles for influence have long shaped policies and alliances. In the twenty-first century, many Arab states face challenges from Islamist groups, like Hamas and Hezbollah, which operate within state systems rather than outside them and whose local politics and ideologies have had regional and transnational implications. Across the Arab world, state control and media regulation coexist with highly imaginative forms of mediated political resistance. Indeed, despite the absence of democratic practices and the persistence of authoritarianism, Arab societies have vibrant and complex political cultures and use diverse media forms that extend the definition of the political into the personal, gendered and social realms: there is street art in Palestine; satire in Syria that contests state hegemony; daring television programmes that discuss socially taboo issues such as sex, homosexuality and pornography; songwriters and musicians whose modes of expression challenge received traditions; new media spaces that give voice to minorities within, and diasporas outside, national boundaries, and an expanding blogosphere, like Egypt's, which serves as a vital site of political discourse and a space in which to criticise government and practice social interaction.

How the Arab state is studied

Academic interest in the Arab (and the Middle Eastern) state gained momentum in the 1980s, spurred on, in part, by the democratisation of the remaining authoritarian regimes in southern Europe and ongoing similar processes in Latin America. Regime openings in East and Southeast Asia and, to a lesser extent, Africa, and the dramatic transformation of former communist regimes in Eastern and Central Europe, also helped sustain an explosion of new scholarship on the so-called 'third wave' of global democratisation.[18] In this scholarship, debates have focused on whether the modern Middle Eastern state is compatible with the 'Western' nation-state or whether the Middle East state could be democratic, often using the Eurocentric models of democracy that emerged in specific historical formations in the West and their particular forms of politics and socio-cultural formations, as a baseline for analysis. Historically speaking, the modern Arab state emerged as an imported entity, partly under colonial pressure and partly as an outcome of de-colonisation and the nation-building processes. As Khiabany rightly notes, however, though de-colonisation was certainly an historical transformation, this process needs to be treated with some caution particularly in contemporary contexts, and to be considered as distinct 'with many others, including the balance of forces and the particular interest of the ruling classes in each country, to gain a more coherent and comprehensive knowledge of the state'.[19] The state's role as an instrument of the ruling class is central, he argues, which means we need to ensure that any attempt to address the relationship between the state and communication considers the particular interests of the ruling classes, who themselves played a key role in the actual creation of the state, often drawing on a considerable pre-history of organisation and political development and on existing 'cultures of communication'.[20]

In terms of structure, the modern Arab state is not that much different from Western counterparts, which constitutes what Sami Zubaida calls the 'compulsory model' that was behind the establishment of new political units outside Europe, if only for the lack of alternatives.[21] In fact, in the wake of their emergence as sovereign entities, mostly following the end of colonial rule in the second half of the twentieth century, Arab countries moved fairly quickly in adopting the structural features of the European state and its bureaucracy – the majority of the states rest on socio-economic foundations that are the necessary outcome of modern capitalist development. These moves coincided with state-building processes aimed at fostering strong and effective states to enforce dominance and generate support from broad, ethnically-varied and divided constituencies through the cultivation of a sense of 'national' membership[22] that transcends ethnic, religious and other differences.

A majority, if not all, of Arab states used, and continue to use 'national' imagery and nationalist, as well as pan-Arab nationalist, discourse as frames of reference to make sense of experiences, to make claims about power and agency and to produce 'taken-for-granted' discourses that set the limit for what 'will appear to be rational, reasonable, credible, indeed sayable or thinkable',[23] as Stuart Hall famously suggested. In authoritarian Arab republics, for example, Syria, Egypt, Algeria and Tunisia, states have consistently used nationalist discourses based on anti-colonial, anti-imperialist and anti-Israeli sentiments to legitimise their hegemony. In contemporary Syria, where I started fieldwork on the relationship between the state and cultural politics, one immediately senses, through the predominance of slogans and posters, if not through a cursory reading of the press, how the Syrian state privileges and uses 'nationalist' discourse to reinforce and legitimise its self-constructed image and identity as the only remaining bastion of Arab nationalism, and the last steadfast Arab country among the so-called frontline states confronting Israeli and US plans for the region. This image and identity has been a cornerstone of the populist discourse of the ruling Ba'ath Party since it came to power in 1963, which went hand-in-hand with strategies aimed at dissolving divisive class, regional and religious differences and disseminating the ideology of pan-Arabism.

As Aurora Sottimano notes: 'The Ba'athist road to modernization was characterized by strong nationalism; the perception of the state as the prime mover of economic activity; an economic programme based on nationalisations, land reform, subsidies, the allocation of government resources to reward followers and punish opponents ... and a professed aim of restoring stability to the country and some dignity to politics.'[24] Building on the notion of the Arab nation and its unity, the Ba'ath leadership envisaged an Arab-Syrian society that was still to be forged in terms of identity and national interests, and that therefore needed state-building processes. Discourses about the economy, politics and the nation were constructed as another 'terrain of struggle' between new state institutions and old structures, therefore helping the 'transformation of the ordinary Syrian citizen into an agent of progress' and 'ultimately creating a new sociability and a sense of "nationhood" '[25] through a strategy of domination based on compliance. This strategy involves a substantial financial, institutional and discursive focus on culture, producing guidelines for acceptable speech and behaviour in public, defining and generalising a particular type of 'national' membership that fits in with state discourse and reproduces it, while enforcing 'obedience and complicity by creating practices in which the public are themselves accomplices in the creation of state power'.[26] The Syrian state, of course, is not alone in focusing on culture and cultural production to produce citizens adaptable to nation-building processes and discourses. As Jessica Winegar suggests, in Egypt too: 'culture came to be an established field of modern governance, increasingly defined not just as knowledge of reading and writing (the common connotation of *thaqafa*), but also as a knowledge of the arts more broadly, and as a set of cultural sensibilities that reflect and engender a civilized national subject'.[27]

How do states come to occupy such a central role in culture? How can they enforce obedience? How do subjects become obedient? How do 'forces from below', the marginal and ordinary people, re-produce state discourses and under which circumstances? What are the possibilities of resistance in authoritarian states? How can we address and understand counter-hegemonic discourses or imaginative forms of mediated political resistance in authoritarian and strong states; ask about the cultural fields or spaces in which hegemonic, counter-hegemonic and imaginative forms of politics co-exist; question how journalists, bloggers, artists and intellectuals play with or accommodate state 'red lines'; explore how censorship is experienced and overturned in formal and informal spaces of politics; find out what people are talking about in the cafés, the street and the mosque? These questions, as well as some others, this chapter suggests, need to be addressed though a holistic approach, combining a 'thick' historical analysis of the state, as a system of power that is rooted in discursive practices, with a thick understanding of cultural practices over time and in diverse contexts and conjunctions.

Concluding thoughts

At the end of the first decade of the twenty-first century, the political landscape in the Arab world sees postcolonial states grappling with the dynamics of the new global capitalist order and the demands of modernity. The Arab world continues to be redrawn and imagined in different and potentially divisive ways: Iraq remains divided, Lebanon faces the increased dominance of Hezbollah, and Egypt is worried about Islamists and liberals and represses bloggers seeking a greater role in politics. Increasingly, Arab states – and these are diverse and varied – are trying to make sense of varied ideological and religious affiliations within and outside national boundaries, and deal with rapid advances in communication technologies and ways of communicating culture that can potentially pose a threat to the status quo. Deregulation by a number of Arab states is likely to increase the number of private media players and outlets, and though this might privilege economic elites and ruling classes, there is no doubt that Arab publics have more media choice than at any other time.

At the beginning of this chapter, I suggested that media studies and international communication scholarship has largely sidelined the state and, more specifically a theory of the state as a system of power, in much of its analysis. I have argued that grounded theory and research must not ignore the state as an evolving and adaptive system of power that is rooted in discursive and other practices, nor its dynamic links to culture, which, as a system of meaning, can be articulated and re-articulated by various actors and in different spaces, across time. Given the essentially 'Eurocentric' roots and assumptions of media studies, I suggested using grounded analysis, informed by both history and grounded empirical work, to explain the shifting and complex relationship between the state and cultural practices, while avoiding the Orientalist and/or essentialist claim of the Arab world's uniqueness and peculiarity. I proposed that in order to overcome these problematics, we need to disassemble monolithic and static notions of the state, which have often obfuscated the understanding of the state as a contradictory entity that is in itself subject to competing interests and struggles.

Indeed, an articulation of the state as a changing and evolving system of power that is rooted in discursive practices – in other words, culture – allows the scholar to focus on elements of state discourse, its formation and transformation against, and along with other contexts and other discourses and practices over time and space, raising questions on how the state produces and reproduces power through diverse means and practices, including socio-economic structures, co-option of elites and subjects, and cultural or symbolic production. This approach does not ignore the relationship between the state and structure, which underpins the normative assumptions of the political economy paradigm, nor other state strategies, including state-led introduction of democratic institutions, such as the legalisation of multiple parties and competitive elections that aim at building legitimacy. Instead, it proposes that addressing these dynamic links, in their fluidity and complexity, can help problematise power and agency/resistance in authoritarian regimes; explain how the state has come to occupy such a central role in culture, how cultural strategies remain central planks of states' avowed goals of modernisation and, crucially, why cultural formations can both produce power and, paradoxically, invite contestations of power. Indeed, my intervention does not negate or undermine resistance cultures or the existence of marginal politics in authoritarian Arab states, nor does it deny agency to subjects who have often been depicted as the 'passive poor', 'submissive women', 'apolitical peasants' and 'marginalised groups'. Rather, I use it to suggest a broader research agenda, or, as Annabelle Sreberny argues, a conversation between paradigms, 'a post-paradigmatic conversation that can pose new questions, even new methods for accessing the answers, an intermingling of voices from the outside and the inside, and can push our understanding further'.[28]

Notes

1. Tarik Sabry, 'In Search of the Present Arab Cultural Tense' in N. Sakr (ed.) *Arab Media and Political Renewal: Community, Legitimacy and Public Life*, London: 2007, pp. 154–168.
2. Michel Foucault, 'Nietzsche, Genealogy, History' in *The Foucault Reader*, New York: 1984, pp. 76–100.

3. Discourse, as Michel Foucault has articulated in *Discipline and Punish*, is understood here as a set of norms, presuppositions, definitions and shared systems of meaning that cannot be understood in isolation from power. As such, discourse systematically forms the object of which it speaks; constructs priorities and hierarchies; classifies and differentiates social experiences and creates systems of exclusion which establish certain concepts and construct them as truth.

4. Gholam Khiabany, *Iranian Media: The Paradox of Modernity*, London: 2009, p. 9. Khiabany makes an interesting, and not dissimilar argument, in his instructive analysis of the state and media in contemporary Iran. In his argument, he moves beyond the liberal focus on the coercive role of the state to highlight the complex nature of the Iranian state in the field of cultural production.

5. Roger Owen, *State, Power and Politics in the Making of the Modern Middle East*, London: 2004.

6. See Asef Bayat, *Life as Politics: How Ordinary People Change the Middle East*, Stanford: 2009.

7. Cited in Owen, 'State, Power and the Making of the Modern Middle East', p. 1.

8. Hesham al-Awadi, *In Pursuit of Legitimacy: The Muslim Brothers and Mubarak 1982–2000*, London: 2004.

9. Nazih Ayubi, *Overstating the Arab State: Politics and Society in the Middle East*, London: 1995 [2008].

10. Tamim Al-Barghouti, *The Umma and the Dawla: TheNation State and the Arab Middle East*, London: 2008.

11. See Owen, 'State, Power and the Making of the Modern Middle East'.

12. Nicola Pratt, 'Democracy and authoritarianism in the Arab World', London: 2007.

13. Barghouti, '*The Umma and the Dawla*', pp. 33–37.

14. See, for example, Bernard Lewis, 'Islam and Liberal Democracy', *Atlantic Monthly* 271.2: 89–98.

15. See Owen, 'State, Power and the Making of the Modern Middle East'.

16. See Dale Eickleman and Jon Anderson (eds), *New Media in the Muslim World*, Indiana: 1999 and Gary Bunt, *Virtually Islamic*, (Cardiff: 2000).

17. See, for example, Hamid Mowlana, The New Global Order and Cultural Ecology', *Media, Culture and Society* 15 (1993): 9–27.

18. For example Rex Brynen, Bahgat Korany and Paul Noble (eds) *Political Liberalization and Democratization in the Arab World*, Boulder: 1995.

19. Khiabany, *Iranian Media*, p. 12.

20. See Atef Alshaer in this book.

21. Sami Zubaida, *Islam, the People and the State: Political Ideas and Movements in the Middle East*, London: 1989/2009.

22. Lisa Wedeen has discussed this in relation to Syria in *Ambiguities of Domination: Politics, Rhetoric and Symbols in Contemporary Syria*, Chicago: 1999. In her

study of Syria, Wedeen uses a broadly Foucaultian approach to examine the ways in which the cult of the late Syrian President Hafez al-Asad is effective in producing obedience and compliance by citizens.

23. See Stuart Hall, 'The Toad in the Garden: Thatcherism among the Theorists' in *Marxism and Interpretation of Culture*, Urbana: 1988, p. 44.
24. Wedeen, *Ambiguities of Domination*, pp. 7–8.
25. Ibid: 9.
26. Ibid: 6.
27. Jessica Winegar, 'Culture is the Solution: The Civilizing Mission of Egypt's Culture Palaces', *Review of Middle East Studies* 43 (2009): 191.
28. Annabelle Sreberny, 'The Analytical Challenges of Studying the Middle East and its Evolving Media Environment', *Middle East Journal of Culture and Communication* 1.1 (2008): 18.

Bibliography

Al-Awadi, Hesham (2004) *In Pursuit of Legitimacy: The Muslim Brothers and Mubarak 1982–2000*, London: I.B.Tauris.

Al-Barghouti, Tamim (2008) *The Umma and the Dawla: The Nation State and The Arab Middle East*, London: Pluto Press.

Al-Hassan, A. (2003) 'Communication and the Postcolonial Nation-State: A New Political Research Agenda' in M. Semati (ed.), *New Frontiers in International Communication Theory*, Lanhan, MD: Rowman and Littlefield.

Ayubi, Nazih (1995/2008) *Overstating the Arab State: Politics and Society in the Middle East*, London and New York: I.B.Tauris.

Bayat, Asef (2010) *Life as Politics: How Ordinary People Change the Middle East*, Stanford: Stanford University Press.

Brynen, Rex, Bahgat Korany and Paul Noble (eds) (1995) *Political Liberalization and Democratization in the Arab World*, Vol. 1, Boulder: Lynne Reiner Publishers.

Bunt, Gary (2000) *Virtually Islamic*, Cardiff: University of Wales Press.

Eickleman, Dale and J. W. Anderson (eds) (1999) *New Media in the Muslim World*, Bloomington: Indiana University Press.

Foucault, Michel (1984) 'Nietzsche, Genealogy, History' in *The Foucault Reader* Paul Rabinow, New York: Pantheon Books, pp. 76–100.

—— (1979) *Discipline and Punish: The Birth of the Prison*, New York: Vintage Books.

Hall, Stuart, 'The Toad in the Garden: Thatcherism among the Theorists' in *Marxism and Interpretation of Culture,* Cary Nelson and Lawrence Grossberg (eds), Urbana: University of Illinois Press.

Khiabany, Gholam (2009) *Iranian Media: The Paradox of Modernity*, London: Routledge.

Lewis, Bernard (1993) 'Islam and liberal democracy', *Atlantic Monthly* 271.2 (February): 89–98.

Mowlana, Hamid (1993) 'The New Global Order and Cultural Ecology', *Media, Culture and Society,* 15.1: 9–27.

Owen, Roger (2004*) State, Power and Politics in the Making of the Modern Middle East*, 3rd edn, London: Routledge.

Pratt, Nicola (2007) *Democracy and authoritarianism in the Arab world*, London: Lynne Rienner Publishers.

Sabry, Tarik (2009) 'Media and Cultural Studies in the Arab World: Making Bridges to Local Discourses of Modernity' in D. Thussu (ed.), *Internationalizing Media Studies*, London: Routledge, pp. 196–214.

—— (2007) 'In Search of the Present Arab Cultural Tense' in N. Sakr (ed.), *Arab Media and Political Renewal: Community, Legitimacy and Public Life*. London: I.B.Tauris, pp. 154–68.

Sottimano, Aurora (2009) 'Ideology and discourse in the era of Ba'athist reforms' in A. Sottimano and K. Selvik (eds), *Changing Regime Discourse and Reform in Syria*, St Andrews Papers on Contemporary Syria: 3–40.

Sreberny, Annabelle (2008) 'The Analytic Challenges of Studying the Middle East and its Evolving Media Environment', *The Middle East Journal of Culture and Communication*, 1.1: 8–23.

Wedeen, Lisa (1999) *Ambiguities of Domination*, Chicago: University of Chicago Press.

Winegar, Jessica (2009) 'Culture is the Solution: The Civilizing Mission of Egypt's Culture Palaces in Culture Concepts in Political Struggles', *Review of Middle East Studies*, 43.2: 189–98.

Zubaida, Sami (1989/2009) *Islam, the People and the State: Political Ideas and Movements in the Middle East*, London: I.B.Tauris.

7

The Necessary Politics of Palestinian Cultural Studies

Helga Tawil-Souri

Politics runs in our blood

(Palestinian idiom)

On one of my research trips to the Palestinian Territories, I attended a photography exhibition at the Khalil Sakakini Cultural Centre in Ramallah. A dozen large-scale photographs portrayed close-ups of fabrics demarcating non-existent doorways between one 'house' and another in a local refugee camp. At the reception afterwards, I overhead two men talking: both disappointed that the photographer had chosen to focus on colourful textiles rather than the ugliness of Palestinian refugees' lives. Certainly, the colours were jumping off the walls in a vibrant spectrum that spoke nothing of refugees' political conditions. There were no Palestinians in the photographs, no wide-angle shots of the camps, no explanation of the refugees' status. Did there need to be, I wondered?

On numerous trips to Palestine, I went to as many cultural events as I could: concerts, films and theatre productions. I did the same in Nablus, Jenin, Jericho, Jerusalem, everywhere – often with little success, as not many cultural events were available. In Gaza, I found an array of graffiti, met multimedia artists, interviewed staff at the Palestinian Broadcasting Company (PBC), and attended more films. It struck me that most cultural modes were crudely jingoistic, wallowing in Palestinian losses since 1948.

The photography exhibition at Sakakini was anomalous. The two complainers would have been content with the other cultural forms I came across.

I had my own complaint: that contemporary cultural artefacts shared a common 'lack' of creativity. Most incorporated similar symbols: the black, white, red and green colours of the flag, a dove, a *kuffiyah*, barbed wired, or the Dome of the Rock, referring to *al-Nakba* (the 1948 catastrophe), to sieges, checkpoints, or the ugliness of camps. I found it stifling that the cultural records of Palestine only reflected its political horrors, with occupation, exile, loss, violence. I exaggerate, but only a little. The conversation I overheard strengthened my observation that cultural expressions – photographs, feature films, graffiti, musical compositions, or what have you – weren't deemed 'Palestinian' or Palestinian 'enough' if they didn't depict political 'realities'. I later read an interview with Elia Suleiman, a Palestinian filmmaker who has portrayed 'Palestine' in absurdist, vague and ironic ways, much to the dismay of Palestinian audiences. Suleiman lamented how, after a screening of his 1996 *Chronicle of a Disappearance*, 'in the West Bank the public took offense because these people [in the film] didn't take up arms! [...Suleiman was criticised] for not showing them [Palestinians] more as targets of Israeli violence'.[1] Suleiman's films are extremely political, they're just not crudely so. In his words, he produces films 'beyond the ideological definition or representation of what it is to be Palestinian... Any artistic creation expresses the identity of a person – a political being – but an identity constantly seeking itself, in perpetual transition, antinationalist. It's in this sense that art is political'.[2]

In countless Palestinian films, there were explicit political tropes from which it seemed impossible to break free. Again, Suleiman was an anomaly; I wondered what this meant about Palestinian cultural expression. Was there something intrinsic in the Palestinian (political) condition that made only a specific kind of cultural expression and hermeneutics possible?

Palestinian cultural studies does not formally exist as an accepted field of study: there is no scholarship that addresses the idea comprehensively. There are neither journals devoted to the subject matter, nor such an academic 'major'. There has of course been a substantial amount of scholarship on Palestine, on the Palestinian-Israeli conflict, and issues relating to them; but a focus on culture has largely been secondary. The absence of cultural studies and of culture that is 'apolitical' (that is not related to any political/

national 'cause') seemed obvious when I reflected on a reason: they have to do with the preoccupation with political aspects that are deemed to be more important. After all, Palestinians still lack the fundamental contemporary political condition of a nation-state. They live either in exile, in refugee camps, or in Bantustans surrounded by walls and checkpoints. Who has time to 'create', let alone to study culture when there are more important – *political* – issues to contend with?

I let about a decade pass following these observations. I went back to the origins of cultural studies and the debates on the relationship between culture and 'non-culture', between culture and politics, between base and superstructure. It helped that over this past decade an increasing number of scholars – Palestinian, Israeli and others – were fomenting the beginnings of what can be termed a Palestinian cultural studies. This body of work is anything but 'apolitical', for it explores the everyday manifestations of Palestinian politics in a range of cultural and media artefacts and, more importantly, expresses the relations and tensions between culture and politics. I recognised that the *strength* of both Palestinian cultural production and the study thereof is precisely in – often overt, sometimes, unfortunately, crude – *the focus on the political*. There were irreducible historical-spatial conditions that made it so. This was not something to lament but to embrace.

My focus in this chapter is precisely on the relationship between the cultural and the political. My argument is that, first, the very act of 'creating culture' in the contemporary period is a form of political resistance – a problematic statement which I attend to by explaining the political conditions against and with which Palestinians have to contend. Second, given these conditions, the study of Palestinian culture is also a form of political resistance. I argue that the resistance at the heart of the two 'analytics' (culture and cultural studies) – which are naturally inter-related – are imperative.

Creating culture is political resistance

The Palestinian people do not exist. Golda Meir.
Sunday Times, London, 15 June 1969.

The study of culture cannot take place outside the historical, political, geographical and socio-economic contexts that determined it, nor the theoretical formations that shaped it. As Hall (1980) observed, the dominant paradigm in cultural studies

> conceptualizes culture as interwoven with all social practices; and those practices, in turn, as a common form of human activity: sensuous human praxis, the activity through which men and women make history ... It defines 'culture' as *both* the meanings and values which arise amongst distinctive social groups and classes, on the basis of their given historical conditions and relationship, through which they 'handle' and respond to the conditions of existence; *and* as the lived traditions and practices through which those 'understandings' are expressed and in which they are embodied.[3]

In other words, I take heed of Raymond Williams' argument that culture is 'a whole way of life'.[4] To study culture, then, is to study the relationships between the elements of the sum of the inter-relationships of this whole way of life, and not to deny the dialectic between the cultural and the political, nor to approach them as separate entities. This approach, however, has almost entirely disappeared from contemporary cultural studies. As Paul Smith argues, in its appropriation of structuralism in the 1970s, cultural studies chose to collapse the political into the cultural, or, at best, place them at a great distance from each other.[5] This bifurcation defused cultural studies' critical practice, led scholars to abandon a materialist understanding of culture, and to retreat from what they saw as the (economic) over-determination of Marxism.[6] The debate continues, receding in the rear-view mirror, between proponents of cultural studies and political economists,[7] although, on the whole, contemporary studies of culture are often void of larger political discussions.[8]

In the Palestinian landscape, the opposite is true: there is an *inherent* and *on-going* relationship (sometimes a *tension*) between the political and the cultural. 'Palestinian sociology has been enveloped by incessant intrusions of politics into its agenda, its motifs, and even its methodology'.[9] The same is true of Palestinian cultural studies. In order to understand why this is, it is essential to address historical conditions. The intellectual formations of scholars engaged in the study of Palestinian media and culture, implicitly or explicitly, respond to a particular historical moment: that of the *Nakba*. As Joseph Massad (2008) and others[10] have claimed, however, the *Nakba* is not simply a catastrophic historical event of the past, but is 'pulsating with life and coursing through history by piling up more calamities upon the Palestinian people [...] The history of the *Nakba* has never been a history of the past but decidedly a history of the present'.[11] Palestinian cultural studies – as Palestinian culture itself – is a means to this on-going catastrophe, to make known and slowly redress the dispossession at the heart of the Palestinian experience.

Countering erasures

Various forms of repression impinge upon Palestinian cultural production: by Zionist narratives, the Israeli state, Arab 'host' governments, such as Lebanon and Syria, an Orientalist and Islamophobic environment in the diaspora, corruption and nepotism within the Palestinian Authority (PA). Of the measures attempting to silence Palestinians, both in the territories and on the global landscape, none are as harsh as Zionist/Israeli measures, particularly as concerns the West Bank, the Gaza Strip, Jerusalem, and Palestinians within Israel. As the cultural anthropologist, Ted Swedenburg, observed over two decades ago: 'because Israeli policies concentrate so ferociously on disintegrating all cultural forms that evoke the national reality, Palestinians carefully protect the memory of those same symbols'.[12]

The historian, Gabriel Piterberg, shows how Zionism is built on foundational myths that have erased Palestinians, beginning with the land and the discourse of that land.

> The land, too, was condemned to an exile as long as there was no Jewish sovereignty over it. It lacked any meaningful or authentic history, awaiting redemption with the return of the Jews. The best-known Zionist slogan, 'a land without a people for a people without a land', expressed a twofold denial: of the historical experience both of the Jews in exile, and of Palestine without Jewish sovereignty [...] The Zionist settlers were collective subjects who acted, and the native Palestinians became objects acted upon.[13]

This is the case not only with the land, but also in all 'geographies' of Palestine: economic, political and cultural. As the film scholar, Haim Bresheeth, notes, Israel 'has consistently refused to allow the Palestinians to commemorate their own history. Power is not only exercised over the land and its people, it also controls the story, its point of view, and the meta-narrative of *truth* and *memory*.[14] Bresheeth continues to explain that, 'the narrative of Palestine in the cultural arena carved by Zionism is, first and foremost, a story of erasure, denial, and active silencing'.[15]

The traumatic disposition of fighting against the notion that they do not exist, and against their real and symbolic erasure from the land, has informed and shaped Palestinian cultural works. It is in response to these attempted erasures that scholars, such as Edward Said, have asked for 'permission to narrate' (1984) against the fact that 'so much of our history has been occluded. We are invisible people'.[16] In similar vein, Hamid Dabashi, when denoting Palestinian cinema, speaks of an 'aesthetic of the invisible' (2006). Countering this hegemonic attempt at silencing and erasing, the very act of 'creating culture' is a form of political resistance. By saying this, I am not pitting 'culture' against 'non-culture'.[17] Culture is what is created, performed, negotiated, disseminated in everyday lived experience – from cooking to folklore, from cinema to music, by the bourgeoisie and the *fellaheen*. In that sense, much of what we do is the process of creating culture, but given Palestinians' political condition, their cultural praxis – whether of the everyday, the institutional, the mundane, or the monumental – is an act of resistance, because it *de facto* attempts to reverse Golda Meir's fiat that Palestinians do not exist. More complicated than that, it attempts to negate subjugation and silencing. Palestinian culture is the attempt to re-voice the silences of the witnesses, victims, and historical 'losers' (i.e., Palestinians) to 're-write' the historical truth of events in Israel/Palestine, before and after 1948.

Most forcefully, when under direct occupation by Israel between 1967 and 1991,[18] Palestinians were forbidden expression of anything deemed 'nationalist': drawing the flag was forbidden, graffiti were forbidden, the production of local media was forbidden (with the exception of highly controlled and censored news, which the Israeli military allowed as a means of feeling the pulse of political moods). By no means did the 'end' of official occupation in 1991 and the arrival of the PA in 1993 mean that efforts to silence and erase Palestinians have stopped – if anything, they have sometimes taken a more ruthless form. Regardless of the lifting of the ban on cultural/media production inside the Territories, silencing policies continue. An example from the period of the Second Intifada will suffice to make my point. During West Bank incursions by the Israeli defence

Forces (IDF) in the spring of 2002, cultural institutions were ransacked (including the Sakakini Centre where I had seen the photography exhibition). The national radio station building and transmission tower were bombed;[19] television stations were destroyed or their transmissions 'interrupted' by the Israeli military (broadcasting pornographic material in some instances!); Internet companies' computers were smashed or stolen; local and international TV stations' headquarters were shot at, their archives stolen ('confiscated' in IDF parlance); radio stations were under continuous gun-fire – in its foray, the IDF also razed refugee camps; destroyed streets and houses; killed civilians; uprooted trees, and much more.[20] That the IDF chose to target its destruction and violence on cultural institutions is not only reminiscent of similar events in Beirut in 1982 (when official Palestinian archives were confiscated by the IDF, and still today lie under Israeli military 'protection'), but are indicative of Israel's policy of erasing Palestinian history and silencing Palestinian culture (especially poignant in the theft of archives). These moments are markers in the enduring attempt by the Zionist/Israeli 'machine' to write history according to its own vision or, at least, to erase anything that is counter to its narrative.[21] As such, any effort by Palestinians to do the opposite is nothing short of resistance.

In the global landscape, Palestinians' history is still marginal and often actively marginalised (most obviously in the USA). Palestinians continue to be vulnerable victims of history, belonging to a world politics larger than themselves, in which they have very little control over their own image.[22] Their story is continuously co-opted by others (and for various reasons): Zionists, Israel, Arab governments, Hezbollah, foreign media, foreign peace activists, Islamists, news sound bites, and so on. Only recently have the tables begun to turn, although the task still seems Sisyphean.

The 'creating of culture' has also taken nationalised, institutional form since the PA came into power in 1993 in the Territories – before that, the PLO and other political parties supported cultural activities in exile. Although the PA's ideological and political reasons for encouraging cultural expression are complex, this did signify the authorisation and sanctioning of official Palestinian self-expression, on Palestinian land, for the first time in modern history. The creation of the PBC (the national TV station) and the financing of cultural projects, for example, should be understood within this context.[23]

The ramifications of the political on Palestinian culture are formidable. It is no wonder, then, as Said explains, that even the most private forms of cultural expression are political: 'there is no necessary contradiction between aesthetic merit and political themes. In the Arab and specifically the Palestinian case, aesthetics and politics are intertwined.'[24] Due to ever-present repression, obstruction, control, surveillance and silencing, the task of Palestinian culture has become the negotiation between the every-day and the extreme; between the continuation of normalcy (as all cultural expression somewhat is), and a battle against eradication. Resistance is imperative.[25] Consequently, Palestinian cultural expressions serve multiple political functions: a mnemonic device, an elegiac operation, a testimony, a form of self-identification, a voice for mobilisation – for Palestinians and other audiences. They are not simply about the transformative power of culture to liberate Palestine from colonial occupation, but about resisting annihilation. What Palestinian cultural studies scholars are doing, then, is keeping a record – for those who will want to hear and see it – of creative expression and life under political conditions that would normally result in a peoples' erasure.

Palestinian cultural and media studies

> The situation for us [Palestinians], since 1948, has been heavily political, in the sense that our self-expression as a people has been blocked. So since every poet in a way answers to the politi-cal and historical needs of the time in some way [...] there is an implicit relationship to the political, even in the most nonpoliti-cal of all forms, a relation of negativity. Edward Said, *Culture and Resistance*, 2003: 163–164

Countless cultural forms have been deemed emblematic of 'true' Palestinian culture: the poetry of Mahmoud Darwish; the literature of Ghassan Kanafani; the cartoons of Naji Al-Ali; folksongs, like *We'hn 'A Ram'Allah*; the *dabke* dance; styles of embroidery (*tatrizz*); the *kuffiyah*; particular forms of stone architecture. Many of these have been co-opted by nation-alist discourses or movements. For example, Naji Al-Ali's child-witness, Handhala, is an icon of Palestinian nationalism and an unofficial mascot for socialist-leaning parties; Handhala paraphernalia is ubiquitous across Palestinian communities (in the Territories and beyond), as are the flag, pictures of the Dome of the Rock, or maps of 'all' of Palestine. Of course, to suggest that there is 'true' Palestinian culture brings up numerous problems. First, it begs the questions: what are Palestine and Palestinians? These become highly complex and de-territorialised following the events of 1948, when the majority of Palestinians no longer reside on Palestinian land and subsequent generations continue to label themselves Palestinians, yet hold no citizenship, nor are they permitted to return to the homeland. Second, it pre-supposes that all cultures are homogeneous, static, and not influenced by any 'external' processes, which is obviously not the case.

My purpose here is not to describe Palestinian culture or cultural forms, but to focus on scholarship that does. My objective is to map Palestinian cultural studies by highlighting scholarship on Palestinian culture and media. I focus primarily on the period since the early 1990s, because Palestinians in the Territories have only had the 'freedom' to create media since then. I include studies that focus on the Territories and/or are created by Palestinians who reside there. This is obviously problematic, for neither is the majority of Palestinians in the Territories, nor is the Palestinian condition so neatly geographically bound, but I limit myself for purposes of brevity and because the nation-state – on that particular piece of land – continues to be an important ideological-political and spatial form for Palestinians. By doing so, however, I am not suggesting that a national, spatially limited paradigm for understanding Palestinian culture is necessary, nor is it preferred. Finally, there are, of course, more scholars and a wider range than those I am including on cinema, music and broadcasting; I chose those below for they generally analyse *and* problematise the fact that 'cultural production and resistance form an important component in the continuing struggle for Palestinian political rights'.[26]

Cinema

Like the two other cultural forms I discuss, the development and study of cinema have paralleled political conditions. Cinema was prevented from developing within Palestine and emerged in exile, mostly after 1967. Films created in the 1960s and 1970s were usually produced under the auspices of political parties in exile, intended as instruments for the promotion of, or propaganda for, the national cause, the registering of revolutionary events and the depiction, most often, of life in refugee camps. In its glaring connection to armed struggle, the slogan of the *Palestinian Cinema Manifesto* (published in Syria in 1968) of a camera in one hand and a gun in the other is indicative of film's political purpose of national definition, recognition, and (armed) mobilisation. The films of this period had unremitting nationalist objectives and tone. As important as their content, is the fact that they 'disappeared' after the 1982 Israeli invasion of Beirut, where they were housed in an unofficial archive, and still today no one knows how or why these films were lost; what remained has since been gathered in the *Dreams of a Nation* archive.[27]

Palestinian-Israeli filmmakers emerged in the 1980s, usually trained and living in Europe, marking the arrival of contemporary Palestinian cinema. Michel Khleifi brought about an aesthetic language of cinema, still firmly tied to a political project of searching for and asserting Palestinian identity, by way of folklore, memory and attachment to land. Khleifi was joined by feature filmmakers, such as Rashid Masharawi (a refugee from Gaza), Elia Suleiman (from Nazareth) and Hany Abu-Assad (in Europe), and documentary filmmakers, such as Mai Masri (mostly working out of Lebanon), Sobhi al-Zobaidi (a refugee in the West Bank), and Annemarie Jacir (out of the USA).[28] While the films of the 1980s and 1990s often projected a unified image of Palestine that superseded internal conflicts and problems, echoing the often-heard mantra among Palestinian politicians (even today) of 'getting rid of occupation first, then fixing internal problems', more recent films have attempted to break away from an over-riding nationalist project of unification. They are still, however, all political, and they incorporate a gamut of conditions, expressions and concerns, from checkpoints and suicide bombings, to refugees and disappeared villages inside Israel.

Arguably, it is the analysis of Palestinian cinema that has garnered the most and earliest attention among scholars interested in culture.[29] Hamid Dabashi's edited volume (2006) is the best collection of essays on Palestinian cinema to date. Contributors – scholars, filmmakers, and collectors – explain and problematise cinema's relationship to the political across historical periods. Other scholars delineate Palestinian cinema's different themes and forms, and situate Palestinian film-making along cinematic movements, such as nationalist, third worldist or exilic cinema;[30] or analyse how 'national affiliations and international awareness affect film production in a society dominated by national conflict'.[31] Livia Alexander focuses on two dominant trends in cinema: the motif of land, and the more geographically loose films on individuals and their liberation. Similarly, I have argued that:

> Palestinian filmmakers are only slowly inching beyond thinking of film as a political project – whether of embracing national unity of challenging it. Of course this may have to do with the fact that one could equally think of Palestinianness as still having to do with a political project: Palestine is simultaneously a nation coming into being and a nation being lost to exile, and its films represent both these contradictory aspects.[32]

More recently, Bresheeth argues that contemporary Palestinian films point to a continuity of pain and trauma and a continuity of struggle since 1948. As such, Palestinian films 'offer a voice to the unsung and unheard continuing tragedy of Palestine, constructing a possible space for national and individual existence and identity today. In telling the story of Palestine, they counter the enormously powerful narrative of Zionism that occupied centre stage for most of the second half of the twentieth century'.[33] In his typological observations, Bersheeth shows how Palestinian cinema deals with the story of Palestine as a strategic defence move designed to recapture ground lost to Zionism and its dominant narrative.

All scholars recognise Palestinian cinema's connection to the political and why the connection is imperative. Dabashi suggests that Palestinian cinema shares 'the paramount feature [of] a subdued anger, a perturbed pride, a sublated violence. What ultimately defines what we may call a Palestinian cinema is the mutation of that repressed anger into an aestheticised violence – the aesthetic presence of a political absence. The Palestinians' is an aesthetic under duress'.[34] In Palestinian films, the duress of erasure and eradication is multi-layered: that of the nation/country, that of the locale (a village or town), that of the family, and that of the individual, 'hence the dispossession brought about by conquest is even deeper and more painful that just losing home and country. The ultimate loss is that of one's story, losing the right to tell one's own story and history'.[35] As such, some scholars argue that: 'Palestinian film-making will continue to be a description of a continuous human tragedy [...] Palestinian documentation is an explanation of loss, necessarily political. A chagrin for lost earth and lost lives, a lost future'.[36] Palestinian cinematic production is more complicated than simply a lament for what has been lost; it is also, especially in its documentary form, a project of certification and the certifying a past history, 'a form of visual "J'accuse"', and a sustained record of an endangered memory in the absence of a state.[37] It is necessarily a response to the Zionist attempt to silence Palestinians. Bresheeth explains:

> The narratives of Zionism, annulling Palestine, denying its oppression by Israel, and telling the one-sided story of Zionism as a liberation movement, decimated the space for Palestinian cultural work after decimating the physical space that was Palestine. First it conquered and subdued the physical space. Then it renamed and reassigned it, thus erasing its past, its history, its story. Fighting the injustice of such narratives has to take place in the cultural arena – not as a replacement for the arena of the physical, but as its compliment.[38]

On a personal level, Palestinian filmmakers are transforming memoirs into evidence. On a collective level, they challenge the hegemonic Zionist/Israeli account of history and ongoing experiences of the Nakba, as well as other forms of hegemonic narratives that have largely left the Palestinian invisible, silent or misunderstood. The cinematic project is also about countering the 'invisibility' and stereotypes of 'the Arab' in Western and Israeli films, thus serving as a complex corrective measure against different discourses of erasure. Filmmaker Sobhi al-Zobaidi (2009) explains that the object of Palestinian cinema is to loosen images' connections to the cultural and ideological assumptions that lie behind that cinema's production and intended consumption/reception, so that it can be re-produced, re-negotiated, and can allow for an alternative reading. This multifold strategy is not the case only with cinema.

Music

Palestinians have a long history of musical expression and performance, and more recently production. Unfortunately, this remains an under-studied area. With the exception of Joseph Massad's 2005 essay, there exists no 'major academic engagement with the overall history and the role of patriotic, nationalist, or revolutionary songs in the modern Arab world [...] nor with their role in the Palestine tragedy specifically'.[39] This is beginning to change with the emergence of Palestinian rappers who have garnered scholarly interest.

Palestinian youth began experimenting with rap and hip-hop in the late 1990s, marked by the emergence of two Palestinian bands inside

Israel: DAM (Da Arabian MCs) from Lod, and MWR from Acre. Both groups began rapping about Israeli discrimination against Palestinians, and widened their repertoire to a range of 'angry' political expressions: from being slighted by Arab nations to addressing internal social problems, such as drug-use and misogyny. Rap has gained popularity across the West Bank, the Gaza Strip, and diasporic communities 'fuelled in part by internet sites where groups can upload songs, and chat in forums devoted to Palestinian and Arabic rap'.[40] There are now countless Palestinian hip-hop groups. Hip-hop has become the 'Palestinian Al Jazeera' (echoing Chuck D of Public Enemy, who labelled hip-hop 'the Black CNN').[41] It has become a tool for sharing news of social and political realities, as well as a tool for political critique and mobilisation.

Scholars have taken interest in this 'new' form of cultural/political expression. Maira (2008) traces the underlying politics of Palestinian and Palestinian-American rap, situating it as a poetics of displacement and protest. Charles Kurzman claims 'DAM's moral blindness is a weapon of the weak. Like suicide [bombing], DAM's radicalism is also a self-eradicating art – in a cultural rather than a physical sense'.[42] This is debatable, since DAM is credited with starting, popularising and influencing Palestinian rap. DAM's lyrics evoke anger, hatred and dispossession, but it is the Palestinian 'structure of feeling' that DAM is expressing and responding to (and arguably instigating further). As Massad argues, DAM's songs 'address not only the horrors of Israeli colonial racism, but also the disunity of the Palestinian population within'.[43] DAM's lyrics have become more sophisticated over the years. With that maturity, scholars have moved beyond simply complaining about Palestinian rap's violent discourse, and the overwhelming focus on DAM itself. For example, Ela Greenberg (2009) writes about a lesser-known hip-hop outfit from *Shu'afat* refugee camp, on the outskirts of Jerusalem, and argues that rap is becoming a space of non-violent resistance against the emasculation that is a consequence of Israeli occupation and racism.

Massad situates rap in a longer tradition of revolutionary and underground Arab political songs since the 1950s, many of which supported Palestinian liberation, mixing nationalist poetry with hybrid Arab-Western musical instrumentation. Massad traces how songs came to be inserted into the political field of nationalism, and how the history of songs parallels the history of the Palestinian struggle: the support of liberation in the 1950s, support for pan-Arabism and Nasserism in the 1960s, the despair and defeat of guerrilla movements post-1967, the loss of Jerusalem, etc. The way in which cinema tracked political changes in the Palestinian landscape was also echoed in music. Songs reflected popular sentiments and generated such sentiments, making the political internal to culture, 'not epiphenomenal or subservient to the political, but [...] generative of political sentiment'.[44] For example, 1970s songs often named and mapped lost villages, expressing nostalgia and functioning to continue the presence of specific geographies, thus playing a role in political resistance.

There is no doubt that Palestinian music, and contemporary rap especially, is imbued with politics, and functions as a cultural tool of political expression. Not surprisingly, some rappers have found the expectation that they be nationalistic stifling, at odds with their desire to be 'purely' artistic. Maira quotes one rapper who expresses this frustration: 'sometimes I feel selfish but it's not always about Palestine ... It doesn't make you feel like an artist, singing the same thing'.[45] She explains that 'there is no inherent contradiction between art and politics, but there is a *tension* that has long been experienced by committed artists who are part of the global movement of Palestinian resistance art [...] while continuing to use literature, music, film, visual art, and multimedia technology for "the cause"'.[46] This demonstrates a core tension in Palestinian cultural expression and the study thereof: is there a way to divorce this from the political? Is there a need to? It also shows the difference, albeit in the diaspora, of what Will Youmans (himself a rapper) calls *Arab American hip hop* versus Arab Americans *in* hip-hop, where the first incorporates Arab identity into its music, while the other identifies only with the broader category of hip-hop.[47]

In the study of Palestinian rap, we see how cultural forms have strenuous relationships with the political. On the one hand, rap is a form of resistance; on the other, its political (over)tone may be what stifles it. The advent of rap complicates both Palestinian culture and its study on at least another level: it is by definition hybrid, open to outside influences, even if it is also co-opted as a 'hyper' nationalist form of expression. Here, the tension between expressing Palestinianness and being open to external cultural influences disappears.

Broadcasting

Broadcast media within the Territories was only permitted after the Oslo Accords in the early 1990s. Through television and radio, 'for the first time, [Palestinians could] speak for themselves and represent themselves, [gaining] the 'legitimacy' of doing so within a public space without sanction of any kind'.[48] Against the hegemonic global order in which they had been silenced or, at best, (mis)represented by others, the allowance of broadcasting allowed for a space in which Palestinians could have self-expression. As Lena Jayyusi argues, 'the electronic media suggested the possibility of Palestinian self-production, and self constitution. Through them, a Palestinian world could be depicted, transmitted and rebuilt'.[49] Like music, broadcasting remains an under-studied area of Palestinian media studies. Jayyusi's work questions the extent to which broadcasting functions as a public sphere[50] and to what extent the discourse of and within the media and, in Jayyusi's research, specifically the PA-run radio station Voice of Palestine, 'is embedded in, and productive of, an organisation of institutional and state directed objectives and concerns'.[51] Jayyusi shows how the creation of radio was connected to both processes of nation-building and state-building and the contradictions at the heart of media discourses and the Oslo Accords themselves. My work looks at the impact of the Accords on the realm of policy and television specifically, which resulted in the proliferation of dozens of private, quasi-illegal channels across the West Bank.[52] I argue that by illegally rebroadcasting satellite channels and being limited by Israel in their use of airwaves, Palestinian television channels are both globalised and forcefully localised.

The broadcast media emerged during the period of the formation and power consolidation of the PA, roughly from 1994 to 2003. Jamal (2004) argues that clear structural pluralism existed in the realm of television – in the dozens of channels for example. I suggest that this was a 'tolerated plurality – officially illegal but permissible [...] an indication of the PA's political strategy to "divide and control" the population'.[53] The landscape changed when, in 2005, Hamas launched its own television channel, which scholars such as Salama (2005) and Warshel (2008) focus on; the first describes the rise of the channel; the second situates its relative lack of popularity among Palestinian audiences. Scholars have yet to look at the production aspects of broadcasting (see Bishara 2006, for an ethnography of Palestinian cameramen who work for foreign news organisations), or conduct ethnographic audience studies. Amal Jamal's work remains the most comprehensive in covering a range of issues from PA censorship (and internal censorship by media professionals) to representations of women. Jamal's works critiques how 'the communication order in Palestine serves not only as a means of control, but also as a field of contention between different political agents'.[54]

He also analyses how, despite the growth of women's efforts and move-ments, Palestinian media continue to hold a conservative view of gender issues.[55] Although a nascent object of study, this scholarship does not sim-ply point a finger at Israel, but looks at the various levels of obstructions and opportunities within the Palestinian media field.

The kinds of hermeneutics, practices and theories that are addressed collectively in the scholarship described above point to the beginnings of a Palestinian cultural studies. Collectively, this work is important, both politi-cally and otherwise, for the Palestinian 'nation'. First, they demonstrate that the political is not simply what takes place in the realm of governments or legal agreements, but in the practice of everyday life and, as such, justify future studies on that 'thing' deemed less important than politics: culture. Second, they demonstrate how the Nakba continues to shape Palestinian life and cultural production, compounded by subsequent political events. Third, their contribution is in putting the political back in culture and cul-tural studies. Finally, they serve as bulwarks against historical erasure, an intellectual means of resistance that is not just in the realm of the abstract but has very real consequences.

Reclaiming history, re-shaping the future

> *Don't grab a gun but grab a pen and write*
> from the song *Ng'ayer Bukra* (Change Tomorrow) DAM, 2006

The Palestinian cultural struggle is not only the 'commemoration' of the Nakba, but also the desire to be visible, to be heard, and to be documented. In their cultural praxis Palestinians preserve the(ir) past and reproduce its images and its discourse, and simultaneously represent and recreate the present, whether in exile, in refugee camps, in ghettos or open-air pris-ons. Given the political necessity of this cultural praxis, the project of Palestinian cultural studies is itself a mode of consciousness reclaiming history, dismantling the mythic Zionist/Israeli narrative. This becomes the task – conscious or not, explicit or not – of scholars such as those above. As Edward Said eloquently puts it:

> One of the roles of the intellectual at this point is to provide
> a counterpoint, by storytelling, by reminders of the graphic
> nature of suffering, and by reminding everyone that we're

talking about people. We're not talking about abstractions [...]
One has to keep telling the [Palestinian] story in as many ways
as possible, as insistently as possible, and in as compelling a way
as possible, to keep attention to it, because there is always a fear
that it might just disappear.[56]

Resistance is at the heart of Palestinian cultural studies, ascertaining that
Palestinians are not silenced, not erased, not 'disappeared'.

This 'responsibility' on the part of scholars is reminiscent of Gramsci's
'war of position', which involves social organisation and the development
of cultural predominance. The war of position is intellectual, focused on
the cultural realm in which anti-capitalist politicians seek to gain the dominant voice in the mass media and across civil society. Once achieved, this
position can be used to amplify class-consciousness, teach revolutionary
theory and inspire revolutionary organisation. Winning the war, communist leaders would then have the necessary political power and popular
support to begin the armed insurrection against capitalism – the war of
manoeuvre. The same is true here (and depending on one's ideological
leanings, one could choose to replace the words capitalist and communist
with, or simply *add* them to, Zionist/Israeli and Palestinian). In Gramsci's
words, 'a human mass does not "distinguish" itself, does not become independent in its own right without, in the widest sense, organising itself: and
there is no organisation without intellectuals [...] But the process of creating intellectuals is long and difficult, full of contradictions, advances and
retreats, dispersal and regrouping'.[57] The quest and contribution of cultural
and media 'intellectuals' is a long struggle of laying the groundwork for a
'larger' insurrection: to reclaim the past and reshape the future.

There is, of course, an inherent tension within Palestinian cultural studies and it is the predicament of the political. On the one hand, it continues
to be hostage to the political conditions of the culture is it studying; on
the other, the political is an order it is trying to negate. Cultural producers
and scholars recognise this, and have expressed the tension in various ways.
Straightforwardly, Said beckons: 'we have to go beyond survival to *the battle of culture and information*'.[58] The rapper who feels stifled by nationalist
responsibility is expressing the same sentiment. DAM suggests something
similar in the lyrics above in that, for Palestinians, the battle is not in armed
struggle, but on an intellectual/cultural level. Elia Suleiman explains this in
terms not at all unique to film: 'there is still some work to be done about

"dismantling the flag". I am trying to deconstruct this imposed national image, this image constructed by all these cultural actors who are always droning on about what Palestine means to them and who seem to fear that if this image disappears their artistic inspiration will disappear with it'.[59]

Finally, the same can be said of culture more broadly, and of Palestinian cultural studies as Massad hopes for cinema: 'that Palestinian cinema will not only remain a *weapon of resistance* but that it will also become a *weapon and an act of culture'.*[60] However, the political conditions that would allow for this kind of 'freedom' are nowhere near happening. Tensions continue. Various forms of repression and silencing persist; and yet there is no denying the power of new forms of expression, their reach to wider audiences, and their potential for wider political change – in mediated platforms, whether in cinema, rap, television or the Internet.

What sets *Palestinian* cultural studies apart is the coercion of the political back into cultural studies generally (and with that the overcoming of the division that has occurred in cultural studies over the past three decades, of negating the legacies of what the forefathers of cultural studies were seeking to achieve in the first place), and the preservation of a past that is reflective of a (hyper)modern condition of de-territorialisation, fragmentation and dispersal. These tensions are reflective of the Palestinian condition: neither an accepted discourse, narrative, history or nation-state, nor a willingness to be silenced and erased. The dialectic between art and politics continues, and nowhere is it more vibrant in the region than in the Palestinian context.

To return to the photography exhibition at the Sakakini, of course, the photographs didn't need to focus on the political reality of refugees; the photographer was pushing Palestinian culture out of its political box. Hers will continue to be a rare feat, one that can only come with privilege, distance, and a forceful divorcing of culture from the political. For the foreseeable future, however, this photographer is likely to remain anomalous. She is also likely to be forgotten in the annals of Palestinian culture. For the strength of Palestinian culture and cultural studies is precisely in merging the political with the cultural, doing so in a particular way and under particular conditions. The heritage, to date, of Palestinian culture and its study is the creation of a record of life under political hardship and against the constant threat of annihilation. Whether in responding to the theft of the archives in 1982, to dispossession of their land, to unremitting racism and apartheid, to repression at the hands of Arab regimes, to continued conditions of exile, to chronic misrepresentations in the global media, Palestinians' contributions to the world are necessarily political. The legacy that a Palestinian cultural studies will leave behind is the formidable task of national self-expression, self-representation and self-realisation under conditions continuously preventing them from actualisation. Until the political 'problem' of Palestinians is resolved, their culture, and their cultural studies will continue to be a culture of active resistance.

Sa'di and Abu-Lughod write that 'Palestinian memory is, by dint of its preservation and social production under the conditions of its silencing by the thundering story of Zionism, dissident memory, counter-memory. It contributes to a counter-history'.[61] The way Palestinian memory is, at its core, political, so is Palestinian culture. Both Palestinian culture and Palestinian cultural studies are attempts to fight historical amnesia and create a more equitable future. Palestinian cultural studies, then, is a counter-cultural studies. The objective, as it stands today, of cultural praxis and cultural studies, is to ensure that Palestinians do not become footnotes in the longer cultural and political history of humanity.

Notes

1. Suleiman 2000: 101.
2. Ibid: 99.
3. Hall 1980, 63; original emphases.
4. Williams 1961, 1977, 1983.
5. Smith 1997: 59.
6. See Peck 2001 for a genealogy and critique of this shift.
7. See Garnham 1995 and Grossberg 1995.
8. Of course the tensions have to do with Marxism, and thus rather than simply with the political, with the *economic*; or if one prefers, or with the 'base' which many cultural studies scholars, from the early 1980s onwards, were critiquing for being approached over-determinatively. While I am not addressing the economic here, I am arguing that the spatial-political conditions of Palestinians function similarly to the 'base' and do in many ways determine the 'superstructure' of the cultural realm.
9. Hammami and Tamari 1997: 275.
10. Sa'di and Abu-Lughod 2007.
11. In fact, Massad argues that the term Nakba – which has been translated, as catastrophe, cataclysm, or disaster – is rather inappropriate. Because Palestinians don't just suffer from a historical event that has passed but are still reeling from it, Palestinians should be called *mankubin*, closer to meaning 'catastrophe-d or disaster-ed people' (Massad 2008).

12. Swedenburg 1989: 268.
13. Piterberg 2001: 32.
14. Bresheeth 2007: 165; original emphases.
15. Ibid: 179.
16. Said 2003: 20.
17. See Thompson 1980; Hall 1980.
18. First, the end of official occupation was really an end on the part of the Israeli government to be responsible for Palestinian life; Israel still remains in ultimate control. Second, I am not suggesting that with the 'end' of occupation this policy is actually over; if anything, it has become more forceful and widespread through different forms *since* 1991. Third, I am not denying the strength of silencing under the control of the Jordanian and Egyptian regimes in the West Bank and the Gaza Strip, respectively, between 1948 and 1967; nor on behalf of Arab governments such as Lebanon and Saudi Arabia, or the larger international community throughout the twentieth and twenty-first centuries.
19. See Jayyusi 2002.
20. See Abdelhadi 2004 for the impact on a Nablus-based radio station.
21. I do not want to make it my object here to delineate all the ways in which Palestinians are silenced and erased; examples are countless, whether in the shape of their territorial exile or the dominance of the pro-Israeli lobby in the West.
22. See Bishara 2008 for an example in the realm of international news.
23. A number of problems arise with the arrival of the PA and the corruption and nepotism manifested in the cultural realm; these are beyond the scope of this chapter. Here I only want to bring attention to the PA's attempts – however feeble and problematic – to assert a Palestinian voice (for critiques of PA censorship, control and relationship to media see Jamal 2001, 2005; Tawil-Souri, 2007; Nossek, H. and K. Rinnawi (2003) 'Censorship and Freedom of the Press Under Changing Political Regimes: Palestinian Media from Israeli Occupation to the Palestinian Authority'. *Gazette* 65.2: 183–202.
24. Said 2003: 163–64.
25. Here it is apt to bring in a common term from the Palestinian context, that of *sumud* (steadfastness), which has been the foundational ideological justification, political strategy and everyday experience at the heart of the Palestinian struggle beginning with the first intifada. See the 2009 special issue of *Middle East Journal of Culture and Communication* 2.2 and my editorial in it, Tawil-Souri, H. 'Towards a Palestinian Cultural Studies', 181–85.
26. Davis: 4. There are studies of Palestinian cultural forms that pre-date the 'peace years' (1991 onwards), that focus on the First Intifada (1987–91), on the period of formal Israeli occupation (1967–91), on the decades between 1948 and 1967, on the British Mandate period (pre-1948); the majority of

these were conducted within more 'traditional' fields such as history, sociology and political science. There also exists a history of attempting to develop village social histories and compiling different aspects of folk culture – proverbs, folk tales, folk medicine, child-rearing practices, superstitions, and aspects of peasant technology and material culture – based 'on collecting and categorising folk artefacts as exemplars of an unchanging national character, with little or no treatment accorded to the social dynamics of change [... and suffering from a general] absence of critical frameworks identifying internal contradictions and historicity' (Hammami and Tamari 1997, 277). Finally, there is scholarship that could be incorporated into the fold of cultural studies focused on the Palestinian Territories that I have chosen to omit: Peteet's analysis of graffiti (Peteet, J. (1996) 'The Writing on the Walls: The Graffiti of the Intifada'. *Cultural Anthropology* 11.2: 139–59); work on the material culture of architecture (Al-Ju'beh, N. (2009) 'Architecture as a Source for Historical Documentation: The Use of Palestine's Built Heritage as a Research Tool'. *Jerusalem Quarterly* 36: 48–65); Feldman's research on 'visibility practices' as manifested in different kinds of objects such as keys, ID cards and modes of discourse (Feldman, I. (2008) 'Refusing Invisibility: Documentation and Memorialization in Palestinian Refugee Claims'. *Journal of Refugee Studies* 21.4: 498–516); Yaqub's essay on political cartoons (Yaqub, N. (2009) 'Gendering the Palestinian Political Cartoon'. *Middle East Journal of Culture and Communication* 2.2: 187–213); and a recently growing body of work on the role of the Internet and digital media in the political: Tawil-Souri, H. (2007) 'Move Over Bangalore. Here Comes ... Palestine? Western Funding and "Internet Development" in the Shrinking Palestinian State' in P. Chakravartty and Y. Zhao (eds) *Global Communications: Toward a Transcultural Political Economy.* Boulder: Rowman & Littlefield: 263–284; Tawil-Souri, H. (2007) 'The Political Battlefield of Pro-Arab Video Games on Palestinian Screens'. *Comparative Studies of South Asia, Africa and the Middle East* 27.3: 536–51; Aouragh, M. (2008) 'Everyday Resistance on the Internet: The Palestinian Context'. *Journal of Arab and Muslim Media Research* 1.2: 109–30.

27. See Dabashi 2006.

28. All of these filmmakers produce *both* feature and documentary films, I am classifying them here according to what they are most well-known for.

29. Studies exist on facets on Palestinian culture that have preceded that on film, particularly news, literature and theatre. Scholarship on Palestinian literature and theatre is substantive. These fall outside the purview of the kind of cultural studies I am focusing on here – as my interest is on the more explicitly mediated. Rashid Khalidi's study on Palestinian nationalism includes a good analysis on early newspapers and their connection to political consciousness and identity formation (Khalidi, R. (1998) *Palestinian Identity: The Construction of Modern National Consciousness*, New York: Columbia University Press). More recent studies on news, news-gathering and news-production have been

rather narrow in their scope: focusing either on various forms of censorship by Israel, and later by the PA (see Nossek, H. and K. Rinnawi, 2003; op.cit), or on ethnocentrism and violence that emerge in news coverage (Wolsfeld, G., P. Frosh, and M. Awadby (2008) 'Covering Death in Conflicts: Coverage of the Second Intifada on Israeli and Palestinian Television'. Journal of Peace Research 45.3: 401–17).

30. Naficy 2001; Tawil 2005.
31. Alexander 2005: 151.
32. Tawil 2005, 137.
33. Bresheeth 2007: 165–66.
34. Dabashi 2006: 11.
35. Bresheeth 2007, 180.
36. Tawil 2005: 137.
37. Dabashi 2006: 12.
38. Bresheeth 2007: 178–79.
39. Massad 2005: 176.
40. Greenberg 2009: 232.
41. Maira 2008: 162.
42. Kurzman 2005: 72.
43. Massad 2005: 193.
44. Ibid: 177.
45. Maria 2008: 184.
46. Ibid; emphasis added.
47. Youmans 2007: 45.
48. Jayyusi 1998: 190.
49. Ibid: 191.
50. See also Jamal 2001, 2005.
51. Jayyusi 1998: 193.
52. Tawil-Souri 2007.
53. Ibid: 11.
54. Jamal 2005: 2.
55. Jamal 2005: 107–138; Jamal, 2004.
56. Said 2003: 187.
57. Gramsci 1971: 334.
58. Said 2003, 81; emphasis added.
59. Suleiman 2000: 99.
60. Massad 2006: 44; original emphases.
61. Sa'di and Abu-Lughod 2007: 6.

Bibliography

Abdelhadi, Amer (2004) 'Surviving Siege, Closure, and Curfew: The Story of a Radio Station', *Journal of Palestine Studies* 34.1: 51–67.

Alexander, Livia (2005) 'Is There a Palestinian Cinema? The National and Transnational in Palestinian Film Production' in R. Stein and T. Swedenburg (eds), *Palestine, Israel, and the Politics of Popular Culture*, Durham: Duke University Press, pp. 150–72.

Al-Zobaidi, Sobhi (2009) 'Memory, Documentary and History' in I. Nassar and R. Salti (eds), *I Would Have Smiled: Photographing the Palestinian Refugee Experience*, Beirut: The Institute of Palestine Studies, pp. 101–19.

Bishara, Amahl (2008) 'Watching U.S. Television from the Palestinian Street: The Media, the State, and Representational Interventions', *Cultural Anthropology* 23.3: 488–530.

—— (2006) 'Local Hands, International News: Palestinian Journalists and the International Media', *Ethnography* 7.1: 19–46.

Bresheeth, Haim (2007) 'The Continuity of Trauma and Struggle: Recent Cinematic Representations of the Nakba' in A.H. Sa'di and L. Abu-Lughod (eds), *Nakba: Palestine, 1948, and the Claims of Memory*, New York: Columbia University Press, pp. 161–87.

Dabashi, Hamid (ed.) (2006) *Dreams of a Nation: On Palestinian Cinema*, New York: Verso.

Davis, Rochelle (2006) 'Palestinian Cultural Expression through Political Turmoil', *Jerusalem Quarterly* 25: 3–4.

Garnham, Nicholas (1995) 'Political Economy and Culture Studies: Reconciliation or Divorce?' *Critical Studies in Mass Communication* 12: 62–71.

Gramsci, Antonio (1971) *Selections form the Prison Notebook*, edited and translated by Quintin Hoare and Goffrey Nowell Smith, London: Lawrence and Wishart.

Greenberg, Ela (2009) ' "The Kind of the Streets": Hip Hop and the Reclaiming of Masculinity in Jerusalem's Shu'afat Refugee Camp', *Middle East Journal of Culture and Communication* 2.2: 231–50.

Grossberg, Lawrence (1995) 'Cultural Studies vs. Political Economy: Is Anybody Else Bored with This Debate?', *Critical Studies in Mass Communication* 12: 72–81.

Hall, Stuart (1980) 'Cultural Studies: Two Paradigms', *Media, Culture & Society* 2: 57–72.

Hammami, Rema and Tamari, Salim (1997) 'Populist Paradigms: Palestinian Sociology', *Contemporary Sociology* 26.3: 275–79.

Jamal, Amal (2005) *Media Politics and Democracy in Palestine: Political Culture, Pluralism, and the Palestinian Authority.* Portland: Sussex Academic Press.

—— (2004) 'Feminist Media Discourse in Palestine and the Predicament of Politics', *Feminist Media Studies* 4.2: 129–46.

—— (2001) 'State-building and Media Regime: Censoring the Emerging Public Sphere in Palestine', *Gazette* 63.2/3: 263–82.

Jayyusi, Lena (2002) ' "Voicing the Nation": The Struggle over Palestinian Broadcasting' in *INTERSections* 2.3/4: 39–49.

—— (1998) 'The "Voice of Palestine" and the Peace Process: Paradoxes in Media Discourse After Oslo' in G. Giacaman and D.J. Lonning (eds), *After Oslo: New Realities, Old Problems*, Chicago: Pluto Press: 189–211.

Kurzman, Charles (2005) 'Da Arabian MC's', *Contexts* 4: 70–72.

Maira, Sunaina (2008) '"We Ain't Missing": Palestinian Hip Hop – A Transnational Youth Movement', *CR: The New Centennial Review* 8.2: 161–92.

Massad, Joseph (2008) 'Resisting the Nakba', *Al-Ahram Weekly* 897 (15–21 May) (http:// weekly.ahram.org.eg/2008/897/op8.htm).

—— (2006) 'The Weapon of Culture: Cinema in the Palestinian Liberation Struggle' in H. Dabashi (ed.), *Dreams of a Nation*. New York: Verso, pp. 32–44.

—— (2005) 'Liberating Songs: Palestine Put to Music' in Stein, R. and T. Swedenburg (eds), *Palestine, Israel, and the Politics of Popular Culture*, Durham: Duke University Press: 175–201.

Naficy, Hamid (2001) *Accented Cinema: Exilic and Diasporic Filmmaking*, Princeton: Princeton University Press.

Peck, Janice (2001) 'Itinerary of a Thought: Stuart Hall, Cultural Studies, and the Unresolved Problem of the Relation of Culture to "Not Culture" ', *Cultural Critique* 48 (Spring): 200–49.

Piterberg, Gabriel (2001) 'Erasures', *New Left Review* 10: 31–46.

Sa'di, Ahmad and Abu-Lughod, Laila (eds) (2007) *Nakba: Palestine, 1948, and the Claims of Memory*, New York: Columbia University Press.

Said, Edward (2003) *Culture and Resistance: Conversations with Edward W. Said* (Interviews by David Barsamian), Cambridge, MA: South End Press.

—— (1984) 'Permission to Narrate', *Journal of Palestine Studies* 13.3: 27–48.

Salama, Vivian (2006) 'Hamas TV: Palestinian Media in Transition', *Transnational Broadcasting Studies* 16 (http://www.tbsjournal.com/ Salama.html).

Smith, Paul (1997) *Millennial Dreams: Contemporary Culture and Capital in the North*, New York: Verso.

Suleiman, Elia (2000) 'Interview: A Cinema of Nowhere', *Journal of Palestine Studies* 29.2: 95–101.

Swedenburg, Ted (1989) 'Occupational Hazards: Palestine Ethnography', *Cultural Anthropology* 4.3: 265–72.

Tawil-Souri, Helga (2005) 'Coming Into Being and Flowing Into Exile: History and Trends in Palestinian Film-Making', *Nebula* 2.2: 113–40.

Tawil-Souri, Helga (2007) 'Global and Local Forces for a Nation-State Yet to be Born: The Paradoxes of Palestinian Television Policies', *Westminster Papers in Communication and Culture* 4.3: 4–25.

Thompson, E.P. (1980) *The Making of the English Working Class*, London: Gollancz.

Warshel, Yael (2008) 'It's All About "Tom and Jerry", Amr Khaled and "Iqra", Not Hamas' Mickey Mouse: Palestinian Children's Television Viewing Habits and Their Parents' Related Preferences', Paper Presented at *Middle East Studies Association* (24 November), Washington, DC.

Williams, Raymond (1983) *Culture and Society*, New York: Columbia University Press.
—— (1977) *Marxism and Literature*, New York: Oxford University Press.
—— (1961) *The Long Revolution*, New York: Columbia University Press.
Youmans, Will (2007) 'Arab American Hip Hop' in A. Ameri and H. Arida (eds), *Etching Our Own Image: Voices from within the Arab American Art Movement*, Newcastle: Cambridge Scholars Publishing: 42–59.

8

Rethinking Gender Studies: Towards an Arab Feminist Epistemology

Layal Ftouni

This chapter calls for an Arab feminist re-assessment of 'the modern' enterprise, not only in terms of its material and discursive manifestations on local gender politics and feminist projects in Arab societies, but also in terms of its methodological and critical analytic framework, which is at work in a substantial body of Arab feminist scholarship. It proposes the need to rethink the binaries that sustain the modern critique (traditional vs. modern, epistemic vs. the political, material vs. the discursive) whilst at the same time questioning the viability of postmodern anti-essentialist paradigms that have recently gained unprecedented acceptance in the developing field of Arab and Middle Eastern Gender Studies. First, the chapter will qualify the theoretical and methodological modalities at work in Arab feminist scholarship, which I shall divide into two camps, reactionary and deconstructive. By referring in detail to particular examples of hermeneutic/literary critical, anthropological and socio-historical research, I investigate the ways in which feminist scholars from both camps have dealt with questions of power/patriarchy, agency, subjectivity and experience. This discussion will proceed in three, thematically divided yet overlapping, sections, one dealing with socio-historical and literary critical scholarship on gender in Islam, another with feminist strategies for recuperating agency in ethnographic research and its links to debates on submission vs. resistance, and the third addressing feminist writings of Her-story.

The chapter expresses an urgent need for an Arab feminist epistemology, one that regards the existential reality of 'being a woman' as *a priori* to becoming Arab (Muslim, Jew, Christian, secular, heterosexual, homosexual).[1] An epistemology that refuses to forget, but that takes the act of not forgetting as the basis from which to develop alternative forms of subjectivities;[2] an epistemology whose objective is to retrieve the agency of Arab women, who are excluded from, or misrepresented within the narratives of History, culture, politics and knowledge. But also one that takes off and starts again with 'different re-departures, different pauses, different arrivals.'[3] An Arab feminist epistemology, I argue, requires a strategic double move, to both *empiricise* the lived experiences of women in Arab societies, and to *theorise* new ways of knowing and representing.

The modern/tradition debate again...

Over the last three decades, many feminist scholars have investigated the extent to which gender-politics, feminist projects and thought in the Arab world and the wider Middle East are imbricated in modern and traditional discourses on religion, culture and the nation.[4] Prevalent amongst this body of work is a significant shift in the methods used to study gender from modernist and Orientalist perspectives postulated on stark defined binaries between tradition, as indigenous and repressive of women; and modernity, as Western and progressive. Through a re-assessment of the oppositional categories of tradition and modernity associated with the East/West divide, feminist scholars have opened up new spaces for the rethinking of Arab women's experiences, gender politics and feminist projects. Feminist theoretical and empirical explorations of the politics of modernity and the traditionalist responses to it have not only been central to research *on* gender in the Arab world, but have also reconfigured the paradigms through which we conceive of and deploy the categories of modernity and tradition *for* the study of gender. Despite the diversity of methods by which scholars have challenged these oppositions, one can decipher two predominant approaches of dissension at work in the field, which I shall address as the reactionary and the deconstructive. Reactionary accounts, I argue, are concerned with a critical unmasking of modernity's 'false consciousness' through a reversal of its oppositional logic and hierarchies of power, in an attempt to inscribe an indigenous, culturally-specific, feminist or Islamic alternative. Deconstructive accounts, on the other hand, call for a move that goes beyond binary frameworks and adopts notions such as hybridity, translation and syncretism. By dismantling the rigid boundaries of modernity and tradition, deconstructive approaches stress the heterogeneity of, and the multifaceted encounters between both sides.

Reactionary feminist scholarship remains trapped in the hegemonic divisions of modernity; the modern against the traditional, epistemic against political, assimilation against difference. Reactionary voices, although quite heterogeneous, are singular in their *opposition* to essentialising narratives of women's subjugation as intrinsic to 'traditional' Arab societies and cultures. The opposition mostly proceeds by reclaiming women's experiences as local and culturally specific; Islamic *ideals* as emancipatory, and/or, following the logic of causality, by studying the constraining effects of power, reified in the discriminatory narratives and practices of colonial and neo-colonial intervention, as well as local patriarchy, on gender relations and feminist projects in the Arab world.[5] Methodologically, this oppositional stance is a critique that takes as its object the rejection of stereotypes; and/or one that studies gender oppression as an effect of Western and local patriarchal ideologies. The agency of the feminist critic here not only performs a reversed denunciation, thus turning what modernity regarded as backward (Arab women, Islam) into progressive and liberal, (Islamic ideals as modern, Muslim women have agency), but also draws *causal* connections between women's oppression/ resistance and structures of power.

On the other hand, deconstructive accounts tend to move beyond binaries of modernity vs. tradition. Deconstructive voices no longer believe in the premise of the modern critique, rejecting its practices of oppositional and hierarchical denunciation, but have then turned to the hybrid that the constitution and condition of modernity rejected but continued to proliferate.[6] This scholarship emphasises the dialogical relationship between the secular and the religious, modern with the traditional, and the East and West.[7] Some deconstructive voices go further, to problematise the conception of the identity of the gendered subject as a *causal* category that exists outside the multiple, and sometimes overlapping discourses that produce them. This approach mostly follows theories of performativity (the notion of the performative agent within language),[8] and/or theories of power/ knowledge (the productive capacity of the power of discourse to produce agents from within).[9]

Gender in Islam

The 1980s and 1990s witnessed a proliferation of publications, conferences and seminars that investigated issues such as women's rights, gender relations and practices in Islam. Taking into account Islam's centrality in interpolating Islamic gendered subjectivities and practices in the Arab world, and bearing in mind the West's ongoing hostility towards Islam, as essentially 'oppressive' of women, many feminist scholars felt an urgent need for studies that re-assessed gender relations and women's status in Islam. Scholars addressing gender discourses in Islamic socio-cultural traditions adopt divergent positions, some are critical of its patriarchal values and others recommend it as ensuring women's dignity and security.[10] Regardless of the divergences in positions around whether Islamic traditions are patriarchal or not, this scholarship shares an Islamic feminist hermeneutic perspective that affirms the egalitarian nature of 'true' Islamic ideals.[11]

Feminist scholars, most notably Fatima Mernissi and Leila Ahmed, critical of the way in which Qur'anic texts and the *Hadith* have been codified to serve androcentric interests, argue that these codifications have averted the ethical and egalitarian message of Islam.[12] Mernissi examines the *tafsir* of the Prophet's *Hadith* and the Qu'ran, arguing that these commentaries contradict the original intent of the Prophet Mohammad. According to Mernissi, the Prophet's message intended to break with misogynist, pre-Islamic traditions. This represented a challenge to the patriarchal male élite who, since the early days of Islam, had deployed the science of *Isnad* to interpret the Prophet's *Hadith* and the Qur'anic *suras* in a manner that served their own political and sexual interests. Mernissi shows how the institution of the *hijab* and the segregation of the sexes, as part and parcel of Islam, is a patriarchal fabrication that was later maintained during the colonial period by Arab nationalists, and is maintained today by some Islamist groups as a way to secure their dominion in the face of change. The Western modern outlook to the future, according to the author, has instilled a sense of anxiety within Muslims, who then turned to the language of patriarchal past in order to ensure their residence 'in the present as an interlude in which [they] were little involved'.[13] Throughout her study, Mernissi returns to the original sources of the Prophet's *Hadith* and the Qur'anic suras in order to counteract the biases put forward by patriarchal interpretations.

Similarly, Ahmed, in her seminal work *Women and Gender in Islam: Historical Roots to a Modern Debate* (1992), draws a distinction between what she terms 'establishment Islam' and 'lay Islam'. Ahmed argues that 'establishment Islam' is the language of the politically powerful; a legalistic and culturally authoritarian version of Islam that is hostile to women, and suppresses all other readings of Islamic gender relations as 'heretical'.[14] According to Ahmed, 'establishment Islam's' claim that it follows authentic Islamic ways is problematic, as this is predicated on the presumption that the Prophet's sayings and the Qur'anic scripts are 'ascertainable in a precise and absolute sense', and that the meaning of gender, as articulated in the written corpus of establishment Islam, is the only possible uncontested one.[15] This, she further accentuates, silences the ethical and egalitarian voice of 'lay Islam' that many Muslim women, marginalised and less privileged groups speak. According to Ahmed, 'it is because Muslim women hear this egalitarian voice that they declare (generally to the astonishment of non-Muslims) that Islam is nonsexist'.[16]

One could argue that these accounts open up a space for the articulation of 'indigenous feminisms' that do not rely on Western sources or influences.[17] However, one need not disregard the paradoxes at work in their methods. For, on the one hand, this scholarship stands, explicitly or implicitly, in opposition to Orientalist and Islamic patriarchal discourses but, on the other, it continues to deploy the oppositional categories of the traditional versus the modern, and the epistemic vs. the political, that has sustained the legacy of modernisation and modern social critique.[18] This is not a call to refrain from the premise of critique, but rather it is to problematise the logic of modern social scientific denunciation that is at work in such a critique. Mernissi, throughout her work, tends to replace the science of *Isnad*, set out to serve patriarchal interests, with that of the science of socio-historical research, sorting out what is 'true' from that which is a product of ideology. Mernissi equates her own re-interpretation, or as Zayzafoon righteously described it, 'her re-authentication' of the Prophet's *Hadith*, with the 'true' message of Islam.[19] The pitfalls in such a methodology lie in its attempt to answer the modern universal question: 'what is an "authentic" Islam?' by posing an hermeneutic approach to the Prophet's *Hadith* and the *Qu'ran* (what do they truly mean?) in order to unmask patriarchal ideologies. In other words, Mernissi is more interested in reclaiming the 'true' substance of Islam, one that bears no relation to the way it is interpreted by Muslim rulers and ideologues, than in examining the complex relationship between the 'constitutive processes' of the concept of Islam, and the 'regulative' ones that designate certain practices as

Islamic and others as not.[20] Ahmed, on the other hand, despite her aware-ness of the impossibility of an absolutist, true interpretation of the *Hadith* and the *Qu'ran,* then turns to 'lay Islam' as the ethical voice that is only heard by the marginalised.

Both Mernissi and Ahmed stand in opposition to Orientalist and patri-archal Islamic scenarios on gender and women's status in Islamic societies by finding refuge either in the idealisation of the past, referring to the origin of the message of Islam as democratic and gender-egalitarian (Mernissi), or in the fetishisation of the marginalised (women and less privileged groups) as the only truly enlightened faction of Muslim society as opposed to the more Westernised and modernised upper-classes (Ahmed). Mernissi reverses the logic of modern temporality that seeks to break from the static past by showing that Islam, in its earliest stages, was progressive. However, she then complies with modernity's progressive temporality by critiquing Muslim and nationalist leaders' return to the patriarchal past, through the imposition of segregation and veiling, as an obstacle to true 'democracy'.[21] Mernissi thus couples the practice of unveiling with democracy, and veiling with tradition, reiterating a long-established narrative held by Arab nation-alists, Western liberal feminist and Orientalists against the practice of seg-regation in Islam. Ahmed opposes the modern conception of an ahistorical Islam (that regards Islam as detrimental to Muslim women's acquisition of liberal rights) through the revelation of its ethical and egalitarian vision, to which, she argues, less privileged Muslim women adhere.

Whereas these scholars have been aware of the androcentric aspects of Islamic socio-cultural traditions, others have accepted the Islamic framework in total, recommending it as a 'home-grown and culturally appropriate alternative to feminism, Marxism and the liberal humanist project'.[22] Islamic feminists, Moghissi argues, face a daunting task: they need to establish a counter-discourse method against anti-Islamic preju-dice without getting caught up in an 'apologetic or self-denying defense of Islamic gender practices or a justification of the oppressive discourses of Islamist ideologues and rulers'.[23] This scholarship tends to conflate Western thought with the project of modernity, launching criticisms, explicitly and implicitly, against what they pigeonhole as 'Western' feminism, 'Western' sexual conduct and gender relations, whilst leaving the categories 'West', and 'modernity' untouched. Even the accounts that are critical of tradi-tional patriarchal Islam for its breach of 'true' Islam's democratic and gender-egalitarian ideals do so without questioning how we can theorise and conceptualise 'the democratic' in relation to Islamic gender relations and practices. Surely these issues cannot simply be resolved by pointing to the 'universal values' of democracy and equality as intrinsic to the original message of Islam. In doing so, we are in danger of succumbing to what Al-Azm termed 'Orientalism in reverse'.[24] The danger lies in elevating a self-glorifying image (by affirming a democratic and modern vision of 'true' Islamic ideals) that stands in *opposition* to Western narratives about Islam as ahistorical and traditional, consequently reproducing and fixating power in the West.

Working with deconstructive and postmodern femininst theories, the literary critic Lama Zayzafoon, in her book *The Production of Muslim Women: Negotiating Text, History and Ideology*, complicates the possibility of a reverse Orientalism by arguing that all cultures are inventions, that 'Islam' is heterogeneous, and that the 'Muslim woman' is an unfixed and plural signifier. The author clearly sets her examination of the notion of cultural difference against anthropological notions of culture as a set of cultural and social practices specific to a particular locale. Zayzafoon turns away from a liberal feminist study of patriarchy through the logic of causality; that is, as an imposition of systems of subordination on a pre-existing reality (e.g., veiling as an imposition on women's bodies). Rather, patriarchy is examined in terms of its different configurations of power through which the category 'Muslim woman' is discursively enunciated. According to Zayzafoon, the 'Muslim woman' is a 'semiotic subject', that is produced and reproduced in Islamic, Orientalist, nationalist and feminist discourses.[25]

While taking *a priori* such an anti-essentialist stance may be politically effective, it remains delimiting for the project of an Arab feminist epistemology in two ways. Deconstruction may be useful for a textual/discursive *analysis* of women's representations, but it restricts the possibility of a feminist politics that enunciates the *lived experiences* of the female subject. Second, it problematises the production of situated knowledge(s), since knowledge is, in the first place, doubted. By reducing our existential reality to a mere analysis of language, a position prevalent amongst deconstructive and postmodern feminists, we are at risk of obliterating the objective of feminist projects.[26] For, as Al-Ali asks, 'what can we demand in the name of women if "women" do not exist?'[27] This is not a call for a return to the liberal feminist premise of women's oppression as a 'unitary phenomenon',[28] or to the logic of causality in the critique of patriarchy and the binary oppositions that sustain it (oppressor vs. victim; resistance vs. submission). What is proposed is that we acknowledge that our subjectivity, both female and male, stands in a relation of proximity to different configurations and modalities of power (social and cultural) that *affect* us on the level of experience, albeit differently, and that in order to enunciate a feminist political and epistemological position, we need to re-affirm our lived experiences as women. Whilst reactionary socio-historical research on gender and Islam is caught in a critique of patriarchal structure and the deconstructive in deconstructing representation, both omit the subjective experience of women and gender. I will return to this, but let me first address some of the scholarship dealing within women's experiences and agency in Arab cultures.

Experience, agency and resistance

Aware of the fact that negative codifications of women were crucial to the West's hegemonic positionality in relation to the Orient, many scholars carrying out ethnographic and social historical research sought to present the complex realities of gender and women in Arab societies, in a manner that emphasises women's strengths and struggles as political and social agents.[29] Feminist scholars' main task, whether writing about themselves or their subjects, was to rescue the agency of women who had been marginalised in the narratives of history and culture. One of the earliest examples is Warnock Farnea and Qattan Bezirgan's edited volume *Middle Eastern Women Speak,* published in 1977. Western ethnographic observers and Orientalist scholars, the authors argue, failed to address the multifaceted layers of gender relations in Middle Eastern society and have arrived at totalising doctrines based on the evidence of family and tribal customs, or of an analysis of historical texts and the origin of Islam, to understand its nineteenth- and twentieth-century manifestations. The editors go about combating such stereotypes by returning to primary sources, such as autobiographical and biographical statements by and about Middle Eastern women, chosen from different historical periods and regions of the Middle East.[30] Other examples that have studied and recorded women's experiences, achievements and struggles include Lila Abu-Lughod's ethnographic work on Awlad Ali in *Writing Women's World: Bedouin Stories* (1991), Homa Hoodafar's socio-historical study *Between Marriage and the Market: Politics and Survival in*

Cairo (1997), and Katherine Bullock's *Rethinking Muslim Women and the Veil: Challenging Historical and Modern Stereotypes* (2002).

Although many of the above-mentioned feminist scholars are aware of their position in framing the experiences and voices of other women, the question we need to ask ourselves, Abu-Lughod remarks, is 'what Western Liberal values are we *unreflectively* validating by proving that Middle Eastern women have agency, too?'.[31] While the focus on women's agency has played a central role in challenging debates on gender in non-Western societies beyond the registers of submission, one needs to be wary, Mahmood argues, of the unproblematic enterprise of coupling agency with liberal feminist notions of women's resistance and struggle.[32]

Raising critical questions about feminist work whose objective is combating stereotypes, including her own ethnographic account in *Writing Women's World: Bedouin Stories* (1993), Abu-Lughod argues that as long as feminists are writing against the Western episteme about their own 'othered' voices, they remain implicated in projects that ascertain the authority of the West.[33] Abu-Lughod warns against romanticising resistance as external to power structures and calls for a reassessment of resistance as 'diagnostic of power'.[34] However, despite Abu-Lughod's understanding of resistance as an act inscribed in power relations, she fails to problematise, according to Mahmood, the universality of the category of resistance; one that is premised on the desire for emancipation from patriarchal traditions. Mahmood questions whether it is even possible for acts of resistance to exist outside the ethical and political conditions within which such acts *acquire* their meaning.[35] She further asks:

> Does the category of resistance impose a teleology of progressive politics on the analytics of power – a teleology that makes it hard for us to see and understand forms of being and action that are not necessarily encapsulated by the narrative of subversion and reinscription of norms?[36]

Mahmood's provocative and sophisticated ethnographic account of the Egyptian urban women's mosque movement poses several conceptual challenges to the trajectories of liberal feminist politics. Grounding her research in a deconstructive critique of the humanist autonomous subject, Mahmood points to the limitations of liberal feminist insights when applied to women whose conceptions of the self are shaped by non-liberal traditions. Mahmood draws on Butler's theorisation of the subject as one that is interpolated through language, but that is also constantly performative through a repetitive enactment of regulatory norms. Through the act of re-enactment, the subject performs certain exclusions necessary to its self-realisation. While Mahmood is largely indebted to feminist poststructuralist theory in its distinction between the notion of self-realisation and the liberal version of autonomous will, she nevertheless, departs from their premise that agency resides in the act of the subversion of the norm.[37] Mahmood turns to Foucauldian ethics to understand agency in terms of its capacities and skills, through which the subject transforms herself to achieve a particular state of being within a particular moral discourse. Focusing on articulations of desire, emotion, reason, and bodily expressions, Mahmood shows how women *inhabit* norms as an act of self-realisation, one that is not defined through the logic of subversion or consolidation, but by consummation.

Similarly, Lara Deeb, in her ethnographic research on the *Enchanted Modern* (2006) explores the embodied and discursive forms of public piety amongst Shi'i Muslim women in Lebanon as processes of 'authentication' of Islam. Unlike Mahmood, Deeb explores how processes of authentication are linked to the notion of material and spiritual progress; as 'a move "forward", away from "tradition", into a new kind of religiosity, one that involves *conscious* and *conscientious* commitment'.[38] The importance of Deeb's and Mahmood's theses lies in their conceptualisation of women's agency outside liberal feminist notions of resistance vs. submission, but also in their approach to the inter-relationship between the bodily material and the discursive in the constitution of subjectivity.[39] However, while Deeb regards the subject's discursive negotiation and embodiment of the pious modern as signs of change, Mahmood departs from the notion of the body as simply a sign, to explore the power that 'corporeality commands on the making of subjects'.[40]

Whereas Mahmood and Deeb's theoretical propositions are important and challenging, one need not shy away from questioning the specificity of the examples they explore in relation to the discourses and practices of piety. No matter how compelling and urgent these arguments might be, the authors do not address women's engagement in the realm of *realpolitik* and the complex interrelationship between the social, cultural, political and religious power structures in the constitution of subjectivity. Moreover, is

Mahmood's critique of liberal feminist values of resistance not in danger of reinscribing the master's narratives by way of a detour through women's discourses and bodily practices of piety? Mahmood's discussion on women's aspirations to inhibit norms through specific modes of being, leaves the realm of fantasy, the unconscious repository, and questions of belongingness, untouched. Do we not risk abandoning the language of feminism and the critique of patriarchal power structures and discourses by *uncritically* accepting the empirical character of our observation and fieldwork as a window into the 'realities' of women's experiences? I am not suggesting that we need to dispose of empiricism, but rather to acknowledge the impossibility of knowing the other in her totality. To assume that we can know the other is to risk dismissing that which escapes us in our encounter with the other. It is also to disregard the processes of politicisation involved in the production of knowledge. The dilemma remains, how do *we speak the language of feminism* in a manner critical of both Western discourses and local patriarchy without getting locked into the dialectical causality of victimhood versus resistance?

Feminist movements and the re-inscription of Her-Story

Nowhere can one so vividly point to approaches in which reverse oppositions are at work in feminist scholarship than in reactionary accounts that discuss the claims and initiatives of Arab feminist projects and thought. Not only, as Kandiyoti argues, has the preoccupation with Islam as a marker of cultural identity 'constrained the discursive possibilities of feminist scholarship', but the Middle East's encounter with the imperial West and the flawed nature of nationalist discourses in regard to women's issues have also 'established styles of debate that exhibit remarkable resilience through time'.[41] This is largely visible in the fact that critical exploration of the intersection between feminism, the colonial legacy and local nationalist discourses are still on the agenda of feminist scholarship, most notably in work that studies the history of Arab feminist movements, as well as studies that assess the rhetoric of nationalist intellectuals and reformists on women's issues in Arab culture and society. Scholars' views have varied between those who reject the premise that local feminism(s) began with men, or have any links to Western colonial projects and ideas, and those who have argued that women's issues were primarily put forward by male reformist intellectuals calling for the abandonment of local misogynistic practices to follow the values and beliefs of European culture, consequently replacing local patriarchy with Western style patriarchy. This dichotomy is clearly discernable in discussions on Egyptian feminism. Margot Badran, in her extensive socio-historical study, expounds that feminism in Egypt began with women, has been indigenous, and transcends local political and class divisions. Although condemned by local patriarchy as being Western, Egyptian feminism since its inception, Badran states, has never been Western, for Egyptian feminists had to 'juggle their feminist struggle with anti-colonial and anti-imperial ones, a dual battle unknown to Western feminists'.[42] Whilst such an exploration affirms the positivity of female subjectivities as agents for political and social change, an approach, as discussed earlier, relevant amongst feminist ethnographers; to argue that Egyptian feminism transcends, and for that matter exists *a priori* to local and colonial/Western gender discourses is rather problematic. Whereas the articulation of an Egyptian feminist identity is necessary to serve political ends, one needs to be wary of implying that it exists prior to politics. As Lloyd argues, identities are 'generated on the field of power and that part of their production entails their naturalisation so that they *appear* to pre-exist politics'.[43]

Conversely, Leila Ahmed argues that the interconnectedness of women's issues and culture made their formal entry into Arabic discourses with the publication of Qasim Amin's *Tahrir Al-Mar'a,* whose rhetoric has its provenance in the language of colonial feminism. According to Ahmed, colonialists who rejected the ideas of feminism at home have 'captured the language of feminism and redirected it, in the service of colonialism, towards Other men and the cultures of Other men'.[44] This is reflected in Cromer's rhetoric that seemed to champion the liberation of Muslim women,[45] a rhetoric reiterated in the native voice of Amin calling for fundamental transformations in culture and society that were symbolised by the abolition of the veil. Later in her book *Women and Gender in Islam,* Ahmed discusses Egyptian feminist discourses that emerged after the publication of *Tahrir Al Mar'a,* raising critical doubt about the dominant voices of feminism enunciated by upper and middle class women who promoted Western feminist ideas, most notably the voice of Huda Sha'rawi and her Egyptian feminist movement.

Reactionary approaches to the study of feminism in the Arab world, be it those who celebrate feminism as indigenous, or those who undermine its Western influences as oppressive, each represent one side of the same coin. They both argue, explicitly or implicitly, for an alternative external to Western feminist essentialist discourses that reduce otherness to the Same or, in other words, that universalise their concerns as those of 'All women'. The universality of the category 'woman', as introduced by Western feminists, is thus confronted by projects that attend to notions of national and cultural difference amongst women. However, such projects, as Narayan argues, tend to counter gender essentialist discourses, but then replace them with culture-specific, essentialist generalisations such as, 'Western women', 'Indigenous women', 'Muslim women'.[46] Even within the one culture, divergent groups are dichotomised between the secular Westernised and the religious Islamic. This disregards the fact that Western feminist universal paradigms, especially when thought of in terms of their links to colonial legacies, often proceed not only by the 'insistence on Sameness' but also by means of an 'insistence on Difference'.[47] Following this argument, Arab feminist scholars' emphasis on *difference* as a site of empowerment can become a process of appropriating the feminist colonial legacy in reverse, as opposed to deconstructing the ontologised binaries of West versus East, or indigenous and imported feminisms. Whereas this is a viable critique, binaries at work in Arab socio-historical feminist scholarship, cannot, for several reasons, be simply rejected as conceptually and methodologically faulty. Firstly, whereas we celebrate deconstructive strategies that seek to destabilise difference by reducing it to language, to disregard the fact that categorical differences have structured, and continue to structure, the fabric of regional, cultural, and political life and feminist projects, is to risk implying that women's movements and projects stand free of their own history. Secondly, feminist historical research is both a project of recuperating histories and experiences and an analysis of texts on/by women in Arab societies. Interpretative free play remains the luxury of literary critics and philosophers. Feminist historians, as Abu-Lughod argues, 'feel bound to represent the particular interests and lives of those they study, a commitment sometimes inconsistent with grand theoretical gestures'.[48] The use of deconstructive textual strategies *in toto* would inevitably transform feminist critical historiography into a critique of historical episteme and what that entails in a critique of the 'subject' of humanism. The result is a problematisation of the female subject as an agent of her-story, and for that matter a critique of the possibility of historical representation *per se*. The modern vision of the subject of humanism as universal and autonomous has been subject to scrutiny by post structuralist feminist theories.[49] Whereas this critique has been productively employed by many postcolonial feminists in order to undermine the autonomy of the white, Western, Eurocentric male,[50] to deploy the same critique against the possibility of reclaiming the status of subjects for those who were denied it (women, the marginalised) is problematic. Whether we should reclaim women's subjectivities and experiences or not, is not the question. It is our responsibility to do so. Rather, the question is how do we *relate* to the experiences of other women?

Towards an Arab feminist epistemology

Feminist epistemology is a project that was initially set out by feminists (mostly white) in the mid-1980s and includes the works of Harding (1986, 1991), Haraway (1989), Hekman (1987) and Duran (1994) to name but a few.[51] The fundamental thesis of this area of research has resonance amongst many third world and black feminist writers whose work has paralleled, or even preceded, the field's inception under the rubric of 'Feminist Epistemology'. Despite the different political and epistemological models that feminists have introduced to the enterprise of feminist epistemology, one of the fundamental questions it poses is 'whose knowledge is it?'[52]

On a basic level, feminist epistemology is primarily concerned with the re-affirmation of our being in the world as women, giving the different experiences amongst and within women priority.[53] It seeks to challenge the male-centred epistemologies from which women have either been excluded or in which they have been misrepresented. Feminist epistemology, Narayan states, proposes that women's contributions to male dominant bodies of knowledge is 'not merely adding of details, it will not widen the canvas, but result in a shift in perspective allowing us to see a very different picture'.[54] It resembles the efforts of 'third world' women writers who reclaim their 'experiences as different from the norm and asserting the value of that difference'; of historians rewriting their histories against the traditional historical episteme.[55] It is also analogous to the work of black and third world critics and theorists, who propose new methods for rethinking and re-inscribing racial, ethnic and gender subjectivities and experiences. Examples of these arguments can be seen in the work of black and third world feminists such as bell hooks, Patricia Hill Collin and Gayatri Spivak.[56]

Looking at Arab feminist scholarship, one can witness the becoming of an Arab feminist epistemology. However, on taking a closer look, one can also point to deficits in the research methods that might preclude the possibility of situated knowledge. First and foremost, Arab feminist scholarship, as argued in previous sections, continues to rely on mainstream theories and critical discourses. With few exceptions, the scholarship mostly either relies on modern methods of socio-historical scientific critique that reproduce oppositions of tradition vs. modernity (reactionary), or on postmodern, anti-essentialist methods celebrating in-betweenness, hybridity and dialogism between the traditional and the modern (deconstructive).

In support of reactionary socio-historical and anthropological accounts, one could argue that these studies have arrived at a new understanding of gender relations and politics in particular socio-cultural and historical contexts; that they are based on empirical research and have presented new 'truths' about Arab women's lives and experiences. One could also argue that reactionary accounts critical of Islamic traditions, have, through sustained scientific research, devalued patriarchal claims, and unfolded the egalitarian nature of 'true' Islam. The question that those protective of modern epistemology might ask here, as Harding observes: why is it necessary that feminists establish a *distinctively* feminist epistemology when their research, already 'provides the same good old empirical evidence that has been regarded as sufficient for claims to count as plausible, well supported, less false, better confirmed than their rival, and so on'?[57] From this perspective, feminist socio-historical research that explains social relations between the sexes and that unmasks sexist beliefs is justified in familiar, uncontroversial ways. So why, modern epistemologists would ask, is it necessary to establish distinctively feminist ways of knowing?

The issue becomes more complex when we point to the links established between modern epistemological methods, especially in the social sciences, and the colonial legacy. As Castro Gomez argues, 'social sciences developed in the space of modern/colonial power, and in the ideological knowledge it generated'.[58] The social sciences, he further argues, 'did not produce an 'epistemological rupture' with respect to ideology. Instead, the colonial imaginary permeated the entire conceptual system of the social sciences from their inception'.[59] Taking this into account, do we, as Arab feminists, simply abandon the rules of social scientific research and critique which permit us to speak back from within the specificity of our cultures and our experiences as women, especially when acknowledging that it is these methods that have been directed against us to legitimate and essentialise the inferiority of our culture and gender?

The recent debates in social sciences and anthropology on the positionality of the female researcher/anthropologist and her epistemic privilege are far more promising than the invisible voice of God that modern epistemology permeates. Arab feminist scholars have undoubtedly been agents in these shifts in the social sciences. However, acknowledging our position *vis-à-vis* our research and the women we are speaking for is not enough. The challenge remains: how do we re-inscribe our gender and cultural specificity through social scientific and historical research without falling into the traps of sexism, ethnocentrism or reverse Orientalism?

On the other hand, and in support of deconstructive/discursive scholarship, one could argue that the methods of deconstruction and discourse analysis allow for new spaces of negotiation to emerge beyond the homogenising narratives of differences, cultural or sexual. They permit us to see the ethnocentric core of social sciences that had constructed Arabnness as an essence that defined our culture. These methods destabilise the fixed categories of East and West, Tradition and Modernity. Deconstructive/ Discursive strategies de-essentialise the epistemic logic (cultural or religious) that regulates our gendered bodies. It allows us to realise that the 'condemnation of feminism as an inauthentic Western import is just as inaccurate as celebrating it as a local or an indigenous project'.[60] Taking into account the liberating potential of deconstruction/discourse theory, and its scepticism about essentialist knowledge claims, the question an orthodox deconstructivist might ask here: why should one then argue for a feminist epistemology, let alone an Arab one?

It is by attending to this chiasmus that we can see the urgent necessity for the beginning of an Arab feminist epistemology. An Arab feminist epistemology is both local and worldly. For an Arab feminist epistemology to be effective, it needs to make links with the project of feminist epistemology elsewhere. It is worldly, for it shares with members of the feminist community 'a common epistemological and ethical bond: a feminist cogito'.[61] A cogito that refuses to universalise our different experiences of womanhood in the world, but that takes the ontological basis of 'sexual difference' – 'being a woman' – as the grounds from which to enunciate feminist politics. The objective of our political action is not a homogenous one either; it differs according to differences amongst and between women, such as the socio-cultural context in which we live, our ethnicity, race and sexual orientation. The point of consensus, however, is that we consider 'being a woman' as the 'ontological pre-condition for [our] existential *becoming as subject*'[62] and from which we can enunciate a feminist epistemology. This, however, is not to be confused with liberal feminists' universal demands for women's emancipation, premised on a singular homogenising definition of what counts as women's oppression. It is rather to acknowledge our ethico-responsibility towards *the other as woman,* but also to all *othered others* who are excluded within the logos of phallocentrism. Acknowledging this responsibility allows us to relate to the other woman in a non-totalising way.[63]

It is after recognising the worldliness of the project of an Arab feminist epistemology that we begin to localise it. For it is not only our 'being a woman' that is at stake here, it is also our being and becoming in language, culture and society. It is the aim of an Arab feminist epistemology to create new modes of thinking, ways of knowing and of representing Arab women that take women's lived experiences as a foundation to knowledge. The project of an Arab feminist epistemology involves a double task; first we need to re-invent, to use Fuss's terminology, 'the essentialist spaces'[64] from which we Arab women, in all our diversity (political affiliations, class, sexual orientation) can speak; to *empiricise* our experiences and to raise critical consciousness about the histories, cultures and systems of knowledge that have negated us. Since feminism is a project of change and transformation, our second task is to reconstruct. Reconstruction is a process of redefining and theorising the terms of our political project from within those experiences. What is 'the democratic', 'the egalitarian' in the context of gender relations in Arab cultures and societies? How can we open up the space for new forms of representation from 'the conditional present'?[65] Here, the task shifts from *speaking about* to *speaking to*.[66] As historians, anthropologists, literary critics and social scientists, by *speaking to*, we displace the semantic distance between the self and the other woman, between oneself and the text, merging the two in a speech act that bounces back and forth. Our political project is thus, using Min-ha's words, a 'work-in-progress':

> [it] is not a work awaiting a better, more perfect stage of real-ization. Inevitably a work is always a form of tangible closure. But closures need not close off; they can be doors opening onto other closures and functioning as an ongoing passage to an

elsewhere (within-here). Like a throw of dice each opening is also a closing, for each work generates its own laws and limits, each has its specific conditions and deals with a specific context [...] Thus every work materialised can be said to be a work-in-progress.[67]

Notes

1. The existential reality of 'being as women' is not to be mistaken with biologism or to be understood in terms of fixed masculine and feminine essences. It is rather to acknowledge, as Braidotti argues, that sexual difference is both a fact, but also a sign that has for a long history been regarded as a mark of pejoration. According to Braidotti, 'that one be socially constructed as feminine is an evidence, that the recognition of the fact may take place in language is clear, but that processes of construction of femininity fastens and builds upon anatomical realities is equally true'. It is the positive project of feminism, she further adds to turn the negative conceptualisation of sexual difference into strength. See Rosi Braidotti, 'The Politics of Ontological Difference' in Teresa Brenan (ed.) *Between Feminism and Psychoanalysis* (Routledge, 1989), p. 101.
2. Rosi Braidotti, 'Nomadism with Difference: Deleuze's legacy', *Continental Philosophy Review*, 29. 3 (July 1996): 312.
3. Trinh T. Minh-Ha, 'Cotton and iron', in Russell Ferguson et al. *Out there: Marginalization and Contemporary Cultures* (New Museum of Contemporary Art and MIT Press, 1990), p. 328.
4. I do not use the term 'feminist' as a definitive label, especially since many women scholars and activists, critical of the project of feminism as Western, do not label themselves as 'feminists'. Rather I, use the term with its explanatory value that describes scholars who write about women and gender relations. By 'Arab feminist scholarship', I am referring to work that addresses gender in Arab cultures and societies. The work cited is not limited to authors from the region.
5. See, for example, Margot Badran, *Feminists, Islam and Nation* (Princeton, 1995); Keddie and Baron (eds) *Women in the Middle East History, Shifting Boundaries in Sex and Gender* (Yale University Press, 1981); Katherine Bullock, *Rethinking Muslim Women and the Veil: Challenging Historical and Modern Stereotypes* (International Institute of Islamic Thought, 2002); Margot Badran, 'Independent Women: More Than a Century of Feminism in Egypt', in Judith Tucker (ed.) *Arab Women: Old Boundaries, New Frontiers* (Indiana University Press, 1993); Fatima Mernissi, *The Veil and the Male Elite: A Feminist Interpretation of Women's Rights in Islam*, trans. Mary Jo Lakeland (Addison-Wesley, 1991).
6. Bruno Latour argues that 'We have never been modern'. Latour distinguishes between two sets of practices designated by the word 'modern'. The first is that of translation and mediation that creates hybrids, and the second is the work of

purification that maintains difference and contradictions. The hybrids are those which the constitution forbids yet continues to proliferate. The modern constitution forbids hybrids, because it is premised on the re-creation and the designation of two distinct ontological zones, nature/culture, West/Non West. The constitution continues to proliferate hybrids, for without the practice of translation there will be no reason to purify. See Bruno Latour, *We Have Never Been Modern*, trans. by Catherine Porter (Harvard University Press, 1993).

7.   See for example, Lila Abu-Lughod, *Remaking Women: Feminism and Modernity in the Middle East* (Princeton University Press, 1998); Mervat Hatem, 'Towards the Development of a Post-Islamist and Post Nationalist Feminist Discourses in the Middle East' in J. Tucker (ed.) *Arab Women: Old Boundaries, New Frontiers* (Indiana University Press, 1993).

8.   See for example Lara Deeb, *An Enchanted Modern: Gender and Public Piety in Shi'i Lebanon*, (Princeton University Press, 2006); Saba Mahmood, *Politics of Piety: The Islamic Revival and the Feminist Subject* (Princeton University Press, 2005). Mahmood both engages with theories of performativity and also departs from them. I will be discussing this later in the chapter.

9.   See for example Lamia Ben Youssef Zyzafoon, *The Production of the Muslim Woman: Negotiating Text, History and Ideology* (Lexington Books, 2004).

10.   Haideh Moghissi, *Feminism and Islamic Fundamentalism: The Limits of a Postmodern Debate* (Zed Books, 1999), p. 84.

11.   This scholarship is quite wide ranging. For example, see, Fadwa El Guindi 'Feminism comes of Age in Islam' in Suha Sabbagh (ed.) *Arab Women: between Defiance and Restraint* (Massachusetts, 2003); Fatima Mernissi, *The Veil and the Male Elite*.

12.   Mernissi, *The Veil and the Male Elite*; Leila Ahmed, *Women and Gender in Islam: Historical Roots of a Modern Debate* (Yale University Press, 1992).

13.   Mernissi, *The Veil and the Male Elite*, pp. 19–20.

14.   Ahmed, *Women and Gender in Islam*, p. 239.

15.   Ibid: 238.

16.   Ibid: 238.

17.   Deniz Kandiyoti 'Contemporary Feminist Scholarship and the Middle East' in Deniz Kandiyoti (ed.) *Gendering the Middle East* (I.B.Tauris, 1996), p. 10.

18.   I am well aware of the pitfalls in generalising modernity as an exclusive possession of the West, or that *all* Western modernisation projects were imposed to the detriment of Islamic cultures. However, I am here referring to modernity's civilisational mission that was mobilised for the expansion of colonial rule and which privileged Europe as the insinuator of this global process. The consequence of this was the production of a body of knowledge about the Orient supported by social scientific, anthropological and historical research that positioned Europe as the rational modern entity in relation to the barbaric East and the religion of Islam.

19.   Zayzafoon, *The Production of the Muslim Woman*, p. 15

20. This critique is very much influenced by Talal Asad's response to Caton Yemeni. Talal Asad states: 'My concern is in the conditions of possibility of religion than in its substance. I refer primarily to its constitutive processes (that which makes the concept of religion) and its regulative processes (that which enables practices to be properly religious). There is a complicated relationship between the two that certainly includes coercive force, but not always and never only. Talal Asad, 'Responses', in David Scott and Charles Hirschkind (eds) *Powers of the secular modern: Talal Asad and His Interlocutors* (Stanford University Press, 2006); Talal Asad, *Genealogies of Religion* (John Hopkins University Press, 1993).

21. Mernissi, *The Veil and the Male Elite*, p. 25.

22. Moghissi, *Feminism and Islamic Fundamentalism*, p. 40.

23. Ibid: 37.

24. Sadik Jalal al-'Azm, 'Orientalism and Orientalism in Reverse' in A. L. Macfie *Orientalism: A Reader* (New York University Press, 2000), pp. 217–38.

25. Zayzafoon, *The Production of the Muslim Woman*, p. 2.

26. Nadje Al-Ali, *Gender Writing/Writing Gender: The representation of women in a selection of modern Egyptian literature* (The American University in Cairo Press, 1994), p. 12.

27. Ibid.

28. Kandiyoti, 'Contemporary Feminist Scholarship and the Middle' East, p. 5.

29. Lila Abu-Lughod, 'Orientalism and Middle East Feminist Studies', *Feminist Studies* 27.1 (Spring, 2001: 103).

30. Elizabeth Fernea and Basima Bezirgan (eds.) *Middle Eastern Muslim Women Speak* (University of Texas Press, 1976).

31. Abu-Lughod, 'Orientalism and Middle East Feminist Studies', p. 105.

32. Mahmood, *Politics of Piety*, p. 17.

33. Abu-Lughod, 'Orientalism and Middle East Feminist Studies', p. 105.

34. Lila Abu-Lughod, 'The Romance of Resistance: Tracing Transformations of Power Through Bedouin Women', *American Ethnologist* 17.1 (February 1990: 41). Also cited in Mahmood, *Politics of Piety*, p. 8.

35. Mahmood, *Politics of Piety*, p. 9.

36. Ibid.

37. Ibid: 22.

38. Lara Deeb, *An Enchanted Modern: Gender and Public Piety in Shi'i Lebanon* (Princeton. University Press, 2006), p. 5.

39. Deeb's exploration of a Muslim subject's negotiation between the modern and the pious as a marker of change, could also be regarded as a move beyond the registers of submission vs. resistance. I particularly disagree with Mahmood's putting together processes of change along acts of resistance, disregarding that 'organic dialogism' also involves change (*pace* Bakhtin 1975; see also Young 1995).

40. Mahmood, *Politics of Piety*, p. 166.

41. Kandiyoti, 'Contemporary Feminist Scholarship and the Middle East', p. 8.

42. Margot Badran, 'Independent Women: More Than a Century of Feminism in Egypt', in Judith Tucker (ed.) *Arab Women: Old Boundaries, New Frontiers* (Indiana University Press, 1993), p. 130.

43. Moya Lloyd, *Beyond Identity Politics: Feminism, Power and Politics* (Sage, 2005), p. 15.

44. Ahmed, *Women and Gender in Islam*, p. 151.

45. Leila Ahmed presents an illuminating discussion on Cromer's rhetoric on the veil, citing several sources. See, for example, Earl of Cromer, *Modern Egypt*, vol. 2 (Macmillan, 1908); A. B. Guerville, *New Egypt* (London, 1906).

46. Uma Narayan, 'Essence of Culture and a Sense of History: A Feminist Critique of Cultural Essentialism' in Narayan and Harding (eds). *Decentering the Center: Philosophy for a Multicultural, Postcolonial and Feminist World* (Indiana University Press, 2000), p. 82.

47. Ibid: 84.

48. Lila Abu-Lughod, 'Contentious Theoretical Issues: Third World Feminism and Identity Politics', in *Women's Studies Quarterly, Internationalizing the Curriculum* 26.3/4 (Fall–Winter 1998): 25.

49. See Chris Weedon, *Feminist Practice and Poststructuralist Theory* (Blackwell Publishing, 1997). For a good discussion on the limits of poststructuralist critique for feminist politics, see Susan Lurie, *Unsettled Subjects: Restoring Feminist Politics to Poststructuralist Critique* (Duke University Press, 1997).

50. See for example, Reina Lewis and Sara Mills, *Feminist Postcolonial Theory: A Reader* (Routledge, 2003).

51. See, for example, Sandra Harding, *Whose Science? Whose Knowledge? Thinking From Women's Lives* (Cornell University Press, 1991); Donna Harraway *Primate Visions: Gender, Race, and Nature in the World of Modern Science* (Routledge, 1989; Verso, 1992), Susan Hekman, 'Feminization of Epistemology, Gender and the social sciences' in Maria Falco (ed.) *Feminism and Epistemology: Approaches to Research on Women and Politics* (Haworth Press, 1987). See also Jane Duran, *Knowledge in Context: Naturalized Epistemology and Sociolinguistics* (Rowman and Littlefield, 1994).

52. See Harding, *Whose Science?*

53. Rosi Braidotti, 'The Politics of Ontological Difference' in Teresa Brenan (ed.) *Between Feminism and Psychoanalysis* (Routledge, 1989), pp. 89–106.

54. Uma Narayan, 'The Project of Feminist Epistemology: Perspectives from a NonWestern Feminist', in *Feminist Theory Reader: Local and Global Perspectives*, Carole McCann and Seung-Kyung Kim (eds) (Routledge, 2003), p. 308.

55. Ibid: 309–400.

56. See, for example, bell hooks, *Ain't I a Woman? Black Women and Feminism* (London, 1981); Gayatri Spivak, *Outside in the Teaching Machine* (Routledge, 1993); Patricia Hill Collins, *Black Feminist Thought: Knowledge, Consciousness, and Politics* (Routledge, 2000).

57. Harding, *Whose Science?*, p. 108.
58. Santiago Castro Gomez, 'The Social Sciences, Epistemic Violence and the Problem of the 'Invention of the Other'', in Saurabh Dube and Ishita Banerjee-Dube (eds) *Unbecoming Modern: Colonialism, Modernity and Colonial Modernities* (New Delhi, 2006), p. 218.
59. Ibid.
60. Lila Abu-Lughod, 'Orientalism and Middle East Feminist Studies', *Feminist Studies* 27.1 (Spring, 2001): 106.
61. Rosi Braidotti, 'The Politics of Ontological Difference' in Teresa Brenan (ed.) *Between Feminism and Psychoanalysis* (Routledge, 1989), p. 100.
62. Ibid: 102
63. See Luce Irigaray, *This Sex Which is not One*, trans. by Catherine Porter (Cornell University Press, 1985); Luce Irigaray, *The Ethics of Sexual Difference*, trans. by Carolyn Burke and Gillian C. Gill (Continuum, 2003).
64. Diana Fuss, *Essentially Speaking: Feminism, Nature and Difference* (Routledge, 1989), p. 118.
65. Rosi Braidotti, 'The Politics of Ontological Difference', p. 103.
66. Minh-Ha, 'Cotton and iron', p. 327.
67. Ibid: 329.

Bibliography

Abu-Lughod, Lila (2001) 'Orientalism and Middle East Feminist Studies', *Feminist Studies* 27.1: 101–13.
—— (1998) 'Contentious Theoretical Issues: Third World Feminism and Identity Politics', *Women's Studies Quarterly, Internationalizing the Curriculum* .26.3/4 (Fall-Winter): 24–29.
—— (1998) *Remaking Women: Feminism and Modernity in the Middle East*, New Jersey: Princeton University Press.
—— (1990) 'The Romance of Resistance: Tracing Transformations of Power Through Bedouin Women', *American Ethnologist* 17.1: 41–55.
Al-Ali, Nadje (1994) *Gender Writing/Writing Gender: The Representation of Women in a Selection of Modern Egyptian Literature*, Cairo: The American University in Cairo Press.
Al-'Azm, Sadik. Jalal (2000) 'Orientalism and Orientalism in Reverse' in A. L. Macfie (ed.), *Orientalism: A Reader*, New York: New York University Press, pp. 217–38.
Asad, Talal (1993) *Genealogies of Religion: Discipline and Reasons of Power in Christianity and Islam*, Baltimore: John Hopkins University Press.
Badran, Margot (1995) *Feminists, Islam and Nation*, New Jersey: Princeton University Press.
—— (1993) 'Independent Women: More Than a Century of Feminism in Egypt' in Judith Tucker (ed.), *Arab Women: Old Boundaries, New Frontiers*, Bloomington: Indiana University Press, pp. 129–48.

Bullock, Katherine (2002) *Rethinking Muslim Women and the Veil: Challenging Historical and Modern Stereotypes*, London: IIIT.

Braidotti, Rosi (July 1996) 'Nomadism with Difference: Deleuze's Legacy', *Continental Philosophy Review* 29.3 (July): 305–14.

Braidotti, Rosi (1989) 'The Politics of Ontological Difference' in Teresa Brenan (ed.), *Between Feminism and Psychoanalysis*, London and New York: Routledge, pp. 89–105.

Deeb, Lara (2006) *An Enchanted Modern: Gender and Public Piety in Shi'I Lebanon*, New Jersey: Princeton University Press.

Duran, Jane (1994) *Knowledge in Context: Naturalized Epistemology and Sociolinguistics*, London: Rowman and Littlefield.

El Guindi, Fadwa (2003) 'Feminism Comes of Age In Islam' in Suha Sabbagh (ed.), *Arab Women: between Defiance and Restraint*, Massachusetts: Olive Branch Press, pp.159–61.

Fernea, Elizabeth & Bezirgan, Basima (1976) (eds), *Middle Eastern Muslim Women Speak*, Austin: University of Texas Press.

Fuss, Diana (1989) *Essentially Speaking: Feminism, Nature and Difference*, London and New York: Routledge.

Gomez, Santiago Castro (2006) 'The Social Sciences, Epistemic Violence and the Problem of the "Invention of the Other" ' in Saurabh Dube and Ishita Banerjee-Dube (eds), *Unbecoming Modern: Colonialism, Modernity and Colonial Modernities*, New Delhi: Esha Beteille, pp. 211–27.

Haraway, Donna (1989) *Primate Visions: Gender, Race, and Nature in the World of Modern Science*, London: Routledge.

Harding, Sandra (1991) *Whose Science? Whose Knowledge? Thinking from Women's Lives*, New York: Cornell University Press, 1991.

Hatem, Mervat (1993) 'Towards the Development of a Post-Islamist and Post Nationalist Feminist Discourses in the Middle East' in J. Tucker (ed.), *Arab Women: Old Boundaries, New Frontiers*, Bloomington: Indiana University Press, pp. 29–48.

Hekman, Susan (1987) 'Feminization of Epistemology, Gender and the Social Sciences' In Maria Falco (ed.), *Feminism and Epistemology: Approaches to Research on Women and Politics*, New York: Haworth Press, pp. 65–83.

Hill Collins, Patricia (2000) *Black Feminist Thought: Knowledge, Consciousness and Politics*, Second Edition, London & New York: Routledge.

hooks, bell (1982) *Ain't I a Woman? Black Women and Feminism*, London: Pluto.

Irigaray, Luce (2003) *The Ethics of Sexual Difference,* trans. by Carolyn Burke and Gillian C. Gill, London & New York: Continuum.

——(1985) *This Sex Which Is not One*, trans. by Catherine Porter, New York: Cornell University Press.

Kandiyoti, Deniz (1996) 'Contemporary Feminist Scholarship and the Middle East' in Deniz Kandiyoti (ed.), *Gendering the Middle East,* London: I.B.Tauris, pp. 1–28.

Keddie, Nikki & Baron, Beth (1981) (eds) *Women in the Middle East History, Shifting Boundaries in Sex and Gender,* New Haven: Yale University Press.

Latour, Bruno (1993) *We Have Never Been Modern,* trans. by Catherine Porter, Cambridge: Harvard University Press.

Lewis, Reina and Mills, Sarah (2003) *Feminist Postcolonial Theory: A Reader,* USA and Canada: Routledge.

Lloyd, Moya (2005) *Beyond Identity Politics: Feminism, Power and Politics,* London: Sage.

Mahmood, Saba (2005) *Politics of Piety: The Islamic Revival and the Feminist Subject,* New Jersey: Princeton University Press.

Mernissi, Fatima (1991) *The Veil and the Male Élite: A Feminist Interpretation of Women's Rights in Islam,* trans. Mary Jo Lakeland, Reading MA: Addison-Wesley.

Minh-Ha, Trinh T. (1990) 'Cotton and Iron' in Russell Ferguson et al. (eds.) *Out there: Marginalization and Contemporary Cultures,* New York: New Museum of Contemporary Art and MIT, pp. 327–36.

Moghissi, Haideh (1999) *Feminism and Islamic Fundamentalism: The Limits of a Postmodern Debate,* London: Zed Books.

Narayan, Uma (2003) 'The project of Feminist Epistemology: Perspectives from a Non-Western Feminist' in Carole McCann and Seung-Kyung Kim (eds), *Feminist Theory Reader: Local and Global Perspectives,* London and New York: Routledge, pp. 308–17.

—— (2000) 'Essence of Culture and a Sense of History: A Feminist Critique of Cultural Essentialism' in Narayan and Harding (eds), *Decentering the Center: Philosophy for a Multicultural, Postcolonial and Feminist World,* Bloomington: Indiana University Press, pp. 80–100.

Scott, David & Hirschkind, Charles (2006) (eds) *Powers of the Secular Modern: Talal Asad and His Interlocutors,* Stanford: Stanford University Press.

Spivak, Gayatri (1993) *Outside in the Teaching Machine,* London and New York: Routledge.

Zayzafoon, Lamia Ben Youssef (2005) *The Production of the Muslim Woman: Negotiating Text, History and Ideology,* New York: Lexington Books.

9

Disarticulating Arab Popular Culture: The Case of Egyptian Comedies

Iman Hamam

In 2008 the Lebanese artist Raed Yassin made a video entitled *The New Film*. It comprised of a montage of scenes from Egyptian films. In each, the portrait of President Hosni Mubarak is hanging on the wall of an office in a police station or government building. The door opens and the official is greeted: repeat. The officer slams down the telephone: repeat. The suspect is kicked out of the office: repeat. The suspect pleads with the authority: repeat. Yassin's arrangement of graphic, spatial and verbal matches – with comic effect – is made possible precisely because of the commercial and formulaic nature of mainstream films produced since the early 1980s, made manifest in the irony of the title, the exaggerated acting (highlighted in isolation) and the absurdity of the dialogue. The soundtrack plays a song by eccentric sha'abi singer Shaaban Abdel-Rahim entitled 'Amrika ya Amrika' (America O America). By 2005 – ever sealed in the minds of Egypt's population as the year Hosni Mubarak made some troublesome constitutional amendments and campaigned for election – the comedy actors Alaa Walieddin, Mohamed Hineidi, Hany Ramzy, Ahmed Helmy and Mohamed Saad had become megastars.[1] The decline in cinematic production during the 1990s has been explained in terms of the series of transformations that the entertainment industry underwent during this period – the rise in satellite television, the wide dissemination of pirated discs (VCDs), the 'video clip', the Internet,[2] but these same media forms have also worked to disseminate film culture and the recent wave of investment in Egyptian cinema has largely met with its success in producing comedies, romances and action films.[3] Local critics have derided Saad's films in particular as an insult to cinema, a base popularisation of the medium and the industry at large, which has been ridiculed for its weak attempt to replicate the Hollywood form and narrative content.[4] Despite these objections, Egyptian comedies are massively popular, and with Saad's name now synonymous with his fictional character al-Limby, the film industry has manufactured a 'new' hero.

These films constitute what might be called a sha'abi genre – aligning them with the music culture and modern settings occupied by the 'everyday' city dweller. In their affinity with a satellite-based entertainment industry, Egyptian comedies are formulaic and fragmentary, with awkward beginnings, abrupt endings and unconvincing plots. They are apparently meaningless. Yet the video clip format reproduced in many of the films' musical episodes is also useful in thinking about the 'randomness' of sha'abi culture and how the experience of time has been revised by modern modes of interaction – satellite television, mobile phones and electronic communication. Disparate and contradictory, sha'abi culture is captured in these films in terms of a temporal dislocation, and is marked by a haphazardness of events and the arbitrary fate of both central and marginal characters. In their warped portrayal of the sha'abi predicament, the films provide a distorted view of an already distorted reality. Typical of the comedy genre and its carnivalesque exaggerations, these films highlight common social concerns relating to a compromised masculinity amidst corruption and unemployment. The hero's excessively unruly behaviour mocks social conventions, ruthless authority figures and the disturbed pretensions of class. As with sha'abi music, the popularity of the films provides a sense of cultural approval or authenticity in their apparent subversiveness, while at the same time reaffirming the status quo and maintaining the validity of those same institutions they mock. Social mobility, frequently articulated through physical transmutations and the typical comedy 'body-swap' scenario, is also portrayed through a shift in the performance of an urban vernacular and a contrivance of English and classical Arabic. These comedies refashion convention, musical tradition and their own film history.

Egypt's adoption of the comedy genre has been far from naïve. Deeply rooted in a studio and star system, a number of early performers were characterised according to their comic personae, most notably Ali al-Kassar, Naguib al-Rihani, Shokookoo, Ismail Yassin, Fouad El-Mohandis, Shewikar and (of course) Adel Imam. The resurgence in comedy films over the last ten years easily aligns with previous instances in Egyptian cinema and theatre performances.[5] The films have also re-borrowed the narratives of Abdel-Halim Hafez's romantic musicals popularised during the 1970s.[6] Egyptian comedy is clearly related to national, social and political issues. Class has been so tightly bound with Egyptian cinema at large that it is almost absurd to draw attention to it.[7] For some reason, the 'socially mis-placed person' doesn't want to unstick himself from Egyptian comedies, yet critical discussions of the genre remain largely descriptive.[8] Indeed, it is fascinating to see how these films manifest a series of serious anxiet-ies while generating such a popular form of humour. Like the black and white comedies of previous eras in Egyptian cinema, these comedies have responded to Egypt's new set of escalating social problems, in particular a stark class divide, rampant corruption and a generation of youth con-fronted with unemployment and marginalisation.

Defining popular culture – and popular comedies – presents a series of difficulties.[9] I think that comedy is confusing (and difficult) because it is so absurd. However, from Bakhtin's reflections of comedy in the renais-sance, to Steven Neale's exploration of comedy in film and television, the situations that comedy creates (whether verbal or visual gags, wisecracks, or sketches) still give rise to meaning. Egyptian comedies show manifest similarities with carnival culture and 'grotesque realism'. The films feature 'images of the body…in an extremely exaggerated form': disguise, scatol-ogy, fragmentation, and distortion, the breakdown in social norms and propriety and associations with 'the street'.[10] Comedy is, as Bakhtin makes clear, inherently deviant. Comedy abandons the respectable – and the rul-ing classes that define it – in favour of the 'deviant classes and their lives'. It situates 'all kinds of impropriety' associated with those whose 'power [is] limited and local, and whose manners, behaviour and values were consid-ered by their betters to be either trivial, vulgar, or both'.[11] This affiliation with the popular classes clearly resonates in the Egyptian context. In an ongoing spirit of street festivities and public celebrations, none of the films appears without musical interludes in which the heroes perform in com-munal gatherings. It is perhaps no coincidence, then, that recent scholarly writing has defined the term 'sha'abi' almost exclusively with reference to a particular style of music.[12] By extension, the definition of sha'abi cannot be applied to film without bringing with it these musical associations. Sha'abi films then, like sha'abi music, are films 'of the people' but, as Hall warns, 'just as there is no fixed content to the category of "popular culture", so there is no fixed subject to attach to it – "the people".[13] There is, perhaps, a sha'abi genre, but this is also a 'ventriloquised' version of the 'manners and customs' of the Egyptian people in 'traditional quarters', produced by elites within a culture industry that is secure in the mass production of its ideologies. The phenomenon of Egyptian comedies relates to the 'culture of the oppressed, the excluded classes' – the 'labouring classes'.[14] At the same time, it is able to mock class conventions and situate them in inappropriate settings. Popular cultures and comedy both have a capacity for both 'containment and resistance'.[15]

In an atmosphere of stark alienation, physical proximities, language and dress differentiate class lines most severely. The 'hero' in these films is frequently downtrodden, unemployed and in need of money. Unlikely inversions of class, gender and socio-political boundaries are common. To draw even broader strokes, the protagonists are all unfortunate, endearing and simple minded. Their masculinity is always put into question. They are simultaneously (and not paradoxically) both cowards and thugs. Mohamed Saad first appeared as al-Limby in *al-Nazir* (The Headmaster, Sherif Arafa, 2000) at his own wedding. His bride passes round a tray of joints while he belly dances with a bottle of beer on his head. Reference to the character within the film seems to allude to a seemingly already established legendary and 'saya3'[16] (street wise, tough guy, or cool deviant) status. Following *Ambulance 55* (in which Saad acted alongside Ahmed Helmy), *al-Limby* (2002) has Saad in the central role.[17] Mostly episodic, the film is generally about al-Limby's struggle to find enough money to pay off his debts and marry his girlfriend. His best friend, Bach (Hassan Hosny) is a violinist with whom he spends his evenings smoking hash. His mother Faransa (Abla Kamel) is a feisty no-nonsense-type widow who runs a local bicycle rental shop. Each of al-Limby's attempts to make meaningful cash fail and just as it looks as though his girlfriend's father has managed to sabotage their relationship, the families agree to set up the couple's wedding so that they can receive as much gift money as possible. Al-Limby is generally drunk, stoned, dishevelled, demented and despairing. In *al-Baily Ballak* (You Know Who/You Know What, 2003) al-Limby ends up in jail after attempting to steal back his inheritance from a greedy paternal uncle. He escapes (almost by mistake) and crashes into the car of his prison warden, Riyad El-Manfalouti. Following the collision, the two bodies are confused in emergency room surgery and al-Limby's brain is placed in the warden's body. He is persuaded to pretend that he is actually the prison warden; moves into his mansion, falls in love with his wife and ultimately restores order to the corruptible institution of which he is in charge. Such unlikely inversions of class, gender and socio-political boundaries are common. These comedies reveal that social roles and positions are composed of distorted styles, behaviours and modes of speech, and that these can be feigned, mocked, and interchanged.

In *3okal* (2004), Saad plays two roles, his own mother 'Atata' and a downtrodden car body repairman, '3okal', who half way through the film accidentally (he is drunk) falls asleep in a coffin that ends up being transported to Turkey. When there is no physical transmutation, there is instead a change of the entire setting – he stays the same, but his surroundings alter dramatically. He wakes up disoriented and lost, but is luckily taken in by an Egyptian (again Hassan Hosny) who has been living in the country for several years. He falls in love, opens a small business, escapes death at the hands of a mafia-style gang and gets married. In *Booha* (2005), Saad travels from Qalubiya to Cairo to find a rich butcher who is in possession of his inheritance. He ends up caught in a battle between a powerful butcher, Ma31im Farag (Hassan Hosny), and a young girl, Kotta, and her mother, Sitt Halawiyat (Libliba). The women take him in. He falls in love with Kotta, and is employed by the police to work undercover in order to expose the corruption of the powerful Ma3alim. He escapes false imprisonment and gets married. In *Katkoot* (2006), he narrowly escapes death, as prescribed by the village matriarch, when he is kidnapped by the police and trained to impersonate a renowned arms dealer named Youssef Khoury, who is planning to blow up a central Cairo metro station. Saad's drink/drug induced, or otherwise mental state, brings him in conflict with figures of authority, power and patriotism. Rituals and taboos are materialised and mocked. The films feature a wedding brawl, obscene bodily functions, mistaken identities and cross-dressing.[18]

Despite a sense off continuity across texts, many of the films come across as disjointed. The narratives are fragmentary and story lines shift abruptly a third of the way through the film. The tempo is erratic. Why is there such looseness of plot and what does it mean? How can we 'account' for such unconvincing causality? How is this related to Hollywood comedy, which has been called 'capitalistic America's finest cinematic hour', in light of Egypt's specific circumstances?[19] The plot line takes illogical turns, the pacing shifts dramatically, and the endings seem abrupt. This 'use of non-causal forms of motivation and digressive narrative structures' is characteristic of comedies in general. The comic scenes are episodic, 'local, specific, and, often, momentary'.[20] It is likely that these films have been discredited precisely because '[t]hey can exist … as self-contained units, or as units linked loosely into sequential (rather than consequential) strings'.[21] Actors play formulaic roles that reveal a general lack of narrative continuity from one film to the next, with the flow of events at times being retroactive or illogical. In *al-Limby*, Abla Kamel is al-Limby's mother 'Faransa'. In *al-Bailly Ballak* (dubbed *al-Limby 2*), she is the surgeon. Hassan Hosny is his friend Bach in *al-Limby*, and the corrupt prison official, Adham, in *al-Bailly Ballak*.[22] In each film, the love interest starts afresh and ends in marriage with a different woman. This illogicality of continuity in concurrence with character transmutation is sustained within the film texts. Narrative continuity is sacrificed for 'the sake of comic effect'.[23] Such a highly episodic structure is also characteristic of a tradition of orally composed narratives and contemporary forms of music video clips, which have spread so swiftly through the infrastructure of popular culture, especially apt for the programming of satellite television and other media sound bites. Sheila Nayar shows that films with an episodic structure derive meaning through repetition, catering to an audience who rely on memory, rather than those who must resort to textual forms of documentation. Such films present 'the thought processes and personality structures that distinguish a non-writerly mindset and its narrative creations'.[24] Inevitably, engagement in this kind of medium brings about peculiar shifts in the experience of time.

The comedies are steeped in music, song and dance – traditionally viewed as moments in which the film narrative is 'suspended' for the sake of spectacle. These festive moments are central components of the film texts precisely because this is where sha'abi culture is situated. Music and song enable the performers to communicate and connect with 'the people'. Take, for example, the film, named *Qisat* (the story) *al-Hayy* (the district) *al-Sha'abi* (the people) and translated as 'Inner City Story' on the English-subtitled DVD.[25] Importance is deliberately granted to the troupe as a community ('my family, my friends, my neighbours'). The group sit around on the rooftops and smoke hash pipes (goza), drink beer and crack jokes until they pass out. So, in case you were wondering, says the trailer, 'this is who we are: very, very, respectable people'. This is what sha'abi/ popular actually means. The film mocks and mimics what Armbrust has called the 'the presumably low brow culture of the uneducated'.[26] When the group performs (and this is a Melody-channel style musical – so they sing a lot), everybody comes together in the streets to join them. In al-Limby, the song, al-biskileta, culminates in a massive street party. Popular 'street' weddings and funerals comprise appropriations of public space, as mobile tents with stages and chairs are set up around the city and country.[27] In Ayez Haqqi (I Want my Rights, 2004), the wedding is literally set in motion as three parallel lorries drive the bride and groom, their guests, the band and entertainment, around the city. Such ceremonies and occasions in the films mark a sign of public authentication – and authenticity. In Qisat al-Hayy al-Sha'abi, Layali (the Lebanese singer, Nicole Saba) establishes her status as a true inner city 'sha'abi' or 'baladi' woman when she succeeds in performing as a singer and dancer on the wedding circuits. Her person is differentiated across lines of musical reference, dress style, and physical location. It isn't strange that she is so blatantly out of place (the peroxide hair, the tight dress, etc.) because the narrative is precisely about authenticating her presence. This culminates in a street fight between her and another woman living in the area. The showdown is verbal rather than physical. In the final song, she declares: 'Baladi is going to win. Not European, not Western ... I'll be saideeya [upper Egyptian woman], an Alexandrian, a Cairean, a rural girl, a 'chique' [stylish] girl'. Comedy bears a strong relation to 'the people'. So, what is it that these films are telling us? If comedy is so popular, then it seems that we, 'the people', like bodies and faces that contort. We laugh at words that come out wrong. We like dancing and joking about shit. We like getting drunk and stoned and dressing up as women. The scenes in these films are not so much shockingly vulgar, as they are pure – for want of a better word – *randomness*.

The wedding scene – a standardised generic component of the comedy – is one such random occurrence which exposes comedic disarray. In al-Limby, the wedding scene at the end is disturbingly illogical and abrupt. Al-Limby and his bride go to their wedding dripping wet after the wedding dress is set on fire. Their belly dancer has an identity crisis. In Karkar the wedding night too carries a sense of heightened melodrama. Like *al-Hayy al-Sha'abi*, *Karkar* also begins with a wedding that ends in a disaster ten minutes into the film. As he showers, Karkar is electrocuted and goes instantly mad, before scaring the wits out of his bride who then jumps out of the window and dies. The mayhem continues throughout the film. There is drink, sex, debauchery, dance, fighting. There is, given the stage and the chairs and the sound system, a ritual public event. This is what has been referred to as a 'lower class life cycle celebration' – as drugs are a lower class life style recreation. These films provide a staging of the sha'abi spectacle, but this is also a studio-manufactured reproduction of public space and the people who inhabit it. Saad 'performs' in all types of public spaces and institutions. Al-Limby works as a bodyguard, a kibda stand vendor, and his mother runs a bicycle rental shop. Reda repairs tyres and Booha is a butcher. In *Wesh Egram* (The Face of Crime, 2006), Taha (Hineidi) works as a pizza delivery boy, a security guard, and a tea boy in a bank. These might be 'traditional' quarters, but the happenings are as Walter Armbrust has put it 'very much part of the modern world'.[28] No list of professions in these films can be exhaustive, but it might be indicative of what constitutes sha'abi culture.

Comedy is comprised of ill-timing, inappropriate behaviour and words – like charging the mourners for their drinks at a funeral or saying 'Happy Birthday' in response to condolences, or even putting up a sign that declares that the deceased is clinically dead. Characters are misplaced and relocated in unlikely settings that make them altogether out of step with themselves and their surroundings. What they wear is 'outlandish', how they move is strange, their public behaviour is 'odd', what they say is jumbled up. They transmute, their bodies are split, disturbed, and are forced to appear in two places at the same time, generating astute jokes of equivocation. In *al-Bailly Ballak*, this is something that is played out in a body swap – something for which Egyptian comedies in previous decades have also shown a liking.[29] It is through accidents, often ones that contain serious physical damage that the comic character 'comes to be'. Enabled by the randomness of narrative structure inherent to the genre, comedy stars can play multiple roles: in 30kal Said plays both Atata and 30kal, and in *Karkar* (2007), he plays four different characters, including Reda, a car repair man with an exceedingly high-pitched voice whose mother forces him to dress up as a woman so that he may marry his rich cousin. Typically of the genre, these comedies also provide opportunities

for actors to perform multiple roles in the same text, to cross dress and
to exhibit a comic crisis of masculinity. A 'men in drag' tradition has
been standard in film comedy also, the latter immortalised in the roles of
Ismail Yasin in *Miss Hanafy* (1953), and Abdel Moniem Ibrahim in *Lady
Sugar* (1960). In *Yana, ya Khalti* (It's Me or My Aunt), Mohamed Hineidi
performs the role of Taymour, a young contrabass player who dresses up
as a baladi sorceress named Khalti (Aunt) Noosa in order to convince
his girlfriend's highly superstitious mother that he is an eligible suitor.
He winds up in the famous Qanatir jail for women and is propositioned
by his own father. He has to deal with the problem of having to be at
two places at the same time.[30] This is as much about intertexuality as it is
about literacy. The films 'show' and 'tell': the characters are often riddled
with grotesque and excessive distortions.

Mohammed Saad, as al-Limby, 30kal, Katkoot, and Karkar, undergoes
dramatic physical transformations. Karkar becomes crazed and demented.
Why? Why does al-Limby have a car accident with his traffic warden? Why
does Katkoot have to become Mister Youssef and go undercover? The answer
is irrelevant. In *Yana, ya Khalti*, Taymour is 'just' a boy who wants to marry
his girlfriend and concocts a series of ploys in order to make that possible.
Katkoot grows hair (a wig), shaves his moustache ('But that's my manhood
you are shaving off! If I shave I'll go backwards/regress. It's what keeps me
straight as I walk ...'), and splutters out words in English. Booha is pulled up
the ranks by Ma31im Farag who gives him a make-over and the 'new look'
of a modern fashionable urbanite and he becomes 'al-Ma3alim', Booha al-
Sabah. Frequently, the shift is 'up', as the character feigns an elevated social
class (or its concurrent empowerment), and the behaviour associated with
it. This is one class masquerading as another, and what Vipin Kumar, writing about Malayalam comic film, has referred to as 'fraudulence'.

> In the comic film, the prevailing notions of social res-pect ... and
> the failure to gain it are factors that force the character to assume
> a fraudulent behaviour. In the beginning itself, the falsity/fraud-
> ulence is disclosed to the viewer through an apparent mismatch
> between his/her manners and the level one expects for his/her
> assumed character. However, the reality of the falsity is not
> revealed to most of the other characters in the film. Within a nar-
> rative, s/he is always split into two: his/her own character and the
> character s/he 'acts'. The fraud does not 'live' his/her own role, but

'acts' the role of someone else who is not literally another person in particular, but a whole social profession or class in general: the fraud imitates the 'myth' of a respected character.[31]

The fraudulence occurs in the open, in that it is clear that this is one class feigning to be another. Through costume and language the characters alter their status – but it remains clear that 'he also does not really possess the dress he wears ... Laughter here means the various possibilities of the mockery and "misuse" of social (elite and upper caste) conventions'.[32] Identity is not an issue, it's the joke. When al-Limby, impersonating Riyad Basha, first meets the inmates, it is obvious that he is not the same person. He is clearly changed. Immediately following the operation, Adham Basha visits his boss in the hospital. Lying in bed, al-Limby sits up and screams: *I am al-Limby!* It is a self-affirmation that leaves little doubt that he is absolutely not Riyad Basha. He is cross-eyed, and an inarticulate fool. Hassan Hosny tries to get him to stop shouting so loudly. He expresses concern with the 'delusion' that Riyad Basha is not himself and attempts to reason with him before conspiring with al-Limby to perform the role of Riyad Basha. He explains to al-Limby that he has undergone a 'body transplant'. The comedy ensues from that: al-Limby's marked difference in behaviour. Katkoot wakes up in hospital following the switching of his body with the real Youssef Khoury, and finds a note from his trainer: *I beg of you, please don't cross your eyes as you speak,* but he can't seem to help it. Through self-affirmation he inflates his own legendary status as a hero who manages to trick the system precisely as he tries to fit in. He is out of place.

The comedy is derived from the different ways in which the heroes become 'men' and negotiate their relationships with (the) Authorities in the context of poverty, corruption and unemployment. All are suspects.[33] Work is informal and subject to the whim of superiors in a long chain of subordination. In *Wesh Egram*, Taha complains to his parents that looking for a job *is* a full time job. His father has been laid off and his son aspires to become a security guard – an urban profession. In the first scene of *al-Limby*, he is stopped by a police general who demands to see his national identity card. He doesn't have one (which is apparently illegal). Instead, he holds a youth club membership card, which the official tears into pieces. This is the criminalisation of all existence. In *Yana, ya Khalti*, both father and son's honour as men is put into question as they are accused of being crooks, while in *Fuul al-Seen al-Azeem* (The Great Fuul of China, 2004), Mohy comes from a family of criminals. In *Booha*, almost every scene culminates in heavily exaggerated violence; the narrative is largely set in the 'butcher's district' in Cairo. He seems to return to the police station throughout the film as though it were some kind of centre of gravity. The officer in charge declares: *This man is so stupid he carries around his cousin's ID* (instead of his own). This kind of randomness confirms that not only has masculinity gone awry, but also that it does so in the context of institutionalised power, in which authority is expressed through excessive aggression.[34] Inasmuch as unemployment impacts on 'manhood', the social inversions that occur in the films pivot around institutionalised crime. Through fraudulence, the characters perform the role of the institutionalised authority: frequently a non-sensical, ruthless and highly-strung figure. *Wesh Egram* features an interrogation scene in which Taha practices his role as a central security officer, parodying scenes that have granted Egypt an international reputation for torture (as well as for mass arrests and the detention of children, political activists, Islamists and protestors).[35] Institutions – police stations, schools, hospitals, and prisons – have a strong presence. As sites where the narrative shifts, and plots thicken, these absurd institutions house corruption and incompetence. In *al-Bailly Ballak* and *Yana, ya Khalti*, both heroes end up in jail. In *3okal*, an entire records office burns down. These are images of a grossly bureaucratic society in which the media typically sensationalises the mundane in its view of the man on the street. In *Bailly Ballak*, al-Limby is interviewed by a television channel for a (fictional) programme entitled *Sabaah el-khir ya gareema* (Good Morning Crime) in which the presenter excitedly announces the presentation of a new inmate and a new crime: *Why don't you work for a living?* He responds: *I don't have time. Why are you a thug? Someone with a friend called Ali Aloowka and Ashraf Kokha – what do you expect me to be? A pilot?*[36] These are institutionalised jokes. The recurrence of scenes on, by, or about television reflects an understanding of what makes a person 'important' and is pertinent to the air of authority around them that is provided by the media. Taymour takes off his Khalti Nossa disguise and confesses his own 'criminality' on the *Hala Show*, live on television. In *Bailly Ballak*, al-Limby delivers a speech to an international press conference on Human Rights, held in the prison:

> *Bism Illah El-Rahman al-Rahim. I would first like to thank the 'human being' who spoke before me. I want to say that I will be*

'sterilizing' [using 3qam instead of 3qab: commenting] *on two points. The first one is al-tasharud al atfal* [homeless, street children]. *I want to say that it is not only a problem here. On the contrary, 'Absolutely'. This homelessness is present on a global level. In Ataba, Midan Abdeen Giza, I would like to direct my speech to the sir in charge of the 'Foot' Committee* [using rigl instead of lagna] *for Human ' showering'* [using homoom: problems instead of hoqooq: rights], *that today the pound beats any id/membership card* [el gineah ghalab al-carneh]. *We have to be a bit more long-sighted. I mean we can start to think about what is this clean/healthy air/atmosphere that this man is talking about. 'Clean air' is, like, difficult. Today, the young boy, regarding homelessness, is holding a plastic bag under the Malek el Saleh Bridge and is sniffing glue* [kolla] *until his face looks like a plimsoll. And then he goes home and sniffs his brother's feet. So where is this clean air going to come from? Sort it out. Find them a solution. Give them homes. Build houses and give them ishta* [cream] *and halawa sandwiches. I want to direct my speech to the 'unwell' mister* [using mass200m instead of mass300l: in charge], *the man in charge of 'Burning' Humans* [using horooq instead of hoqooq al insan: human rights], *that there have to be ahead of you one of two solutions: either make more houses available, or make more kola* [glue] *available. Wa salaam alaykum wa rahmut allah wa barakatu.*

We think it's funny to mock power and figures of authority. We know they are corrupt, but even though he is directly speaking to an authority, he can only do so while he is feigning empowerment – rendering his efforts and speech ineffective, perhaps not even genuine. Not so in the film's ending, in which the corruption and neglect that al-Limby is responsible for is 'corrected'. As Kumar argues (2008), all comedy is sacrificed for melodrama and it is precisely at the moment when the identity 'crisis' ends and al-Limby becomes 'himself' that the dominant and corrupt institution is 'broken' and exposed. Melodrama takes over and restores 'morality' and 'justice' to the system. Of course, this too is ridiculous. At the end of *Karkar*, he regains his sanity and laments that his own family cheated him in an emotional song *Toz to* (to hell with) *the world*. Again, Kumar (2008: 13–28) observes: '[the] melodramatic "performance" begins where his true representation of a "socially acceptable" profession/role fails'. This break with the comedy in Saad's films is consistent. In *Booha*, he makes a moving speech in the courtroom explaining that he is just a poor man who wanted to get his inheritance. In *Katkoot,* he makes a moving speech in which he declares that he was a coward before, but he is willing to die for his country. In *al-Bailly Ballak,* he makes a moving speech in which he declares that the corruption and deceit must end. In all of them, he has real, true tears in his eyes. It's not meant to be funny or ironic at all. In a moving patriotic speech in *Ayiz Haqqi,* Saber al-Tayeb decides *against* literally selling his 'share' of the country (his 'right' as a citizen and member of the sha'ab). These are moments when the films speak for The People. We have problems. We have concerns. Fraudulence addresses corruption in the ultimate melodramatic moment. The fantasy of transmutation provides an acknowledgement of housing problems, unemployment and the 'melodrama' of everyday life in a modern context. The films demonstrate the ways in which people respond to, and engage with, the modern world around them.

If there is anything about al-Limby that strikes the viewer, it is his manner of speaking, his performance. The language he uses is 'coarse, unrefined'.[37] Different modes of articulation are situated (expressed) in the physiognomy of the characters/performers themselves. Ismail Yassin was famous for his big elastic mouth. In Saad's case, the demented, distorted manner in which he speaks is a central feature of the texts. Never more so than in *al-Bailly Ballak* in which, shortly after the operation, al-Limby stands in front of a mirror and examines his face. He expresses immediate surprise, and exclaims: *Have they cut my lip off or what? Where has my lip gone?* He looks more closely into the mirror and searches for his lip in vein. His eyes look for it. His nose looks for it. His eyes look for it again. To no avail, he declares: *It's disappeared completely!* More contortions. *How is this possible? Is it possible for a lip to just fly off like that?* Why is the disappearance of this man's lip a necessary part of the transformation that occurs following the operation? Katkoot legitimates his status as Youssef Khoury in a song, which states: *I've had the forensic examination* (bil tibb shara3y) *and they have opened up my throat* (or made me open my mouth/throat – wa bi fat7 zoori). *I am, I am, I am Youssef Khoury.* The transformation has to manifest itself on his person and the way he speaks. This form of 'linguistic humour [is] ... the product of linguistic or cultural ignorance, some kind of physical impediment, deafness, for instance, or a stammer or an uncontrollable psychological propensity for mixing metaphors, perhaps, or for mispronunciation' showing a 'disturbance in the communication process'.[38]

The films are rife with verbal insults, the language of the 'street', and classical Arabic itself, are often the brunt of the jokes made, simultaneously mocking and mimicking the 'ideologically conditioned perception of sharp differentiation between a written classical language and a spoken colloquial'.[39] Not only are these films meaningful, they are, in their humour and performance of the comedy, sophisticated in their manner of articulation. It is not clear whether al-Limby is very, very stoned all the time, or has a speech impediment, or actually is using very clever and specific distortions of particular words. Feigning to be of another class is usually about how you speak. The fraudulent process is so obvious (the difference between class behaviour so marked) that the impostor attempts (and fails) to alter his manner of speaking in order to compensate. Al-Limby, standing before the prison inmates for the first time acting as the warden, blurts:

> *You are the lowest/dirtiest of society, the children of the insect.*
> *Donkey! Don't think that the accident has had an effect on me*
> [dimaghi – my head/brain]. *On the contrary. 'Absoluootley'. I*
> *had an effect on the accident. The accident gave me a high* [again:
> dimagh] *and a strong high as well [wa dimagh gamdah]. So now*
> *I have two heads* [dimagheen]. *In long summary* [bil mukhtasar
> il-mozeed], *if you respect the law, you will be my friend and loved*
> *one and equal. You have no idea who Riyad el-Bantalony* [liter-
> ally: trousers]. *I've taken my heart out and replaced it with a box*
> *of tar!*

Katkoot also changes his manner of speaking. Following the switch, 'Youssef Khoury' leaves the hospital and yells aggressively at his driver. *I've been waiting here for an hour. People (dead people) have been coming in and out, and I have been standing here watching them.* He throws his bag at him and then reprimands him for coming in the limousine. *Stupid nonsense, low manners and rudeness.* (The driver has said nothing). He enters the hotel and declares (in English). 'I am very busy, very, very busy'. To act rich is to act arrogant and pretentious. Pretending to be a rich Gulf Arab, Taymour pays the con-sorcerer, Bashandi, a visit. He enters the 'clinic' and asks his two assistants: *Are these poor people* (masakeen)? *Then get out the money. Distribute my money.* His generosity is obscenely excessive. He asks Bashandi: *Have you got a watch? Have you got a car?* He gestures to his assistant to give him both before they begin the consultation. He confesses to ruthlessly killing his wife and son merely because he suspected them of ill intent. Khalti Noosa wields her power from her ability to communicate with her two fake, just as she is fake, spirits. Through the fraudulent process that pushes the narrative forward, language plays a crucial role in the delineation of class and status.

While in the past classical cinema employed a vernacular that promoted a national culture, today's films are consolidating an urban slang that localises classical and non-Egyptian references. The characters are not only articulate they are *vernacu*late. Written text, usually in classical form, is written in Egyptian dialect. In *The Great Fuul of China,* an elderly Chinese woman holds up cards, giving Mohy (Hineidi) instructions to poison a judge in an international cooking competition. When he objects, she holds up a card that reads: *Ikhras qata3 lisanak* (shut your mouth). This is an elderly Chinese woman who is communicating silently through text, in Egyptian 'street style' (perhaps even 'homie') Egyptian Arabic. In *Yana, ya Khalti,* Taymour and his girlfriend are first seen on a felucca sailing the Nile, both playing a classical tune on the contrabass and clarinet. Once they have completed their performance, Taymour, exalted with the recital, declares: *I feel like eating Hawawshy* (which is a greasier and altogether rougher version of a Cornish pasty, made with minced meat and onions and spices). In many films, classical music references are made in 'vulgar' contexts. Drunk and stoned, al-Limby staggers home trying to recite a classic song by Omm Kulthoum. This is what drugs do to a person's speech. He can't get the words quite right. The vernacularisation is complete when, at his wedding, he performs a remix sha'abi version of her song *al-Hobb eh.* In *Katkoot,* the saidiee and his cousin, Ghareeb, hum the music of an Omm Kulthoum song that they cannot get out of their heads. He plays the pipe of a goza as though it were a flute. Derived from mispronunciations, miscommunications and general word play, the films target classic musical or literary references. *Al-Limby's* character is, like the sha'abi music it parallels, perceived as unintelligible to elite audiences. Booha has to repeat himself because he is persistently not understood, and cannot understand what is being said to him. However, as the speech about street children above shows, these incomprehensible statements do mean something, after all. This is also manifest in the adoption of English words.

Jokes delivered through language are also jokes *about* language. The fraudulence takes place in an 'oral universe'.[40] The mispronunciations are deliberate. The comedy characters can speak English and are aware of its local currency. Their references are derived from a modern setting in which Egyptians are exposed and interacting with language on a number of levels: television, cinema, tourism, and pay-as-you-go mobile phones. Call it globalisation, call it China, whatever. Atata, the old hag of a mother in *3okal*, sits in a circle of women and laments the disappearance of her son. *For the dead, people wear black, for the living, people wear white. But what do you wear for the missing? Adidas? Adidas?* In other instances, the references are distorted back into Arabic. As al-Limby borrows the words of love being exchanged at the table beside him, his repetition of '*Believe me, believe me*' is turned into '*boloubeef, boloubeef*' (corned beef). By targeting a specific manner of speaking, the humour that adopts English words also targets the pretensions associated with the language. In *Katkoot*, the woman who is 'picked up' in a bar by Youssef Khoury orders a 'Black Label with soda'. He exclaims: *You took the drink right out of my mouth!* (As he was going to order the same thing) *It was on my lips.* She adds: *And 2 shalemon* (straws). *Will you take a shalemon?* He replies: *No I don't want to ruin my appetite. I heard that recent research has revealed that it brings on headaches. It's better to get the pill version.* As Armbrust explains: 'humour comes at the expense of the English, not at the expense of the language'.[41] So it seems not to be so irrelevant or meaningless, then, that al-Limby's name is derived from a British General, Sir Edmund Henry Hynman Allenby (1861–1936). Wikipedia holds that he was nicknamed the 'Bloody Bull' because of his physical stature.[42] His manner of ruling was one which inspired confidence, though it was especially cruel towards his subordinates. So, whether the viewer is informed or not, the comment remains articulated in that an English general is turned into a local – and somewhat demented – hero. Maybe al-Limby doesn't have a speech impediment (or defect) after all. A tourist asks: *Do you speak English?* Al-Limby replies: *Yes. I am donkey.* Who is mocking whom? His mother interjects: *Ana ismi* (my name is) *Faransa. You dunt tunderstand wala tunderstand wala ta3mili feeha ghabiya.* (Don't pretend you don't understand) *Get out the dollars.* And to al-Limby: *Collect their money, boy.*

But the most wicked reference to the modern vernacular mode occurs at the end of *al-Limby*, when the belly dancer at his wedding has an existential crisis prior to her performance. Horrified at the sight of the rowdy crowd, she says she feels that she is not understood. *Sir, I am not a dancer in the traditional sense of the word. I perform expressive dance*

(literally: communication through movement) *These people won't understand what I am going to do. These are drunk people. All they want is for
a naked woman to dance to any drum beat.* She is certain that nobody
in the crowd has an email address, or *even an ICQ account.* She dances
professionally because she wants nothing more than to be able to afford a
better deal on her mobile phone. She never wants to hear the words: *You
have run out of credit.* He tries to engage, to which she responds:

> *Inta hadritak bitikallim kidda leh?* [Why are you talking like
> that?]. *Gihaz il natq a3ndak – your pronunciation mechanisms*
> [physiologically speaking] ... *Yaani, alfaz – I mean your manner
> of speaking. Tab fe doctor 'phonetics' kwayis awi arafo* [I know a
> really good phonetics doctor]. *Ideeni 'el-email address' beta3ak
> wa'ana aba3tlak nimreto. Give me your email address and I'll
> send you his number. I am Zizi@hotmail dot com.*
>
> Al-Limby: *Yanhar azrak* [oh hell]. *They've brought me a pre-
> senter from Nile TV. Look here, good woman, I will leave you to
> get rid of the illness and diseases that you have, because one way
> or another, you will dance. How, I don't know. You could smoke
> a couple of pipes. Turn around in a bottle of beer. Do whatever
> you want, but what's important is that I come back and find you
> sweating it out and rolling about on the stage.*

Some events just occur as though in a vacuum. This episode is one such
occasion. In two shots following the pseudo-monologue above Zizi, we get
a close up of her hand and then a long shot of her on stage with the wedding
guests in the foreground. No audience reaction shots are provided. There
is no follow-up or recollection of the event. The scene just ends – *toz* to
her expressive dance. *Toz* to her expressing anything. People are random.
Buildings are random. Time is random. The temporality of these narratives
is already in 'disarray' because of their episodic and fragmentary nature,
more so because it describes a real, general state of existence. The opening
shot is of al-Limby throwing a cigarette into his mouth and then closely
examining his wristwatch before using it to light up (it's a novelty device).
How is time 'spent'? How does the sense of waiting for something to happen inform the narrative endings? Isn't it strange that the endings of epic
scale cultural texts are, as Armbrust has shown with the comedy drama
School of Troublemakers, 'forgotten'.[43] How come the happy ending is also
presented as the most ridiculous of all possible endings, rather than the

most 'realistic' or likely? In *al-Limby*, a montage sequence of al-Limby, now married with a son, is standing beside a chalkboard and teaching him the alphabet. This is al-Limby – remember? In both English and Arabic the arrangement is, of course, distorted. This is not the correct alphabet and al-Limby's pronunciations, or even his recognition of the letters, is incorrect, but that doesn't matter. The image of the future is as fictional as it is unlikely. Katkoot dreams of completing his passport application before he gets killed so that he can travel to the Gulf and secure his future. Again, it's illogical. In *Karkar,* a faceless figure, the owner of a Nile-side casino, goes up in flames. *Isn't that your father?* al-Hinawy asks the tea waiter. No explanation is offered, again as though in a vacuum. This is the world we live in, one of video clips and mobile phone text messages, of phone credit running out. In *Yana, ya Khalti*, Taymour, in utter despair at being forced to wear his father's suit, tries to explain that the jacket is 'style adeem (old)' and pointing out his fashionable hair spikes and the amount of hair gel he has put in, asserts: *I am Funky!* Following Taymour's live-on-air confession, the 'real' Khalti Noosa takes over the *Hala Show* studio and, addressing the spirits with whom she is in communication, declares: *Now we've got control of the airwaves!* She centres the camera on her face.

How knowing are these films? Does the 'power' of Egyptian comedy lie in its specificity to Egypt, to the in-jokes it makes, which are then dissipated in Egyptian society. Is the ignorance of the Western or non dialect-speaking viewer necessarily part of its process? Is it silly and 'meaningless' simply because it is an in-joke that mocks those who don't understand it? Culture is best shown in the proverbial market – coffee shops (the newer ones play pop music), dry cleaners, boutiques, phone shops, and grocery stores, they all carry a television screen. It is possible that mall culture and hypermarkets are also eroding this screen presence, but these reference points constitute the popular imagination, how people spend their time, and the places they inhabit. Call it leisure time, boredom, body building or work. Perhaps this vernacularisation also presents an idea of self-reflexivity within Egyptian culture, and a debasement that underpins Egypt's mechanisms of survival. The word sha'abi's double meaning is used in music 'as both a marker of authenticity intrinsic to national identity, and at the same time as a marker of social traits undesirable for a modern sensibility – to create a rich tradition of public dissent and cultural commentary'.[44] So, in viewing these films, are questions of authenticity also sticky ones, especially when claims are being made about who understands what humour and what licence we are given to find something amusing? This is equally tricky when thinking about how we explain cultural 'phenomena', and to whom. Who are we to be explaining anything anyway? Maybe this is what I see because I have a speech impediment of my own. Maybe it is reassuring to think that others, even if they are fictional characters, have one too. In either case, there is a communication process, *you tunderstand walla you dunt tunderstand*. It wouldn't be 'funny' if it were articulated in the 'correct' way.

Can we rush to conclude that this too, then, might constitute what Hassan Khan calls a 'breath of hope in a largely stultified deadly bourgeois culture that constantly betrays its anxiety and class aspirations in every pop video clip, every mobile phone advertisement'?[45] If *Karkar* is anything to go by, then this is far from 'canned and neutralized demotic populism',[46] but they are certainly mainstream commercial products. Kumar, whose filmic references remain obscure to me, makes another resonant point: 'The viewers' laughter, which makes them perhaps forget themselves, cannot be then ruled out simply as that which lulls them into resignation. If it means resignation, it is a resignation from the bourgeois rupture, which dumps somewhere those objectives of modernism articulated through the cinematic apparatus'.[47]

Again, comedy 'works' because it is understood. Kinds of humour are commonly attributed to particular cultures, but they also draw on a storehouse of comic sketches that are easily familiar to non-Egyptians. There is, of course, something decidedly Egyptian about the comedies discussed here. As we are flailing for universalism, comedy waves it in our faces at the same time as it laughs at our desire to 'understand' its concepts. We have to be careful: 'Any attempt to read the level of irony that they are employing inevitably implicates the reader: the more you read their jokes ironically the more the aggression in them is turned back on you'.[48] Comedy mocks us, even, because we don't know who 'we' are, or because we suspect – or it suspects – that we do. We act as if we know who we are and comedy calls us in on this joke of presumptions.

Notes

1. The films are widely known and understood as reference points for Egyptians and have consolidated star personae for both mega stars and secondary roles in Egyptian cinema; stars frequently become lead performers following a series

of minor and secondary roles. Many of what I refer to as 'stars' are derived from the popularised Egyptian form of reference to these figures as *nogoom*, who earn around 5 million LE for each film, rather than what Richard Dyer would call 'stars'. In 2001, Hineidi held first and fourth place in Egypt's top ten biggest grossing films of the year, Al-Limby held first place in 2002. The summer of 2005 saw the release of three comedy films: *Yana, ya Khalti* (Me or Aunt, Said Hamed), starring Heniedi; *Booha* (Rami Imam) starring Mohamed Saad, *Al-Sifara fil Imara* (The Embassy in the Apartment Building, Amr Arafa) starring Adel Imam. 'Egypt Box Office Index 2002–2009'. *Box Office Mojo International*. Available at http.//www.boxofficemojo.com/intl/egypt/ See also Fouad Al-Tohami, 'Rules of the Game', *Egypt Almanac: The Encyclopaedia of Modern Egypt*, 2003 edn, p. 76.

2. Film critics and journalists held the 1997 film *Ismailiya Return Ticket* (directed by Karim Diaaeddin), a star-driven narrative featuring pop singer Mohamed Fouad (with Mohamed Hineidi in the supporting role) and *An Upper Egyptian in the American University* (1998, Said Hamed, starring Hineidi) accountable for the resurgence of the film industry. See Rehab El Bakry, 'Reeling Them in', *Business Monthly*, July 2006. Available at http.//www.mafhoum.com/press9/283C34.htm; Mohamed Assyouti, 'A Consumerist Amnesia' *Al-Ahram Weekly* 16–22 June 2005. Available at http.//weekly.ahram.org.eg/2005/747/cu4.htm.

3. There is, of course, a difficulty in defining genres, given that their boundaries are so fluid and permeable. In a publication entitled 'Genre in Egyptian Cinema' the author acknowledges the lack of any 'pure' genres. Ali Abu Shadi, 'Genre in Egyptian Cinema' in *Critical Film Writing from the Arab World*, Alia Arsoughly (ed. and trans.) (Quebec: World Heritage Press, 1996), p. 85.

4. The journalist Hani Mostafa commends Mohamed Saad's versatility and performance, but laments the 'absence of a convincing plot and meaningful material', 'A Grotesque Cacophony' *Al-Ahram Weekly* 23–29 August 2007. Available at http.//weekly.ahram.org.eg/2007/859/cu5.htm. The problem does not seem to be that the films are detached from relevant social and political concerns but that the films themselves are 'mindless' – poorly scripted, episodic and 'vulgar'. Walter Armbrust has discussed extensively and demonstrated how important it is to consider how what is understood as 'low brow' culture communicates meanings. See his chapter on 'Vulgarity' in *Mass Culture and Modernism* (Cambridge: Cambridge University Press, 1996) and 'New Cinema, Commercial Cinema, and the Modernist Tradition in Egypt' in *Alif: Journal of Comparative Poetics* 15, *Arab Cinematics: Toward the New and the Alternative* (1995): 81–84. James Twitchell points out that 'We don't need Marxists to tell us that much of what constituted taste [is] based on the separation of classes in a society'. In *Carnival Culture: The Trashing of Taste in America* (New York: Columbia University Press, 1992), p. 18.

5. Theatre is widely understood as bearing the roots of Egyptian cinema and remains a popularised form. Shafik traces what she calls 'Egyptian farce' back to cinema's roots and the first two decades of the twentieth century in theatre

performances, which were known to carry a strong tradition of 'improvisation...'loose plot' and 'mere farce', stating that 'It has been rather verbally oriented, using a lot of jokes and wordplay, and relying on the generally clumsy
behaviour of its protagonists and their schematized personae'. Viola Shafik,
'Egypt' in *Companion Encyclopaedia to Middle Eastern and North African Film*,
Oliver Leaman (ed.) (Taylor and Francis, 2001), p. 51. Drawing from the experience of improvised Egyptian theatre (*al-masrah al-murtajal*), improvisation
techniques are still employed in contemporary comedy films. In reference to
the comedy drama *School of Troublemakers*, Armbrust calls these instances of
improvisation, where the actors 'literally hijacked the script'. In 'Terrorism and
Kabab: A Capra-esque View of Modern Egypt' in Sherifa Zuhur (ed.) *Images of
Enchantment: Visual and Performing Arts of the Middle East* (Cairo: American
University in Cairo Press, 1998), p. 291. Improvisation was also characteristic of
native Arabic drama performed in public spaces, rather than in purpose built
structures. See Mark Bayer, 'The Martyrs of Love and the Emergence of the Arab
Cultural Consumer', *Critical Survey* 19.3 (2007): 18.

6. *Ismailiya Return Ticket* is a romantic musical comedy which structured its narrative according to a traditional 1970s set of films starring Abdel-Halim Hafez.
Not surprisingly, then, these film formulas 'worked' – *Ismailiya Two Way Ticket*
was a star driven narrative, featuring pop singer Mohamed Fouad in a story
that reworked the 'classic' film narratives and starring Abdel-Halim Hafez. In
Andaleeb El-Dokki (The Dokki Nightingale, 2007), Hineidi parodies the Abdel-
Halim Hafez figure, this time as an aspiring singer who can't actually sing, rather
than the Halim character who is typically a talented aspiring singer. Hineidi
also plays the role of his estranged twin brother, a grossly rich Gulf-style busi-
nessman living in the United Arab Emirates. See Joel Gordon, *Revolutionary
Melodrama: Popular Film and Civic Identity in Nasser's Egypt* (Chicago: Middle
East Documentation Centre, 2002), pp. 117–26, for an extensive analysis of
Abdel-Halim's films and his legendary status as the Nightingale.

7. Viola Shafik has examined comedies in terms of their depiction of minorities, the portrayal of Islamic fundamentalism and the emphasis on gender and
class relations in *Popular Egyptian Cinema: Gender, Class, and Nation* (Cairo:
American University in Cairo Press, 2007).

8. On comedy, Ali Abu Shadi states that 'in all its artistic and conceptual levels,
and in its range from the sophisticated to the vulgar, [the comedy film] has
seen many waves of innovation, imitation, and decline, but it has remained a
mainstay of Egyptian cinema since the twenties'. ('Genre in Egyptian Cinema',
p. 96). Writing on Malayalam comic films, Vipin Kumar has pointed out that
'the aesthetic seriousness of realistic themes' – in Egypt's case this would be
the concern of the new realist directors, or *auteurs* such as Youssef Chahine –
'is not the only sign of a politically conscious creativity in filmmaking today'.
Vipin Kumar, 'Politics of Laughter: An Introduction to the 1990s' Malayalam
Popular Comic Film' *South Asian Popular Culture* 6.1 (April 2008): 13.

9. On defining popular culture, see Stuart Hall, 'Notes on Deconstructing the Popular' in *People's History and Socialist Theory*, Raphael Sauel (ed.) (London, Boston, and Henley: Routledge & Kegan Paul). John McCallum states that 'comedy touches, in one way or another, on a vulnerable social nerve. Questions are at stake here concerning difference and power, the negotiation of complex social positions and relations, and different ways of reading the work available to a large heterogeneous audience'. John McCallum, 'Cringe and Strut: Comedy and National identity in Post-War Australia' in *Because I tell a Joke or Two: Comedy, Politics and Social Difference* (London and New York: Routledge, 1998), p. 201. The amount of material on American and British comedy is so vast that, instead, it has been useful to look elsewhere at how condensed views of other comedy films have distilled into a few, more manageable, perhaps, notions. The story of Egyptian comedy might start like this: An American, an Indian and a Russian walk into a bar. Except in this version they walk into an Egyptian coffee shop ...

10. Mikhail Bakhtin, *Rabelais and his World*, translated by Hélène Iswolsky (Bloomington: Indiana University Press, 1984), p. 18. While Bakhtin was looking at a specific instance of Renaissance culture, his analysis has since been used to think about subsequent manifestations of similar tendencies, including nineteenth-century hysteria and the 'crude vernacular tradition' of street performances, feasts and ceremonies that took place in Egypt prior to Napoleon's expedition (Bayar, 18). See Allon While 'Hysteria and the end of carnival: Festivity and bourgeois neurosis' in *The Violence of Representation: Literature and the History of Violence* (Routledge, 1989), pp. 157–70. These features of carnival were also apparent in the bizarre tales of *Alf Layla wa Layla* (1001/Arabian Nights) and *al-Hikayat al-ajiba* (The Wonderful Tales). See Ulrich Marzolph, 'Narrative Strategies in Popular Literature: Ideology and ethics in Tales from the Arabian Nights and Other Collections' *Middle Eastern Literatures* 7.2 (July 2004): 171–82. Roberta L. Dougherty, 'Badi'a Masabni, Artist and Modernist: Egyptian Print Media's Carnival of National Identity' in Walter Armbrust (ed.) *Mass Mediations: New Approaches to Popular Culture in the Middle East and Beyond* (Berkeley, Los Angeles, London: University of California Press, 2000), pp. 243–68, which provides a brilliant analysis of a series of cartoon strips in the 1930s magazine *El-Masri*. Dougherty shows how this mode of 'carnivalesque' transpires throughout the series in which 'nothing happens the way it should'. The strip includes celebrity figures, hysteria and musical interludes, drug taking (hashish, always hashish). As the cartoons in *El-Masri* show, comic occurrences have a lot to do with the setting in which they occur and the language employed.

11. Steve Neale, *Popular Film and Television Comedy* (Florence, KY: Routledge, 1990), p. 12.

12. As a phenomenon, attention has been paid to a series of singers who have popularised the *sha'abi* music genre (Adawiya, Saad El-Soghayar, Shaaban

Abdel Rahim...). See Walter Armbrust, 'The National Vernacular: Folklore and Egyptian Popular Culture' *Michigan Quarterly Review* 31.4 (1992): 525–42; James R. Grippo, 'The Fool Sings a Hero's Song: Shaaban Abdel Rahim, Egyptian Sha'abi, and the Video Clip Phenomenon', *Transnational Broadcasting Studies* 16 (2006). Available at http://www.tbsjournal.com/Grippo.html; Jennifer Peterson, 'Sampling Folklore: The "re-popularization" of Sufi inshad in Egyptian dance music', *Arab Media and Society* 4 (Winter 2008). Available at http://www.arabmediasociety.com/?article=580. See also Hassan Khan, 'Hysteria' in *Dictionary of War* (Presentation available at http://dictionaryof-war.org/concepts/Hysteria). Grippo explains: 'As is the case with its common English translation of "popular", the word "sha'bi" comprises various shades of meaning. It derives from the word "sha'b", meaning "people", and is used variously to imply "populist", "popular" as in enjoying great popularity, and "popular" as in being "of the people" – of being local, vernacular, and from the proverbial "street". "Sha'bi"is also used as a virtual synonym of "folkloric", for example in the context of "sha'bi" or "popular" arts such as folk dancing, the narration of epic tales, and other traditional "folk" genres'. Peterson elaborates: 'Like its counterpart "baladi", an adjective describing "low-class" urban culture of rural origin, and essentially meaning "native" or "cottage-industry", "sha'bi" is held both in high regard and abhorrent disdain depending on who is doing the naming and the context at hand. On the positive side, it is used to suggest authenticity, savvy, cleverness, and an engaged connection to one's humble yet honoured origins and social environment. At the negative end of the spectrum, however, it can imply being poor-quality, grossly impoverished, unsophisticated, and downright uncouth'.

13. Hall: 239.
14. I borrow the term 'labouring classes' from Alison MacEwen Scott's *Division and Solidarities: Gender, Class and Employment in Latin America* (London and New York: Routledge, 1994), pp. 7–8. There is a surprising lack of material about the terminology used to refer to social and economic class in Egypt in reference to informal housing districts ('ashwaiyaat'). In Cairo, residents have been referred to by the same term, as 'ashwaiyeen'. The word literally means 'random'. See Asef Bayat and Eric Denis, 'Who is afraid of ashwaiyyat? Urban change and politics in Egypt', *Environment and Urbanization* 12.2: (October 2000): 185–99. Available at http://eau.sagepub.com/cgi/content/abstract/12/2/185. In Egypt, statistics vary depending whether informal labour has or has not been factored in, as does the nature of the organisational body making the claim. Numbers range between 9 and 23 per cent. Journalists have decried the state of the youth, sitting around coffee shops and loitering on street corners with nothing to do. Graduate certificates are mocked as meaningless pieces of paper while others scramble to find connections for their children to get a job in some company or some office anywhere possible. See Neshmahay Sayed, 'Better Days Ahead' *Al-Ahram Weekly* 28 May–3 June 2009. Available at

http.//weekly.ahram.org.eg/2009/949/ec3.htm and Magda Shahine, 'Confronting Unemployment' *Al-Ahram Weekly* 12–18 Feb. 2009. Available at http.//weekly.ahram.org.eg/2009/934/op22.htm

15. Hall: 228.
16. I use '3' as in the word 'saya3' throughout the chapter to compensate for the Arabic letter and sound 'ع' that have no equivalent in the English language.
17. The film was written by Ahmed Abdallah and directed by Wael Ihsan though, when filming, Saad also had a great deal of input. Ahmed Abdallah has written a number of popular comedies: *Aboud ala el hedoud* (Aboud on the Border, 1999) *El Nazer* (The Headmaster, 2000), *55 esaaf* (Ambulance 55, 2001), *Ibn ezz* (Son of Wealth, 2001), *al-Limby* (2002), *Mido mashakel* (Mido Problems, 2003), *Askar fi el-mu'askar* (Askar at the Camp, 2003), *Ghabi mino fih* (2004), *Fuul al-Seen al-Azeem* (The Great Fuul of China, 2004), *Yana, ya khalti* (2005), *Lakhmet ras* (2006), *Ahlam alfata al tayesh* (Rash Boy Dreams, 2007), *Karkar* (2007), information and credits available at http.//www.imdb.com/name/nm1583960/.
18. In the films that star Ismail Yassin, the comedy is derived from his physical form, his happy-go-lucky character, and the unfortunate situations in which he finds himself; Adel Imam's films have also highlighted the plight of the downtrodden, as the emphasis shifted to the corruption and materialism that emerged as a result of Sadat's Open Door policy during the 1970s, which appears to have encouraged a lack of government accountability, greed and corruption, and a widening class divide. Depictions of a greedy and corrupt nouveau riche became common in Egyptian cinema during the 1980s.
19. Andrew Horton, *Comedy/Cinema/Theory* (Berkley, Los Angeles, London: University of California Press, 1991), p. 15.
20. Neale: 17.
21. Neale: 17.
22. Veteran actors Abla Kamel and Hassan Hosny have become important features of the recent wave of comedy films. During the 1980s and '90s, the two actors performed in films directed by new realist directors: Abla Kamel in Khairy Beshara's *Bitter Day Sweet Day* (1988), and Hassan Hosny in Atef al-Tayeb's *The Bus Driver* (1982) and *Blood on the Pavement*, as well as Mohamed Khan's *Wife of an Important Man* (1987) and *Why Violet*, Radwan al-Kashef (1993) and *Pavement Demons*, Osama Fawzy (1996). They both acted in *Sareq al-Farah* (The Stolen Joy, Daoud Abdel Sayed, 1994) and in several comedy dramas and television serials in 1999, Hosny starred in Sherif Arafa's *Aboud Ala El Hoddod* (starring Alaa Walieddin) and has been a mainstay of comedies ever since. Abla Kamel took the title role as Fanransa in *Khalti* (Aunt) and *Faransa* (2003).
23. Neale: 32.
24. It is through this mode of viewing popular (in Nayar's case, Hindi) cinema that the ghosts of stereotypical plot structure, the recurrence of character types, repetition and borrowing can finally be put to rest. This episodic and cyclical

structure has also been attributed to the literary style of traditionally oral cultures. See David A. Wacks. 'The Perfomativity of Ibn Al-Muqaffa's Kalila wa-Dimna and al-Maqamat al-luzumiyya of al-Saraqusti'. *Journal of Arabic Literature* XXXIV, 1–2: 183.

25. Most films are released in VCD format, the film split onto two discs. Rotana releases 'official' copies of films with subtitles, but their selection is extremely limited. Of the films discussed, only Hayy Sha'abi, Karkar and Andaleeb El-Dokki were purchased as DVDs in Cairo.

26. Armbrust, 'National Vernacular', p. 525.

27. See Omar Nagati, 'Competing Urban Orders in Cairo: A Historical Perspective' Kharita 01: Symposium on Urban Trajectories in Cairo. 16 January 2009. Video of presentation available at http.//v2v.cc/v2v/Omar_Nagati%3A_Competing_ Urban_Orders_in_Cairo%3A_A_Historical_Perspective

28. Armbrust, 'National Vernacular', p. 533. This is again noted by those writing on popular music trends. Grippo states that sha'abi is a 'quintessentially modern concept'. In the *Encyclopaedia of Popular Music of the World* street music, wedding singers and cassette culture are grouped together. Peterson observes that 'mulid songs are also used in more individual, arguably more "modern" ways, as the listening choice of drivers in various forms of public transportation, the soundtracks to outings in horse-drawn carriages, or Nile pleasure boats, or the music selection of friends and family dancing in the living room to entertain each other'.

29. This brain transplant was also generated the narrative of a 1984 film, entitled *Beasts Race*, in which Mahmoud Abdel Aziz is convinced by a rich man who cannot have children to undergo surgery to transplant the part of his brain which controls fertility. The anterior lobe, as the cutting-edge Egyptian scientist (played by former UN Ambassador of Good Will, Hussein Fahmy) calls it, is later called the Canteloupe. The operation leaves Abdel Aziz distraught and al-Sherif's wife still barren.

30. The recurrence of cross-dressing in comedies might confirm that 'subversion and transgression are institutionalized generic requirements'. Neale: 4. See Garay Menicucci, 'Unlocking the Arab Celluloid Closet. Homosexuality in Egyptian Film'. *MERIP*, no. 206 (Spring 1998): 32–36.

31. Kumar: 22.

32. Kumar: 24.

33. Raed Yassin's 'The New Film' features a full length preview to Samir Seif's 1980 film, *The Suspect*, which stars Adel Imam and Souad Hosny.

34. 'All comedy is to some extent about power, involves elements of aggression and malice, and is often rebellious or debunking'. (McCallum: 202). Following the tradition of Ismail Yassin comedies, directed by Fateen Abdel Wahab, in Alaa Walieddin's *Aboud 31-Hoddod* (Aboud on the Border, 1999), Aboud is forced to complete his military service by his father (instead of getting excepted) so that he can become 'a man'.

35. Images of torture and abuse of detainees have also been captured using mobile phone technology and distributed on Youtube.
36. This clip is available on Youtube: 'saba7 21 5eer ya garema' (21 lemby fee 21 segn fee 5alf 21 2swar – al-Limby in Prison behind bars) Posted by thevampireofearth on 8 April 08 2007. http.//www.youtube.com/watch?v=cfaqdldZh70
37. Armbrust, 'National Vernacular', p. 534.
38. Neale: 49.
39. Armbrust, 'National Vernacular', p. 526.
40. Nayar: 21.
41. Armbrust, *Mass Culture and Modernism*, 46.
42. 'Edmund Allenby', Wikipedia http.//en.wikipedia.org/wiki/Edmund_Allenby
43. Armbrust, *Mass Culture and Modernism*, p. 169.
44. Grippo, http.//www.tbsjournal.com/Grippo.html
45. Hassan Khan, 'Based in Cairo: Interview with Hassan Khan' *Local Folk* 5 (April 2007): 6–8.
46. Hall: 233.
47. Kumar: 18.
48. McCallum: 215.

Bibliography

Abu Shadi, Ali (1996) 'Genre in Egyptian Cinema' in Alia Arsoughly (ed.) and trans, *Critical Film Writing from the Arab World*, Quebec: World Heritage Press, pp. 84–129.

Adorno, W. Theodor (1991) *The Culture Industry: Selected Essays on Mass Culture*, London and New York: Routledge.

Al-Tohami, Fouad (2003) 'Rules of the Game' in *Egypt Almanac: The Encyclopedia of Modern Egypt*, 2003 edn.

Armbrust, Walter (2002) 'Islamists in Egyptian Cinema', *American Anthropologist* 104.3: 922–30. Available on anthrosource: http.//www. anthrosource.net/loi/aa

—— (2000) *Mass Culture and Modernism: New Approaches to popular Culture in the Middle East and Beyond*, Cambridge: Cambridge University Press.

—— (1998) 'Terrorism and Kabab: A Capra-esque View of Modern Egypt' in Sherifa Zuhur (ed.) *Images of Enchantment: Visual and Performing Arts of the Middle East*, Cairo: American University in Cairo Press, pp. 283–99.

—— (1995) 'New Cinema, Commercial Cinema, and the Modernist Tradition in Egypt' *Alif: Journal of Comparative Poetics*, No. 15, *Arab Cinematics: Toward the New and the Alternative*: 81–84.

—— (1992) 'The National Vernacular: Folklore and Egyptian Popular Culture' in Michigan Quarterly Review: 31, 4, pp. 525–542.

Assyouti, Mohamed (2005) 'A Consumerist Amnesia' in *Al-Ahram Weekly* 16–22 June 2005, available at http.//weekly.ahram.org.eg/2005/747/cu4.htm

Atia, Tarek (2000) 'Hooligan with a Heart' in *Al-Ahram Weekly* 14–20 September 2000, available at http.//weekly.ahram.org.eg/2000/499/tim1.htm

Bakhtin, Mikhail (1984) *Rabelais and his World*, trans. Hélène Iswolsky, Bloomington: Indiana University Press.

Bayat, Asef and Eric Denis (2000) 'Who is Afraid of ashwaiyyat? Urban Change and Politics in Egypt', *Environment and Urbanization* 12.2 (October): 185–99.

Bayer, Mark (2007) 'The Martyrs of Love and the Emergence of the Arab Cultural Consumer', *Critical Survey* 19.3: 6–26.

Darwish, Mostafa (2003) 'Staving off Stagnation', *Egypt Almanac: The Encyclopaedia of Modern Egypt*, 2003 edn, pp. 73–77.

Dougherty, L. Roberta (2000) 'Badi'a Masabni, Artise and Modernist: Egyptian Print Media's Carnival of National Identity' in Walter Armbrust (ed.), *Mass Mediations: New Approaches to Popular Culture in the Middle East and Beyond*, Berkeley, Los Angeles, London: University of California Press, pp. 243–68.

El Bakry, Rehab (2006) 'Reeling Them in', *Business Monthly*, July 2006. Available at http.//www.mafh oum.com/press9/283C34.htm

Gordon, Joel (2002) *Revolutionary Melodrama: Popular Film and Civic Identity in Nasser's Egypt*, Chicago: Middle East Documentation Centre.

Grippo R., James (2006) 'The Fool Sings a Hero's Song: Shaaban Abdel Rahim, Egyptian Sha'abi, and the Video Clip Phenomenon', *Transnational Broadcasting Studies* 16 (2006) Available at http.//www.tbsjournal.com/Grippo.html.

Hall, Stuart (1981) 'Notes on Deconstructing the Popular' in Raphael Samuel (ed.), *People's History and Socialist Theory* London: Routledge, pp. 227–40.

Hollows, Joanne and Jancovich, Mark (eds) (1995) *Approaches to Popular Film*, Manchester and New York: Manchester University Press.

Horton, S. Andrew (1991) *Comedy/Cinema/Theory*, London: University of California Press.

Karnick, K. Brunovska and Jenkins, Henry (eds) (1995) *Classical Hollywood Comedy*, London and New York: Routledge.

Khan, Hassan (2007) 'Based in Cairo: Interview with Hassan Khan' in *Local Folk* 5 (April): 6–8.

—— (2007) 'Loud, Insistent and Dumb', *Bidoun* Issue 11 (2007): 82–83.

Kumar, Vipin (2008) 'Politics of Laughter: An Introduction to the 1990s' Malayalam Popular Comic film' in *South Asian Popular Culture* 6.1 (April 2008): 13–28.

McCallum, John (1998) 'Cringe and Strut: Comedy and National identity in Post-War Australia' in *Because I tell a Joke or Two: Comedy, Politics and Social Difference*, London and New York: Routledge, pp. 200–18.

Menicucci, Garay (1998) 'Unlocking the Arab Celluloid Closet. Homosexuality in Egyptian Film', *MERIP*, no. 206 (Spring 1998): 32–36.

Mukerji, Chandra and Scuhdson, Michael (eds) (1991) *Rethinking Popular Culture: Contemporary Perspectives in Cultural Studies*, London: University of California Press.

Mustafa, Hani (2007) 'A Grotesque Cacophony' in *Al-Ahram Weekly* 23–29 August, available at http.//weekly.ahram.org.eg/2007/859/cu5.htm.

—— (2005) 'The Puny hero Prospers' in *Al-Ahram Weekly* 29 Dec. 2005–4 Jan. 2006, available at http.//weekly.ahram.org.eg/2005/775/sp142.htm.

Nagati, Omar (2009) 'Competing Urban Orders in Cairo: A Historical Perspective, 'Kharita 01: Symposium on Urban Trajectories in Cairo, 16 January 2009. Video of presentation available at: http.//v2v.cc/v2v/Omar_ Nagati%3A_Competing_ Urban_Orders_in_Cairo%3A_A_Historical_Perspective

Nayar, J. Sheila (2004) 'Invisible Representation: The Oral Contours of a National Popular Cinema', *Film Quarterly* 57.3 (Spring): 13–23.

Neale, Steve (1990) *Popular Film and Television Comedy*, Florence, KY: Routledge.

Peterson, Jennifer (2008) 'Sampling Folklore: The "re-popularization' of Sufi inshad in Egyptian dance music" ', *Arab Media and Society*, issue 4 (Winter). Available at http.//www.arabmediasociety.com/?article=580.

Qasim, Mahmoud (2004) *Mawsouat al-Momathil fial-Sinima al-Arabiya*, Cairo: Madbully.

Sayed, Neshmahay (2009) 'Better Days Ahead' in *Al-Ahram Weekly* 28 May–3 June 2009. Available at http.//weekly.ahram.org.eg/2009/949/ec3.htm.

Shafik, Viola (2001) 'Egypt' in *Companion Encyclopaedia to Middle Eastern and North African Film*, Oliver Leaman (ed.), London: Taylor and Francis, pp. 23–129.

Shafik, Viola (2007) *Popular Egyptian Cinema: Gender, Class, and Nation*, Cairo: American University in Cairo Press.

Shahine, Magda (2009) 'Confronting Unemployment' *Al-Ahram Weekly* 12–18 February 2009. Available at http.//weekly.ahram.org.eg/2009/934/op22.htm

Strinati, Dominic (2000) *An Introduction to Studying Popular Culture*, London and New York: Routledge.

Twitchell, James (1992) *Carnival Culture: The Trashing of Taste in America*, New York: Columbia University Press.

Ulrich, Marzolph (2004) 'Narrative Strategies in Popular Literature: Ideology and Ethics in Tales from the Arabian Nights and Other Collections', *Middle Eastern Literatures* 7.2 (July 2004): 171–82.

Van Nieuwkerk, Karin (2003) 'Egypt' and 'Cairo' in *Encyclopaedia of Popular Music of the World*, London: Continuum, pp. 197–205.

Wacks, David (2003) 'The Perfomativity of Ibn Al-Muqaffa'z Kalila wa-Dimna and al-Maqamat al-luzumiyya of al-Saraqusti', *Journal of Arabic Literature*, XXXIV.

Weltman-Aron, Brigitte (2004) 'The Politics of Irony in Fanon and Kristeva', *The Southern Journal of Philosophy* XLII: 42–47.

While, Allon (1989) 'Hysteria and the end of carnival: Festivity and bourgeois neurosis' in *The Violence of Representation: Literature and the History of Violence*, Routledge, pp. 157–70.

10

Placing Political Economy in Relation to Cultural Studies: Reflections on the Case of Cinema in Saudi Arabia

Naomi Sakr

The age-old question of 'determination'

'Culture', remark the editors of a collection entitled *Cultural Political Economy*, 'is a notoriously polysemic term'.[1] It can refer to a way of life and its associated categorisations, to processes of intellectual, spiritual and aesthetic development, or to artistic activity. Its very complexity reflects, in Raymond Williams' words, 'a complex argument about the relations between general human development and a particular way of life, and between both and the works and practices of art and intelligence'.[2] Among those arguments is a question that has often arisen in discussions about the political economy of culture: namely, whether it is culture that ultimately determines politics and economics or whether, as implied by the sequence of terms in the phrase 'political economy of culture' (where 'political' is relegated to adjectival status), even to utter the phrase 'political economy of culture' is to imply that the economic is somehow really determinate.[3]

There are obviously ontological and epistemological issues at stake in this long-standing debate, in the sense that scholars take differing positions on whether social phenomena are foundational or socially constructed, and whether relationships between those phenomena are directly observable or can only be interpreted, by people who are themselves influenced by social or even discursive constructions of 'reality' and whose interpretations in turn affect outcomes.[4] It is also important to note from the outset that a political economy approach inherently challenges the possibility of conceptualising politics and economics separately. This chapter starts by exploring distinctions and overlaps between a political economy of culture and cultural studies, with particular reference to analytical issues arising in an Arab context. It goes on to apply a political economy perspective to five years of struggle (2005–09) over the future of cinema in Saudi Arabia. Insights from the initial review and the case study allow conclusions to be drawn about cinema's place in Saudi power relations and about political economy's distinctive research agenda.

Disciplinary divergence and wary co-existence

To say what is meant by a political economy approach is relatively simple. It involves studying the social, political and economic arrangements that affect systems of production, distribution and consumption and the mix of values they reflect.[5] Those arrangements, as Susan Strange put it, are the 'result of human decisions taken in the context of man-made institutions and sets of self-set rules and customs'.[6] Classical political economy, which predated the establishment of a separate discipline of scientific economics, is said to have come of age with the publication of Adam Smith's *Inquiry into the Nature and Causes of the Wealth of Nations* in 1776. It reached a turning point in 1857–67 when Karl Marx, having set out to critique John Stuart Mill's 1848 *Principles of Political Economy*, produced first the *Grundrisse* and then *Das Kapital*.[7] The simplicity of political economy's enduring analytical and normative proposition – that we should discover who pays and who benefits in the exercise of authority/allocation of values, in order to identify both the distributional consequences and conceivable alternatives[8] – seems to have been clouded when economics started to branch out as separate academic discipline in the 1870s, borrowing mechanical analogies and models of explanation from that period's development of physics.[9] The notion of 'the economy', in the sense of a general structure of economic relations implicitly aligned with the construct of the nation state, was a 'new discursive object' formed as late as the 1930s with the emergence of economic modelling and econometrics.[10] In classical political economy, 'economy' referred to restrained use of resources.

In other words, if proponents of political economy felt a need in the 1970s and '80s to make a case for the interdependence of power, values and material conditions, this was in part due to the impact of disciplinary boundaries on thinking during the twentieth century and a spreading assumption that the political and economic are functionally independent of each other. In the interdisciplinary field of culture and communication, appeals for a political economy approach were a response to what the British academic, Nicholas Garnham, called the 'dominance of idealism within the analysis of culture and the mass media'. He was concerned that under-reported changes in the ownership and finance of cultural industries could lead to a vertically integrated international cultural monopoly that would have long-lasting 'cultural consequences'.[11] With cultural studies established as a field in the UK by the founding, in 1964, of the pioneering Centre for Cultural Studies at the University of Birmingham, and its status in the USA reflected in the 1987 launch of the journal *Cultural Studies*, edited by Lawrence Grossberg from the University of Illinois, Garnham urged the 'elaboration of a political economy of culture' as part of a necessary 'major revision within cultural theory'.[12] In 1990, noting shifts in the regulation of broadcasting, along with prioritisation of communication and information industries by Western governments formulating new economic and industrial policies, Garnham judged that the need to elaborate a political economy of culture had become more urgent than ever. Yet, he observed, media and cultural studies had moved 'ever further...from political economy'.[13]

Meanwhile, US government moves to force services related to information and culture onto the agenda of bilateral and multilateral trade agreements prompted calls among US and Canadian scholars for research to pay far more attention to trade policies and their cultural impact, given what they saw as the crucial role of communication in how human beings think and act.[14] Yet evidence of a refocusing of culture and communication research agendas remained limited, despite the appearance in other fields during the 1990s of work on what its advocates termed 'new political economy'.[15] Hence Robert McChesney's *cri de coeur* in 2000, bemoaning US universities' marginalisation of studies examining media ownership, advertising or government policies on communication, and blaming a lack of funding for research in these areas on the fact that such research is inconvenient to 'moneyed interests'.[16] Hence also Andrew Calabrese's 2004 declaration that 'much remains to be done in advancing [a historical materialist political economy of communication and culture]', even though some cultural theorists had by that time turned their attention to issues of policy analysis, citizenship and the commodification of audiences that might previously have been seen as the political economists' preserve.[17]

In essence, the potential for synergies between political economy and cultural studies continues today to depend on the extent to which culture is seen to be linked to materiality. For as long as ideas and theories grouped under the umbrella of poststructuralism were dominant in cultural studies, focusing on language and semiotics without reference to a material basis, there was no chance of healing the rift with political economy. In the aftermath of the poststructuralist turn, space opened up for a return to the critical 'cultural materialism' represented in Raymond Williams' work in the 1970s and thus, in the view of Williams' admirers, for dialogue or even integration between cultural studies and political economy.[18] But conceptualising the relationship between culture and political economy still poses the challenge of avoiding the twin traps that Garnham summarised as economic reductionism and 'idealist autonomization of the ideological level'.[19] When sociologists claim that 'meaning is constitutive of structure', because '[d]istinctions have material consequences', causing 'culture' to become 'formidably powerful',[20] there would seem to be a risk of implying the autonomy of ideas. The French anthropologist Maurice Godelier described the risk succinctly. 'Any analysis that commences by isolating thought from the other components of social reality... and then attempts to deduce the latter from the former' will, he said, 'inevitably box itself into a corner'. By the same token, however, he warned that the same was true of the 'vulgar materialist approach'.[21]

When it comes to analysing the political economy of Arab affairs, the tendency to do so through the lens of 'culture' has been quite marked across the decades. Clearly, this phenomenon deserves closer scrutiny, not least because it is often manifest in the work of Arab scholars. It is relatively easy to discount what Aziz Al-Azmeh calls the 'vast industry of misrecognition', sustained by a 'traffic in mirror-images between re-orientalizing orientals speaking for authenticity and orientalising neo-orientalists', which construes Islam as a culture that 'over determines' Muslim economies, societies and non-religious cultures.[22] But aside from this 'pseudo-sociology' of 'culturalist differentialism',[23] there are works by Arab thinkers about articulations of power and society in Arab countries that are notable for the way they privilege political culture over political

economy. In the colonial era this was arguably attributable to a preoccupation with gaining national independence; Albert Hourani, survey-
ing schools of thought during the century-and-a-half to 1939, noted
that the 'content of nationalism in this period included few precise ideas
about social reform and economic development', since foreign domination was seen as the immediate problem to be resolved.[24] According to
Abdullah Laroui, in his early 1980s writings on the concepts of liberty and
the state,[25] foreign administrations were one reason why state machinery
remained 'alien' to local populations, giving Arab intellectuals little incen-
tive to engage with its workings. Nazih Ayubi, seeking to trace some of the
social bases of politics in the Middle East, cites several examples of scholarship that highlight supposedly significant aspects of Arab education, or
a distinctive Arab 'personality' or 'mentality'. These include, in chrono-
logical order of publication: Ali Zayour's *Qita' al-Butula w'al-Narjasiyya
f'il-Zat al-Arabiyya* (The Heroism and Narcissism Sector in the Arab Self,
1982), Al-Sayyid Yassin's *Al-Shakhsiyya al-Arabiya* (The Arab Personality,
1983), Hisham Ju'ait's *Al-Shakhsiyya al-Arabiyya al-Islamiyya* (The Arab
Islamic Personality, 1984), Hisham Sharabi's *Al-Binya Al-Batrakiyya* (The
Patriarchal Structure, 1987), and Fuad al-Khuri's *Al-Dhihniyya al-Arabiyya* (The Arab Mentality, 1993).[26] The point about these works is that they
are mostly non-essentialist, insofar as they attempt to explain political
culture by reference to particular collective histories or social formations,
such as tribal survivalism or colonial bureaucracy.

Ayubi himself, pondering whether to explain the regional historical
heritage of despotism in terms of political culture or political economy,
veers towards the latter. But he is resolved not to overlook the 'significance
of "political culture"'.[27] He argues that what are sometimes seen as characteristics of a distinct political culture are, in fact, the mechanisms of
adjustment from one mode of production to another. Thus, for example,
'although patronage and clientelism have a long history and an elaborate
vocabulary in the Middle East, they are not the inevitable outcome of certain essential and permanent cultural traits' but are 'in reality behavioural
correlates to articulated modes of production'.[28] Ayubi takes modes of production as his starting point but, drawing on Ernesto Laclau's 1977 exposition of the theory of 'articulation' of different modes of production, which
helps to account for situations in which two or more modes of production
coexist and interlink,[29] he argues that culture cannot be treated simply as a

reflection of the economic base. Culture 'changes much more slowly than the economy', being influenced not only by the mode(s) of production but by many geographically and historically contingent factors, which together may be described as a *conjuncture*.[30] As evidence, he suggests that tribalism may be expressed socially and politically even after the disappearance of its economic base, and that – for example – the bureaucratic, centralised traditions of a society dependent on river management may persist even when irrigated agriculture is no longer either a chief source of livelihood, or state-owned.[31] That is to say: there may be little *correspondence* among the various manifestations of structural power in society.[32]

Articulation offers a way to grapple conceptually with non-correspondence and contradictions. It was taken up by cultural theorists as 'a way of characterising a social formation without falling into the twin traps of reductionism and essentialism',[33] a way of avoiding economic determinism without de-historicising. Stuart Hall expressed it as 'the form of the connection that can make a unity of two different elements, under certain conditions. It is a linkage which is not necessary, determined, absolute and essential for all time. You have to ask, under what circumstances can a connection be forged or made? ... Thus, a theory of articulation is both a way of understanding how ideological elements come, under certain conditions, to cohere together within a discourse, and a way of asking how they do or do not become articulated, at specific conjunctures, to certain political subjects.'[34]

As a theory of contexts, articulation is said to provide 'a way to talk about the power of the discursive and its role in culture, communication, politics, economics, gender, race, class, ethnicity and technology',[35] along with a recognition of 'the inability to know in advance the historical significance of particular practices'.[36] After a heated debate at the 1993 meeting of the International Communication Association, which testified to a 'great divide' between political economy and cultural studies, Lawrence Grossberg rebuffed any reconciliation of the two on the grounds that, in cultural studies, relations between production, consumption, politics and ideology are principally theorised through articulation.[37] Since that time, however, attempts at reconciliation have continued, sometimes with reference to Raymond Williams' own insistence that 'any ruling class devotes a significant part of material production to establishing a political [and social] order'.[38] It has been pointed out that the material/symbolic dualism or dichotomy, which continues at times to be mutually reproduced in opposite ways by both political economy and cultural studies, can be superseded if culture and economy are conceived alike as the 'meaningful, practical activity of human beings'.[39]

One question, then, in thinking through the political economy of the struggle over cinema in Saudi Arabia, is how much political economy can add to our understanding, given the theoretical tools and multidimensional perspectives already afforded by cultural studies. It is proposed here to attempt an historical materialist political economy, which requires the probing of structures and pressures that are neither self-evident nor directly observable. The task of the international political economist, in the words of Susan Strange, is to try to 'untangle the complex web of overlapping, symbiotic or conflicting authority', along with the 'interlocking, interacting bargains' in 'any sector or on any who-gets-what issue'.[40] As summarised by Graham Murdock and Peter Golding, a critical political economy of culture and communication is 'especially interested in the ways that communicative activity is structured by the unequal distribution of material and symbolic resources'.[41] It sets out to show how 'different ways of financing and organizing cultural production have traceable consequences for the range of discourses, representations and communicative resources in the public domain and for the organization of audience access and use'.[42] With these tasks in mind, and since space is limited, the following section attempts to incorporate three interwoven elements.

The first element pays attention to what makes the period 2005–09 historically specific in terms of control over filmmaking, distribution and exhibition in Saudi Arabia. The second deals with the significance of cinema in the material reproduction of Saudi Arabia's political and social order. The third considers how capital seeks to use cinema in Saudi Arabia to increase its value and how the 'smooth circular flow' of capital, in which 'the moment of consumption is part of the production process', may encounter obstructions.[43] In the Saudi case, acute contradictions exist through the state's heavy reliance on rents from a single main export commodity, which locks it into the world capitalist system, at the same time as its relations of production and the role of its rulers in distribution follow a logic derived from decades of dependence on oil rents.[44] Taken together, these threads of exploration should lead at least to a glimpse of where and how power is exercised, and with what outcomes, in a particular area of Saudi cultural production.

Saudi cinema: forbidden, desired, promoted, repressed

The Intercontinental Hotel in Riyadh made headline news in November 2005 when it opened its doors to the public for three hour-long showings per day of Arabic cartoons, on a cinema screen. The screenings, part of festivities marking the end of Ramadan, continued for no more than a fortnight and were restricted to audiences of women and children. But they were newsworthy in having been formally allowed by the Riyadh authorities.[45] As such, they seemed to signal the possibility that cinemas might be permitted in Saudi Arabia after a *de facto* nationwide ban that had lasted for around 25 years.

Sources are generally unclear about the precise starting point of the ban on cinemas in the Kingdom. An account of Saudi Arabia's media landscape under King Faisal, whose 11-year reign ended with his assassination in 1975, indicates that Faisal countered religious conservatives' objections to the introduction of television by saying that it could be used to transmit the word of God. Regarding cinema, in contrast, he reportedly sided with the conservatives, who objected both to the foreign content of films and to the way movie theatres would bring men and women together.[46] Faisal's formal co-optation of religious clerics as state functionaries, achieved through the use of growing oil rents to fund public sector employment, reflected a fusion of his personal religious faith with a political strategy designed to counter internal and external threats to the Saudi monarchy.[47] A royal decree dating from 1964 and banning the screening of movies in public places was later cited by opponents of cinema. But it seemed to be undermined by another decree transferring cases against cinemas not to the courts, but to the Committee on Commercial Disputes.[48] Against this legal confusion, film screenings for mixed audiences continued during the 1970s,[49] being organised by large oil and armaments contractors and through private rental of projectors. In 1979, however, religious dissidents' siege of the main mosque in Makkah, in protest at the government's alleged moral degeneracy, triggered a decisive backlash against liberalisation of public media. For Saudi film lovers, the effect of the clampdown was mitigated by the subsequent rise in the local market for video recorders and videocassettes, available for use in private homes.[50]

If the outlawing of cinema during the 1960s–1980s was gradual and more rigidly enforced for some Saudis than for others, the faltering return of cinema screenings during and after 2005 was arguably equally contingent on a sequence of blurred trade-offs involving the religious authorities, ruling princes and the princes' business interests. The latter are complicated by the sheer number of descendants of Abdel-Aziz al-Saud, Saudi Arabia's first king, who fathered 45 recorded sons by at least 22 different mothers, between 1900 and 1953.[51] As generations of princes occupied key posts in all tiers of government, contacts with government figures came to be seen as essential to running a business in Saudi Arabia.[52] Investment interest in developing the cinema business in the Kingdom can be viewed in light of princely patronage. Even so, most Saudi-owned media production is based abroad to avoid the stringent constraints that hard-line clerics are allowed to impose on domestic media content in return for bestowing religious legitimacy on rule by the Al-Saud. From 2003 onwards, the two main distributors of film to Saudi audiences via satellite TV were the MBC Group, owned by Walid al-Ibrahim, a brother-in-law of King Fahd (ruler of Saudi Arabia from 1982 to 2005), and Rotana, owned by Prince Alwaleed bin Talal, a nephew of King Fahd and a shareholder in US companies, including Time Warner, Disney and News Corporation. Alwaleed started the Rotana network of music and film channels from studios in Beirut and Cairo after becoming sole owner of the Rotana recording label in 2003, thus acquiring the world's largest library of Arabic music and film. The MBC Group, based in Dubai from 2001, launched its first free-to-air film channel in January 2003 and added others later. MBC showed mostly Hollywood movies subtitled in Arabic. Rotana Cinema and Rotana Zaman screened Arabic films.

Against the background of the post-2003 surge in availability of film through television in Saudi Arabia, the most significant political event to predate, and possibly precipitate, the Eid al-Fitr screenings at the Riyadh Intercontinental in November 2005 was Abdullah's accession to the Saudi throne, in August 2005, upon the death of his long-incapacitated half-brother Fahd. The changeover was presented through the media as heralding a move to greater openness,[53] which many Saudis attributed to King Abdullah's interest in reforming a country that had become stigmatised internationally as the home of 15 out of the 19 perpetrators of the 9/11 atrocities in the US in 2001. On the other hand, the significance of the accession should not be overstated. For one thing Abdullah had already held prominent roles in government over many years, as Crown Prince,

First Deputy Prime Minister,[54] Commander of the National Guard and Head of the Higher Economic Council. For another, evidence indicates that neopatrimonialism had by this time fragmented the Saudi state into a collection of personal fiefdoms, reflecting competition among senior princes for influence over bureaucratic, security and societal structures.[55] It has been suggested that this competition had started to moderate after 9/11 and a series of bombings in Saudi Arabia itself, as efforts to shore up the Saudi political system prompted the country's rulers to 'unite and survive', while seeking active support from a wider section of the population. Hence, attempts were made (through such means as the National Dialogue, launched in June 2003)[56] to bridge divisions entrenched through decades of custom and practice, between sects (Sunni, Shia), between the sexes, and between regions.[57] This renewed project of nation-building implicitly challenged the vision – conveyed in Orientalist literature and policy documents circulating in Washington in December 2002 – of Saudi Arabia as an unstable amalgam of disparate groupings, ripe for partition.[58]

After the cinematic breakthrough in 2005, things moved quite quickly on the cinema front, with film apparently deployed to stimulate a national conversation about social conventions. In March 2006, Rotana released its first film, under the title *Keif el-Hal?* (How Are You?). Written by an Egyptian, filmed by an Arab-Canadian director in Dubai, and restricted to distribution on DVD in Saudi Arabia because of the absence of Saudi cinema screens, *Keif el-Hal?* could claim to be a Saudi film because of its Saudi actors. But it was distinctively Saudi in other ways too. Its associate producer was Saudi film director, Haifaa al-Mansour,[59] who had gained international recognition in 2003–04 for her own films dealing with domestic Saudi issues.[60] The role of the lead female character's best friend was played by a 25-year-old Saudi woman, Hind Mohammed, previously known only for her acting voice and not her appearance, because Saudi dramas had relied hitherto on non-Saudi actresses.[61] The film's theme was unmistakeably Saudi, telling the story of a Riyadh family whose members differ over the correct path for a newly-graduated daughter. It may also have been no coincidence that the central character, Sultan, dreams of becoming a movie producer, since this dream was taken to represent 'liberal tendencies' among Saudi youth.[62] In fact, the narrative power of forbidden desire put cinema at the heart of another Saudi-directed film to premier outside Saudi Arabia in 2006. This was Abdullah Al-Eyaf's 40-minute documentary,

Cinema 500km. Shot partly in Riyadh and Khobar, with official permission from the Saudi Ministry of Culture and Information, the film traces the journey of a young man who loves watching movies on the small screen and is forced to travel 500km to neighbouring Bahrain in order to experience watching one in a cinema.[63] Eyaf's account was no exaggeration. Bahraini officials say that Saudi nationals account for some 85 per cent of tickets sold by Bahrain's 90 movie theatres, boosting traffic on the Saudi Arabia–Bahrain causeway by around 30,000 vehicles during holidays and weekends.[64]

With this sequence of events in 2005–06, filmmakers and investors alike expressed confidence that a loosening of restrictions on cinema was inevitable. A leading cleric, Salman al-Odeh, had declared, on an MBC channel in January 2006, that Saudi cinema would be a 'good thing' because, in contrast to Western cinema, it would 'do justice to Islam'.[65] The lucrative business openings were obvious. After the Intercontinental screenings, entrepreneurs had quickly applied for permission to open cinemas at the Coral Beach Resort, near Jeddah, and in Dammam. Even though these projects failed to get off the ground,[66] there was keen awareness of the potential for box office takings in a country with an estimated population of 23.6m and per capita GDP of $22,000 in 2006. Prince Alwaleed was anxious to reap the financial rewards of his investment in *Keif al-Hal?* and in a second film, *Menahi*, which featured a popular television character, a goat herder, being enticed to Dubai by the promise of easy riches. Ayman Halawani, general manager of Rotana Studios, complained that the lack of distribution outlets meant 'You cannot monetise a Saudi movie'.[67] Rotana's own response was to show *Menahi* to segregated audiences in specially hired halls in Jeddah and Taif over a 10-day period in December 2008, having obtained permission to do so from the pro-liberalisation provincial governor, Prince Khaled al-Faisal. Audiences were so eager that showings numbered eight per day, and even then there was overcrowding in Taif.[68] Meanwhile, those with a stake in bringing Hollywood movies to the Saudi public, including the Arabian Anti-Piracy Alliance and Walid al-Ibrahim's MBC Group, saw the opening of cinemas as an overdue solution to film piracy.[69] Rotana demonstrated its commitment to Hollywood when it added Fox Movies to its network of channels in 2008. Encouraged by the *Menahi* screenings and by the Dammam Literary Club's inaugural Saudi Film Competition in May 2008, the Saudi Arabia-based production house SilverGrey Picture and Sound revealed that it planned major expansion in anticipation of a big surge in local film production.[70] Construction of an Imax theatre in Khobar, and plans for others in Jeddah and Riyadh, added another reason to plan for growth, as did the 64 Saudi films submitted to the Gulf Film Festival in Dubai in April 2009, out of about 200 entries in total.

In July 2009, however, the outlook changed again, just when investors with a stake in a Saudi film industry were coming to see the formal acceptance of cinema in the Kingdom as simply a matter of time. Al-Ibrahim had taken steps to create an MBC film division by investing in a new US company, the Film Department, in 2007, with the aim of 'learning the business'.[71] Rotana, in line with its other initiatives, had stepped in to sponsor the Jeddah Film Festival, an event that started in July 2006, under the title 'Jeddah Visual Show Festival', on advice from the Ministry of Culture and Information not to use the word 'film'.[72] The festival, repeated in 2007 and 2008, was due to be held for the fourth time in July 2009, barely three weeks after the head of the Mass Media Department at King Saud University in Riyadh had announced plans to start teaching drama to students to prepare them to make films.[73] The fourth Jeddah film Festival was due to last a week and include a competition among eight Gulf-made feature films, including two from Saudi Arabia. Out of a total of 100 films to be screened, including animations, documentaries and shorts, nearly half were Saudi.

In the end no films were shown. On the eve of the event, the organisers received instructions from the Governorate of Jeddah to call it off; an official at the Ministry of Culture and Information said the cancellation order had been issued by the Ministry of the Interior.[74] The order came as a shock, because King Abdullah had only recently appointed reformers to some key posts and removed the head of the religious police after he spoke about the evils of film. What the order seemed to signal was the continuing power of the 'old guard' in the religious establishment, their enduring alliance with the highly conservative interior minister, Prince Nayef bin Abdel-Aziz, and the persistence of competing spheres of influence. In March, 2009, Abdullah had formally named Nayef, his half-brother, as the person who would take over the government whenever the King and Crown Prince were both out of the country – a move that put Nayef next in line to be Crown Prince. This private decision was questioned disapprovingly by Alwaleed's father, Prince Talal, a half-brother of both the King and interior minister.[75] It cast doubt on the standing of internationally active media moguls, like Alwaleed bin Talal and Walid al-Ibrahim, relative to policymakers at the heart of Saudi government.

Conclusion

It can be seen from this account that cinema in Saudi Arabia, as a medium of expression and entertainment, is also a means by which investors seek to make financial gains, and figures endowed with political or religious authority try to shape the future of the country. All these aspects are fused, so that, far from determining outcomes, economics and the flow of capital are subject to obstacles created by rule-making structures that were put in place half a century ago. On the other hand, the cultural economics of the regional market play a vital role, because the use of Arabic across the region allows aspiring players in a Saudi film industry to gain a business foothold through activities conducted in Cairo or Dubai. It remains significant that the making and showing of Saudi feature films was dominated during 2005–09 by a single company, Rotana, owned by a member of the ruling family. The most prominent challenge to the ban on cinemas was thus directed through the activities of someone with a vested interest in other aspects of the Kingdom's political and economic status quo. Indeed, a national conversation conducted through film about liberalising social mores could be seen as smothering a potentially more threatening exchange about political restructuring. As Mohammed Abbas, literary critic of *Al-Riyadh* newspaper, once said of a television satire on Saudi customs: 'reality is a big joke that we have all helped tell, but that we have neither the right nor the power to change.'[76] Sudden cancellation of the Jeddah Film Festival in 2009, after it had already run in each of the three previous years, reinforced a sense of unpredictability and disempowerment among its supporters. In this way film, by its fraught combination of presence and absence, made a material contribution to reproducing the social and political order of the ruling Al-Saud.

On the more general question of what can be achieved by a political economy approach to understanding culture, these details from an eventful period in the history of Saudi cinema point to possible outcomes of the research tasks identified by political economists, cited earlier in this chapter. That is to say: an exploration of geographic and historic contingency can help to untangle the complex web of bargains made by those who exercise authority and uncover the unequal distribution of communicative resources. The bargains and resource allocations discussed here show that the moments of production, distribution and consumption of film are analytically inseparable.

Notes

1. Jacqueline Best and Matthew Paterson, 'Introduction: Understanding cultural political economy', in Jacqueline Best and Matthew Paterson (eds) *Cultural Political Economy*, London: Routledge, p. 5.
2. Raymond Williams, *Keywords: A Vocabulary of Culture and Society*, London: Croom Helm, pp. 80–81.
3. R.B.J. Walker, 'Conclusion: Cultural, political, economy', in Best and Paterson (eds), *Cultural Political Economy*, p. 226.
4. David Marsh and Paul Furlong, 'A skin, not a sweater: Ontology and epistemology in political science', in David Marsh and Gerry Stoker (eds) *Theory and Methods in Political Science*, Basingstoke: Palgrave Macmillan, pp. 17–41.
5. According to Vincent Mosco, 'one can think about political economy as the study of the social relations, particularly the power relations, that mutually constitute the production, distribution and consumption of resources'. See Mosco, *The Political Economy of Communication*, London: Sage, p 24.
6. Susan Strange, *States and Markets*, London: Pinter Publishers, p. 18.
7. Anthony Payne, 'The genealogy of new political economy' in Anthony Payne (ed) *Key Debates in New Political Economy*, London: Routledge, pp. 2–3.
8. Susan Strange, *The Retreat of the State: The Diffusion of Power in the World Economy*, Cambridge: Cambridge University Press, pp. 38, 42 and 99; Andrew Gamble, 'The new political economy', *Political Studies* XLIII (September), p. 517.
9. Philip Mirowski, *Against Mechanism: Protecting Economics from Science*, Lanham MD: Rowman & Littlefield, quoted in Timothy Mitchell, 'Fixing the economy', *Cultural Studies* 12.1: 85–86.
10. Mitchell: 'Fixing the economy', p. 88.
11. Nicholas Garnham, 'Contribution to a political economy of mass-communication', in Richard Collins et al. (eds) *Media, Culture and Society: A Critical Reader*, London: Sage, p. 10.
12. Garnham, 'Contribution to a political economy', p. 9.
13. Nicholas Garnahm, *Capitalism and Communication*, London: Sage, p. 20.
14. E.g. Sandra Braman, 'Trade and information policy', *Media, Culture & Society* 12.3 (July): 377–78; Edward A. Comor 'Introduction: The Global Political Economy of Communication and IPE', in Edward Comor (ed.) *The Global*

Political Economy of Communication: Hegemony, Telecommunications and the Information Economy, Basingstoke: Macmillan Press, pp. 3 and 15.

15. See examples in the tenth anniversary volume of the journal, *New Political Economy*, in December, 2005.
16. Robert W. McChesney, 'The political economy of communication and the future of the field', *Media, Culture & Society*, 22.1 (January): 113.
17. Andrew Calabrese, 'Toward a political economy of culture', in Andrew Calabrese and Colin Sparks (eds) *Toward a Political Economy of Culture*, Lanham MD: Rowman & Littlefield, p. 9.
18. E.g. Janice Peck, 'Why we shouldn't be bored with the political economy versus cultural studies debate', *Cultural Critique* 64 (Autumn 2006). In the same vein, Peck cites Eileen Meehan's 'Commodity, Culture, Common Sense: Media Research and Paradigm Dialogue', *Journal of Media Economics* 12.2. See also Robert E. Babe, *Cultural Studies and Political Economy: Toward a New Integration*, Lanham MD: Lexington Books, e.g. p. 72.
19. Garnham, *Capitalism and Communication*, p. 23.
20. Elizabeth Armstrong and Mary Bernstein, 'Culture, power, and institutions: A multi-institutional politics approach to social movements', *Sociological Theory* 26.1 (March 2008), p. 83.
21. Maurice Godelier, *Mental and Material*, London: Verso, cited in Peck: 'Why we shouldn't be bored', p. 92.
22. Aziz al-Azmeh, 'Postmodern obscurantism and 'The Muslim Question'', *Journal for the Study of Religions and Ideologies*, 5 (Summer 2003): 23 and 25.
23. Azmeh, 'Postmodern obscurantism', p. 40.
24. Albert Hourani, *Arabic Thought in the Liberal Age 1798–1939*, Oxford: Oxford University Press, pp. 344–45.
25. Abdullah Laroui, *Mafhoum al-Dawla* (The Concept of the State, 1981) and *Mafhoum al-Huriyya* (The Concept of Liberty, 1983), both published in Casablanca by Al-Markaz al-Thaqafi al-Arabi.
26. Nazih N. Ayubi, *Over-Stating the Arab State: Politics and Society in the Middle East*, London: I.B.Tauris, pp. 166–67.
27. Ayubi, *Over-Stating the Arab State*, p. 2.
28. Ibid: 167–68.
29. In *Politics and Ideology in Marxist Theory*, London: New Left Books, 1977.
30. Ayubi, *Over-Stating the Arab State*, p. 29; italics in original.
31. Ibid.
32. Ibid: 26–27; italics in original.
33. Jennifer Daryl Slack, 'The theory and method of articulation in cultural studies', in David Morley and Kuan-Hsing Chen (eds) *Stuart Hall: Critical Dialogues in Cultural Studies*, London: Routledge, p. 113.
34. Lawrence Grossberg, 'On postmodernism and articulation: An interview with Stuart Hall', *Journal of Communication Inquiry* 10.2 (June): 53.

35. Slack, 'The theory and method of articulation', p. 122.
36. Lawrence Grossberg, *Bringing It All Back Home: Essays in Cultural Studies*, Durham NC: Duke University Press, pp. 177–78.
37. Lawrence Grossberg, 'Cultural studies vs. political economy: Is anybody else bored with this debate?', *Critical Studies in Mass Communication* 12.1 (March): 72–81 (p. 73).
38. Raymond Williams, *Marxism and Literature*, Oxford: Oxford University Press, p. 93.
39. Peck, 'Why we shouldn't be bored', p. 112.
40. Strange, *The Retreat of the State*, p. 99.
41. Graham Murdock and Peter Golding, 'Culture, communications and political economy', in James Curran and Michael Gurevitch (eds) *Mass Media and Society*, London: Hodder Arnold, p. 62. Previous editions of *Mass Media and Society* (1996, 2000) include earlier versions of the same article.
42. Murdock and Golding, 'Culture, communications and political economy', p. 60.
43. Garnham, *Capitalism and Communication*, pp. 45–46.
44. Ayubi, *Overstating the Arab State*, pp. 224–27.
45. According to the Saudi-owned London-based newspaper *Asharq al-Awsat*, 18 October 2005, quoting Kamal Al-Khatib, head of the Media Committee of Riyadh Council.
46. William A. Rugh, 'Saudi mass media and society in the Faisal era', in W. A. Beling (ed.) *King Faisal and the Modernisation of Saudi Arabia*, London: Croom Helm, pp. 131–32.
47. Madawi Al-Rasheed, *A History of Saudi Arabia*, Cambridge: Cambridge University Press, pp. 124–25.
48. Sabria S. Jawhar, 'Conservatives impede progress in opening theaters', *Saudi Gazette*, 16 November 2005.
49. Naomi Sakr, 'Women and media in Saudi Arabia: Rhetoric, reductionism and realities', *British Journal for Middle Eastern Studies* 35.2 (December): 392.
50. Douglas A. Boyd, *Broadcasting in the Arab World: A Survey of the Electronic Media in the Middle East*, Ames: Iowa State University Press, pp. 170–71.
51. According to *Burke's Royal Families of the World*, Vol II, quoted in David Holden and Richard Johns, *The House of Saud*, London: Pan Books, p. 552.
52. Tim Niblock and Monica Malik, *The Political Economy of Saudi Arabia*, London: Routledge, p. 152.
53. Sakr, 'Women and media in Saudi Arabia', p. 394.
54. The post of Prime Minister was always held by the King.
55. Steffen Hertog, 'Shaping the Saudi state: Human agency's shifting role in rentier-state formation', *International Journal of Middle Eastern Studies*, 39.4 (November): 556–57; Iris Glosemeyer, 'Checks, balances and transformation in the Saudi political system' in Paul Aarts and Gerd Nonneman (eds) *Saudi Arabia in the Balance: Political Economy, Society, Foreign Affairs*, London: Hurst & Company, pp. 218.

56. Details in Sakr, 'Women and media in Saudi Arabia', pp. 393–94.
57. Glosemeyer, 'Checks, balances and transformation', pp. 224–27.
58. Pascal Ménoret, *The Saudi Enigma*, London: Zed Books, p. 31.
59. Sam Dagher, 'Saudi Arabia's first film blazes taboo-breaking trail', *Middle East Online*, www.middle-east-online.com, 21 March 2006.
60. Andrew Hammond, *Popular Culture in the Arab World*, Cairo: AUC Press, p. 140; *Le Monde Diplomatique*, 'The first director of Saudi cinema', September 2004, p. 13.
61. Hassan Fattah, 'Daring to use the silver screen to reflect Saudi society', *The New York Times*, 28 April 2006.
62. Elaph, 'First Saudi film in Egyptian cinemas', www.elaph.com, 24 October 2006.
63. Mirza Al-Khuwaylidi, 'Interview with Saudi film director, Abdullah Al Eyaf', *Asharq al-Awsat* English website, 3 January 2007, www.aawsat.com/english/news.asp?section=7&id=7530 [accessed 4 January 2007].
64. Data gathered by *Al-Riyadh* newspaper and reported by Habib Trabelsi in 'Hardliners reject cinema in Saudi but want it elsewhere', *Middle East Online*, www.middle-east-online.com, 15 February 2010.
65. Quoted in 'Saudis put cinema ban in the frame', *aljazeera.net*, 23 February 2006.
66. Jawhar, 'Conservatives impede progress'.
67. Quoted by Roula Khalaf in 'Clerics lament as Saudi film draws crowds', *Financial Times*, 23 March 2009.
68. Reuters, 'Saudi religious police eases criticism of cinema', www.arabianbusiness.com, 22 December 2008.
69. Scott Butler of the Arabian Anti-Piracy Alliances is quoted by Patrick Elligett in 'Unveiling the Kingdom', www.digitalproductionme.com, 22 February 2009. Al-Ibrahim is quoted by Ali Jaafar in 'Sheikh Waleed al-Ibrahim expands media empire' *Variety*, 21 November 2007, www.variety.com/article/VR1117976421.html.
70. Patrick Elligett, 'SilverGrey set to capitalise on KSA cinema revival', www.digitalproductionme.com, 7 January 2009
71. Ali Jaafar, 'Oil gives way to film in Middle East', *Variety* 10 March, 2010, quotes Al-Ibrahim as saying: 'The whole idea for us is to learn so we can be part of the film industry and it can be part of our business', www.variety.com/article/VR1118016308.html
72. According to Saudi director Mishael al-Enazi, quoted by Andrew Hammond in 'First Saudi film festival opens despite clerics', *Middle East Online*, www.middle-east-online.com, 14 July 2006.
73. Iman al-Khaddaf, 'Drama to be taught in Saudi Arabia for the first time', *Asharq al-Awsat* English website, www.asharq-e.com/news.asp?section=7&id=17188
74. Reuters report by Souhail Karam from Riyadh, published in the *Independent*, 20 July 2009.

75. Prince Talal's statement, faxed to Reuters, was reported by Samia Nakhoul, 'Saudi prince questions royal appointment', www.arabianbusiness.com, 28 March 2009.
76. Quoted by Pascal Ménoret in 'Saudi TV's dangerous hit', *Le Monde Diplomatique*, September 2004, p. 13.

Bibliography

al-Azmeh, Aziz (2003) 'Postmodern obscurantism and "The Muslim Question"', *Journal for the Study of Religions and Ideologies* 5 (Summer): 20–46.

al-Rasheed, Madawi (2002) *A History of Saudi Arabia*, Cambridge: Cambridge University Press.

Armstrong, Elizabeth and Mary Bernstein (2008) 'Culture, Power, and Institutions: A Multi-Institutional Politics Approach to Social Movements', *Sociological Theory* 26.1 (March): 74–79.

Babe, Robert E. (2008) *Cultural Studies and Political Economy: Toward a New Integration*, Lanham MD: Lexington Books.

Best, Jacqueline and Matthew Paterson (2010) 'Introduction: Understanding Cultural Political Economy' in Jacqueline Best and Matthew Paterson (eds), *Cultural Political Economy*, London: Routledge, pp. 1–25.

Boyd, Douglas A. (1999) *Broadcasting in the Arab World: A Survey of the Electronic Media in the Middle East*, Ames: Iowa State University Press, 3rd edn.

Braman, Sandra (1990) 'Trade and Information Policy', *Media, Culture & Society* 12.3 (July): 361–85.

Calabrese, Andrew (2004) 'Toward a Political Economy of Culture' in Andrew Calabrese and Colin Sparks (eds), *Toward a Political Economy of Culture*, Lanham MD: Rowman & Littlefield, pp. 1–12.

Comor, Edward A. (1996) 'Introduction: The Global Political Economy of Communication and IPE' in Edward Comor (ed.), *The Global Political Economy of Communication: Hegemony, Telecommunications and the Information Economy*, Basingstoke: Macmillan Press, 2nd edn, pp. 1–18.

Gamble, Andrew (1995) 'The New Political Economy', *Political Studies* XLIII (September): 516–30.

Garnham, Nicholas (1986) 'Contribution to a Political Economy of Mass Communication' in Richard Collins, James Curran, Nicholas Garnham, Paddy Scannell, Philip Schlesinger and Colin Sparks (eds), *Media, Culture and Society: A Critical Reader*, London: Sage, pp. 9–32.

Glosemeyer, Iris (2005) 'Checks, Balances and Transformation in the Saudi Political System' in Paul Aarts and Gerd Nonneman (eds), *Saudi Arabia in the Balance: Political Economy, Society, Foreign Affairs*, London: Hurst & Company, pp. 214–33.

Grossberg, Lawrence (1997) *Bringing It All Back Home: Essays in Cultural Studies*, Durham NC: Duke University Press.

—— (1995) 'Cultural Studies Vs. Political Economy: Is Anybody Else Bored with This Debate?', *Critical Studies in Mass Communication* 12.1 (March): 72–81.

—— (1986) 'On Postmodernism and Articulation: An Interview with Stuart Hall, *Journal of Communication Inquiry* 10.2 (June): 45–60.

Hammond, Andrew (2007) *Popular Culture in the Arab World*, Cairo: American University in Cairo Press.

Hertog, Steffen (2007) 'Shaping the Saudi State: Human Agency's Shifting Role in Rentier-State Formation', *International Journal of Middle Eastern Studies* 39.4 (November): 539–63.

Holden, David and Richard Johns (1982) *The House of Saud*, London: Pan Books.

Marsh, David and Paul Furlong (2002) 'A Skin, Not a Sweater: Ontology and Epistemology in Political Science' in David Marsh and Gerry Stoker (eds), *Theory and Methods in Political Science*, Basingstoke: Palgrave Macmillan, 2nd edn, pp. 17–41.

McChesney, Robert W. (2000) 'The Political Economy of Communication and the Future of the Field', *Media, Culture & Society* 22.1: 109–116.

Ménoret, Pascal (2005) *The Saudi Enigma*, London: Zed Books.

Mitchell, Timothy (1998) 'Fixing The Economy', *Cultural Studies* 12.1: 82–101.

Mosco, Vincent (2009) *The Political Economy of Communication*, London: Sage, 2nd edn.

Murdock, Graham and Peter Golding (2005) 'Culture, Communications and Political Economy' in James Curran and Michael Gurevitch (eds), *Mass Media and Society*, London: Hodder Arnold, pp. 60–83.

Niblock, Tim and Monica Malik (2007) *The Political Economy of Saudi Arabia*, London: Routledge, 2007.

Payne, Anthony (2006) 'The Genealogy of New Political Economy' in Anthony Payne (ed.), *Key Debates in New Political Economy*, London: Routledge, pp. 1–10.

Peck, Janice (2006) 'Why We Shouldn't Be Bored with the Political Economy versus Cultural Studies Debate', *Cultural Critique* 64 (Autumn): 92–126.

Rugh, William A. (1980) 'Saudi Mass Media and Society in the Faisal Era' in W. A. Beling (ed), *King Faisal and the Modernisation of Saudi Arabia*, London: Croom Helm, pp. 125–44.

Sakr, Naomi (2008) 'Women and Media In Saudi Arabia: Rhetoric, Reductionism and Realities', *British Journal for Middle Eastern Studies* 35.2 (December): 385–404.

Slack, Jennifer Daryl (1996) 'The Theory and Method of Articulation in Cultural Studies' in David Morley and Kuan-Hsing Chen (eds), *Stuart Hall: Critical Dialogues in Cultural Studies*, London: Routledge, pp. 113–30.

Strange, Susan (1996) *The Retreat of the State: The Diffusion of Power in the World Economy*, Cambridge: Cambridge University Press.

—— (1994) *States and Markets*, London: Pinter Publishers, 2nd edn.

Walker, R.B.J. (2010) 'Conclusion: Cultural, Political, Economy' in Jacqueline Best and Matthew Paterson (eds), *Cultural Political Economy*, London: Routledge, pp: 225–33.

Williams, Raymond (1977) *Marxism and Literature*, Oxford: Oxford University Press.

——(1976) *Keywords: A Vocabulary of Culture and Society*, London: Croom Helm.

11

The Saudi Modernity Wars According to 'Abdullah Al-Ghathami: A Template for the Study of Arab Culture and Media

Marwan M. Kraidy

When the British-educated Saudi literature professor and cultural critic 'Abdullah Muhammad Al-Ghathami published *al-Khati'a wal-Takfir* (*Sin and Excommunication*) in 1985, a literary biography of the Saudi modernist poet Hamza Shahata, he triggered an impassioned public polemic about modernity and Islam in Saudi Arabia. A motley crew of hostile critics hailing from the country's clerical establishment, establishment press and conservative intelligentsia mounted a sustained assault on Al-Ghathami's work and person. Al-Ghathami's opponents launched a campaign consisting of op-ed pieces in newspapers, scathing articles in literary journals, petitions to the authorities, mosque sermons and political manoeuvring in Saudi Arabia's myriad local literary clubs, attacking Al-Ghathami's theoretical bearing, smearing his character and accusing him of the worst possible offences against Islam and Saudi Arabia, respectively – apostasy and treason. As a result, Al-Ghathami was transferred from his position in Jeddah, the Kingdom's most socially and intellectually liberal city, to the capital city of Riyadh, where he still teaches at King Sa'ud University. Al-Ghathami is perhaps one of the least known Arab modernist intellectuals in the West, most likely because, to my knowledge, his important works have not been translated from the Arabic original into any major world language. One of the objectives of this chapter is therefore to introduce a snapshot of Al-Ghathami's thought to a non-Arabophone readership.

In 2004, Al-Ghathami published *Hikayat al-Hadatha fil Mamlaka al-'Arabiyya al-Sa'udiyya* (*The Tale of Modernity in the Kingdom of Saudi Arabia*), an autobiographical account of the Saudi modernity wars. In addition to the story of a fascinating culture war that gripped one of the world's most socially conservative societies, the book is an intellectual and literary history of Saudi modernism, which has developed in a context of continuous and broad-ranging social change since the 1920, but became especially pronounced after the oil boom of the 1970s. This chapter does not focus on *The Tale of Modernity in the Kingdom of Saudi Arabia* (2004) because the book reflects a transcendental theoretical sophistication, or because it captures the minutiae of its author's thought; rather, Al-Ghathami's intellectual autobiography is important because of the ways in which it articulates theoretical discussions of modernity through the rough and tumble of the actual modernity wars that raged in Saudi newspapers, magazines, cultural and literary clubs, and universities from the mid-1980s to the mid-1990s, through the author's personal experience as a protagonist in those wars. The implications of that contentious decade continue to unfold in what can perhaps be described as a Saudi culture war, the latest episode being the Saudi chapter of the pan-Arab reality television polemics.[1]

A compelling picture of the litigious and abiding debate over the elaboration of an Arab-Muslim modernity emerges from *The Tale of Modernity in the Kingdom of Saudi Arabia*'s articulation of literary theory, cultural criticism, and social action through autobiography in the particularly daunting Saudi context. My objective in this chapter is to elucidate that picture through a systematic analysis, citing copiously from the book to reflect as much as possible the author's own voice, of Al-Ghathami's definition and theorising of modernity, then move on to analysing the role of the media in the struggle over modernity, as Al-Ghathami sees it, and finally to use some of his ideas as a prism through which contentious debates about media, culture and identity in the Arab world can be comprehended. Notably, I explore the heuristic potential of Al-Ghathami's notion of the 'symbolic event' for Arab thought about media and culture, taking into account that Saudi Arabia's position as Arab media's politico-economic centre of gravity gives Saudi debates broad pan-Arab resonance and influence on Arab cultural production at large, even if most Arab societies are less socially conservative than the Kingdom of al-Sa'ud. By thinking through some of the implications of the Saudi modernity wars for their regional context, I hope to tease out theoretical elements that could be significant for the development of Arab media/cultural studies as a theoretical project.[2]

Defining modernity

Despite countless debates over its definition, it is generally agreed that modernity entails a process of critical distancing and the recasting of established ways of thought and life. Whereas Giddens (1990) argues that modernity is 'manifestly incompatible with religion as a pervasive influence upon day-to-day life',[3] other thinkers counter Giddens' ontological ethnocentrism with evidence that religion has, in fact, not only been compatible with, but is actually necessary for, modernity. Gillespie (2008), for example, argues that Western modernity has theological origins, and Eickelman (1998) claims that religious speech enabled early European modernity. The lives of modern, yet pious, Muslim communities has been amply documented by scholars from multiple disciplines: Adelkhah (2000) on Iranians, Blanks (2001) on the Dodi Bohra in India, and Deeb on Shi'i Muslims in Beirut (2006). More sweepingly, Aziz al-Azmeh theorises the manifold connections between Islam and modernity in his revealingly titled treatise, *Islams and Modernities* (1993). What is perhaps most poignant about Saudi Arabia's experience with modernity is the backdrop – the extreme conservatism of the clerical-religious regime, the geo-historical status of the country as the cradle of Islam and the locus of the global *hajj*, and the decisive impact of oil wealth – against which battles in favour and in opposition to the modern have unfolded.

Al-Ghathami distinguishes six stages in the development of the *recent* Saudi modernity war (recent, because his chronology begins in the mid-1980s and therefore excludes the slow development of poetic modernism since the founding days of the current Saudi state). The first stage occurred in the early to mid-1980s, when initial debates about modernist poetry underwent a 'radical qualitative'[4] shift to focus on critical theory (*al-Nazhariyya al-Naqdiyya*). In the 1990s, the second stage witnessed an expansion of the purview of critical theory from poetry and literature to cultural, social and political criticism that addressed hot-button issues, such as women, language and cultural discourse. Within the same decade, new intellectuals, many of them returning from doctoral studies in the United States and France, initiated a third stage, with Mu'jab al-Zahrani returning from the Sorbonne in the early 1990s to introduce dialogism (*al-Hiwariyya*), while critics returning from the USA, like Abdulaziz al-Sabil and Hassan al-Naʿmi, introduced narrativism (*al-Sardiyya*) to the Saudi intellectual sphere. Not only were these critics young, but they also included some women, like Fatima Al-Wuhaybi. The forceful emergence of the Saudi novel in the 1990s, with its bold treatment of social issues, signalled a fourth stage. At the same time, Saudi prose poetry was published in Beirut in protest over rejections by Saudi publishers.[5] A fifth stage emerged with a heightened visibility of the debate over modernity, the rise in the number of women involved in the debate, and the emergence of the idea of a national dialogue focusing on momentous social, cultural and political issues. Al-Ghathami sees the Internet as contributing to the emergence of a sixth stage in the Saudi modernity wars, which disabled censorship and circumvented intellectual gatekeeping, opening Saudi society broadly to the heated polemic surrounding modernity.

In Al-Ghathami's account, Saudi cultural modernity harks back to the formative years of the modern state in the mid-1920s, and was forged in poetry. According to Al-Ghathami, 'modernity is *al-tajdid al-waʿi* [aware, attentive or self-reflexive renewal]. This means that modernity is an awareness of history and of the present'.[6] His definition is grounded in the Saudi experience, which 'uncovers a very early project of modernity, going back to the founding (of the Kingdom). This means that we do not restrict modernity to one discourse with no others, since all discourses are necessarily exposed to *al-tahdeeth*' [literally, 'modernisation', but in this context 'renewal' is a more apt translation].[7] He is thus espousing an approach sympathetic to the multiple modernities thesis, which rejects a necessary link between modernity and the West. Al-Ghathami then argues that modernity means different thing to different intellectuals and in different contexts, using as an example the Arab literary figures Adonis and Khalida Saʿid, who despite being married to each other, hold different definitions of modernity. In Chapter Two, Al-Ghathami gives his own detailed definition of modernity:

> It is certain methodologically that there is no (single) definition of modernity, but that it is *Hala Fikriyya Shamila* (an all-encompassing mental/intellectual state), encompassing ideas and awareness as it encompasses styles of living and management. Every social or intellectual environment has its specific definition (of modernity); even every modernist has his own specific definition that no one shares with him.[8]

In the socially conservative context of Saudi Arabia, Al-Ghathami argues that 'the stand towards modernity is the stand towards the new, is the stand towards *al-tari*'[9], which could be translated as extraneous, contingent, unforeseen. A distinctive feature of Saudi modernity, he argues, is the extreme publicness of the debate about modernity, what he calls the 'explosion of social modernity',[10] implicitly counter-posing cultural modernity, which has been restricted to literary elites since the mid-1920s, to social modernity, which, from the mid-1980s, included broader social groups.

Saudi modernity, in Al-Ghathami's opinion, reflects a socio-cultural schizophrenia. Firstly, it will remain incomplete because it is not entirely indigenous. Since Saudis achieved modernity through others, theirs will be a non-native modernity. This contrasts sharply, in the author's view, with the East Asian countries that are known as the Asian tigers. 'Though deeply steeped in tradition', Al-Ghathami writes of these countries, they 'became industrial, modernist, productive societies'. Saudis made what Al-Ghathami considers a 'fatal mistake when [they] decided to modernise [their] society as rapidly as possible, even if that meant that [they] resorted to others to accomplish this, and this is undoubtedly a fatal mistake'.[11] Second, in a Hegelian moment, Al-Ghathami faults the oil boom of the 1970s for hindering the accomplishment of a fully-fledged Saudi modernity:

> A kind of schizophrenia occurred when we abandoned manual and technical labour and accomplishment to imported hands, and we became high-minded masters who issue orders. But this is a mastery of paper and not a mastery of sweat; meaning it is not a mastery over the self and the circumstance, which makes it momentary, formal, and illusory. The boom did not become a positive modernist element and did not produce a modernist society, but only a modernity of appearances. The modernity of means did not become a modernity of mental modes and human conceptions…a total schizophrenia between the building of place and the building of human beings, and development became that of space and not that of people, with its human dimension ripped out of it.[12]

Warning that the modernisation of Saudi Arabia's infrastructure and the adoption of the technological gadgets of modern life reflected only a skin-deep foray into the modern, one that is epiphenomenal to being modern,

Al-Ghathami does not mince words. Saudi modernity, he wrote tersely, is 'a modernity of means and a reactionism of minds'.[13]

The main counter-veiling force opposing modernity and sapping its development is what Al-Ghathami calls '*al-Nassaq al-Muhafizh*', the conservative mode, a deeply entrenched 'structure of feeling' characterised by an ontological rigidity so fundamental that it makes it unable to contemplate the possibility of change. As Al-Ghathami described it, 'because of its strong transformation of knowledge production, the project of modernity at the theoretical, methodological levels was the source of a deep modal fear, which made it forbidden to mention structuralism or deconstruction and textualism in the Arabic (university) department in Jeddah, since that would be tantamount to apostasy'.[14] The deep and unyielding obscurantism of the conservative mode pre-empts the emergence of critical thinking, which in Al-Ghathami's view, made constructive dialogue impossible, because the debate over modernity was 'a battle of modes and not a battle of ideas'.[15] He continues:

> Were it a battle of ideas, then debate and dialogue would have been beneficial; but the mode does not dialogue and does not think; it becomes agitated and rejects and eliminates, and that is what happened...Courageous intellectual, critical, cultural clashes are necessary for a society to get to know itself and reveal its defects.[16]

In a modern nation-state of the size and tribal and regional diversity of Saudi Arabia, it is only through the mass media that the population experiences the consequential public battles about which Al-Ghathami writes.

The role of the media

In Al-Ghathami's retelling of the historical evolution of Saudi modernity and the polemic surrounding it, media institutions played a decisive role. Saudi Arabia is not unique in this regard, since newspapers, and in a later period television, played an important role in mediating and contesting Arab experiences with modernity. In the nineteeth century, reformers advocating selective adoptions from Western modernity throughout the Arab world effectively used newspapers as platforms.[17] The Moroccan poet, Muhammad Bennis, crystallised the opinions of many critics when he called the Arab press the midwife of modernity, spreading the 'alphabet of light'[18] to the Arab population. Decades later, as the twentieth century began, newspapers in

Aleppo and other Ottoman cities carried broad-ranging discussions about the meanings and implications of modernity.[19] Indeed, in the press, Arab modernisers found an effective platform for their ideas, especially with the development of the newspaper column, a development to which Al-Ghathami devotes considerable attention, as we shall see later in this chapter.

Television carried the role of the press in mediating modernity further, by broadening access to the debate to Arabs whose illiteracy, rural location, or meagre means shut them out of newspaper discussions. As the debate became more public, television reflected various shades of Arab ambivalence towards modernity. Egyptian television drama is a case in point. With Egypt's *infitah* (open door economic policies) television promoted consumption while also highlighting consumerism's harmful implications. Since the 1970s, Egyptian *musalsalat* have featured characters who are 'educated, sophisticated, worldly, and at the same time clearly tied with *asala* (authenticity)', reflecting a desire for national renewal while maintaining continuity with the past.[20] By fomenting individual emotionality, television drama is one of the 'technologies of modern self-making'.[21] Similarly, Moroccans' ambivalence towards Morocco has been exacerbated by satellite television which, by introducing cosmopolitan lifestyles rooted in consumerism, created what Sabry (2005) called 'mental migration'. Finally, the recent pan-Arab reality television controversies are best understood as a contentious episode in the historic debate around Arab modernity.[22]

It is not surprising, then, according to Al-Ghathami, that the mass media – both newspapers and television – have been instrumental in the forging of Saudi modernity. Though he does not organise them this way, from his book one can glimpse how fundamental tensions of modernity are articulated and contested in and through the media. These include the individual/social nexus, the rural/urban divide, the role of intellectuals, and the role of women. Since these dimensions are intricately interlinked and, to be faithful to Al-Ghathami's treatment of these issues, which weaves them together in an autobiographical narrative, I will analyse them in conjunction with each other and how they are articulated in media discourses.

The press was decisive in recasting the individual/social nexus in Saudi Arabia. Al-Ghathami describes how the appearance of the newspaper column in his country in the 1950s embodied:

> [...] a modal change in the individual's position towards himself and in his relation to the world. The individual used to be a

cell in a relationship deferring speech to the lord of the people, who did not require evidence to back what he said. But, in the column, the individual came to change the ways of expression and topple the boundaries of the permissible [...] The column [is] a foundation for the constitution of an independent, individual opinion.[23]

In Al-Ghathami's reading, the journalistic column had a revolutionary impact because it re-cast the individual social nexus by embodying 'the rise of the individual and individualism, which is not a normal thing in a conservative traditional society whose most important features are concealment and consent, on the one hand, and deference to the group on the other'.[24]

The mutual encroachment between the private realm and public life, which has become increasingly manifest in the Arab media sphere, is symptomatic of modernity.[25] Al-Ghathami considers this momentous issue in its broad social and cultural contexts, writing that a 'contradictory position between personal opinion and social opinion is a widespread practice of all selves at any moment when the self is exposed to another culture or to a new experience'. He discerns the same tension in Saudi sartorial styles:

A similar difference can be seen in our clothes, between those for outside and those for inside... we wear the robe and the headdress in Saudi Arabia, and pants and shirts abroad, starting from the steps of the airplane. How deviant we would be if we were to wear shirt and pants and went out in our society, while this is normal when we go out of our society. And so is the situation of the ideas we wear. As if we faced a local culture, like our clothes, and a foreign culture, like our travelling clothes.[26]

This 'schizophrenia between our personal position and the depicted social position',[27] Al-Ghathami seems to say, dooms our modernity to a protracted inability to become complete.

By recasting how individuals relate to society, the press enabled the rise of Saudi intellectuals, especially female intellectuals, and contributed greatly to the unification of myriad rural and tribal identification markers in the emerging national identity of Saudi Arabia, the latter being a centripetal force symptomatic of modernity. One of the most important contributions of the press was to displace cultural debate from literature to society and politics. Though newspapers existed in Saudi Arabia before the rise of the modern state, in the 1950s a new breed of journalists appeared, often coming from the rural hinterlands, and they were unshackled from the traditionalising effects of money, tribal notability [wajaha], and the journalistic experience which publishes newspapers out of intellectual adventuring and commercial ambition. These included newspapers in Jeddah [al-Adwa' (The Lights) and al-Ra'id (The Pioneer)], Dhammam and the capital Riyadh, which competed head-on with press owned by Saudi notables. Though intellectual work now enjoyed a multiplicity of platforms, the thoughts and writings of modernist intellectuals did not coalesce into a definable project. In Al-Ghathami's words, the archetype of Saudi Arabia's pioneering public intellectual was:

> [...] modernist [...] no doubt – but his consciousness of modernity was not developed... Though he tended towards social reform, he was not ready for intellectual and mental reform, because he was a momentary intellectual [muthaqqaf zharfi], meaning that he is a product of his own need as an individual to make a living first... But he did not have a full awareness that would enable him to turn his predilection into an intellectual project... a social, critical, or creative theory. As a result, his work remained cumulative and quantitative; one can barely survey the number of columns that have been written since then, but all of them do not amount to a theory to which one can refer and on the foundations of which one can build.[28]

Though the lack of a cumulative, organic project has pre-empted the emergence of a fully developed Saudi modernity, young newspapers opened up the journalistic field to female intellectuals. It is poetically and politically resonant that in 1965 the first issue of the al-Riyadh daily newspaper published the first column written by a Saudi woman, Khayriyyah al-Saqqaf, three years after education became available for Saudi girls, following a contentious battle with conservative opponents of the measure. In Al-Ghathami's lyrical telling, the 'young woman emerges with her own consciousness, to express herself, and to announce her first step in reaching for her hopes and ambitions'.[29] In that pioneering column, al-Saqqaf wrote:

> With the rise of the new Hijra year, and with hopes that it will be a year of happiness, well-being and tranquility, with the shining morning, eyes wide open, taking her first breath, breathing ambition, a fragrance spreading to fill her path with

desire... the desire that will lead her to her sought after goal, which is success.[30]

Al-Ghathami imputes to this column the emergence of a public feminine consciousness readying itself to enter into a dialogue about modernity with the hitherto exclusively male voices. Al-Saqqaf concluded her column by saying:

> I make the first step, whose traces will descend on a section of al-Riyadh's pages in the form of printed words in my corner, and al-Riyadh has more appeals, and readers, male and female, have many wishes.[31]

She thus conjures up an imagined community of women readers, rendering it visible in public space for the first time, and accessing public space for the first time as a female voice.

> Here appears a mention of female readers alongside male readers, which is especially symbolic... there was still no women's cultural constituency. But the writer spoke the language of the future and of hope, and of the first step.[32]

In Al-Ghathami's reading, al-Saqqaf's column was revolutionary, because:

> A column by a young woman who registers her name alongside her male colleagues was tantamount to a feminine alphabet, a new birth, a living birth with eyes and breaths... which eventually will write a new women's history in a society that for long has marginalized women... with expressions... that feminize the event itself [...][33]

The symbolism of that column, in Al-Ghathami's eyes, more than compensated for the fact that it was, after all, only one woman who published one column, in one newspaper in a national press with many newspapers and with numerous male writers publishing myriad columns. Nonetheless, Al-Ghathami summed up the event's symbolic significance when he wrote: 'with the column of Khayriyyah al-Saqqaf a new page of our cultural memory opened up.'[34]

The growing visibility of women intellectuals in Saudi Arabia enabled the emergence of a women's discourse that struck a balance between 'declaration and concealment, elaborating a language between two languages, between spoken language, which is women's language originally, and the written language, which was originally a male domain'[35]. This new language was distinctly modernist, and served to expose the injustice inherent in the conservative mode, gesturing towards the necessity of alternative social and gender arrangements, by bringing to the fore the oppression of women in Saudi society (poignantly, Khayriyya al-Saqqaf used the byline 'human' before signing the aforementioned *al-Riyadh* column with her real name).

In addition to unsettling the 'private–public' and 'male–female' discursive binaries of the conservative mode, the Saudi press also contributed to the undermining of the 'rural–urban' divide in the Kingdom of al-Sa'ud. Newspapers gave an important platform to rural voices, helping to integrate the nascent Saudi nation. Al-Ghathami tells the experience of 'Ali al-'Umayr – who left the Southern *rif* town of al-Jaradiya to become a nationally prominent journalist – holding a daily newspaper for the first time in his life:

> It was a moment of unprecedented awe when he held *Umm al-Qura* newspaper to read it, as he started from the first word in the right column and read word by word towards the left, and felt as his eyes went over it that words began to be fragmented, and that sentences were transformed from one meaning to another, and he was astonished to see blank space between a line in this column and contiguous lines from a contiguous column. This was not poetry for divisions to exist between one part and another. He was unable to figure out a link between lines atop columns, and did not understand that the right column was to be read vertically, and did not comprehend that the next line was the one below the first. It took him not a short time to figure out that the newspaper column is written vertically ... but a new problem confronted him when he reached the end of the right column on the first page, how to proceed [...]! He switched to the second page, but word flow was interrupted; then he thought of reading from the start of the second column on the left of the same page, and discovered that words flowed well and he figured out the layout of the page, and discovered that the newspaper was not like the book, neither in page layout, nor in text arrangement, nor in the presence of living writers in it (the newspaper), including pictures of people as if you could see them.[36]

This moment, Al-Ghathami writes, tantalised al-'Umayr to imagine himself as a writer in a newspaper, because he was attracted by the simple, direct and seemingly spontaneous writing style. This triggered a chain of events, with al-'Umayr moving to Riyadh to write for Al Jazeera magazine, eventually rising to the position of Editor-in-Chief.

The newspaper thus echoed the processes of urbanisation and sedentarisation of Saudi society, playing an important role by facilitating the rise of thinkers and writers through the socialisation of the newly urbanised classes. Al-Ghathami establishes a metaphorical link between media and modes of social organisation, describing:

> [...] the transformation of the *rif* into a city, and corresponding upheaval in mentality and vision ... the village is horizontal and proximate (*'ufuqiyya mutajawira*), based on a union that is held together like a bound book with compressed pages, whereas the city is vertical and has complicated relationships that are not based on simple proximity. It is a complicated construction whose unbinding requires complex mental tricks, as happened to this rural dweller as he discovered differences between the book and the newspaper ... this urbanised rural dweller is a blend of the old and the modern, whose story reflects the journey of transformation from tent to nation.[37]

Echoing the media historians and theorists Harold Innis and Marshall McLuhan, in addition to Benedict Anderson's famous notion of the nation as 'imagined community', Al-Ghathami produces a media ecology that undergirds the social and political transformations brought by Saudi modernity.

If the shift from book to newspaper sped up the process of unifying Saudi Arabia's tribally and geographically fractious population into a nation, television took centre stage in the polemics over modernity by broadening the reach of the mass media to a near-universal penetration in Saudi Arabia, where more than 97 per cent of the population has access to television. The modernity wars of 1985–95 coincided with an expansion in Saudi television.[38] Unavoidably in such a convergence, specialised talk shows on the national television service hosted discussions about modernity. In the early 1980s, for example, Saudi state television broadcast a show called *al-Kalima Tadduqqu al-Sa'a* (The Words Strike the Hour) that hosted leading Egyptian, Iraqi and Lebanese modernists. Though popular in the

Saudi intellectual environment, the show never hosted Saudi modernists and it was promptly cancelled. Al-Ghathami described the talk show as 'a strange event on a conservative channel, as if it were a momentary mistake, since it was not repeated'.[39] Nonetheless, his final verdict was that the programme 'contributed to the situation of modernity in its Arab dimension in a confrontation with the Saudi public'.[40]

Television itself also became the subject of attacks by conservative clerics for content that they deemed 'un-Islamic'. With the intensification of the modernity war, the Ministry of Culture and Information banned the use of the word 'modernity' in all Saudi print and broadcast media in 1988. Al-Ghathami described how his articles would be edited to replace any mention of modernity through the use of variants like *tajdid* (renewal), *tatwir* (development), or *taqaddum* (progress). Contention around television in the modernity wars intensified as Saudi Arabia grew increasingly entangled in the pan-Arab media sphere, whose productions and transmissions were funded by Saudi moguls, princes and notables, but whose content could not be controlled by the Saudi clerical establishment. With the Saudi-owned Middle East Broadcasting Centre (MBC) initiating satcasts from London in 1991, followed by the Lebanese channels Lebanese Broadcasting Corporation and Future TV in 1996, and by dozens of satellite channels – general entertainment, music, and women's channels[41] – whose content violates the Wahhabi norms predominant in Saudi Arabia, the stage was set for the Saudi modernity war to become embroiled in regional battles over popular culture. The 'Saudi-Lebanese connection', a combination of Saudi capital and Lebanese creative know how, undergirds to a large extent the reality television polemics of 2003–08, with the Saudi chapter of those controversies being an extension of the Saudi modernity wars of 1985–95.[42] At this point it is useful to recapitulate two crucial ingredients in Al-Ghathami's vision of Saudi modernity. First, he advances a notion of modernity that is only contingently linked to Western modernity. Though I do not doubt Al-Ghathami's theoretical integrity, his notion of modernity is politically useful in his battle against the guardians of what he calls the conservative mode, since it pre-empts Al-Ghathami's opponents from depicting him as a Westernised intellectual, alienated from his own culture (this is not unique to Al-Ghathami, since most Saudi liberals are deeply grounded in local culture and politics, with outside influence being relatively small). His focus on the elaboration of a specifically Saudi modernity locates him within the multiple modernities literature. Second, Al-Ghathami, in line with other Arab historians and intellectuals, considers the media an important arena in which the battle of modernity is fought. While the newspaper column enabled the development of male, and then female, public intellectuals in Saudi Arabia, who entered the fray of the modernity war, since the 1980s television has broadened the reach and scope of the debate. In this context, it is now time to focus on some of Al-Ghathami's potential conceptual contributions to the study of culture and media.

The symbolic event

In his autobiographical account of the Saudi modernity wars, Al-Ghathami develops a concept that is worth considering as a building block in the project of Arab media and cultural studies: *al-Hadath al-Ramzy*, or the *symbolic event*. Though it bears some resemblance to concepts like media scandals, moral panics, and media events, or even the contentious politics approach, the notion of the 'symbolic event' stems from the specificities of the Saudi context. As Al-Ghathami describes it:

> Among the features of a symbolic event is that it encounters public opposition, and the stronger the opposition, the stronger the symbolism. As to events that do not elicit reactions, they remain outside the scope of intellectual and mental (awareness), and people remain neutral as if the event had not occurred.[43]

The symbolic event is important because it constitutes an important polemical effervescence in society. Taking his own case as an example, Al-Ghathami describes how a symbolic event unfolds:

> The attack on modernity and its model *Sin and Atonement,* expanded … intensifying from 1985 to 1990, and Arab residents in Saudi Arabia entered the debate, which became a topic to which were attributed all the problems of the nation and all the dangers of the future, until it reached mosques' pulpits, and animated Friday sermons, and became material for preachers, missionaries, *fatwa* makers, cassette-tapes, publications and posters. Books were published and *fatwas* were issued, and [*Sin and Atonement*] became the talk of councils and societies, and was the talk of Saudi society for five full years.[44]

This intensity is crucial in a country like Saudi Arabia, whose social conservatism can only be shaken by extreme outbursts of controversy. Al-Ghathami situates his argument comparatively when he writes:

> Undoubtedly, some of the most advanced societies, like France and the United States, suffer from conservative ways, but the difference between our traditionalism and their conservatism is that we only have one predominant mode, with no co-present modes with which it enters into dialogue and with which it can be mutually held accountable. The proximity of modes leads to a modernisation of society and its ways of thinking through exchanges ... the absence of such proximity reinforces the sovereignty of a single mode, and keeps a sensibility of elimination and rejection, which leads to breaking any progress.[45]

As a result of the doctrinal rigidity of the conservative mode, public debates do not move forward, but face a bewildering array of attacks, which reduces progress to cosmetic entrapments. 'We face this cultural tragedy', writes Al-Ghathami, 'which consists of a move from simple symbolic progress to a regression; this crisis of culture reveals that our cultural awareness remains weak and unable to withstand a counter-revolution'.[46] Clearly, in Al-Ghathami's view, Saudi Arabia suffers from a permanent crisis of culture, in which modernist ideas introduced into public discourse face opposition of such power and intensity that they inflict severe setbacks on the cause of modernity.

In this debilitating context, the symbolic event serves the important purpose of unmasking those who pretend to be modernists while holding reactionary ideas. Within that group, two types can be glimpsed in Al-Ghathami's book. First, is the Saudi business figure who emerged during the 1970s with the oil boom, who Al-Ghathami calls 'the new individual':

> He is selfish, materialist, and acquisitive; with a language compatible with the conditions of change, their possibilities and their value systems ... lying entered the real estate market until it became an acknowledged feature. It became taken for granted that real estate peddlers were not to be believed, and it became noticeable that their vocabulary created fixed forms that constituted a market discourse employed by market movers, its victims the innocent who still use the native [fitri][47] social language, with its innocence, transparency and credulity. They do

not notice the transformation of the discourse, so they fall into the cracks in expression.[48]

Though Al-Ghathami does not explicitly focus on the distinction between modernisation, modernism and modernity, this case clearly reflects a modernisation of the Saudi socio-economic system in which the values of financial accumulation and conspicuous consumption took centre stage. (He does ask the rhetorical question: 'Is the modernization of means sufficient for the modernization of mentalities'... ?).[49] The new, boom-produced Saudi individual embodies a new kind of work where:

> [...] earning was not a result of individual genius, or special skills, or competitive training; it was rather linked to circumstance, on the one hand, and to linguistic metaphor which relies on a separation between the word and the deed, and between truth and reality. It carries predictable marketing lies, and fake exaggeration [...] This was the individual with modernist features, but only metaphorically modernist, unrealistic and irrational.[50]

This metaphorical modernism (*hadathiyya majaziyya*) was the playground not only for budding Saudi businessmen and investors, but also for Saudi intellectuals who pretended to be modernist, and by doing so played directly into the hands of the conservative mode. Al-Ghathami cautions against the phenomenon where

> [...] you find a reactionary author using modernist language, decorating his sayings with the modern notion. This is a modal trick, which makes the author appear, on the surface, to be in synch with the modernist discourse, and fool himself into thinking he is one of them [the modernists].[51]

It is here that Al-Ghathami makes the distinction between literary critics who claim to be modernists, but who restrict themselves to non-controversial and non-consequential issues, and cultural critics – the real modernists in his view – who are not afraid to enter the fray of broad-based and contentious social and cultural debates. 'When I consider the question of the boom to be related to the question of modernity', Al-Ghathami explains, 'it is because I am practising 'cultural criticism', which is the criticism of social modes and the way that these modes deal with the self and with the other'.[52] It is precisely this *social* mode of address that distinguishes the *cultural* critic and *public* intellectual from the literary critic that explains the intensity of the opposition to Al-Ghathami. Notably, his nemesis, al-Milibari, was motivated in his critique of proponents of modernity, as Al-Ghathami explained, by the fact that 'the matter was no longer modern poetry and modern taste, but rather a mental and methodological transformation, a project to reconsider and criticise rational discourse, and to deconstruct the culture in its entirety, and this is the beginning of deconstruction, its signal and its theoretical foundation'.[53]

Conclusion

Al-Ghathami sees the struggle over the definition, impact and implications of Saudi modernity as a battle of modes (*Sira' al-Ansaq*): 'the tale of modernity here', he writes, 'is a tale of culture and the movement of modes'.[54] Clearly, therefore, he sees the elaboration of modernity as a contentious process that involves societies and cultures broadly, beyond the confines of the halls of academe, literary periodicals and poetry recitals. *A major contribution of Al-Ghathami therefore consists in his call to expand the purview of modernist scholars from the literary through the cultural, leading ultimately to the political.* His notion of the symbolic event, therefore, resonates with his concerns that the politics of modernity should exceed rarified debates about modernist aesthetics. Ironically, his autobiography is a clear illustration of his call. His publication *Sin and Excommunication* (1985) is essentially a treatise about the modernist poetics of Hamza Shahata, and triggered an impassioned culture war that moved the debate about modernity into Saudi society at large. *The Tale of Modernity in the Kingdom of Saudi Arabia* (2004) can thus be read contrapuntally to *Sin and Excommunication* (1985), the former acting as a book-end to a series of chapters opened by the latter.

If, as Paddy Scannell eloquently wrote, US communication research in the 1930s, and British cultural studies three decades later, were shaped by specific historical experiences and can be best understood as a 'determinate effect of the historical process; responses to the pathologies [the disorders] of modernity',[55] then Al-Ghathami's work stands a great chance of emerging as foundational for Arab cultural and media studies. Arab cultural studies will not necessarily follow intellectual trajectories initiated in Birmingham, nor will it necessarily tackle the same topics that emerged from British cultural studies. As an emergent and scattered assemblage of infant intellectual energy, Arab cultural and media studies risks being over-determined if we carry the comparison with the well-established, relatively coherent, and far older Anglo-Saxon variants. Nonetheless, there is a great deal to be learned from comparing these different, but similar experiences. In that context, categories of analysis used in *The Tale of Modernity in the Kingdom of Saudi Arabia* (2004) could emerge as key concepts in Arab cultural studies. Gender, for example, is an important dimension of Al-Ghathami's work. He clearly sees women and the media to be symbiotically connected in the contentious emergence of Saudi modernity. Future research could focus on explaining the ways in which gender concerns in the study of culture in the Arab world, and build on but modify gender-based analysis in the West. How does Al-Ghathami's analysis of the rural–urban divide in Saudi Arabia, and the tribal connotations that it carries, inform a theorisation of class identity in Arab cultural studies that differs from Marxist UK/US analyses? Finally, to what extent can Al-Ghathami's notion of the symbolic event inform our analysis of the numerous contentious episodes – past, present and future – that characterise the painful but necessary processes of social, political, cultural and intellectual change in the Arab world?

Answering these questions requires thoughtful, polyphonic, multi-sited, sustained efforts on the part of scholars of Arab media and cultural studies. As we pursue this path, there is a lot we can learn from Al-Ghathami's experience. Through his adoption of a version of the multiple modernities thesis, Al-Ghathami, in effect, enacts an intellectual agenda that reaches beyond merely theoretical and gestures towards a political horizon. Separating modernity from Westernisation is a strategic rhetoric that robs his opponents in the Saudi culture wars of the most potent weapon in their arsenal: the discourse of authenticity and its resonant rejection of Western influence in any shape or form. In this, Al-Ghathami is an important voice within the still emergent literature on multiple modernities, not least because of his articulation of British training and Saudi positionality, and of his combination of a proclivity for theory and his willingness to engage in contentious public intellectual work. After Al-Ghathami was moved from Jeddah to Riyadh, his opponents claimed victory in the Saudi modernity wars. Critics of Al-Ghathami, like Mohammed 'Abdallah al-Milibari, Ahmad al-Shibani, and Sa'id al-Ghamdi, claimed credit for 'extinguishing modernity in Saudi Arabia'.[56] Al-Ghathami disagreed with his critics' claims. For the chief protagonist in the battle that inspired the book discussed in this chapter, even if 'the open struggle centered on modernity as a notion and as an arena of

struggle and discussion' had come to an end, 'modernity remained, interacting in various ways, and multiplied in various fashions'.[57]

The picture that emerges from *The Tale of Modernity in Saudi Arabia*
is that of a thinker synthesising various worldviews and multiple cultural
sensibilities, and translating theoretical insight into socio-political debate.
Admirably, Al-Ghathami writes in Arabic, is deeply imbued with Saudi
Arabia's social context and intellectual life, and blends effortlessly theoretical insights from structuralism, deconstruction, and Arab poetics. His
importance for the project of Arab media and cultural studies, therefore,
resides less in his *strictu sensu* theoretical work than in his being a role
model. Through his words and actions, Al-Ghathami depicts a productive
way of being a theoretically based, socially engaged, scholar-practitioner of
Arab cultural studies. Said differently, Al-Ghathami offers a template for
how to think and how to be in the protracted elaboration of Arab modernity.
This, in my opinion, is Al-Ghathami's most momentous achievement.

Notes

1. Kraidy 2009.
2. All translations from the Arabic original are mine; unless otherwise indicated,
   all page numbers listed in this chapter refer to Al-Ghathami, M. (2005) *The
   Tale of Modernity in the Kingdom of Saudi Arabia*, Beirut and Casablanca: Arab
   Cultural Centre.
3. Giddens 1990: 109.
4. Al-Ghathami 2005: 288.
5. This is emblematic of the historical relationship that I explore in depth as the
   'Saudi-Lebanese Connection'. See Chapter 3 of *Reality Television and Arab
   Politics: Contention in Public Life*, Cambridge University Press. In that regard,
   Al-Ghathami also writes that 'the first *diwan* by Fawziyya Abu Khaled was
   published in 1973 with the title: *Dense with Meaning: Until They Kidnap You
   On the Wedding Night*, and the *Weeping Rhymes* Diwan by Thurayya Qabel was
   published in 1963, both in Beirut (p. 141).
6. Al-Ghathami 2005: 38.
7. Ibid: 39.
8. Ibid: 35.
9. Ibid: 31.
10. Ibid: 33.
11. Ibid: 171.
12. Ibid: 172.
13. Ibid: 173.
14. Ibid: 231.

15. Ibid: 241.
16. Ibid: 241.
17. See Hourani 1983.
18. Bennis 2004: 121.
19. Watenpaugh 2006.
20. Armbrust 1996: 22.
21. Abu-Lughod argues that Egyptian television serials contribute to a modernist project by shaping national political and social debates and by promoting a 'distinctive configuration of narrative and emotionality' (2005: 113).
22. Kraidy 2009.
23. Al-Ghathami.
24. Al-Ghathami 2005: 126.
25. Kraidy 2009.
26. Ibid: 26.
27. Ibid: 27.
28. Ibid: 126–27.
29. Ibid: 133.
30. Cited in Al-Ghathami 2005: 134.
31. Ibid: 136.
32. Ibid.
33. According to Al-Ghathami, Thurayya Qabel was the first Saudi woman to publish a poetry *Diwan* in 1963. Khayriyya al-Saqqaf had previous appearances in the local press, but this was a symbolically important step, a self-penned column (ibid: 135).
34. Al-Ghathami 2005: 137.
35. Ibid: 137.
36. Ibid: 129–30.
37. Ibid: 130–31.
38. See Kraidy and Khalil 2009.
39. Al-Ghathami 2005: 99.
40. Ibid: 100.
41. See Kraidy and Khalil 2009.
42. See Kraidy 2009, Chapter 3, for a detailed critical discussion of the historical links between Saudi Arabia and Lebanon and their role in pan-Arab media.
43. Al-Ghathami 2005: 100.
44. Ibid: 207.
45. Ibid: 146.
46. Ibid: 146.
47. *Fitri* can be defined as natural, instinctive, innate, native, inborn.
48. Al Ghathami 2005: 162.
49. Ibid: 171.
50. Ibid: 164.
51. Ibid: 168.

52. Ibid: 171.
53. Ibid: 212.
54. Ibid: 219.
55. Scannell 2006: 4, quoted in Sabry, 2008: 241.
56. Al-Ghathami 2005: 285.
57. Ibid: 287.

Bibliography

Abu-Lughod, Laila (2005) *Dramas of Nationhood*, Chicago: University of Chicago Press.
Adelkhah, Fariba (2000) *Being Modern in Iran*. New York: Columbia University Press.
al-Azmeh, Aziz (1993) *Islams and Modernities*. London: Verso.
Al-Ghathami, Abdullah (2005) *The Tale of Modernity in the Kingdom of Saudi Arabia*. Beirut and Casablanca: Arab Cultural Centre. (in Arabic)
Armbrust, Walter (1996) *Mass Culture and Modernism in Egypt*, Cambridge University Press.
Bennis, Muhammad (2004) *Fractured Modernity*. Casablanca: Toubqal Press. (in Arabic) Blanks, Jonah (2001) *Mullahs on the Mainframe*, Chicago: University of Press.
Deeb, Lara (2006) *An Enchanted Modern*, Princeton, NJ: Princeton University Press.
Eickelman, Dale (1998) 'Inside the Islamic Reformation', *Wilson Quarterly* 22.1: 80–89.
Giddens, Anthony (1990) *The Consequences of Modernity*. Palo Alto: Stanford University Press.
Gillespie, Michael (2008) *The Theological Origins of Modernity*, Chicago: University of Chicago Press.
Hourani, Albert (1983) *Arabic Thought in the Liberal Age: 1789–1939*, Cambridge: Cambridge University Press.
Kraidy, Marwan (2009) *Reality Television and Arab Politics: Contention in Public Life*, Cambridge and New York: Cambridge University Press.
Kraidy, Marwan and Khalil, Joe (2009) *Arab Television Industries*, London: British Film Institute/ Palgrave Macmillan.
Sabry, Tarik (2005) 'The Day Moroccans Gave up Couscous for Satellite: Global TV, Structures of Feeling and Mental Emigration', *Journal of Transnational Broadcasting Studies* Volume: 1.1: 197–221.
—— (2008) 'Arab Media and Cultural Studies: Rehearsing New Questions' in K. Hafez (ed.), *Arab Media: Power and Weakness*, New York: Continuum. pp. 238–51.
Watenpaugh, David (2006) *Being Modern in the Middle East: Revolution, Nationalism, Colonialism, and the Arab Middle Class*, Princeton: Princeton University Press.

12

Cultural Criticism: Theory and Method[1]

Abdullah Al-Ghathami
Translated from the Arabic by Muhammad Ayish

A central question frequently raised in criticism circles relates to whether literature possesses features other than those embedded in its 'literary form of expression'. To address this question, I have scrutinised a whole range of the accumulated literary works that have formed the basis of discussion in this chapter. The 'historicisation' of text and the 'textualisation' of history are two central components of a critical theory that has won broad acclaim for its sound conceptual and methodological features.

The deep-rooted meaning of literature as a form of expression is bound to preclude the academic/formal conceptions of its literary features, thus rendering a vision of literature as a discursive arena that is formulated by the cultural establishment and defined by inherited and modern aesthetic and linguistic perfectionism (*Balaghiya* or rhetoric). Amongst other things, this orientation enables us to carry out classifications, inclusions and exclusions in literary forms of expression based on that linguistic perfectionism. In addition, we also tend to conceive of high arts as being followed by more inferior 'low' arts that do not fit the official establishment definition of what high art is. We all know how *One Thousand and One Nights* was widely viewed as catering to an audience of boys, women and 'weak-hearted' persons. This classification scheme is more in tune with the cultural norm that controls how official discourse defines our relationship with 'the other', who happens to be 'different' and 'weak', like women and children. It also has a bearing on how we view the discourse that addresses weak people, something that renders the text as disrespected as it does its envisioned target audiences.

The above classification is just one example of the endeavours that have created two levels of literature: the official and the folkloric. It is clear that this classification scheme has been undermined by the quality of discourse that enables us to see high literature as being divorced from low literature, and accorded superior (snobbish) values that have collided not only with subjects' (people's) views, but also with the critical establishment itself. In this case, high discourse has been conceived only through its aesthetic and snobbish or selfish values. It is by default, aesthetic, and if you wish to be critical of it, you will be constrained by its aesthetic imperatives in aspects that may not be compatible with the rules of rhetoric or with institutional expression conventions, which have long stifled genuine cultural criticism and that have transformed the critic into a guardian for the institution. As a result, critical consciousness has stagnated, because criticism has come to be dominated by the establishment, which owes much of its development to the critic himself. It is not strange, therefore, to see pioneers avoiding the use of the term 'critic' in their classification scheme. Latecomers, when using the term, gave it no critical dimension beyond its aesthetic and institutional features. As a result, the act of criticism remained captive to norm analysis without venturing into exposing the woes of discourse, that embrace the woes of the critical establishment itself and its role in stereotyping acts of reception, taste, interpretation, and the subjection of the act of reading to the conditions of the establishment and its conventions. What was beautiful in the eyes of ancient critics was preserved in the eyes of modern critics, and difference is visible only in the way the aesthetic is addressed and the means by which its new interpretations are generated. Both Abu Tammam and Al Mutanabi have remained towering figures (*Fohoul*) in our poetry traditions as we turned a blind eye to the serious damage they and others had inflicted on our cultural norms. Modern examples include poets like Nizar Qabbani and Adonis, both of whom have shocked us as being regressive, while the critical establishment views them as progressive. In particular, the progressiveness of Adonis has been taken as being sacred and unquestionable. As we analyse the dominant Arab discourse, we will see that both men's works have an amazing affinity with literary forms of expression produced by classical poets.

We call here for the liberation of the term 'Literary features' (*Adabeyya*) from the bonds of institutional conceptions through a reconsideration of the questions of aesthetics and its representations in discourse. In the meantime, it is necessary that we expose the defects of the aesthetic approach and unveil the ugly face of its discourse. As much as we have developed theories in aesthetics, we need also to have theories in 'ugliness' that focus on the defects of the aesthetic.

Criticism, as both a concept and a theory, has the potential to perform functions other than those originally conceived for it in the context of its century-long usage in promoting and rationalising aesthetics and imposing it on cultural consumption patterns. Due to criticism's power to carry out these functions in light of its proven effectiveness in analysis and interpretation, sacrificing it would deprive us of an important instrument of analysis, thus giving way to the domination of a whole array of philosophical premises that shape the depth and breadth of our thinking patterns. This is exactly what has happened to works of criticism shrouded in intellectual terminologies that are intrinsically institutional, even if they may at face value demonstrate the contrary. In this case, we find a discourse embedded in sound intellectual foundations while lacking in critical orientations, yet presenting itself as a parallel discourse. Variations do not seem critical at face value, but when it comes to interpretation and employment, we find embedded discourse norms that, when combined with other equally forceful norms, give rise to a strong sense of submission that many cultural audiences may find uncritical.

It is suggested here that what we need is a qualitative transition that addresses this same question of criticism. This will not be achieved unless this critical tool undergoes some transformations to liberate it from its associations with the literary subjects it seeks to analyse. Criticism is labelled as literary, and here literary features more or less reflect the institutional connotations of the term. Hence, our task is to rid what is literary of its institutional character and to open up venues for other discourses that have remained off limits for the 'kingdom of literature', like narrative genres, and unconventional and un-institutional forms of expression. According to modern sociological thinking, what is significant is an expressive language and discourse, whether it is a motion, an act, a form or a text, all are parts of a discourse norm. As such, there is no distinction between a high and a low discourse, especially when we notice that the un-institutional is the most influential among the masses. Let us compare any modern or ancient poem with other forms of neglected discourse that have not been highly considered from an institutional point of view, like jokes, songs and rumours, and discover which genres produce the greatest effect on people. We should not be inclined to deny the literary value of these forms because they are full of metaphorical, connotative, and symbolic values, and they function within deep and serious discourse norms. The proof of all of this is evident in their huge power, which is unmatched by any official discourse, regardless of how forcefully it is being marketed or established. This is an aspect that has received little attention by critics, and this is mainly due to the limitations of the terminology, which remains captive to classical features of literary expression.

The liberation of the term from its institutional bondage is the prime condition for the liberation of the critical tool since both have an eternal linkage. Our thesis in this chapter addresses this matter and seeks to employ the critical terminology in its non-literal sense by shifting it to the cultural context, something that requires many modifications in the term to fulfil its newly prescribed function against a backdrop of multiple experiences that continue to shape our thinking.

How do we bring about a qualitative shift in critical action from the literary to the cultural fields? To do this, we need a series of procedural operations that embrace:

a)   A transition in the critical terminology itself.
b)   A transition in the concept (norm).
c)   A transition in function.
d)   A transition in application.

The following section addresses each of these transitions.

The terminological transition

It is not wise to assume that the critical terminological system can be manipulated by any single change initiated by a lone, hard-working scholar. We should also not assume possession of a comprehensive knowledge of what critical traditions have come to offer throughout their long and varied history. The best way to address this issue is to extract the defining critical, conceptual and operational foundations of the model we are supposed to develop. To do this, we need to develop creative ways to harness the critical tool which has traditionally been defined as literary, always obsessed with aesthetics in the field of the 'cultural' rather than 'literary' criticism. In this case, we need to view transition as a qualitative process bearing on both substance and tool, as well as on the interpretation mechanisms and material selection methods that we use to classify them, to identify texts and samples long subjected to literary criticism, in its institutional sense.

The terminological transition, being the prime and most important one, includes six terminological areas:

1. Message elements (norm function).
2. Metaphor and holistic metaphor.
3. Cultural puns.
4. Type of signification.
5. The qualitative statement.
6. The double-authored work.

These six foundations will form the basis of our cultural criticism project.

1. *Message Elements (Norm Function)*: Roman Jakobson has undoubtedly come a long way in reinforcing the literary traits of literature, and has contributed to answering the ancient central question about what confers a literary nature on any linguistic text, or what makes a literary text part of literature. Jakobson borrowed the communication model from media studies and transferred it to literature.[2] The model is based on six elements: addresser (sender), addressee (receiver), a message that moves in context and code, and the channel as the communication tool. The function of language varies depending on how it relates to each of these elements. The aesthetic\literary function is achieved when the message focuses on itself. This was a remarkable critical achievement with important implications for literary studies. However, it clearly offers excessive focus on the literary features of texts, something that does not seem to help much in liberating the terminology. Ignoring the model, however, may not be helpful in addressing this issue. I suggest, therefore, the modification of this model by the addition of a seventh element: 'the norm component'. As long as the communication process takes place between a sender and a receiver through a message delivered via diverse channels, and based on codes used by the receiver to understand the message within commonly-shared contexts (which is central to achieving the acts of communication and

interpretation), we achieve an interpretation of the message within a norm context (which we will elaborate on in this chapter).

In this revision, language acquires a seventh function, which is the 'norm function', in addition to its other six functions: the *phatic, emotive, referential, meta-lingual, conative* and *poetic* (aesthetic). We are not inventing a new function for language, just as Jakobson did not invent the six analytical functions, but revealed them for the purposes of scrutiny and research. There is no doubt that all forms of human communication have embedded in them some norm significations that bear on how we understand and interpret messages. Non-literal text has stronger affinity to norm functions, without excluding literal texts from this relationship.

If we agree on the existence of this seventh component (norm) and its function, we are able to focus on norm dimensions that shape our interpretation patterns and discourse. In the meantime, we should bear in mind what is familiar to us as fitting our expectations about what is aesthetic and significant in text and what is conceived of as being relevant to historical and social conditions. Hence, the norm function comes through as part of the norm component. This has very important implications for cultural criticism as elaborated in this chapter, as it offers a basis for the conceptual and operational transition from literary to cultural criticism in which text is viewed as a cultural incident or anecdote and not merely as literary output. After adding the seventh component, the communication model looks like this:
In this case, language has come to embrace seven functions:

- Intra-communication/emotive (when discourse is sender-centred).
- Phatic (when discourse is receiver-centred).
- Referential (when discourse is context-centred).
- Meta-lingual (when discourse is code-centred).
- Conative (when discourse is channel-centred).
- Poetic/aesthetic (when discourse is self-centred).[3]
- Norm functions (when discourse is centred on the norm element as we attempt to develop norm-based criticism).

(Addresser) Sender	Code	(Addressee) Receiver
	Context	
	Message	
	Channel of	
	Communication	
	Norm Element	

2. *Metaphor and Holistic Metaphorism*: The metaphor remains the principal feature of text-based action. However, we need to point out here that a metaphor has a cultural rather than rhetorical or aesthetic value, as is often suggested. Rhetorical portrayals in literature have always dominated the concept and operation of metaphors, turning them into an aesthetic and conceptual institution that defines the production and interpretation of texts. This is contrary to the saying that a word in its pre-usage phase carries no sense of realism or metaphor and its value is rather a function of language usage. This makes usage the basis of critical description and identification, two functions that carry public and collective, rather than individual characteristics; something that suggests usage as a prime action of culture. This requires that we turn usage into a conceptual and theoretical foundation, and that suggests the existence of numerous cultural genres that give rise to new rhetorical genres that define our discourse. It is also central in evolving a new function for usage that defines how it will be employed, something that suggests metaphorical action as intrinsically a product of the cultural contexts and actions that determine the nature of usage. In fact, usage is the operational definition of cultural action that has a public and collective character.

Based on this approach, we now turn to the concept of rhetorical criticism that addresses the metaphor in order to work out a cultural perspective that enhances its operation within a context of usage that lends itself to the norm action and its ramifications.

The rhetorical concept of the metaphor revolves around the use of the single word, although it may embrace the sentence, but can never tackle discourse as a text entity. Since the theory of metaphor is based on the act of signification which we call real rhetoric, and since the metaphor describes how language changes the meanings of words beyond their explicit meanings, we need to take account of this preliminary concept of the metaphor to scrutinise the cultural act in light of the direct expressive functions of language and its indirect influences. If we take into account metaphor functions as they exist and as they have a bearing on our relationship with language, we realise that it is a holistic double phenomenon, rather than a single manifestation at the level of the word or sentence. It is also a dualism that relates to our consciousness of language and its effects on us. This suggests that discourse carries two primary dimensions, one is present in language action, and this is the one clear to us in the aesthetic features of language and its six functions. Whatever is included in the language actions that produces signification and enables understanding and interpretation of that language is an aspect of the present action that can be defined and studied. Even though it may look vague and complex, its operation remains within linguistic reach. This is typically in tune with what we know of critical and rhetorical perspectives and reception and interpretation theories.

The other dimension touches on the embedded rhetorical feature of discourse, which is the real engine of our interactions with states of expression and as such defines our actions as well as our mental and taste patterns. The two dimensions have a holistic character in language and as such, they need a holistic approach if they are to be unravelled. As the concept of rhetoric has proven its power to reveal and identify signification transformations at word and sentence levels, the expansion of the concept will assist us in understanding the more dangerous signification dualism which inhabits cultural discourse in its holistic and collective sense.

Through using the norm element and its norm functions, and by expanding the concept of metaphor as a holistic concept that is not based on the real-metaphorical duality, and does not stop at the boundaries of word/sentence, but can accommodate all norm elements in the discourse, and reception actions, we can argue for the notion of holistic metaphor as associated with the norm function of language, and both concepts are basic to our cultural criticism project as viable conceptual and operational alternatives to literary criticism.

3. *Cultural Puns*: We may safely argue that one of the most significant achievements of rhetoric is the pun, which suffers from some of the defects associated with rhetorical jargon in addition to its preoccupation with intentional and explicit expressive phenomena in the production and interpretation of discourse. Modern criticism has inherited this rhetorical feature, as scholars in the field of cultural criticism become less interested in linguistic consciousness and more in norm-embedded meanings, which may not be revealed by traditional rhetorical or literary critical tools. This should prompt us to bring about changes that would expand our ability to act without depriving ourselves of the benefits of accumulated rhetorical traditions.

In conceiving of puns, we see basic dualism in two signification dimensions: one is direct, the other is imagined. This is an important approach for cultural criticism as problems often arise from the fact that the real concept of the pun refers to its imagined dimensions. By doing so, the whole process is subjected to intentionality and consciousness, which is then transformed into an aesthetic game. This is what dragged rhetoric into the pure aesthetics field, making it a science in language aesthetics, and deprived it from being a tool of criticism or reading discourse norms. This is also the exact case in criticism, where critical action is confined to the realm of what we are conscious of and the critic's mission has not been how to reveal but how to interpret. It does not invent or establish the aesthetic, but only tells us why it is beautiful, as noted in the structural question raised by Lévi Strauss. It guides us to how to imitate the beautiful and taste it, but it fails to uncover the implicit meanings and dilemmas of cultural discourse, because it is constrained by the shackles of aesthetic methodologies.

Puns are based on this dual signification feature of the present and the imagined that we would like to use in the institution of our conceptions of cultural norms in their explicit and implicit dimensions. We need to be cognisant of the fact that the explicit part has generated a good deal of critical discussion, while implicit norms have received the least attention, despite their deep-rooted effects. Transferring the concept of puns from rhetoric to cultural criticism requires the expansion of the concept beyond its present and imagined dimensions, and employing it to denote the state of discourse that embraces two features: the implicit and the unconscious, for both writer and reader. It is an embedded cultural norm that has not been constructed by a single author, but has accumulated through successive processes that feed into discourse. Its revelation requires special tools; it is taken as a pun in its cultural sense based on the signification dualism that seems to fulfil this function. One of the pun's dimensions deals with the present and the explicit, while the other thrives on the imagined and the implicit, and the latter is far more effective than the former. Again, the way puns are used is not an individual act, but an accumulation of discourses and behaviours representing specific genres that embrace acting and acted-upon objects.

4. *Type of Signification*: Literary criticism has been based on text relationship with processes of signification production by sorting out two types of signification: the explicit and the implicit. It is noted that the

text becomes more literary with the dominance of explicit signification. There is no quantitative balance between the two types of signification as we may find one single covert signifier that embraces a full-scale text or group of texts, like the novel or such literary genres as the 'innocent poetry' (*Othri*) tradition, or it may be confined to one statement, as is evident in proverbs, while overt signifiers are associated with sentences and the conditions for linguistic communication.[4]

Based on our view of the seventh element of the communication scheme, we propose a third type of signifier: the norm signifier. While the explicit signifier is contingent on grammar and utilitarian-communicative features, the implicit signifier is connected with the aesthetic function of language. Norm signifiers are connected with networked relationships that have evolved over the years to form a cultural element that has gradually taken shape to develop into an effective component. As a result of their phased development, norm signifiers have managed to penetrate into the deep dimensions of discourse, continuing to move between language and human mentality, creating deep-running effects without any critical reactions as criticism has continued to be pre-occupied with aesthetic aspects of text with the addition of the ability of norm elements to hide. This has empowered norm elements to go unmonitored, thus perpetuating their control over us and our thinking modes. Regardless of the historical and cultural changes taking place, those changes only touch the surface and take up formalistic features due to the profound effects of the norm, something that would turn the modernist into a reactionary and the democrat into an authoritarian, despite claims of 'vanguardism' and pluralism.

What is important here is to evolve a third type of signifier, which is the norm signifier that helps reveal the norm actions within the discourse. Signifiers would be classified as follows:

1. Explicit signifiers, which reflect a communication process.
2. Implicit signifiers, which reflect literary aesthetic features.
3. Norm signifiers, which have a critical cultural dimension connected with the cultural statement, as we will see later.

5. *The Qualitative Statement*: Based on our view of the norm signifier, we need to deal with a special conception of the sentence. If the explicit significance refers to the grammatical sentence, and if the implicit

sentence arises from the literary statement, we need to develop a specific conception to allow for the reproduction of the norm signifier, something we would like to call the cultural sentence. The cultural sentence is the qualitative equivalence of the grammatical and literary sentence. We need to draw out sound distinctions between these categories with a view to the cultural sentence emanating from the peculiarities of cultural formation that generate different expressive manifestations. This requires the development of a methodological model that fits the conditions of this formation and is capable of identifying and criticising it. Hence, we have three types of sentences:

1. The grammatical sentence connected with explicit signifiers.
2. The literary sentence based on high rhetorical and aesthetic values.
3. The cultural sentence arising from the norm action embedded in the implicit signifier associated with the norm function of language.

Here, the concept of culture is aligned with Geertz's definition of culture as being neither a package of sensible behaviour, as is generally held, nor a collection of traditions and norms, but in its anthropological sense, where it is about hegemony, made up of schemes, rules, regulations, like a ready-made meal, or like computer software whose function is to control behaviour. Man is the most dependent on such unnatural programmes to regulate his conduct. What is striking, according to Geertz, is that each of us starts his life aspiring to live a thousand kinds of life, but ends up living only one.[5]

6. *The Double-Authored Work*: In critical action based on the cultural norm approach, the cultural and critical conditions turn into important components of both tool and substance. If this is not fully produced at the lexical and theoretical levels, we end up with writing that claims to be critical while yet carrying no sense of criticism. This has been the case with many studies that have sought to shift their research focus without being guided by a solid method, thus falling into norm entrapments without knowing it. This is the reason why this work seeks to draw on solid theory and method to comprehend the full scale of the research.

Concepts of holistic metaphor, cultural pun, norm function and cultural sentence will open new windows for us, thanks to this methodological vision. Through these theoretical statements, we will be able to liberate ourselves from the dominance of the theoretical/aesthetic, which is an

offshoot of the cultural norm that has deep-running control over critical taste and conventions simply because the critic is already subject to
them and is one of their products, just like those involved in culture at
the level of production or consumption. All of us are cultural products
steered by norms and only methodological discipline will liberate us from
this limitation.

This methodological discipline will enable us to discover two authored
texts: the first is the familiar text which could be implicit, ideal or actual,
and the other is culture *per se,* or what I would like to call the implicit
authored text, which is part of the norm text as noted in norm action and
its implicit effects.

This fact that the explicit authored text is culture *per se* suggests that
the normal authored text is a cultural product that is firstly imbued with
culture, as its inner discourse says something that is neither part of the
author's consciousness nor that of cultural subjects. These implicit matters
suggest meanings that contravene the basic premises of discourse, whether
intended by the author or left to readers' interpretations. What we said
about contradictions between semiotic implicitness and explicit discourse
is central for critical cultural action. Unless this condition is realised, there
will be no cultural criticism that fits the concept we are trying to promote
here. What we would like to emphasise is that the double-authored text
is highly contingent on norm signification, where contradictions seem to
thrive with serious implications and this is exactly what cultural critics
should pursue.

The concept of cultural norm

What is a cultural norm, how do we read it and distinguish it from other
norms? The concept of the norm is frequently used in public and private
discourse and sometimes it is abused in writings in a way that distorts its
signification. It starts out with a simple definition as something based on a
single norm as defined (in Arabic) by the *Waseet* Lexicon. It is sometimes
used interchangeably with structure or a group of interdependent items
forming a unified body, (see de Saussure, 1986). Some Arab scholars have
tried to evolve their own definition of the norm. Though we do not object to
the development of diverse connotations, we present the norm as a central
pillar of our cultural criticism project and, as such, it acquires certain semiotic values and lexical features as follows:

1. A norm is determined by its function rather than by its abstract existence, and the norm function occurs only in a specific and controlled situation that arises when two paradoxical discourse norms emerge, one explicit and the other implicit. In this case, the implicit overrides the explicit. This all occurs in one single text that should have some aesthetic value and mass-oriented outlook. By aesthetic we do not mean the critical and institutional definition but what is being considered by the audience or the public as such.

By applying the public and aesthetic condition in this case, we also exclude the banal and elitist types of text, as well as norm contradictions that occur in different places and in contradictory texts. Our identification of these conditions lends itself to the fact that the cultural criticism project seeks to unveil tricks used by culture to carry its discourse under different guises, with aesthetics being the trick that is the most outstanding when it is used to pass on the most dangerous and domineering norms. The exposition of those tricks is legitimate in cultural criticism and this would be impossible unless we expose explicit norms of expression. The function of the norm materialises when:

a) Two norms occur at the same time in one text.
b) The implicit is antithetical to the explicit, and unless there is an implicit norm beneath the explicit the text will not fall within the domain of cultural criticism as defined in this chapter.
c) The text must have aesthetic qualities and be consumed as such, because the aesthetic quality is the most potent medium for the passing on and perpetuation of cultural tricks.
d) The text must enjoy mass audience appeal in order to enable the development of solid statements about the deep running impact of cultural text on social and psychological structures.

Once the four conditions are met, we will be face-to-face with a norm function that carries an instance of cultural criticism.

2. From an operational point of view, this requires the reading of norms and texts as cultural cases from a cultural criticism perspective, where the text is not viewed as literary or aesthetic material, but rather as a cultural instance. Based on this, the norm signifier will be the anchoring theoretical point of revelation and exploration, while recognising other semiotic features (implicit or explicit) and the artistic value of a text that cannot be downgraded by norm signifiers. We would say, rather, that those signifiers

and the aesthetic values conferred on them serve as guises that enable norms to carry out those of their manipulative functions that have yet to be unveiled by cultural criticism. The conditions we have set are likely to exclude many texts that do not possess this norm signifier quality.

3. The norm, as an implicit signifier, is not written by an author, but rather it is deeply engrained in discourse, while culture is its prime author and its consumers are language users, writers and readers alike, and all are equal regardless of age and gender.

4. The norm here has a narrative nature that moves within a well-designed plot, therefore, it is covert and implicit and able to hide using many disguises, the most outstanding of which are linguistic and rhetorical aesthetics, where norms are passed on safely under this huge masquerade. It penetrates minds and times with amazing effects as we imagine ourselves listening to poetry, jokes or narrated rumour that goes against what we rationally believe, but we find pleasure in emotionally interacting with them and build new patterns reflecting those norms upon them. The authoritarian norm is a cultural production that has flown from the image of the Master Poet (*Fahl*), who is deeply engrained in our culture.

5. These cultural norms are eternal and dominating, normally marked by massive public consumption of their cultural products in a moment of covert norm action that we must unravel. Extensive and rapid responses suggest the workings of an implicit engine that moves peripherals and establishes a norm plot. This may be embedded in songs, costumes, folkloric tales, and proverbs as well as in poetry, jokes and rumours. All of these are rhetorical and aesthetic tricks employing metaphors and puns, and they hide within themselves an implicit cultural norm that we tend to receive conveniently because it seems compatible with an inner norm that has developed within us and not as a new occurrence, but as an ancient germ that rises up for action if conditions allow.

6. This leads us to claim some sort of a symbolic power that is marked by a holistic collective metaphoric, rather than individual nature, as in rhetorical metaphors. It is rather a cultural pun that gives form and shape to the collective implicit. The symbolic power serves as the engine that sets all of the parts in motion in a community's cultural mindset, the hidden component shaping its tastes and dominant norms.

7. I need to make a cautious note about two paradoxical norms in a single text, something that, at face value, does not refer to the text, but to

the discourse, norm of expression or articulation, whether in a single, compound or epic text, an anthology, or behavioural pattern. What is important is that both norms coexist according to the aforementioned conditions (Number 1).

We start here by suggesting that a pun is an essential term in the sense that all cultural discourses, patterns and behaviours are cultural puns with sensible and imagined meanings that we have conceived of as aesthetic art forms with varied signifiers, implicitness, and metaphors. Our interpretation thus varies at the mental and cognitive consciousness level. Beneath that, there is a norm implicitness that carries out its symbolic role as a controlling power within which norm signifiers are formed. The discourse that carries the above features is called norm discourse, and it is distinctive from other discourses in that its scrutiny draws on norm signifiers as being different from explicit and implicit signifiers. This approach also draws on the cultural sentence, as distinct from grammatical and literary sentences, just as much as norm text is different from literary text; something that eventually suggests that cultural criticism is different from literary criticism.

The function of cultural criticism: from text criticism to norm criticism

The function of cultural criticism derives from its being a theory for the critique of cultural consumption (rather than criticising culture at large and exposing its deficits). This means that the moment of cultural criticism is realised at the moment of consumption or audience reception and the acceptance of a certain discourse, which turns it into a public consumption that may not be compatible with our self-conception and views of our mission in life. This happens when the aesthetic stands on a collision course with the rational and when the rhetorical convention is not compatible with intellectual reasoning. A conflict arises between the emotional, as created by the intellectual and rational self-consciousness, and the general emotional set-up created by norm implicitness through which our perceptions and deep responses are controlled. As an example, we cite the rational consciousness that sees women as not only a body, but as a mind and an emotion. However, despite this, there remains a persistent sense of receptivity to any joke or statement that portrays female bodies as objects of lust. This is evident in discourses associated with movies, fashion shows and magazine covers, something that is not generated by men only, but also by women who take part in the production, consumption and representation of those images. This is an example of the implicit norm effect and its ability to control public sentiments. Conscious individual culture is not capable of abolishing the effects of the norm, firstly, because those effects are highly covert and, secondly, because they have been well entrenched since ancient times and their revelation requires deep and normative critical endeavours.

This critical effort is directed at the cultural body and at the norm tricks used by culture to reinforce its signifying values. These tricks are manifested in the following aspects:

a) The downgrading of reason and sentiment: this most dangerous trick of poetry and rhetoric has served as a bridge to pass on many things that foster irrational thinking in our culture and give prevalence to emotional aspects of our life.

b) There is a famous statement, which suggests that the sweetest poetry is that based on lies and hyperbole, and the poet's role is in insulating language from thinking. An implication of these attitudes is that more precedence is given to the aesthetic than to the rational and the intellectual, not only in poetry, but in all aspects of our cultural character, half of which has been overshadowed by poetic features while leaving the other half subject to the deepest effects the norm creates in our cultural consciousness.

c) We were apologetic to every poetic statement and personality until we awoke to see full patterns of values being uncritically instilled in us. They have been perpetuated and accorded a magic status, perpetrated even by those labelled leaders in enlightenment and modernisation. It is not surprising that some people claim that Arab modernism has been dominantly poetic and has left no impact on other discourse patterns in intellectual, political and economic fields – as is evident from the works of Adonis and Ihsan Abbas. They are not aware that poetry continues to be captive to norm deficiencies that make it unqualified to shape the modernisation discourse.

As a branch of general textual criticism, cultural criticism is one of the linguistic sciences concerned with criticising implicit norms that are shrouded in cultural discourse, interpreted by mass consumers, in all its manifestations, patterns and formats. In this sense, it is not concerned with revealing the aesthetic, as in literary criticism, but in excavating what is hidden beneath the aesthetic, and, as much as we have a theory of aesthetics, we need to have a theory of the un-aesthetic (ugliness), with the aim of exposing the regressive role played by norms against critical sense and consciousness.

Cultural criticism is therefore a form of a cause-and-effect science, which investigates discourse defects in body and attribution (as in *Hadith* sciences) and becomes a strict critical practice. The study of discourse deficiencies requires a method capable of dissecting texts, extracting implicit norms and monitoring their movement. As noted in the linguistic connotation of the word *Jameel*, which means 'fat' (*shahm*) as beauty (in Arabic), there is beauty in culture cushioned by fat. As much as fat is beautiful and attractive, it is also lethal and destructive to human health as if its usefulness is the guise that hides its negative effects. Likewise, rhetorical aesthetics hide their harm and ugliness and the need to expose this deficiency often turns into a critical concern.

The critical question then turns to readership as the basis for cultural consumption. The popularity of any discourse does not derive from text-related aesthetic values and practical uses, but from the dimensions associated with the norm. This is basically what cultural criticism is about.

In practice: types of norms

When people say an 'x person' hails from good ancestors, or has no ancestors at all, or somebody is a man or not a man, or a human or not a human, or a woman is original or not, they are using synonyms that denote one signifier: the cultural norm. This suggests implicit conceptions of certain desired characteristics and once these characteristics are available, the person becomes a man or genuine, and when he/she is not there, he/she turns into a beastly or primitive creature. There is a mindset that serves as a benchmark or point of reference for social behaviour.

While the word 'origin' is used to symbolically signify a set of comprehensive traits hidden in implicit meanings, those traits do not themselves alert us except in times of need, which turns them into a self-made haven used to handle those critical and uncertain moments when we seem to lack any other form of language to express the situation. These words flow from our inner subconscious reservoir to speak on our behalf.

The image of ancestral genesis and originality may come in simple forms when persons are known for their generosity, bravery and modesty, as opposed to fake men (with no known family origins), who are described as misers, cowards and self-conceited. Norms do not, however, move at simple levels only, as the situation is far more complex than we think. Social conceptions draw on inherited classifications by creating connotative images representing norm signifiers, as in stereotypes of the Saeedi (from southern Egypt), the Himsi (from central Syria), and the Houthi (from mountainous Yemen), all of whom are erroneously conceived as being mentally inferior people. The same also applies to the image of women as tools of sensual enjoyment, who have the propensity for marginalisation. Culture moves on a similar level, based on well-entrenched foundations embedded in the implicit in a discourse that makes us captive to the dominant norm.

The genesis of those conceptions is as ancient as language itself. Since language has been known as a commodity with no expiry date, with its survival drawing on its repeated use, we tend to ritualistically represent and perpetuate mental values and conventions as engrained in language without being aware of it. We are struck by the fact that a modernist poet, like Adonis, has revived the tradition of the master poet (*Fahl*) with all its old deficiencies, something that resembles a lonely man whose very existence is contingent on a mutually-exclusive vision of the other. This is indeed the image of the despotic character, as known in our ancient and modern culture, and such that that we cannot imagine a poet of Adonis' calibre seeking to reproduce in his works. We see this alarming trend as a good reason for adopting cultural criticism to expose implicit norms that leave the deepest effects on us without our being aware of them.

Here we note the poetic personality as one of the norm origins in our Arab culture, and as a trait of which we continue to be proud and with which we identify. There is no doubt that we are intrinsically poetic by nature, but this will not eventually be good news as we had come to believe. In this chapter we argue that our poetic traits have inflicted serious norm problems on our human and cultural self that we continue to reproduce and live within, something that could perhaps be a prime reason for our cultural underdevelopment. This is especially true when we realise that it is poetry that has undertaken the modernisation project, making it incumbent on us to fail, because poetry is inhabited by a norm that we cannot unravel through our traditional aesthetics-based tools. Though Ali Al Wardi (1994) was the first critic to refer to this feature, his vision was diluted by a dominant poetic mechanism that gained momentum from his failure to offer sound theory and methodology to substantiate his argument.

If we scrutinise Arab *Diwan* (anthology of literature) using our critical implicit norm methods, we would discover that poetry has been the most dangerous powerhouse of those norms, the germ hiding within the confines of aesthetics. It has continued to plague our culture through successive generations, not only in poetic discourse but in all cultural forms of expression, ranging from prose that was poeticised at an early time, to behavioural and value patterns and to communication at intra-and interpersonal levels. All norms have been poeticised as we turned into a nation of poets and poetic language. But our pleasure with all of poetic transformation is no more than a celebration of a norm trick whose implications we have yet to realise. Such poetic domination has not passed without resistance – albeit weak – that has sought to demonstrate intellectual vigour and defiant dialogue. Though that rebellious spirit has not been well harnessed in promoting a broader critical trend, its manifestations in norms of rejection and opposition continue to be visible. We find examples of this in poets' stories: their unrealistic nature has conferred on them some cultural value as they were viewed as mouthpieces of culture in exposition, criticism and revelation. If we were to consider stories told by poets, we would come up with notions of culture trying to use narrative to talk about the marginal and the banal, and this is where we find the other voice.

Each one of the ancient poets had two texts: his reported poetry and the stories mentioned in books, which have not received adequate attention. Should we give them this attention, we would find discrepancies between the language of the human and the marginalised (in stories and anecdotes) and the language of the lone individual with an inflated ego (in poetry). These are not mere poetic hyperboles or artistic aesthetic portrayals; they are configurations of a cultural norm industry that produces a social and political model to be emulated. All of this has taken place in the absence of criticism and that continues to speak favourably of the poet, the poetic language, metaphoric expressions, and the highly revered poetic imagination. These forms are deemed to be far superior to the real and the rational and have allowed for the uncritical infliction of extensive damage on our cultural norms.

The poetic discourse has acquired a degree of sacredness and immunity that has rendered criticism a cultural taboo, under the pretext of safeguarding the nobility and uniqueness of poetic expression. Disciplines dealing with poetry have become closed-minded and isolated, acquiring secondary value because they have accepted the status of servant to the Master Poet. Despite this tradition's huge theoretical and methodological potential and its rich experience in text reading, its focus on poetic aesthetics has made us oblivious to the defects of norm discourses. It has consequently allowed the domination of one of the most dangerous cultural discourses that we have perceived to be the exclusive source of knowledge. By not critically noting its norm qualities, we have failed to study the core component that gives both shape and substance to our cultural behaviour and character.

Notes

1. This is a translation of Chapter Two of the book *Cultural Criticism* by Abdullah Al-Ghathami, published by The Arabic Cultural Centre, Beirut, Lebanon.
2. Jakobson 1960: 357.
3. This last component was added by Jakobson (1960: 357) to explain how language is transformed in the literary sphere.
4. Barthes 1983: 9.
5. Geertz 1973: 44–45.

Bibliography

Alwardi, Ali (1994) *Usturat Aladab Alrafi*, London: Dar Kofan.
Barthes, Roland (1983) *Elements of Semiology*, New York: Hill and Wang.
de Saussure, Ferdinand (1986) *Course in General Linguistics*, London: Open Court.
Geertz, Clifford (1973) *The Interpretation of Cultures*, New York: Basic Books.
Jakobson, Roman (1960) 'Closing Statement' in Thomas A. Sebeok, (ed.), *Style in Language*, Cambridge: MIT Press, pp. 350–77.

13

Language as *Culture*: The Question of Arabic

Atef Alshaer

This chapter aims to highlight the theme of language in respect of its cultural relevance, particularly in the context of the Arab world. It will give an overview of some schools of thought and ideas that have focused on language and will engage with some of the relevant mainstream literature to argue for the cultural consideration of language as a system of communication that expresses social and political orientations and attitudes. In every speech community, there are particular discourses about language which primarily echo cultural and political concerns. This is true for the Arabic-speaking world, where the language is spoken by a large number of people and is rooted in a literary and intellectual history.[1] This chapter thus delves into the cultural history of the Arab world and the location of Arabic within it. For centuries, Arabic remained fundamental to the cultural and political formation of the Arab world. Meanwhile, Arab history has been fraught with ideological fragmentations and political contentions, which were heightened by the nation-state system. The language has not been immune from these cultural and political fragmentations, which are echoed in public statements, publications, media-based debates and local conversations. The centrality of language to culture is captured in the phrase, 'culture of communication', a term with the potential to institute cultural embodiment through language use. In this context, this chapter intends to articulate and suggest methods through which Arabic culture can be studied with the view that the Arabic language is an enduring component and emblem of the Arab people and history.

Language considered

The concept of language has always exercised the imagination of philosophers everywhere. In fact, there is no exaggeration in the claim that language is as fundamental to philosophy as thought is central to it. All life revolves around language as a system of articulation, meaning and communication, hence the continued interest in its nature, makeup, function and value. Language stands at the heart of any philosophical system which involves a totality of human vision and experience, mainly because it is the common guide by which the world is organised into names, entities and categories, ingredients through which our worlds are made intelligible.[2] In addition, language entails action at many levels: epistemological, physical and ideal, socio-cultural and political. Given its majestic totality and infinitude, language is not an easy topic to theorise *tout court,* or about which to make orthodox concrete claims. As Raymond Williams put it, 'a definition of language is always, implicitly or explicitly, a definition of human beings in the world'.[3] Be this as it may, one cannot escape the fact that language is an integral part of each culture. There can therefore be no proper and expansive cultural understanding of any people without knowledge of their language. It is not that language and culture are mirrors of one entity, but they do represent its important essence. Saussure, highly credited for his insights into language at the turn of the twentieth century, mentioned the relevance of the question of language to all scholars/people in a valid manner:

> [...] finally of what use is linguistics? Very few people have clear ideas on this point, and this is not the place to specify them. But it is evident, for instance, that linguistic questions interest all who work with texts – historians, philologists, etc. Still more obvious is the importance of linguistics to general culture: in the lives of individuals and societies, speech is more important than anything else. That linguistics should continue to be the prerogative of a few specialists would be unthinkable – everyone is concerned with it in one way or another.[4]

All civilisations and schools of thought dealt with and thought of the question of language and its relation to (their) culture, the Chinese, Indian, Greek, Roman and the Islamic.[5] Such widespread interest in language confirms its enduring centrality to the lives of cultures and individuals; it's the common medium by which culture is expressed. Indeed, language is the very substance by which human beings know and define each other. This seemingly obvious fact is contested or disregarded altogether. Chomsky, in his original work in the field of linguistics, excluded culture from linguistics' remit, suggesting that language is innately grounded in humans and is therefore to be studied from an inward-looking position, rather than an outward one, where language becomes about conceptual and social constructions on the basis of which (communication) interaction takes place. Chomsky intelligently introduced linguistic models to enable him to discern what he claimed to be universal innate rules that underpin the formation of human language. His position on language is ardently idealist-rationalist. It has no bearing on the empirical world in which we live insofar as it does not accord language enough attention when considering the phenomenon.[6] His stance is unique as it has gone furthest in relating language to an internal mind-related constitution that bears no outward significance. However, I take the position in this chapter that, just as it seems obvious that there are nature-attuned infrastructures to which language is related, there are acquired and culturally-oriented features of language that are equally defining of language, whether on the collective or individual level.[7] These features find vital testimony in people's relationship with, and their intimate sentiment for and use of their language, where history is lodged in the living words and discourses of the present. In this sense, the study of language in the context of culture acquires particular importance as pertaining to power relations, agency, symbolism, aesthetics, identity and consciousness. All these aspects are tightly connected to language as the most expansive sphere of identification and communication through which people are defined and connected. As Fishman writes:

> [...] although many behaviors can mark identity, language is the only one that actually carries extensive cultural content. The distinctive sounds uttered in speaking a particular language encode meaning, and the link between ethnic group and ethnic language becomes much more at this level.[8]

Moreover, many philosophers, such as Giambattista Vico and Ludwig Wittgenstein, and anthropologists, such as Glifford Geertz and Pierre Bourdieu,[9] have come to recognise, through philosophical investigations and anthropological enquiries, the inextricability of languages in cultures. Salvatore writes, summarising their views generally but meaningfully, that 'discursive traditions are then densely complex instances of language in use'.[10] This chapter, therefore, will focus on the Arabic language and its relevance to the formation of Arab culture and identity: how language figures in Arabs' cultural consciousness, and how it is present today.

Culture of communication

The question above can be posed in terms of how language, not as an ontological structure *per se*, but as a system of communication, meaning and signification, figures in culture. I argued in an earlier paper that the relationship between language and culture can be usefully represented in the phrasal term 'culture of communication'. This term is value-laden, insofar as it constitutes history and admits its presence in the formation of language. Metaphorically, history can be understood as the grandmother of language. The resonance of the past in the present, which figures in all cultures in varying degrees, in accordance with the immediacy of the current moment, manifests itself in language in significant ways, as will be demonstrated in the case of Arabic culture. In this context:

> [...] what defines a culture of communication is the process of enactment that stems from the historical-anthropological rootedness of action in language and culture...a culture of communication is a communicated compendium of religious, historical, literary and mythological references used by a community as valid tropes for all times and, as such, are acted upon and treated as having authenticity. Authenticity in a culture of communication serves to manipulate language as a residue of resonant power embodied in culture as an anthropological-historical space in which the powerful, the spiritual and the pertinent (to the moment) are drawn on, selectively, produced, idolised, talked of and visualised.[11]

The integration of language into culture is strongly considered in the philosophy of Jürgen Habermas through his concept of the *Lebenswelt*, lifeworld: 'Lifeworld as represented by a culturally transmitted and linguistically organized stock of interpretive patterns...language and culture are constitutive of the lifeworld itself'.[12] The shift in values, political structures and conditions is often insightfully captured in the study of discourses that preceded and followed the shift, and ultimately this reflects itself in language because it is not passive or impervious to power-relations which underpin cultural and political conditions and changes.[13] The fifteenth-century

Arab thinker, Ibn Khaldun, and the sixteenth-century Italian philologist, Giambattista Vico, paid particular attention to the question of language and its relevance to culture and civilisation in general.[14] Giambattista Vico correlated language changes with historical changes, the result being that different civilisational epochs revealed different modes of speaking. He thus wrote from the standpoint of man-made history:

> Three kinds of language were spoken which compose the vocabulary of this Science (The New Science): (1) That of the time of the families, when gentile men were newly received into humanity.[15] This was a mute language of signs and physical objects having natural relations to the ideas that they wished to express. (2) That spoken by means of heroic emblems, or similitudes, comparisons, images, metaphors, and natural descriptions, which make up the great body of the heroic language which was spoken at the time the heroes reigned. (3) Human language using words agreed upon by the people, a language of which they are absolute lords, and which is proper to the popular commonwealths and monarchical states; a language whereby the people may fix the meaning of the laws by which the nobles as well as the plebs are bound. Hence, among all nations, once the laws had been put into the vulgar tongue, the science of laws passed from the control of the nobles. Hitherto, among all nations, the nobles, being also priests, had kept the laws in a secret language as a sacred thing. That is the natural reason for the secrecy of the laws among the Roman patricians until popular liberty arose [...][16]

In a nutshell, Vico put forward the compelling idea that with each new emerging power, a corresponding idiom of language prevailed. There were the mythic, the poetic, the metaphorical and the rational discourse, which heralded the inception of modernity. Vico's ideas remain pertinent because they reflect how culture is inculcated into language in a way that renders it invisible, yet strikingly present. Edward Said, in his preface to his influential book *Orientalism* (2003), highlighted the power of philology in the interpretation of cultures, in the same manner that Clifford Geertz did in his important book, *The Interpretation of Cultures*. Said wrote, 'philology, in fact, is the most basic and creative of the interpretive arts'.[17] Said meant by philology an interpretive approach to texts which takes into consideration the socio-cultural and political conditions under which a certain text was written or discourse produced. In the Arab and Islamic civilisation, philology, as a method of cultural and linguistic interpretation, whether of the *Qur'an*, poetry, or literary and philosophical treatises, was pre-eminent. Several schools of thought were founded upon the diversity of opinions around different interpretations of the *Qur'an*, poetic or philosophical creations, such as *al-Mu'tazilat, al-Jabriyyah* and *al-Dhahiriyyah* and *al-Batinyya*.[18] Arkoun laid particular emphasis on the cultural value of language when he wrote, by way of introduction to the notion of the blogosphere as:

> [...] the linguistic mental space shared by all those who use the same language with which to articulate their thoughts, their representations, their collective memory, and their knowledge according to fundamental principles and values claimed in a unifying *weltanaschaung*.[19]

There is thus a longstanding historical understanding of language as a manifestation of culture-anchored world. The significance of language is, indeed, starkly evidenced in Arab culture, as will be explained below. Different discourses within a historically-rooted culture project diverse ideologies and attitudes. Language houses diverse discourses by virtue of its cultural expansiveness, from which different groups can draw on the same resources, such as the *Qur'an,* in the case of Arab culture, yet different meanings and values accrue to it. While discourse is thus specific in terms of its representation of one group or another, and it is rooted in the conditions of the present, a culture of communication entails the preservation of history as a source of cultural and civilisational background to be drawn on and selectively used as befits either one's ideological strand or that of another, in the present. The diversity of political and cultural orientations in the Arab world justifies the notion of 'culture of communication' as a meaningful term that interpretively explains the plural facets of one culture. Clifford Geertz insightfully complements this view when he writes:

> [...] the concept of culture I espouse ... is essentially a semiotic one. Believing with Marx and Weber, that man is an animal suspended in webs of significance he himself has spun, I take culture to be those webs, and the analysis of it to be therefore not an experimental science in search of law but an interpretative one in search of meaning. It is explication I am after, construing social expressions on their surface enigmatical. But this

pronouncement, a doctrine in a clause, demands itself some explication.[20]

In what follows, I highlight the relevance of Arabic to Arab culture and civilisation and the diverse ways in which it has been expressed.

Arabic in the fray of culture

The cultural relevance of Arabic to the formation of the Arab people throughout their history, and their consciousness of that history and themselves has been present in notable ways. Albert Hourani, the eminent historian of the Arab world, perceptively captured this at the beginning of his book, *Arabic Thought in the Liberal Age: 1798–1939*, when he wrote:

> More conscious of their language than any people in the world, seeing it not only as the greatest of their arts but also as their common good, most Arabs, if asked to define what they meant by the 'Arab nation', would begin by saying that it included all those who spoke the Arabic language.[21]

This consciousness is born of cultural events, which are at the heart of the formation of the Arabic language. This includes Islam itself, a religion that is constituted and concretised in the *Qur'an* and in the tradition of the *Hadīth*, which encompass the sayings of the Prophet Mohammad. The cultural epitome of Pre-Islamic Arabia was embodied in poetry, an artistic tradition, which still occupies the premier position within the Arab world.[22] The *Qur'an* came as a challenge to the tradition of poetry in the sense, from an Islamic perspective, that it constituted a linguistic miracle *'mu'jazah*. In the Italian phrase, the *Qur'an* represented a state of 'prosa ornata' (ornamented prose), in that it moved between prose and poetry in a way that did not happen before. In the *Qur'an*, Arabic is mentioned in thirteen verses[23] – in twelve verses, according to another source.[24] Arabic gained more importance for the Arab peoples as it put them on the map of world civilisations when several philosophical and scientific treatises were translated from Greek into Arabic during a period of intellectual decline in Europe. In addition, new, original, intellectual and literary works were produced by Arab scholars during the Umayyad (660–750) and Abbasid (750–1258) periods. Intellectually, these two periods constituted important reference points in all those that followed. This is particularly so with the Abbasid period, which witnessed momentous scholarly, literary and translation activities, notable amongst which is the scholarship of Ibn Khaldun, which touched on the question of language and its relevance to culture in interesting ways, as explained briefly above.[25] It is also poetry that continued to mark the identity of the Arabs, giving them a diverse set of idioms that endured throughout the centuries in schools, universities and the public sphere. In a condensed, but perceptive, statement, the eminent Egyptian scholar and thinker, Taha Hussein, regarded as the doyen of Arabic literature, considered the speech of the Arabs as consisting of 'Poetry, prose and Qur'an'. This statement summarises the Islamic and Arab intellectual and literary traditions, and their endowment from the language and imagined sphere of the Arabs of the past. Classical Arabic, the primary constituents of which include the 'Qur'an, early 'ādāb literature, grammatical treatises',[26] remained intact in terms of its literary prestige. It has been suggested that the importance of Arabic to the Arabs, and its relevance to their culture, is echoed in the language of many political groups in today's Arab world. There is hardly any group whose language is divested of religious overtones, even if the intended meaning is not necessarily religious. As Halliday writes, in his book Nations and Religions in the Middle East: 'even the most secular of nationalisms has words of religious origin'.[27] Arabic has thus been at the heart of the Arab world as a cultural and political emblem; its significance predates nationalism in its modern sense, even if nationalism gave the question of language visibility and momentum. Hourani characterises this situation perceptively when he writes:

> That those who speak Arabic form a 'nation', and that this nation should be independent and united, are beliefs which only became articulate and acquired political strength during the [twentieth] century. But as far back in history as we can see them, the Arabs have always been exceptionally conscious of their language and proud of it, and in pre-Islamic Arabia they possessed a kind of 'racial' feeling, a sense that, beyond the conflicts of tribes and families, there was a unity which joined together all who spoke Arabic and could claim descent from the tribes of Arabia.[28]

Furthermore, the importance of Arabic extends far beyond the Arab frontiers to include Muslims who read the Qur'an in Arabic. The Pakistani Islamist leader, Al-Mawdudi, thus wrote in his book Towards Understanding Islam, in a manner that represents an Islamic-orientated view of the Arabic language, like that espoused by Yousef Al-Qaradawi and others, as will be explained later:

> Take also the Arabic language. The more you study its literature, the more you will be convinced that there is no other language more suited to express high ideals, to explain the most subtle aspects of Divine knowledge, and to impress the heart of man and mould it into submission to God. Small phrases and brief sentences express a whole world of ideas; they are so powerful that their very sound can move men to tears and ecstasy. They are so sweet that it is as if honey were being poured into one's ears; they are so full of harmony that every fibre of the listener's body is moved by their symphony. It was a rich and powerful language such as this that was needed for the Qur'an, the Great Word of God.[29]

This statement concurs with what amounts to a tradition of adulation of the Arabic language in Arab and Islamic civilisation. The nexus of religion, Arabism and the Arabic language, is made tangible in the following tradition-anchored statement, which projects the Islamic connection to Arabic: 'I love the Arabs for three reasons: because I am an Arab, the Qur'an is revealed in Arabic and the speech of the people of Heaven is Arabic' (in Suleiman 2003: 44). The modern renaissance of the Arab world is traced to linguistic and literary consciousness, which became notable from the nineteenth century onwards. Tibi diagnosed three distinct stages in the history of Arab nationalism:

> [...] first, the Arabic literary and linguistic renaissance, during which Westernised Arab intellectuals arrived at a form of national consciousness (the Nahda); secondly, the politicisation of this literary renaissance, and the transformation of cultural into political nationalism into the demand for a unified Arab state.[30]

The nineteenth and twentieth centuries thus represent turning points in the cultural history of the Arabs, insofar as they gave rise to new nation-states and state-based nationalism(s) that affected attitudes to the Arabic language.

With the emergence of nation-states in Europe (after the French Revolution in 1789) and the Arab world (after the dissolution of the

Ottoman Empire, which reigned over the Arab world from 1453 until 1918), the question of Arabic became more nuanced.[31] The history of the Arab people in the twentieth century is a history of contested narratives and conflicts of ideologies that had never previously been as visibly acute. The nation-state system made divisions more visible on the political and cultural level, where language was intractable. As Hourani writes, 'there was no need, before, in 1914, for lines to be sharply drawn'.[32] Language became implicated in the acute contentions of the ideologies that beset the Arab world in the twentieth century. Sensing signs of disintegration in the hitherto united Arab world, Sati' al-Din al-Husari, an eminent Syrian educator and nationalist, articulated and propagated with enthusiasm the message of Pan-Arabism on the basis of language. Al-Husari maintained that the Arab language is the very essence through which Arabs can be defined, and through which they can be culturally related and brought together. Al-Husari extolled Arabic linguistically, culturally and politically, deeming it to be a binding knot which, alongside a common Arab history, unites all Arabs: 'the strongest and most effective tie is the national tie, which derives from a common language and history', he wrote.[33] Al-Husari's emphasis on Arabic as defining Arabs came in inclusive statements in which he consolidated his thought on Arabic as primordially binding Arabs:

> Every individual who belongs to the Arab countries and speaks Arabic is an Arab. He is so, regardless of the name of the country whose citizenship he officially holds. He is so regardless of the religion he professes or the sect he belongs to. He is so, regardless of his ancestry, lineage or the roots of the family to which he belongs. He is an Arab [full stop].[34]

In al-Husari's writings on Arab national identity, Arabism thus meant the Arabic language. In the twentieth century, the balance of power shifted to the Western sphere. The Ottoman Empire dissolved, and Europe and America emerged as the powers of the day.[35] In this atmosphere, Arabic was articulated in various ways by different ideological forces within the Arab world. New thinkers emerged who even attributed to Arabic, the language, the Arabs' weakness and decline vis-à-vis the west. The battle of ideologies can largely be drawn as being between those who advocate pan-Arabism from a secular or Islamic perspective, and those who call for the consolidation of the nation-state, with less or complete disregard of the wider Arab world. In this context, several issues were brought to bear on Arabic, e.g., territory (territorial nationalism, as opposed to pan-Arabism) and modernity (a break with the past, as opposed to continuity and the revival of tradition and heritage). Some writers in Egypt, Musa Salama, and in Lebanon, Saeed 'Aql, in particular, have argued for the position that Arabic should be written in Romanised letters or in the colloquial form, rather than the standard/classical Arabic language.[36] Opposing this, mostly intellectual, Westernised or West-awed camp, were secular Pan-Arabists, Muslims and Christians alike, Al-Husari (1880–1968), Nasif al-Yaziji (1800–71), Faris al-Shidyaq (1805–87), Butrus al-Bustani (1819–83), and others. Some Christian pioneers of cultural revival could see no alternative to the unifying force of the Arabic language and its embodiment of their literary, intellectual and scientific heritage. However, with the culture of the nation-state putting down roots in the Arab world, Arabic became the site of ideological divides. The presence of ideology with regard to language in the Arab world, is defined as follows by Suleiman, '[It is] always encoded in discourse, but when it is encoded recursively and explicitly to refer to language itself... it becomes meta-discourse; in this sense, language is the means and the object at the same time.'[37]

Debates about Arabic and its cultural and political relevance continue to find fertile ground in modern discourses. In this context, language is not conceived as a system of communication, innocent of political manipulation. Here, some, envisaging language as being connected wholesale with thought, attribute serious changes to Arabic. Such ideology-driven views find representation in figures such as Fouad Ajami and Moustapha Safouan, to name but two. Ajami writes: '...the connection between political reform and the reform of language was to become one of the prominent concerns of those who wanted to get to the roots of the Arab defeat [meaning the 1967 Arab defeat at the hands of Israel]'.[38] The lack of reform in the area of language, which Ajami does not spell out in detail, explains a political defeat. Ajami's position, among others similar, indicates a lack of understanding of language itself, as a system which is amenable to any use, rhetorical or not; thus the ideological rhetoric that political figures, such as Jamal Abd Nasser, employ, as Ajami implies, does not mean that the language is inadequate, or is not heuristically equipped to express meaningful positions, ideas and ideals. Such a view communicates confusion as to the very dimensions within which language can be sensibly viewed and debated.

In addition, another dimension in which the defence of the Arabic language figures strongly is when it is viewed from an anti-colonialist perspective. The Arabic language in some Arab countries, such as Algeria, and to a lesser extent Morocco, was subjected to laws which favoured the language of the colonisers over Arabic.[39] Similar linguistic strategies were applied in Africa and other places, where English or French dominated the linguistic scene to the extent that local languages were perceived less favourably in economic and cultural terms.[40] This situation led some scholars and activists in the Arab world to adopt strong views against those who propagate policies that concur with the aims of the colonisers, such as the use of the coloniser or colloquial language,[41] as opposed to standard Arabic, or the writing of Arabic in Romanised letters, or the adoption of a new language altogether.[42] Here, the defence of Arabic against outside forces becomes a defence of the Arab nation and heritage in general. In this context, Arabic is regarded as more than a language through which people communicate, it is also a civilisational and cultural well in which historical treasures reside.

Furthermore, given the widespread use of Arabic and its spread over a large territory, the question of mutual linguistic intelligibility among the Arabs arises. Edward Said (1935–2003) reflected on this situation in two posthumously published articles, written about the Arabic language and its civilisational and cultural values, namely 'Living in Arabic' and 'The Language of the People or the Language of Scholar'. He emphasised the richness of the situation in terms of the quotidian linguistic experiences of Arabs in their shift from one linguistic form to another, mainly from the standard to the colloquial, and vice versa. Said characterises the present sociolinguistic situation in the Arab world as follows:

> If I were to try to understand an Algerian, I would get nowhere, so different and varied are the colloquials once one gets away from the shores of the Eastern Mediterranean. The same would be true with an Iraqi, Moroccan, or a deep Gulf dialect. Which is why all Arabic news, broadcasts, discussion programmes and documentaries – also meetings, seminars, mosque sermons and nationalist rallies, as well as daily encounters, between people with different spoken languages – are conducted in a modified, modernised classical language or an approximation of it that can be understood across the Arab world from the Gulf to Morocco.[43]

Said's summary of the situation is apt both linguistically and culturally. The thrust of Said's point in the two articles is that those who call for linguistic reform in the Arab world, along the lines of writing and speaking in the colloquial only, or in the classical form of the language only, demonstrate misunderstanding of the intermixed nature of the two codes: the classical/standard and the colloquial, insofar as modern Arabic is concerned. The question of language in the Arab world gains widespread attention for its centrality to culture. Some favour or defend the use of one form or another. Others, such as Said, interpret the complexity of the situation in a way that does not reflect deep-rooted ideological bias but, rather, highlights the varied nature of the language situation without charging the language with misconceived conceptions.

Media are another arena where the question of language in the Arab world finds echoes. Yousef Al-Qaradawi, the well-known Egyptian Sheikh, in an article entitled *lughatanā al-jamīla wa-I'lām*, cautions against the use of colloquial language in formal contexts and in writing. Al-Qaradawi's article is riddled with statements from the Arabic tradition and Islamic canon, asserting the cultural significance of the Arabic language and its Islamic values, as well as the inseparability of the language from thought. Concerning the dangers facing Arabic, as Al-Qaradawi perceives them, he writes:

> [...] there are two factors that threaten classical/standard Arabic in so far as media is concerned. The first one is the use of the colloquial language, in particular in debates, discussions and drama-based works. And the second factor is the spread of *al-laḥn* 'solecism' and the repetition of mistakes in grammar, declension, vocabularies and styles.[44]

Since the end of the 1970s, political Islam has become a considerable force in the Arab world. Islamism, as a religiously-inspired political ideology, takes the question of Arabic and its cultural significance seriously within what is usually called a 'project of Islamic revival', as often declared by leaders of Islamic movements.[45] Al-Qaradawi's call for adherence to the grammatical rules of Arabic by media outlets, comes under this ideological cover. The reference to solecism in the statement of Al-Qaradawi quoted above is informative. Solecism, *al-laḥn*, was considered a serious deviation from the Islamic tradition; as it amounted to the distortion of the language of the *Qur'an* through grammatical or stylistic mistakes. In addition, the statement highlights the rootedness of the past in the present thinking of Islamic-orientated ideologies.[46]

The issues and examples discussed above in the context of the Arabic language, highlight its rootedness in Arabs' contemporary thought and usage. As much as language is naturally grounded in humans, it also has a socio-culturally and politically construction that means people use, streamline and advance it in various ways. Any philosophy that does not consider these two manifest sides of language, its natural and its constructed sides, runs the risk of being flawed by virtue of its narrow-mindedness and its neglect of what makes language simultaneously natural and inter-subjectively meaningful. The Arabic language is interesting in its own right, for it amply demonstrates the significance of history to language. Its old structure, diction and form remain visible in the life of Arabs today in a way that suggests the continuous presence of the past in the contemporary lives of Arabs, a situation which is telling of its linguistic integration into the cultural milieu of the Arab world.

Culture in the life of another language

We learn from the work of scholars such as Edward Said, Albert Hourani, Kees Veerstegh, etc., that all civilisations and cultures are born of continuous interactions with each other. This is also true of Arab culture, which has benefited from previous intellectual and cultural traditions and has added to them, while spreading them to other cultures and civilisations in which they would acquire a life of their own. Indeed, there is no cut-off point where one culture ends and another begins. Translation activities have been central to the study of other cultures. In fact, any study of culture from an outside perspective amounts to an act of translation. In the context of Arab societies, this begs the question as to how Arabic culture can be studied within other traditions and languages. What are the methods by which one can understand Arab culture and life from an outside, linguistically different, perspective? What forms could an Arab cultural studies programme take within the context of another culture of communication? Could the same language and methods used in Western academia, for example, be applied to Arab societies without appearing to be distant or irrelevant? These questions cannot be ignored if there is to be a serious and critical contemplation of Arab cultural studies.

Against this background (that language is integrated into culture), the starting point for understanding and studying Arabic culture is the Arabic language, the historical repository and emblem of Arab life. However, given the multifaceted nature of Arabic, which is a diglossic language[47] with both a standard and a dialectal/colloquial form, which of these is representative of the culture? Obviously, Arab culture is not monolithic, and language reflects that. Each dialect, whether Palestinian or Moroccan, is interwoven into the cultural and political fabric of its own people. However, since the classical/standard Arabic language is the medium which all Arabs share and understand, it becomes imperative that it be the departure point for deeper engagement with the lives of the dialects, where other forms of particular knowledge and habits reside. Linguistically, Arab dialects are varied, as evidenced by the quote from Said, above, but they also stem from similar sources.[48] In addition, the rise of education and globalisation through media in the Arab world have given rise to new linguistic phenomena, an educated medium of spoken Arabic, called *koine* or *educated Arabic*, a blend of urban and rural forms of Arabic that ultimately amalgamates these into a form of speech that is mutually intelligible to Arabs.[49] A serious understanding and engagement with Arab societies can only happen through a thorough learning of their culture of communication,[50] their shared sources of reference and knowledge, and the infrastructure which underpins the diversity of their discourses. Language, in this context, is like a generous soul with many facets, capable of projecting various aspects of life and civilisation. Arab cultural studies can do no better than to emphasise the significance of understanding Arabic societies through the study of language, and a venture into one or other of the Arab dialects, depending on the general and specific interests and orientation of each scholar. An informed knowledge and familiarity with the classical/standard Arabic language guarantees an understanding that will move towards meaningful interpretations, and that, from my perspective, is what one should hope for from the study of one's own, as well as other, cultures.

Conclusion

This chapter opened with preliminary remarks on language and its centrality to culture. It argued against positions which deny language, in terms of its formation, its cultural and political ambiences. For a useful understanding of language within its cultural realm, the chapter has suggested the use of the term 'culture of communication'. The phrase 'culture of communication' serves the purpose of viewing and asserting the connection between language and culture, as well as highlighting the diversity of cultural practices that are manifested in the diverse discourses that share one language and civilisation. Subsequently, the chapter focused on Arabic in its historical and cultural constitutions. It explained the various conjectures around which Arabic revolves. The diverse discourses in the Arab world emerge from different cultural and ideological convictions, which are themselves reflected in the very use of the language. Though people draw on one language and similar references, they do so differently. In addition, as a result of colonialism and cultural and political evolutions, Arabic has come to be viewed from various standpoints. The differences in views on the Arabic language suggest, more often than not, ideological variations, since they attribute to language ills and charges that conflate language with political and cultural manipulations.

A sensible understanding of language will take into consideration its natural, its cultural and political components, which are shown in various ways within a broader culture of communication. At one level, language is innocent of all charges, because it is a system of communication, but it is in its use that concerns arise. In the latter side of language, it can fall prey to ideological manipulations, where reality is objectified to befit one's view of the matter at hand, rather than the matter as it is (subjectively, inter-subjectively, objectively and worldly speaking). Having established the distinctions above between the ontological and epistemological sides of language, Yasir Suleiman, the great Arab sociolinguist, explains the reforms that are called for, which are cultural and linguistic at the same time, even if they appear to be linguistically-orientated in the first place. Suleiman writes:

> [...] there is a commonly held belief in the nationalist discourses I have examined... that Arabic is in need of modernisation grammatically, lexically, stylistically and pedagogically to make it better participate in the nationalist project in an effective manner. Grammatical modernisation should have as its aim the use of a syntax that is unencumbered by the outmoded and dead rules of the past. Lexical modernisation should aim at increasing the stock of new terminologies available to the language users. It should also aim at culling the excesses

of synonymy in the language, thus freeing some lexical slots for use in designating new meanings. Stylistic modernisation should encourage the development of a new rhetoric in which meaning is not neglected in favour of linguistic virtuosity, but in which the latter is made to serve the functions of the former. Pedagogic modernisation should aim at developing new ways of setting out the facts of grammar for the effective nurturing of grammatical competence in the learners. Some demanded effective nurturing of grammatical competence in the learners. Some demanded that a daring approach be adopted in this area, consisting, among other things, of dropping the desinential inflections [in Arabic grammar, a final short vowel added to a base form to indicate nominative (-u, un), genitive (-i, -in), or accusative (-a, -an) case]. Others considered any such so-called pedagogic simplification of grammar to be an unwarranted intrusion into the very structure – even the soul – of the language. Some nationalist thinkers additionally argued for reforming the Arabic script. Others called for its wholesale abandonment as the Turks had done.[51]

What Suleiman mentions in this paragraph and explains in his book *The Arabic Language and National Identity,* represents a list of linguistic and cultural aspects underpinned by ideological beliefs about the current state of the language and the hypothetical directions it should take. They highlight the diversity of views about language itself, views that are conflated with extra-linguistic factors, rather than rooted in an actual linguistic state. Some of these reforms might indeed be needed, yet this does not invalidate the point that language is a system of communication that is affected by cultural and political structures and attitudes in so far as use is concerned. Structurally, language is capable of expressing whatever human beings will it to express.

Notes

1. It is estimated that 350 million people speak Arabic, distributed over 25 Arab countries and territories. Some Arab countries regard Arabic as an 'official language', and others consider it to be 'the national language'. The Arab League defines an Arab as 'a person whose language is Arabic, who lives in an Arabic-speaking country, and who is in sympathy with the aspirations of the Arabic-speaking peoples'.
2. See Lakoff 1987.
3. Williams 1976: 21.

4. Saussure 1960: 7.

5. See Robins 1997; on the civilisational and cultural embodiment of language, Gramsci wrote, 'language is transformed with the transformation of the whole of civilisation, through the acquisition of culture by new classes and through the hegemony exercised by one national language over others, etc., and what it does is precisely to absorb in metaphorical form the words of previous civilizations and cultures' (cited in Ives 2004: 89).

6. See Chomsky 1971, particularly in his chapter 'On Interpreting the World', pp. 3–51.

7. See Alshaer 2008: 101–21.

8. See Fishman 1991: 31.

9. See Glifford Geertz (1973) *The Interpretations of Cultures*, New York: Basic Books; and Pierre Bourdieu (1992) *Language and Symbolism*, Cambridge: Polity Press.

10. Salavotre 2007: 87.

11. Alshaer 2008: 104.

12. Salvatore 2007: 72–73.

13. See Foucault 1972.

14. Language is considered from a philosophical and historical point of view in the *Muqaddima* of Ibn Khaldun (1332–1406). He considers language as a *malkah*, something that is initially acquired by nature and is modulated and advanced by habit, *'Adah*. His views on language and other historical and cultural issues, though provincially situated sometimes, have universal resonance and implications, sometimes predating many of the modern cultural and philosophy of language theories (for a concise review of the philosophy of Ibn Khaldun, see Abdelselam Cheddadi (1994) *Ibn Khaldun*).

15. Gentile (*gentilis*) in the latinate (Latin, Roman) sense, which Vico highlighted, means belonging to a clan or tribe; in the Biblical sense, it means the non-Israelites tribes.

16. Giambattista Vico, *The New Science*, Para. 33, pp. 3–4.

17. See Edward Said, *Orientalism* (2003 [1978]), p. xviii.

18. These schools emerged to explain different philosophical facets of the *Qur'an* and other texts. *Al-Mu'tazilat* is considered a liberal school of thought that highlighted the *Qur'an* as being created but at the same time inspired; the *mu'tazileets* accrued agency to human beings, whereas the other school of thought, *al-Jabriyyah*, which means 'determinism', did not. *Al-Jabriyyah* and *al-Ashariyya* (another deterministic school of thought) considered the *Qur'an* a literal creation of God without the active mediation of the Prophet Mohammad; so Mohammad was a transmitter, messenger of the words, rather than a mediator whose presence and role is acknowledged. The positions of the schools mentioned above extended to cover areas concerning the agency of human beings and their responsibility for their own acts, which *al-mu'tazilat* emphasises, as opposed to the other deterministic groups, who denied the

agency of human beings and viewed them as creatures acting within the realm of a God-constituted world, both pre-destination and post-destination. The other two schools mentioned, *al-Dhahiryyiah* (the manifest) and *al-Batiniyyah* (the latent), differed on whether the focus of interpretation of the *Qur'an* and other texts should be through the obvious language or the latent language, its hidden meanings and so forth (see Akhavi, 2009).

19. See Arkoun 2002: 19.
20. See Geertz 1973: 5.
21. See Hourani 1962: 1.
22. See Alshaer 2009.
23. Al-Wadghīry 2000: 14.
24. See al-Kitānī 2000: 14.
25. See Versteegh, 1997; al-Muhayri, Sumud and al-Masdi, 1988.
26. Fischer, cited in Owens 2006: 39.
27. See Halliday 2000: 48.
28. See Hourani 1983: 260.
29. Al-Mawdudi 1960: 28.
30. Tibi 1997: xi.
31. See Brown 2001: 112.
32. Brown 2003: 287.
33. Cited in Tibi 1997: 145.
34. Cited Suleiman 2003: 133.
35. See Said 1978.
36. See Suleiman 2003.
37. See Suleiman 2006:79.
38. See Ajami 1992: 33.
39. See Suleiman 1994; Ennaji and Sadiqi 2008: 44–61.
40. See Simpson 2008: 1–25.
41. Some colonial officials, most notably William Willcocks in Egypt, suggested that the Egyptians should use Egyptian Colloquial Arabic and give up on Standard Arabic, regarding the latter as archaically stultifying to the progress of cultural life in Egypt (see Suleiman 2004: 71–79).
42. See Alshaer 2009.
43. See Said, *Al-Ahram Weekly*, 12–18 February 2004, Issue No. 677.
44. See al-Qaradawi 2006.
45. See Alshaer 2008.
46. See Suleiman 2003: 49–55.
47. The term 'diglossia' was given life by Charles Ferguson in 1959. Ferguson (2003: 345) defined diglossia as 'a relatively stable language situation in which, in addition to the primary dialects of the language (which may include a standard or regional standards), there is a very divergent, highly codified (often grammatically more complex) superposed variety, the vehicle of a large and respected body of written literature, either of an earlier period or in another

speech community, which is learned largely by formal education and is used
for most written and formal spoken purposes but is not used by any sector of
the community for ordinary conversation'.

48. See Holes 2003.
49. See Boussofara-Amar 2005: 629–37.
50. Even the translation of the concept of 'culture of communication' into Arabic
is telling. The Arabic equivalent is *Thaqqafa loghawiyya* which means literally 'linguistic culture', and thus embodies a narrower range of meaning than
'culture of communication', which indicates not only language but also the in-
terpretational, visual and other communication-related realms that are embodied in culture. Cultures differ and meet. Human behaviours are finite. They
meet on certain conjectures and diverge on others. Cultural interpretation is,
at some level, an act of translation.
51. See Suleiman 2003: 227.

Bibliography

Al-Muhayri, Abdul-Qādir, Sumūd, Hammādī and al-Massadī, Abdu s-Salām
(1988) *al-Nazariyyah al-Lisāniyyah wa shi'riyah fiat-Turāthal-'arabī min khilāl
an-nusūs* (Readings in Linguistic and 'Poetics' Theory), Tunisia: Dār at-Tunisi-
yyah lil nashr.
Al-Qaradāwī, Yūsif (23.12.2006) *Lughatunā al-jamīlah wa 1-i'lām* (Our Beautiful
Language and the Media), Al-muntadā at-tarbawī.
Al-Wadghīrī, 'Abd al-'Alī. (2000) *al-Lughah wa ad-din wa lhawiyyah* (Language,
Religion and Identity), ar-Rabāt: Dar Nashr al-Ma'rifah.
Ajami, Fouad (1992) *The Arab Predicament: Arab Political Thought and Practice
since 1967*, Cambridge: Cambridge University Press.
Akhavi, Shahrough (2009) *The Middle East: The Politics of the Sacred and Secular*
(World Political Theories), London: Zed Books.
Al-Maudidi, Abu 'Ala (1960) *Towards Understanding Islam*, Pakistan: Al-Murad.
Alshaer, Atef (2009) 'The Poetry of Hamas', *The Middle East Journal of Culture and
Communication* 2.4, Leiden: Brill: 214–30.
—— (2008) 'Towards a Theory of Culture of Communication: The Fixed and the
Dynamic in Hamas's Communicated Discourse', *The Middle East Journal of
Culture and Communication* 1.2, Leiden: Brill: 101–21.
Arkoun, Mohammed (2002) *Islam: To Reform Or Subvert?* London: Saqi
Essentials.
Bourdieu, Peirre (1991) *Language and Symbolic Power*; introduced by John B.
Thompson. Cambridge: Polity Press.
Boussofara-Omar, Naima (2005) 'Diglossia' in M. Eid (ed.), *Encyclopedia of Arabic
Language and Linguistics*, Leiden: Brill Academic Publishers, pp.629–37.
Brown, Carl. A.(2000) *Religion and State: The Muslim Approach to Politics*, New
York: Columbia University Press.

Burke, L. Crowley, T. and Girvin A. (eds). (2000) 'General Introduction' in *The Routledge Language and Cultural Theory Reader*, London and New York: Routledge, pp. 1–13.

Cheddadi, Abdesselam (1994) *Ibn Khaldun* (A.D. 1332–1406/A.H. 732–808), *The Quarterly Review of Comparative Education*, vol. XXIV, 1/2, Paris: UNESCO International Bureau of Education: 7–19.

Chomsky, Noam (2000) *New Horizons on the Study of Language and Mind*, Cambridge: Cambridge University Press.

—— (1971) *Problems of Knowledge and Freedom*, New York: Random House.

Ennaji, M. and Sadiqi, F. (2008) 'Morocco: Language, Nationalism and Gender' in A. Simpson (ed.), *Language and National Identity*, Oxford: Oxford University Press, pp. 44–61.

Ferguson, Charles (2003) 'Diglossia' in B.C. Paulston. and R. Tucker (eds), *Sociolinguistics: The Essential Readings*, Oxford: Blackwell, pp. 345–59.

Fishman, Joshua (1999) 'Sociolinguistics' in J. Fishman. (ed.), *Handbook of Language & Ethnic Identity*, New York, Oxford: Oxford University Press, pp. 152–64.

Foucault, Michel (1972) *The Order of Things: An Archaeology of the Human Sciences*, London: Tavistock Publications.

Geertz, Clifford (1973) *The Interpretation of Cultures: Selected Essays*. New York: Basic Books.

Holes, Clive (2004) *Modern Arabic: Structures, Functions and Varieties*, Georgetown: Georgetown University Press.

Hourani, Albert (1992) *A History of the Arab Peoples*, London: Faber and Faber.

—— (1983 [1961]) *Arabic Thought in the Liberal Age, 1798–1939*, Cambridge: Cambridge University Press.

Ives, Peter (2004) *Language and Hegemony in Gramsci*, London: Pluto Press.

Lakoff, George (1987) *Women, Fire and Dangerous Things: What Categories Reveal About the Mind*, Chicago, London: University of Chicago Press.

Owen, Jonathan (2006) *A Linguistic History of Arabic*, Oxford: Oxford University Press.

Robins, R. Henry (1997) *A Short History of Linguistics*, London: Longman.

Safouan, Moustapha (2007) *Why Are the Arabs Not Free? The Politics of Writing*, Oxford: Blackwell Publishing (Critical Quarterly Book Series).

Said, Edward (2004) 'Living in Arabic', *Al-Ahram Weekly* 12–18 February, Issue No. 677.

—— (2003) 'The Language of the People or of the Scholar: Eloquent, Elegant Arabic', *Le Monde Diplomatique*, 29 August 2004.

—— (2003 [1978]) *Orientalism*, London: Penguin Books.

Salvatore, Armando (2007) *The Public Sphere: Liberal Modernity, Catholicism, Islam*, New York & Houndmills, UK: Palgrave Macmillan.

Saussure, Ferdinand de (1999) 'Arbitrary Social Values and the Linguistic Sign' in Charles Lemert (ed.), *Social Theory: The Multicultural and Classic Readings*, London: Westview Press, pp. 148–57.

—— (1960) 'The Nature of the Linguistic Sign', 'Language and Linguistics', and 'Linguistics Value', in Charles Bally (ed.) and Albert Sechehaye; Wade Baskin (trans.), *Course in General Linguistics,* London: Peter Owen.

Simpson, Andrew (2008) 'Introduction' in A. Simpson (ed.), *Language and National Identity,* Oxford: Oxford University Press, pp. 1–25.

Suleiman, Yasir (2006) 'Arabic Language Reforms: Language Ideology and the Criminalization of Sībawayhi' in L. Edzard and J. Watson (eds), *Grammar as a Window onto Arabic Humanism: A Collection of Articles in Honour of Michael G. Carter,* Harrassowitz Verlag: Wiesbaden, pp. 66–84.

—— (2004) *A War of Words: Language and Conflict in the Middle East,* Cambridge: Cambridge University Press.

—— (2003) *The Arabic Language and National Identity: A Study in Ideology,* Edinburgh: Edinburgh University Press.

—— (1994) 'Nationalism and the Arabic Language: A Historical Overview' in Y. Suleiman (ed.), *Arabic Sociolinguistics: Issues and Perspectives,* Richmond: Curzon Press, pp. 3–25.

Tibi, Bassam (1997) *Arab Nationalism: Between Islam and the Nation-State,* Basingstoke: Macmillan.

Versteegh, Kees (1997) *Landmarks in Linguistic Thought: Arabic Linguistic Tradition* (History of Linguistic Thought), London: Routledge.

Vico, Giambattista (1948) *The New Science of Giambattista Vico, translated by Thomas Goddard Bergin and Max Harold Fisch,* Ithaca and London: Cornell Paperbacks, Cornell University Press.

Williams, Raymond (1983) *Keywords: A Vocabulary of Culture and Society,* Fontana: London.

Wittgenstein, Ludwig (1953) *Philosophical Investigations,* Oxford: Blackwell.

14

Internationalising a Media Studies Degree in Arab Higher Education: A Case Study Arising from an Agreement Between New Zealand and Oman

Susan O'Rourke and Rosser Johnson

On the surface, there are few, if any, meaningful similarities between New Zealand and the Sultanate of Oman. The former is a secular, 'Western' society where several generations have enjoyed access to tertiary education. The latter is a comparatively religious, 'Middle Eastern' country, which is now extending the project of offering higher education to the wider population. Yet in May, 2006, the New Zealand Tertiary Education Consortium (NZTEC) and the Omani Ministry of Higher Education (MOHE) signed a contract detailing how four New Zealand universities were to develop four degrees for delivery in English in Oman.[1] This contract is 'the single largest off shore education project ever undertaken by New Zealand institutions'[2] and the identity of the signatories encapsulates the differences between the two countries.

NZTEC is a private entity established specifically for this project. Its main function is to 'insulate' the four New Zealand universities from direct contact with Oman: legally, the degree writers are sub-contractors and they have no direct connection with those who will deliver the material. By contrast, the MOHE is a government ministry, and one in which the Omani political elite are directly involved. On the one hand, then, we have a public/private structure typical within third-way governance structures.

On the other, we have a more traditional (and arguably responsive) model within which individuals enjoy sufficient agency to meaningfully direct and control events.

Despite the issues that such differences might reasonably produce (such as the challenges of liaising within a multi-layered international communication chain), the project has thus far been remarkably successful. The media studies (or 'communications') degree, for which AUT University has been responsible, has been delivered in full and on deadline, enabling the Omani Colleges of Applied Science (COAS) to begin delivery in July, 2006. At the time of writing, the project is slightly more than 50 per cent complete; the final delivery of material from New Zealand will take place in July 2009, and the degrees will be conferred for the first time in 2010.

This chapter focuses on the 'reversioning' of New Zealand's oldest media studies degree, a Bachelor of Communication Studies, into Oman's first Bachelor of Communications. Following Eisenhardt (1989) and Yin (1994), it will proceed on the basis that, as a case study, it illustrates the decisions that have been – and have needed to be – made during the first phases of the process. In doing so, we will also reflect on the challenges and opportunities involved in 'reversioning'.

Reversioning

The New Zealand media studies degree that forms the basis of this project was designed according to the taxonomy of curriculum development first developed by Benjamin Bloom in the mid-twentieth century (see Bloom, Englehart, Furst, Hill, and Krathwohl 1956). This same basic logic underpins the design of the 'reversioned' degree for delivery in Oman. Drawing on some more recent material (for instance, Krathwohl 2002), the writers were initially faced with two separate but linked tasks. First, they needed to focus on freeing the degree from the inherent biases and cultural practices that are both explicit and implicit within the New Zealand curriculum. Second, they needed to try to understand the cultural, social and educational milieu in Oman. Removing explicit reference to New Zealand (for example, Maori culture) is relatively simple. It is far more difficult, however, to recognise the implicit assumptions that lie behind the writers' words. The reversioning process can therefore be situated along a continuum that involves the writers in New Zealand and the teachers in Oman and works on explicit and implicit axes. In terms of explicit, concrete tasks, the writing team in New Zealand has been required to work within a different structure. This has two dimensions. First, the Omani degree only has three modules per semester (as opposed to four in New Zealand) to allow for English language tuition. This can create some difficulties when trying to ensure adequate coverage is given to the core professional competencies and capabilities of each major. Second, the majors chosen by the Omani Ministry of Higher Education differ considerably from those offered in New Zealand.[3] This has created difficulties when the teaching staff in Oman accessed material available on AUT University's website and point to courses – for example, in broadcasting – that they consider essential.

Since the Omani degree follows a four-year pattern and the New Zealand degree is completed in three years, even those majors that carry the same name are substantially different; the specialised discipline content of the Omani major is of necessity more constrained than the content offered in New Zealand. This does not mean the content will be less suitable for Omani graduates; rather, space has been opened up in the later years of the degree when there is not the same need for extensive English language tuition and students will be offered a choice of minors. Other locally written courses (such as *Arabic Language Skills*, *Islamic Culture*, and *Omani Economic History*) add a further depth of understanding of local and regional mediascapes. There are also significant pedagogical differences between New Zealand and Oman, and these offer significantly more challenge to the degree writers. For instance, progression through the degree in Oman is based upon the credit hours system, which sets a specific number of credit hours per course (three) and then allows students to take on more than the standard four courses per semester if they need to repeat a course. In New Zealand, progression through the degree is limited to students who achieve a passing grade and failing students either repeat that paper in summer school or take more than the standard three years to complete their degree. This is further complicated by differing policies on what constitutes a pass. In Oman, a student who has a D grade may continue in the subject while repeating that course in addition to his ongoing study. In New Zealand, a D grade is a clear fail and students must repeat the paper. Taken together, these issues raise questions for the writing team, none of whom have ever faced developing courses in an environment where students take more than the standard course 'loading'.

Similarly, the process of ensuring consistency of teacher delivery and comparability of student achievement in Oman is very different from New Zealand. The Omani degree is taught at three geographically dispersed colleges and although the basic material delivered from New Zealand is the same, delivery methods and the extent to which the material is contextualised vary according to individual teachers' interests and strengths. Further, the lecturers in Oman come from a range of diverse backgrounds; there are Egyptian, Moroccan, Tunisian, Indian, Malaysian, Bangladeshi, and Pakistani staff in the various colleges. However, because the writers all work at the same institution, these are issues they will never have previously faced. Most obviously, the collegial input and moderation of teaching and assessment standards that are taken for granted in New Zealand cannot be achieved at the same level in Oman. Standardisation can only occur if, as has been mooted, the Omani degree moves to delivery from one centralised site. A significant proportion of the implicit underpinnings of the material delivered to Oman could thereby be made manifest.

'Institutionalising'

Institutionalising the degree in and to Oman is a significant challenge, not least because the project operates over an extended time period (six years from negotiation to the graduating review in 2010). Further, the geographic separation of the writers from the deliverers, differences in core belief systems and cultural paradigms, and differences in the communication practices needed to enable students to be fully functioning citizens, mean that constant dialogue is only the first step in establishing a productive relationship. However, the formal structure (where the main contract is between the MOHE and NZTEC and the curricula are prepared by universities working – in effect – as subcontractors) can, understandably, blur the lines of communication. For instance, if a staff member in an Omani college wants to suggest a change to a course, he or she must contact the Programme Director in Oman, who must then make a request to the NZTEC Board of Directors. In turn, they will then funnel that request through to the appropriate Programme Coordinator in New Zealand, who will implement the change with the writing team. And, of course, this unwieldy process also operates in reverse when staff in New Zealand want to make a change. Suggestions to increase practical elements in the International Communication major (in response to requests by Omani staff) took over seven weeks to finalise because of these multi-layered communication channels.

Within Oman, of course, there are significant challenges. Along with the obvious implications of geographical distance (such as a lack of opportunities to liaise with colleagues face to face), there are also difficulties with recruiting staff and with access to specialist equipment. The comparatively late introduction of the Blackboard e-learning platform (at the beginning of 2008, Year 3 of the project) and the gap between the expectations of such material in Oman and the realities of e-learning materials development in New Zealand, are another barrier to effective institutionalising. A recent initiative, the establishment of an Omani National Quality Assurance Council, will remedy yet another problem: how to achieve consistent coverage of material and comparable academic standards across all colleges.

Design of the project

Just as Quality Assurance mechanisms are now evolving into internal Omani processes, rather than relying exclusively on external New Zealand procedures (such as annual visits by QA staff), so too has the design of the project morphed over time. The original version of the contract included a range of features (such as New Zealand staff assisting local staff in Oman), but was later amended to focus solely on providing teaching materials at the request of the Omani government. These materials are based on existing New Zealand lectures and tutorials and the writing team must take into account cultural and societal differences. From the writers' point of view, this has been seen as largely a process of initial subtraction followed by subsequent addition. So, the first step has been to remove specific New Zealand content (for instance, references to New Zealand law, history, cultural practices, images, place names and so on). This is not as simple as it sounds because most of the writers have never previously been required to question and confront their acculturation to and acceptance of Western cultural, social and pedagogical tropes. The second step has therefore been to contextualise the material sent to Oman and, perhaps understandably, there have been significant differences in how effectively this has been done. On the positive side, contextualisation through the inclusion of an assessment in the *Visual Communication* course about the *falaq* system in Oman and incorporating government programmes, such as *Origin Oman*, into the *Public Relations Communication* course, have been well received.

On the negative side, two entire courses (*Sociology* and *Applied Media Ethics*) have been disappointing to the point of failure. Here, the differences between the pedagogical and philosophical stance of the writers in New Zealand and teachers and students in Oman have resulted in students rating these courses very poorly, with only 18 per cent and 23 per cent respectively of the student body giving positive scores for *Acceptance*, and 27 per cent and 32 per cent respectively for *Relevance to Oman*.[4]

Such negative feedback had been expected by the writing team but, of course, has caused major problems for the teaching team in Oman. It also highlights the different cultural and religious lenses through which these teams view their worlds. For instance, the Terry Schiavo case obviously raises a number of ethical dilemmas for American and other Western media organisations.[5] Equally obviously, however, the same issues were often promptly dismissed in Oman, as this comment to the degree writers shows:

> Now after all the lengthy explanations aiming to generate hot discussions, some of the smarter students responded by saying that there is no need for the discussion because the idea of such debate is not only foreign to them [...] the solution is very simple. That they argued: 'those [to whom the Lord] gives life, [he] takes life back whenever [he] wants. Khalas. So what is there to debate? No debate'.[6]

Alongside these macro-level challenges, the degree writers faced a range of important micro-level challenges as well. On one level, there was a degree of openness to the process – every university was left to decide for itself which method(s) were most useful in reversioning the degrees for which they were responsible. Naturally, the resulting differences (for instance, our school worked on an inclusive model, where senior staff were relatively heavily involved in the design and writing of the courses, while others outsourced these tasks), meant that there were few opportunities for the individual teams to support each other through the process. On another level, there was a remarkable degree of uniformity required with respect to the final product. For instance, the MOHE requires a standard template and consistency across the reversioned material. This involved following a specialised format for lectures, PowerPoints and tutorials, with all resources (including assessments, examinations, marking schedules, readings and media files) provided in digital form. Similarly, high levels of quality assurance (including internal checking within the writers' universities and external checking by a consultant for NZTEC) provides successive deadlines and feedback loops that can dramatically increase the demands on individual staff members. One particular issue here is that in New Zealand semesters run February–June and July–December, while Oman follows the northern hemisphere September–January and February–May pattern. This difference often means that feedback is only provided to the writing team after its usefulness has passed (because of the gap between writing and delivery). Another issue is that the writers tend to use American and British readings to underpin their courses, while NZTEC – and to a degree the Omani deliverers – expect a wider, more international, variety of readings. This difference often means that the writing team needs to provide alternatives and include diverse points of view, while ensuring the material provided is comprehensible to the students in Oman.[7]

Challenges and opportunities of redeveloping the curriculum for an Arab audience

There are many areas of difference that have needed addressing in the reversioning process: between 'eastern' and 'western' perspectives; between Omani and New Zealand societies and cultures; and between an education system strongly based on Islam and one where secular values are paramount. On the surface, these would seem impossible to negotiate and, in some instances, they have been. The project would, of course, have been very different had it involved Arab academic institutions, which could have supplied academic personnel to fulfil such functions as external moderators, external examiners and visiting professors. Arab academics would also be useful as members of advisory boards and as intermediaries in establishing links to the media industries in Oman. They might also have had experience of the huge intellectual and resourcing challenge required when writing an entire degree from foundation to graduation and might therefore have been well placed to understand the burdens that the pace, ferocity and disparate nature of this challenge places upon the writers.

The project would also have been different had it been delayed so that stronger English language foundations were in place throughout the primary and secondary education system in Oman. Such a delay may well have eased the burden on staff and particularly on students, who are dealing with the challenges of studying at higher education level in a language that is not their own. Similarly, ensuring Omani staff understood the broader picture would have been beneficial, especially as that picture related to the constraints and limitations on the writers. Omani students could likewise have been provided with more general information, particularly with regard to the links between the graduate profile of the degree (and therefore the broad areas of employment a graduate might hope to connect with) and the student competencies and capabilities developed within particular courses in the degree.

Finally, the project would have been much improved had some management processes been more substantially engaged with. Clarifying basic differences would have been extremely useful. How exactly did the project leaders envisage the connection between a three-year degree programme in New Zealand and a four-year programme in Oman? Equally, providing opportunities for every writing team to consider their own approach would have been extremely useful. In our own university, views vary from 'Just take it off the shelf and send it', to arguments that the writing team must include dedicated personnel, like an instructional designer, a language expert, a multi-media person, a subject expert, an editor and a graphic artist.

It is no small wonder, then, that miscommunication and dissatisfaction have arisen at times between Oman and New Zealand. Mistakes are inevitable in a cross-cultural, long distance, extended time-period project such as this, and having a process in place which acknowledged the barriers to success and provided a mechanism for removing them would have been immensely valuable for both parties.

Difficulties of cross-cultural and inter-regional communication

Chief among those barriers is a raft of issues that illustrate the complexities of cross-cultural and inter-regional communication. Broadly speaking, these fall into two categories: problems with cross-cultural communication itself, many of which have been foreshadowed (to some degree) and are thus predictable (to a certain extent); and problems with personnel and equipment, which are less predictable and often more difficult to solve.

The long distance nature of the project means that face-to-face communication is only possible twice a year – in February or March in

Oman and in October in New Zealand. These meetings take place under serious time pressures as there is a great deal of material to be covered. Examples of cultural differences arise constantly. Senior Omani officials take mobile phone calls during meetings (which would only happen in New Zealand if there were an emergency) and New Zealand academics needed to be provided with neckties before meeting the Minister of Higher Education in Oman (casual dress being unremarkable in the education sector in New Zealand). Despite this, on most occasions both groups communicate well.

Where difficulties have arisen, they have highlighted a range of predictable issues. First, there have been clear issues regarding the status of the contract. Omanis value relationships more highly and see contracts through that lens; New Zealanders tend to be more legalistic and more driven by the written word. Second, there have been concerns regarding attitudes to communication, especially in making use of email. In Oman, there is often a long gap in time between an email request and response; New Zealanders prefer to use email on a regular basis and respond to written requests from Oman fairly quickly. Third, communication channels are restricted. Communication between Oman and New Zealand exists at the Programme Director to Programme Co-ordinator level, as the project is too complex to allow significant interaction between individual staff members in each country at this stage. Once the first set of graduates has completed the degree, there will be more chance to make inter-country staff connections, to design some assessments across both the Omani and the New Zealand degree, and to use technology to integrate particular teaching and learning practices. There will also be possibilities for future exchanges of staff and students, students studying at postgraduate level in either country, and joint research by staff.

Working relationships – levels and changes

Establishing productive working relationships between the two 'teams' was always going to be a challenge, given the hierarchical nature of the project and the fact that communication channels were always going to be written, asynchronous and problem-focused rather than oral, synchronous and problem-solving.

Communicating effectively through all layers of this structure has always been difficult, particularly as the delivery team and the writing team have little, if any, opportunity to communicate directly. Additionally, in its understandable efforts to facilitate the project (and to allay Omani concerns), NZTEC offers compromises or adds additional tasks for the degree writers (examples include deciding that New Zealand student work should be available to staff in Oman and the language level of courses could be altered and assessed). As such decisions require more effort and time, they have a significant impact on the New Zealand team and the additional requirements can reduce the time available for course development and writing.

A substantial range of issues (including the language used in the courses, the suitability of material for the local Omani environment and culture, and the availability of copyright material) have all affected working relationships at times. From the writers' perspectives, while significant effort can be (and has been) made to simplify and clarify language used in lectures and tutorials, there is little that can be done by individual subject experts to change readings that are considered necessary at the various stages of university study. Likewise, material for Oman is contextualised as much as possible, but this must be augmented by those who are living in, cognisant of, and imbued with that culture. Copyright material is supplied by New Zealanders for the purpose of 'academic review only'; to help Omani staff become familiar with the material. However, New Zealand cannot provide copyright clearance and this is also causing increasing difficulties within the relationship. Perhaps even more significantly, the Omani team are very keen to have copies of student assessments and this also provides challenges on a number of levels. Under New Zealand privacy law, these students must be contacted and their permission given. Further, this exercise could only ever be of extremely limited value. As all assignments and examinations are contextualised to Oman, and because the content of courses has also been altered for cultural reasons, there can be little basis for comparison between the work completed in Oman and that assigned in New Zealand. Furthermore, the differences between the language use of Omani students, who are working at an IELTS level of between 4 and 5.5, and that of native English speakers will be substantial. Expectations and teacher marking may also vary between the two countries and there is no need to apply New Zealand standards to the Omani degree, which will set its own benchmarks and criteria for successful achievement.

Perceptions of the New Zealand team about Arab media and Arab society

Differences in perception are at the heart of this project. For the New Zealand team, perceptions of the Arab world are more likely to be versions of the 'Arab street', derived from Western media or academic accounts informed by, say, Said's views on Orientalism, rather than being based on experiential encounters (and such encounters are limited to a small minority of the project team, only one of whom has worked with Arab colleagues when he studied overseas). There are no Arabs or Arabic speakers on the team, and none has lived and taught in an Arab society. Perceptions are thus both generalised and vague. For example, the writers are respectful of Islam and take care to avoid offence, especially in the choice of images, eschewing situations such as bars and alcohol use and being careful about how to portray male/female interactions. But, of course, this is not enough and even the best-intentioned approaches cannot approach Omani reality. In the informal lecturer feedback received in October 2007, for the *Image and Sound* course, one staff member had understandable difficulty with a diagram:

> Slide 33, 'Evolution theory – transformation from monkey to [necked] man sitting with computer'. We have lots of trouble with necked pictures especially with the girl students. Publically, they are embarrassed ... I think lecturers do not want to been seen as a catalyst propagating or implanting such ideas in the student's mind. If we are seen doing that. We will invite trouble.[8]

From the writer's perspective, this slipped 'under the radar'. They were so attached to their customary gaze that they did not even register that the evolutionary diagram could be offensive, nor that the man was naked. A similar situation arose in the *Applied Media Ethics* course, where it was accepted at the outset that viewpoints would be very different and great care was taken not to offend. However, again there were significant differences, as issues that presented moral dilemmas that were only resolvable in shades of grey in New Zealand, were seemingly perceived as painted entirely in black and white in Oman. For the writers, such an approach is the antithesis of 'becoming educated', which entails learning to discuss an issue, researching different views and theories, and then critiquing those through the development of a logical argument with the aim of creating a new model or paradigm. The writing team thus had much to learn and a long journey to travel in redeveloping their curriculum.

Defamiliarisation from the processes normally followed when developing curricula

The general processes adopted when developing curriculum suggest basing teaching material in the world around the students, and working from the familiar into the new. Clearly, as outlined previously, this option was not available to the writing team: in fact, they had to do the opposite and remove all references to the world around them without having the requisite knowledge to replace it with concrete real world material which would 'speak' to students. Furthermore, for academics, there is an expectation that material progresses from the secondary school curriculum to university study; there are certain compulsory elements that all first year students must have, such as a certain number of credits in numeracy, literacy and science (in addition to specified discipline knowledge). Once again, this baseline knowledge was not available to the writing team, who had no familiarity with the secondary school syllabus in Oman. Thus constructivist techniques of 'scaffolding' new knowledge onto old could not be used.

Curriculum development in New Zealand occurs within a dual heritage society where indigenous people (those of Maori heritage) and the descendants of European settlers (mainly British, initially) are bound by law into a partnership, which necessitates a bicultural approach. Recent immigration and increasing numbers of international students in tertiary education have extended this focus to a more multicultural one in which developing an international curriculum and transferable skills is encouraged. Many New Zealand universities have partnerships with international universities and student exchange opportunities are widespread. Such a focus does not appear to be appropriate in Oman. Similarly, New Zealand staff who expect to be immersed in, or at least aware of, youth culture and popular culture do not have the ability to make similar connections with young people in Oman. As a result, much teaching material must seem foreign, strange and divorced from everyday life in Oman, a point which was neatly acknowledged by one Omani academic:

> Of course it would be too naïve for me to expect the original course writer/s to come up with the local Omani's examples.

This is certainly not possible. People from New Zealand cannot possibly provide examples from the Oman in particular. This is the job of the local College lecturers to take the initiative.[9]

Teaching at university level in New Zealand also operates within a liberal mandate to act as 'critics and conscience of society' and the skills of analytical thought and critique are highly valued in and of themselves. The curriculum therefore is focused on debate, scholarship and a critical approach to reading. This has proven to be difficult for students in Oman. Of course, as we were aware, theirs is an oral rather than a print culture, and there have been major changes in the amount and scope of reading material provided. Nevertheless, the paradigm shift required to develop material for people from such a different cultural background was not sufficiently foreseen. Neither was the writing team sufficiently aware of the ways in which their curricula are implicitly designed for native English speakers, or international students with an IELTS of 6.5 overall, with a minimum of 6 in any band on entry into the degree. This naturally means that curricula need to be developed within narrower linguistic boundaries than 'normal', and this significant additional challenge may not have been met.

Incorporating a number of new perspectives into professional practice

Likewise, attempting to 'de-westernise' teaching material is difficult for a number of reasons. Most notably, there is a telling lack of 'insider' input to the writing process. Also, as recent scholarship (see, for instance, Curran and Park 2000) has shown, there are peculiar challenges set by the fact that the most familiar media studies/cultural studies theoretical frameworks derive from English and American models, and that much of the writing in the field is published in English. For the writing team in New Zealand, such material as is published in other languages is broadly inaccessible in its original form and is rarely translated. However, some pertinent material has been found and incorporated. For example, Mike Davis' *Fear and Money in Dubai* (*New Left Review* September–October 2006) is required reading in the Year Two *Communication and Culture* course. Added to this, the writing team was unsure of the acceptable degree of formality in an Omani classroom for student/teacher relationships and the attitudes to information presented in lectures. In New Zealand, lecturers are addressed by their first names, students are able (and usually encouraged) to ask questions in lectures, and tutorials are often the site of fierce debates. This may well not be the same in Oman. As a result, the writing team developed the convention of addressing notes to their Omani counterparts in the colour sea-green (and adding the Arabic for Oman to them in later iterations so that the material would still stand out when photocopied). These notes were designed to signal that the material might not be suitable for an Omani audience and asked the lecturers to check in advance. These notes were also used to demonstrate where Omani examples would be needed and to suggest that further contextualisation or clarification might be needed. For instance, in the *Applied Media Ethics* course, jihad was mentioned when discussing possible reasons to go to war, but the sea-green note stated: 'NB the concept of jihad could be included and developed here but I will leave this to the lecturer to do as I am in no position to do so, on cultural grounds'.

Clearly, there were some topics that were inappropriate for an Omani audience, and these presented some challenges. For instance, developing a fifteen-week course in *Identity and the Media* without interrogating (or even mentioning) concepts of gender was particularly problematic. Similarly, images were often altered. In the *Image and Sound* course, one lesson discussed how personal media are increasingly used when disasters or other freakish events occur. The writer of that course substituted scenes of the 7 July London bombings with images of natural disasters such as the 2004 Indonesian tsunami. Likewise, when making points about ensemble casts' portrayals of strong female characters on television, the overtly sexualised images from *Desperate Housewives* were replaced with images of the cast of *Grey's Anatomy*. Interestingly, some feedback from Oman (mainly from the Programme Director) has noted that the writing team is perhaps too self-censorious. While taking that on board, it is clear that mistakes can still be made.

Assignments, which link to Omani, or at least Arab society, are provided as much as possible and examination questions such as 'Is there a healthy level of global media present in Omani society? Why or why not?' and 'What are the possible responses to globalization? Which response is best for Omani society?' (from the *Communication and Culture Course*) explicitly involve students in applying theory to their own society. Overall, however, the writing team has been faced with a substantial task, not too dissimilar to developing courses for young adults (rather than those over the age of 18).

Feedback

Until recently, feedback was only provided in an informal fashion through comments from the Programme Director and one set of staff comments. In March 2008, however, the Head of the Communications Department at Ibri College conducted a survey of students and compiled a set of comments from other Communication Heads of Department. The student survey asked students to rate courses from the first and second years of the four-year programme on *acceptability, language level* and *relevance to Oman. Acceptability* ratings ranged from 65 per cent (for *Introduction to Communication*) to 18 per cent for (*Introduction to Sociology*); language level was rated from 79 per cent (again for *Introduction to Communication*) to 11 per cent (again for *Introduction to Sociology*), and relevance to Oman varied from 41 per cent (for *Introduction to Journalism and Public Relations*) to 16 per cent (for *Image and Sound*). This was extraordinarily useful and facilitated a response from the New Zealand Programme Coordinator who could finally deal with specific rather than generic issues.

From our perspective, it is very interesting that some staff in Oman feel there is too much information provided and that they would like more freedom and autonomy with regard to the content and structure of courses. The writing team, however, see themselves as being contracted to deliver teaching materials only. What happens to these materials in Oman and, indeed, what structure the Omani Bachelor of Communications takes in its final form, are entirely Omani decisions. The New Zealand team is happy to help, but are also very aware that many changes will need to be made to their material and that best practice in education is a process of constant modification and alteration to keep up with the latest theory and changes in society.

Conclusion

For a project of its size, duration and complexity, the reversioning of the New Zealand media studies degree for Oman has been remarkably successful. Given the inherent problems in developing curricula for 'others', the writing team has been extremely productive and constantly inventive. Of course, some ideas and initiatives have worked better than others, and some staff have been more able to engage with the deeper levels of the project than their colleagues. That is not surprising – the level of self-reflection and confidence, let alone the time required to absorb the necessary lessons, is not accomplished simply. From our point of view, the encouraging part of the project has been the way in which writers have revisited and redesigned successive portions of a course as their confidence and expertise has grown.

From this – slightly more than midway – point, it has also become clear that our original view of this project was simplistic and limiting. On the surface, the MOHE faced a choice between developing their own degree and purchasing a 'reversion' of a New Zealand one. The former option was not feasible, but the latter, while proving successful, might not have been the best 'fit'.

Had time and resources permitted, it would surely have been possible to extend the exercise away from a 'degree in English for Oman' to 'an Omani degree in English'. This would have required much more time – and resources – and would have needed direct communication between writers and deliverers. However, a true, connected dialogue between them could very well have allowed the writers to use their skills in context, had the deliverers been available (and able) to provide that context for them. The result would bear even less resemblance to the New Zealand degree than does the current 'reversion'. But it would also have been better suited to students in Oman.

Notes

1. The degrees were a Bachelor of Communication Studies and a Bachelor of Design (AUT University), a Bachelor of Information Technology (Otago University) and a Bachelor of International Business Administration (Waikato University). Language support is provided by Victoria University.
2. 'News briefs', 2006: 2.
3. In New Zealand, there are seven majors in communication and media: Advertising, Creative Industries, Digital Media, Journalism, Public Relations, Radio and Television. The MOHE chose Digital Media, Journalism and Public Relations and added Media Management (derived from the Creative Industries major) and International Communication.
4. Omani student survey, March 2008.
5. Terri Schiavo was a 26-year-old American woman who collapsed in her home in 1990 and, after being in a coma, was diagnosed as being in a persistent vegetative state. In 1998, her husband and guardian asked the courts to remove her gastric

feeding tube, which would lead to her death. This was opposed by her parents and led to much ethical and legal debate until the courts agreed, the tube was removed and she died on 31 March 2005.
6. Omani staff feedback, October 2007.
7. An example here might be the NZTEC suggestion to include complicated material about postcoloniality at a stage where the writers believe a more simplified account of the issues is more appropriate for Omani students.
8. Omani staff feedback, October 2007.
9. Omani staff feedback, October 2007.

Bibliography

Bloom, Benjamin (ed.) (1956) *Taxonomy of educational objectives: The classification of educational goals*, Handbook I: *Cognitive Domain*, New York, Toronto: Longmans Green.

Curran, James and Park, Myung-Jin (2000) *De-westernizing Media Studies*, London: Routledge.

Eisenhardt, Kathleen (1989) 'Building Theories from Case Study Research', *The Academy of Management Review* 14.4: 532–50.

Krathwohl, David (2002) 'A Revision of Bloom's Taxonomy: An Overview', *Theory Into Practice* 41.4: 212–18.

'News briefs' (2006) *The New Zealand Education Review*, 25 August.

Said, Edward (1979) *Orientalism*, New York: Vintage Books.

Yin, Robert (1994) *Case Study Research: Design and Methods*, 2nd edn, London: Sage.

Omani feedback material: Individual staff comments, October 2007, Student survey, March 2008 Communication Course review (Staff feedback), March 2008.

Index